'The study of subjective experience is fundamental to
Yet, consciousness has often been treated with circum
characteristic clarity of thought and intellectual rigor that
of the foremost scholars in our field, Morris Eagle tackl
Eagle sifts through a vast body of literature to synthesize, critique, and at times ac...... ...... ,
notions of what subjectivity means and why it is so critically important to psychoanalysis and
to a psychoanalytic psychology. The result of such a monumental undertaking is a remarkable
achievement and a major contribution to the field that is sure to become a classic'.

Christopher Christian, PhD, *editor*, Psychoanalytic Psychology

'Morris Eagle strikes again. Forty years have passed since 1984, when, in a volume that
now is a "classic", he taught us to look at psychoanalysis as a living and evolving theory. A
challenge to which he has returned in the following years, with a series of volumes written
in a lucid and balanced voice, showing us that, despite the irredeemable plurality of the
word "psychoanalysis", it is still possible to think of a unified theory of the mind capable of
accommodating all the major schools of psychoanalytic thought. In this view volume, Morris
captures us with the idea that, despite the centrality of the unconscious, psychoanalytic theory
has room within it to relocate consciousness and subjective experience in a way that does
justice to their centrality in our existence. Once again, he offers us a priceless book that
enriches the way we look at psychoanalysis and, inevitably, at ourselves'.

Vittorio Lingiardi, *University of Rome, Italy*

'Our subjective experience – our consciousness – is all that really matters to us, yet it has
often not fared well in psychological and philosophical theorizing, and its importance is
downplayed – indeed, it is a target of supposition in psychoanalysis. Morris Eagle offers
a brilliant, intellectually kaleidoscopic exploration of the many ways that the importance
of subjective experience has been affirmed or denied, deftly parrying the reductionists
and affirming the centrality of consciousness while acknowledging its elusiveness. Eagle
grapples with myriad provocative puzzles and controversies about understanding subjective
experience across the disciplines of psychology, philosophy, and psychoanalysis, offering
a cornucopia of insights, wise judgments, and, when warranted, devastating critiques of
current views. His analysis leads him to construct a compelling and persuasive path forward
that reinterprets Freudian insights into the unconscious in terms of James's notion of fringe
consciousness, an idea that, he shows, has profound clinical implications and saves us from
much nonsense. This book offers us nothing less than a blueprint for tackling the future of
psychoanalysis that saves psychoanalysis's soul by fully acknowledging ours'.

Jerome C. Wakefield, PhD, DSW, *is professor of Social Work, affiliate professor of
Philosophy, professor of the Conceptual Foundations of Psychiatry (2007–2019),
associate faculty in the Center for Bioethics, and honorary faculty in the
Psychoanalytic Association of New York, at New York University*

'Only Morris Eagle could have written this book. Eagle's unique mix of deep erudition, keen
intellection, and unflagging passion result in a precious outcome: a masterwork that places
subjective experience – consciousness – at the very center of human living. Experimental
psychology, psychoanalysis, philosophy of mind all receive thorough and innovative
treatment, not only illuminating features of conscious life, but also clarifying the nature
of "unconscious" processes. *Subjective Experience* will be of interest to a wide-ranging
audience: from undergraduates and practicing psychoanalysts, to graduate students and
leading academics'.

Mitchell Wilson, MD, *editor-in-chief*, Journal of the American Psychoanalytic
Association

Subjective Experience

Morris N. Eagle explores the understanding and role of subjective experience in the disciplines of psychology, psychoanalysis, and philosophy of mind.

Elaborating how different understandings of subjective experience give rise to very different theories of the nature of the mind, Eagle then explains how these shape clinical practices. In particular, Eagle addresses the strong tendency in the disciplines concerned with the nature of the mind to overlook the centrality of subjective experience in one's life, to view it with suspicion, and to reduce it to neural processes. Describing examples of research in which subjective experience is a central variable, Eagle provides an outline of a model in which the dichotomy of conscious and unconscious is supplemented by subjective experience as a continuum.

This book is essential reading for psychoanalysts, psychoanalytic psychotherapists, psychologists and anyone wishing to gain a deeper understanding of the importance of theories of the mind to therapeutic practice.

Morris N. Eagle is professor emeritus of the Derner Institute of Advanced Psychological Studies at Adelphi University. He is a fellow of the Royal Society of Canada and a recipient of the Sigourney Award for lifetime contribution to psychoanalysis. He is the author and editor of eight books and more than 150 journal articles and chapters in edited books.

PSYCHOLOGICAL ISSUES

The basic mission of *Psychological Issues* is to contribute to the further development of psychoanalysis as a science, as a respected scholarly enterprise, as a theory of human behavior, and as a therapeutic method.

Over the past 50 years, the series has focused on fundamental aspects and foundations of psychoanalytic theory and clinical practice, as well as on work in related disciplines relevant to psychoanalysis. *Psychological Issues* does not aim to represent or promote a particular point of view. The contributions cover broad and integrative topics of vital interest to all psychoanalysts as well as to colleagues in related disciplines. They cut across particular schools of thought and tackle key issues, such as the philosophical underpinnings of psychoanalysis, psychoanalytic theories of motivation, conceptions of therapeutic action, the nature of unconscious mental functioning, psychoanalysis and social issues, and reports of original empirical research relevant to psychoanalysis. The authors often take a critical stance toward theories and offer a careful theoretical analysis and conceptual clarification of the complexities of theories and their clinical implications, drawing upon relevant empirical findings from psychoanalytic research as well as from research in related fields.

Series Editor David L. Wolitzky and the Editorial Board continues to invite contributions from social/behavioral sciences such as anthropology and sociology, from biological sciences such as physiology and the various brain sciences, and from scholarly humanistic disciplines such as philosophy, law, and ethics. Volumes 1–64 in this series were published by International Universities Press. Volumes 65–69 were published by Jason Aronson. For a full list of the titles published by Routledge in this series, please visit the Routledge website: https://www.routledge.com/Psychological-Issues/book-series/PSYCHISSUES

Subjective Experience

Its Fate in Psychology, Psychoanalysis and Philosophy of Mind

Morris N. Eagle

Routledge
Taylor & Francis Group

LONDON AND NEW YORK

Designed cover image: Wesley VanDinter © Getty Images.

First published 2024
by Routledge
4 Park Square, Milton Park, Abingdon, Oxon OX14 4RN

and by Routledge
605 Third Avenue, New York, NY 10158

Routledge is an imprint of the Taylor & Francis Group, an informa business

© 2024 Morris N. Eagle

The right of Morris N. Eagle to be identified as author of this work has been asserted in accordance with sections 77 and 78 of the Copyright, Designs and Patents Act 1988.

British Library Cataloguing-in-Publication Data
A catalogue record for this book is available from the British Library

ISBN: 9781032686943 (hbk)
ISBN: 9781032686950 (pbk)
ISBN: 9781032686967 (ebk)

DOI: 10.4324/9781032686967

Typeset in Times New Roman
by Deanta Global Publishing Services, Chennai, India

I dedicate this book to my wife Rita Eagle who, as always, gets to the heart of the matter and helps me organize what is often somewhat messy.

Contents

Acknowledgments

I want to express my appreciation to my editor, Georgina Clutterbuck, who has been consistently and graciously helpful. I also want to acknowledge the stimulating and clarifying discussions of difficult issues with David Wolitzky and Jerry Wakefield.

Introduction

Although we do not normally give it much thought, what is most valuable and precious about being alive is consciousness, that is, being able to feel, think, and experience the world and oneself and others in it. Indeed, at the core of the dread of death is the fear of ceasing to be, that is, ceasing to experience. Death, Montaigne (1580/1993) tells us, is the limit of experience. As Thomas Reid wrote, 'people are greatly interested in their own personal survival, which they see very much in terms of the continuity of their own consciousness' (p. 2). And Edwards (1966) writes, 'A person thinking of his own death is thinking of the destruction or disintegration of his body and the cessation of his experiences' (p. 416). Let us say you were offered a devil's bargain in which 'you gain unlimited wealth, but must relinquish all subjective feeling. You can act and speak like a zombie, but no more hearing, smelling … loving, hating … wanting, hoping … imagining …' (Koch, 2019, p. xi). As Koch notes, 'From your point of view, you might as well be dead' (p. xi). In short, 'Everything in our life depends on being alive and just about everything in our lives depends on being conscious' (Searle, 2013, p. 10347).

Consciousness and subjective experience have had a checkered career in the history of intellectual thought. As Makari (2015) documents, until the 1700s, the study of the mind, understood in terms of consciousness and subjective experience, was a topic for theology. That is the soul, which included consciousness and subjective experience, belonged to religion. It was mainly the philosophical writings of Hobbes and Locke that secularized the study of mind and thereby made it available for empirical investigation. However, making the mind available for empirical investigation did not necessarily mean that subjective experience would be at the center of the study of the mind.

The philosopher Michael Oakeshott (1933) wrote that '"experience", of all the words in the philosophic vocabulary is the most difficult to manage' (p. 9). He appears to locate this difficulty in the questionable relationship between sensation and judgment in the description of experience (an issue that will be discussed later in the context of the sensation–perception distinction) as well as the different perspectives one can take toward experience. At one point, John Dewey (1944) thought that the term 'experience' should be dropped from philosophical discussion, presumably because of its elusiveness. He wrote to a colleague 'I agree

DOI: 10.4324/9781032686967-1

with what you say about dropping "experience" as not needed' (Letter to Arthur Bentley, May 12, 1944). However, he also wrote: '… we need a cautionary directive word, like experience, to remind us that the world which is lived, suffered, and enjoyed, as well as logically thought of has the last word in all human inquiries and surmises' (p. 372) (as cited in Jay, 2005)

Despite the obvious and stark reality that consciousness and the capacity to experience are at the core of one's existence and the most precious things about being alive, until recently, they have not fared well in the disciplines – psychology, psychoanalysis, neuroscience, and philosophy – that have to do with the nature of mind. Consciousness and subjective experience have been variously viewed in these disciplines as epiphenomena, reduced to neural processes and broken down into their presumed elements. For example, not only were consciousness and subjectivity excluded from the subject matter of the discipline of psychology in the form of behaviorism, but were also given short shrift in the emergence of cognitive psychology, with its emphasis on unconscious computational processes. Thus, Fodor (1983) writes: 'all psychologically interesting cognitive states are unconscious' (p. 86). And Lakoff and Johnson (1999) write that one of three 'major findings of cognitive science [is that] thought is mostly unconscious' (p. 3).

Consciousness and subjective experience fare little better in psychoanalysis, particularly in the Freudian theory of the mind. The reduced significance of consciousness in classical psychoanalysis is reflected in its very definition as the study of unconscious phenomena. Laplanche and Pontalis (1973) write that 'psychoanalytic theory emerges from a refusal to define the psychoanalytic field in terms of consciousness' (p. 84). Further, as will be elaborated in a later chapter, not only is conscious experience viewed as epiphenomenal in the Freudian theory of the nature of the mind, but as (Ricoeur 1970) notes, consciousness is seen as 'false' (p. 33) and replete with 'illusions and lies' (p. 32). That is, conscious subjective experience is mainly a surface façade that hides, disguises, and misrepresents the unconscious motives and forces that truly drive one's life.

A dismissive approach to subjective experience is also common in neuroscience. As Chalmers (1995) puts it, 'for many years … the prevailing view was that science, which depends on objectivity, could not accommodate something as subjective as consciousness' (p. 80).[1] For example, Crick (1994), the Nobel Prize laureate, states

> You, your joys and sorrows, your memories and ambitions, your sense of personal identity and free will, are, in fact, no more than the behavior of a vast assembly of nerve cells and their associate molecules. As Lewis Carroll's Alice might have phrased it: 'You're nothing but a pack of neurons'.
>
> (p. 3)

The neuroscientist Chater (2018) maintains that the positing of an inner world of beliefs, desires, motives, and thoughts is egregiously false. He writes that

'Thoughts, like fiction, come into existence in the instant that they are invented, and not a moment before' (p. 5). He also writes that

> no one, at any point in human history, has ever been guided by inner beliefs and desires, any more than any human being has been possessed by evil spirits or watched over by a guardian angel. Beliefs, motives, and other imagined inhabitants of our 'inner world' are entirely a figment of our imaginations. The stories we tell to justify and explain our own and others' behavior aren't just wrong in detail – they are a thoroughgoing fabrication from start to finish.
>
> (p. 6)

Thus, Chater is not saying that the reasons and motives we give for our behavior do not represent our real reasons and motives. Rather, he is saying that there are no such things as reasons and motives motivating one's behavior.

A radically different position is seen in a phenomenological perspective, which is less concerned with the problem of how a scientific physicalist worldview can accommodate consciousness and subjective experience. Rather, its concern is with the analysis of the structure of experience itself, which, it is argued, needs to be addressed prior to scientific concerns. However, as we will see, it is far from clear that this approach has contributed significantly to our understanding of consciousness and lived subjective experience.

The approach to consciousness and subjective experience in the disciplines I discuss is not monolithic. For example, as exemplified by Gestalt psychology, psychophysics, and other methods that investigate the determinants and correlates of subjective experience, there are approaches that do justice to the nature of actual, lived experience. As we will see, this is also the case in the context of psychoanalytic theory. As for philosophy of mind, there is an ongoing debate in the philosophical literature between those who believe that science must find a way of accommodating 'something as subjective as consciousness' (Chalmers, 1995, p. 80) and those who approach consciousness and subjective experience through various forms of reductionistic and eliminative strategies. On the one side, we have philosophers like Strawson (e.g., 2015) and Searle (e.g., 1992), who argue for the reality, indeed the primacy of consciousness, and who argue that if current science cannot accommodate as central an aspect of the natural world as the existence of conscious experience, it is science that needs to change. On the other side, similar to the neuroscience and philosophical perspectives of Crick and Chater described above, the philosopher Georges Rey (1983) writes that 'The concept of consciousness might turn out to be an excessively simplistic way of viewing our complicated lives ... we would be mistaken in thinking of ourselves, or of anything, as conscious' (as cited in Baars, 2003, p. 14).

In the following chapters, I will elaborate on and critically evaluate various views in the disciplines of psychology, psychoanalysis, and philosophy on the role of consciousness and subjective experience in the understanding of the nature of mind. Before proceeding further, I want to clarify my use of some key terms and some key assumptions: the term 'experience' is equivalent to 'conscious experience'. Whereas mental contents, as well as discrimination and encoding, can be unconscious, unconscious experience is an oxymoron. Normally, consciousness is *my* consciousness and the experiences I have are *my* experiences. That is, they are 'subjective experiences'. However, under certain conditions (e.g., dissociative states, depersonalization, intrusive thoughts), one can have 'not me', ego-alien experiences. Such experiences lack the quality of *subjectivity* and thus, are not *subjective* experiences. These uses and assumptions should be kept in mind in reading discussions of subjective experience throughout the book.

Note

1 Dewey's ambivalent position regarding experience reflects the dilemma that although experience is at the center of existence, and constitutes the foundation for empirical scientific investigation, the phenomenon of conscious experience itself does not readily fit into a scientific worldview.

References

Baars, B. J. (2003). The double life of B. F. Skinner: Inner conflict, dissociation and the scientific taboo against consciousness. *Journal of Consciousness Studies*, *10*(1), 5–25.

Chalmers, D. (1995). The puzzle of conscious experience. *Scientific American*, *273*(6), 80–86.

Chater, N. (2018). *The mind is flat: The remarkable shallowness of the improvising brain*. Yale University Press.

Dewey, J. (1944). Letter to Arthur F. Bentley. In J. Dewey & A. F. Bentley (Eds.), *A philosophical correspondence 1932–1951*. Rutgers University Press.

Edwards, P. (1966). My death. In P. Edwards (Ed.), *The encyclopedia of philosophy* (Vol. 5, pp. 416–419). Free Press and Macmillan Publishing Company.

Fodor, J. A. (1983). *The modularity of mind*. MIT Press.

Koch, C. (2019). *The feeling of life itself: Why consciousness is widespread but can't be computed*. MIT Press.

Lakoff, G., & Johnson, M. (1999). *Philosophy in the flesh: The embodied mind and its challenge to western thought*. Basic Books.

Laplanche, J., &Pontalis, J.-B. (1973). *The language of psycho-analysis*. Hogarth Press.

Makari, G. (2015). *Soul machine: The invention of the modern mind*. W. W. Norton & Company.

Montaigne, M. de (1958). *The complete essays of Montaigne* (D. M. Frame, Trans.). Stanford University Press.

Oakeshott, M. (1933). *Experience and its modes*. Cambridge University Press.

Rey, G. (1983). A reason for doubting the existence of consciousness. In R. J. Davidson, G. E. Schwartz, & D. Shapiro (Eds.), *Consciousness & self-regulation: Advances in research and theory* (Vol. 3). Plenum Press.

Ricoeur, P. (1970). *Freud and philosophy: An essay on interpretation.* Yale University Press.

Searle, J. R. (1992). *The rediscovery of the mind.* MIT Press.

Searle, J. R. (2013). Theory of mind and Darwin's legacy. *Proceedings of the National Academy of Sciences, 110*(Suppl. 2), 10343–10348. https://doi.org/10.1073/pnas.1301214110

Chapter 1

Consciousness and subjective experience in psychology

Titchener's structuralism

Every undergraduate psychology student is taught that psychology became a scientific discipline in 1879, the date that Wundt established the first experimental laboratory of psychological research.[1] Trained by Wundt, Titchener brought the experimental laboratory for research in psychology to the United States at Cornell University. Titchener and his followers defined psychology as the study of conscious experience. His theoretical and research program was called structuralism because it focused on the structure of conscious experience. According to the structuralist perspective, paralleling the approach of the physical sciences of analyzing physical objects into its constituent elements (i.e., atoms and molecules), the task of the psychological scientist is to analyze conscious experience into its constituent elements, which were identified as sensations, images, and feelings. The method of carrying out this analysis was *introspection*; however, this was not ordinary introspection, but rather *trained* introspection, which required the observer to report his or her subjective experience rather than the physical object. The latter was seen as a 'stimulus error'; that is, the observer lapsed from a psychological point of view, in which one introspected and reported one's experience, to a physical point of view in which one described the external physical object. For example, one's report of seeing, say, 'an apple' constituted a stimulus error insofar as it reported a physical object rather than one's sensations (e.g., 'red', 'round'). As we will see in Chapter 3, Titchener's trained introspection bears a strong family resemblance to Husserl's phenomenological approach of bracketing, that is, suspension of the natural attitude in order to describe the structure of experience. In both cases, the observer is suspending or bracketing the natural attitude of reporting the object.

In visual perception, different features of an object (e.g., an apple) such as contour, color, location, and so on, are processed in different parts of the brain. And yet, we do not normally experience these different features separately. Rather, we experience a unitary object in a particular context, a 'binding' product that is highly adaptive in one's interaction with the world. (I will return to the process of 'binding' in Chapter 3.) In its emphasis on breaking down conscious experience

DOI: 10.4324/9781032686967-2

into its presumed elements, and thereby avoiding the so-called 'stimulus error', the trained introspection procedure of structuralism, in effect, attempts to unbind the natural achievement of binding.[2] This is also the case with regard to Husserl's bracketing and suspension of the natural attitude. In both cases, it is not a spontaneous perceptual experience of unified objects that is the object of investigation, but the presumed elements of perceptual experience. This is but one expression of the (misguided) search for the presumed elements of perceptual experience, an issue that we will revisit in a discussion of the sensation-perception distinction.

It is worth noting that prior to the advent of structuralism, a fruitful body of work that came to be known as *psychophysics* (of which Titchener was certainly aware) had been conducted on the relation between reports of subjective experience and variations in physical stimuli. Weber (1834) reported that 'the smallest perceptible difference between two weights can be stated as a ratio between the weights' and further that 'the ratio is independent of the magnitude of the weights' (Boring, 1950, p. 113). This discovery also held for visual and auditory discrimination. Fechner refined and mathematized Weber's findings into what has come to be known as the Weber–Fechner law. In contrast to structuralism, this approach to the investigation of subjective experience was productive and led to important discoveries. This was largely so because unlike the structuralist approach, which focused on the supposed elements of experience, the research on psychophysics investigated the *relations* between experience as it is given and events in the world.[3] Fechner recognized that although we cannot measure sensation itself, we can measure the relations between sensations (e.g., just noticeable differences or JND'S) and physical stimuli (see Boring, 1950, pp. 286–287). There is also the seminal work of Muller (1840) on specific nerve energies and perceptual experience, by Helmholtz on a wide range of perceptual experiences, as well as by many others. As I will elaborate later, a strategy of investigating functional relations between variations in experience and variations in other events such as external stimuli, neural processes, and social has been far more fruitful than approaches that attempt to analyze the structure of subjective experience itself.

Functionalism

The research program of structuralism led to few, if any, important findings or insights.

Following the relative failure of the structuralist project to generate findings of much significance, a new psychological perspective known as functionalism emerged in the United States. Its major figures included Angell, James, Baldwin, and Dewey. Functionalism was characterized, on the so to speak negative side, by a rejection of the elementalism of structuralism; and on the positive side, by an understanding of the mind and its properties in terms of its evolutionary functions. William James (1890), a central figure of functionalism, wrote a great deal about consciousness; not the static and broken down into elements consciousness of structuralism, but the personal, forever changing, and selective consciousness that we experience in our everyday life. Also, as the term functionalism indicates, James' emphasis was not on the elements, but rather on the function of consciousness. He writes:

> Taking a purely naturalistic view of the matter, it seems reasonable to suppose that, unless consciousness served some useful purpose, it would not have been superadded to life. Assuming hypothetically that this is so, this results in an important problem for Psychophysicists to find out, namely, *how* consciousness helps an animal, how much complication of machinery may be saved in the nervous centers, for instance, if consciousness accompanies their action.
>
> (James, 1875/1890, p. 205)

The functionalist approach is clearly summarized by Angell (1907) who described it as the 'psychology of the fundamental utilities of consciousness' in which mind is 'primarily engaged in mediating between the environment and the needs of the organism' (as cited in Boring, 1950, p. 557).[4] Thus, although as was true of structuralism, consciousness was viewed as an appropriate subject matter for psychology, unlike structuralism, the emphasis was on its function, not on its elements. Among other implications, this meant that reduced importance was given to introspection as the primary source of psychological data.

Evolutionary theory exerted a strong influence on functionalism, not only in regard to its emphasis on adaptive functions, but also in its emphasis on the *continuities* between animals and humans. Although the functionalist study of animal behavior initially included inferences to the nature of the animal's consciousness, investigators such as Watson, later to become the originary figure of behaviorism, soon concluded that it was sufficient to limit one's investigations to the animal's behavior without any reference to consciousness. This led to the reasoning that if animal behavior could be investigated and understood without any reference to consciousness, this was also likely to be the case with regard to the investigation of human behavior. In short, the ground was prepared for the full-blown emergence of behaviorism, one major consequence of which was the snuffing out of any reference to consciousness and subjective experience. Based on the evidence that animal behavior could be shaped by Pavlovian conditioning (Yerkes & Morgalis, 1909), it appeared that behavior could be influenced directly, without the mediation of consciousness. As Boring (1950) notes, at least with regard to animal behavior, 'a functional psychology could get along without consciousness' (Boring, 1950, p. 556). The net result was a waning interest in consciousness and an increasing emphasis on behavior itself; thus, the boundary between functionalism and behaviorism became increasingly blurred.[5]

The ambivalent attitude of functionalism toward consciousness went beyond the context of animal behavior. We have already noted Dewey's (1944) ambivalence toward the term 'experience' In his introduction to the 1981 publication of James' (1890) *The Principles of Psychology*, Miller writes that 'The functionalist's attention to behavior was so successful that the subjective aspect of psychology came to seem unnecessary' (p. XXI). Miller is, of course, referring to the link between functionalism and the emergence of behaviorism. However, despite that link, not only James, but the other major founders of functionalism – Angell, Baldwin, and Dewey – never took the explicit step of eliminating subjective experience as the subject matter of psychology. Indeed, it would be mistaken to conclude that James dismissed the importance of subjective experience. Even a casual familiarity with James' writings – particularly his *Principles of Psychology* – would make it clear that subjective experience and its functions are at the center of his theory of the mind.

Given the centrality of evolutionary theory in functionalist thinking, particularly, the idea that the capacity for conscious experience emerged in the course of evolution, it would be difficult for functionalist theorists to fail to recognize that this capacity served vital functions. As James (1890) writes:

> The distribution of consciousness shows it to be exactly such as we might expect an organ added for the sake of steering a nervous system grown too complex to regulate itself. Consciousness ... has in all probability been evolved, like all other functions, for a use it is to the highest degree improbable *a priori* that should have no use.
>
> (as cited in Boring, 1950, p. 515)

Behaviorism

James' cogent evolutionary argument regarding the function of consciousness notwithstanding, the move toward the dominance of behaviorism was inexorable. This meant that the exorcism of subjective experience as an appropriate matter for scientific investigation was inevitable. The emergence of behaviorism was influenced not only by functionalism, but also by the earlier writings of Russian physiologists and psychologists, including Bekhterev and Sechenov, who were developing an 'objective psychology'. Central to objective psychology was the proposition that all psychological life could be understood as reflexes. Sechenov (1863) wrote that 'all acts of conscious or unconscious life are reflexes' (as cited in Boring, 1950, p. 635). Of course, the work of Pavlov, the greatest of the Russian physiologists, on conditioned reflexes, exerted a strong influence on behaviorism. It is important to note, however, that Pavlov did not accept Sechenov's reduction of psychological life to reflexes. He wrote: 'Psychology, insofar as it concerns the subjective state of man, has a natural right to existence; for our subjective world is the first reality with which we are confronted' (Pavlov, 1927, p. 239).

As the contrast between Bekhterev's and Sechenov's 'objective psychology' and Pavlov's statement makes clear, one needs to distinguish between ontological and epistemological behaviorism. The former includes the position of early figures such as La Mettrie (1747), who viewed animals and humans as automations, Hobbes (1651), who interpreted all mental states in terms of matter in motion, and the Russian reflexologists, who reduced all behavior to reflexes. Epistemological behaviorism was mainly motivated by the overriding goal of enabling the scientific investigation of psychological phenomena. Epistemological behaviorists did not argue that consciousness does not exist; only that if psychology was to be a science, it needed to limit its subject matter to the observable. As Skinner (1953) wrote, 'The objection to inner states is not that they do not exist, but that they are not relevant in a functional analysis' (p. 53). (However, as we will see, in the very same paper, Skinner also adopts a position of ontological behaviorism). The basic stance of epistemological behaviorism toward subjective experience is that because it is private and not objectively observable, it is not subject to scientific investigation.[6,7] On this view, the structuralist definition of psychology as the study of the elements of consciousness placed it outside the boundary of scientific study. The sterility of the structuralist project of investigating the elements of subjective experience appeared to support that idea. J.B. Watson's 1913 book *Psychology as the Behaviorist Views It*, marks the birth of behaviorism in the United States and outlines its general program, which is filled out and elaborated in later papers. In one of those papers, Watson (1925) wrote that

> ... the time has come for psychology to discard all reference to consciousness ... it is merely another word for the 'soul' of more ancient times ... the behaviorist must exclude from his scientific vocabulary all subjective terms such as sensation, perception, image, desire, purpose, and even thinking and emotion as they were subjectively defined.
>
> (as cited in Baars, 2003, p. 3)

Echoing Watson's view many years later, Skinner (1953) wrote: '... "mind" and "ideas" are non-existent entities, invented for the sole purpose of providing spurious explanations ... since mental and psychic terms are asserted to lack the dimensions of physical science, we have an additional reason for rejecting them' (pp. 30–31).

Watson argued that principles of animal behavior, such as conditioning, are applicable to human beings. He also 'translated' experiential terms into various forms of behaviors – for example, thinking as subvocal verbalizations; and verbal report as a form of behavior. In view of the fact that we generally report our subjective experiences verbally, the concept of 'verbal behavior', some argued, could be seen as allowing mentalistic terms into behaviorism through the back door. Similarly, in a book entitled *Verbal Behavior*, Skinner (1957) tried to demonstrate that through 'functional analysis' of environmental variables, one could predict and control verbal behavior without any reference to mental states. In what has become a classic, Chomsky (1980) wrote a devastating review of the book, which exposed the utter untenability of Skinner's behaviorist approach to so-called verbal behavior.

Behaviorism justified its approach not only on the ground that observable behavior was the proper subject of psychological science, but also on the ground that focusing on the relation between antecedent (stimuli) and consequent (response) variables – without any reference to subjective experience – enabled successful prediction and control, the presumed primary aims of science. However, aside from the fact that various forms of subjective aims, goals, and desires motivate overt behavior, one can question whether an overriding emphasis on prediction constitutes an accurate description of science. Successful predictions can be made without theoretical understanding and theoretical understanding can occur without prediction. Indeed, one can understand the primary role of accurate prediction in scientific theorizing as an indication one's theoretical account of a phenomenon is likely to be valid, that is, that one has *understood* the nature of the phenomenon being investigated.

Consider conditioning of behavior – a mainstay of behavioral research – which behaviorists assumed is independent of subjective experience. However, there is evidence that this assumption is unwarranted. Whereas a simple response such as an eye blink can occur without awareness of the relationship between the conditioned and unconditioned stimulus, there is evidence that with regard to other responses (e.g., skin conductance), conditioning is dependent on the participants' awareness of the stimulus contingency (Hamm & Vaitl, 1996; Hur et al., 2016). Although there is some controversy on this issue, there is evidence that awareness of the contingency between conditioned and unconditioned stimulus influences evaluative conditioning (i.e., conditioning in which pairing a neutral stimulus with a negative or positive stimulus shifts the evaluation of the neutral stimulus) (Walther & Nagengast, 2006; Field, 2000). There is also evidence that fear conditioning is influenced by other factors such as the availability of executive resources, degree of neuroticism, and attentional focus (Hur et al., 2016). In short, in humans, conditioning is hardly simply an automatic reflex totally independent of subjective experience. Rather, it is influenced by a number of higher-order processes, including focus of attention and most important in the present context, subjective awareness of the contingency between the conditioned and unconditioned stimulus. Thus, ironically, even if one's sole interest is in prediction and control, it appears that taking into account the individual's subjective awareness as a variable enhances predictive success.

In addition to the issue of the role of awareness in conditioning, there is also the question of the degree to which the specific behaviors predicted and controlled in a great deal of behaviorist research have much to do with any important aspects of an individual's life. For example, Hullian behavior theory was mainly preoccupied with rats running mazes The assumption made that such research would yield findings that would be relevant to human learning has always been a very questionable one. And as for behavior therapy, a clinical derivative of behaviorism, was applied to human behavior, the focus in the early literature tended to be on such phenomena as de-conditioning spider phobias, hardly a common life problem. The later development of behavior therapy (e.g., Wolpe, 1961, 1968; Rachman, 1967; Davison, 1968; Salter, 1949) included such techniques and concepts as systematic desensitization, reciprocal inhibition, reinforcement, conditioning, extinction, and so on. However, a majority of the early published papers on behavior therapy continued to deal with specific phobias and fears, an area in which behavioral techniques, in particular, extinction procedures, would be most applicable. Since then, behavior therapy of one form or another has been in wide use in altering behavior in such areas as autism and conduct disorders. With regard to the former, I think it is safe to say that Applied Behavioral Analysis associated with the work of Lovaas (e.g., 1987) (which, in turn, was derived from Skinnerian principles) represents the most widespread to treatment of childhood autism.[8]

Although behavioral techniques may have focused on altering behavior, behavior therapy essentially attempted to alter behaviors through interventions that were directed to subjective experience, namely, the experience of fear and anxiety. This was soon recognized by Beck and his colleagues, as reflected in their development of Cognitive Behavior Therapy (CBT).

Although behaviorism dominated American psychology for many years, its influence began to decline due to a number of factors. One such factor, as I noted above, was the degree to which the behaviorist empirical research program focused on animal behavior, such as rats running mazes – behaviorist research was not infrequently referred to as 'rat psychology' – and pigeons pecking behavior. An obvious question raised was not only the generalization of research findings to human behavior, but the ecological validity of these research findings even to the behavior of *animals* in their natural environments.

Another factor that contributed to the markedly reduced influence of behaviorism was the emergence of research findings that appeared to contradict the stimulus–response drive-reduction formulations exemplified by Hullian theory (e.g., Hull, 1943) to the effect that virtually all learned behavior was due to primary or secondary reinforcement, defined in terms of reduction of tensions associated with primary drives (e.g., hunger). A simple example of primary reinforcement is the enhancement of learning through the reward of food, which serves to reduce tensions associated with the hunger drive. An example of secondary reinforcement is the reward value of the caregiver due to her association with hunger drive reduction. A parade of findings emerged that could not be readily accounted for by either primary or secondary reinforcement. For example, evidence was reported that the mere opportunity to observe a novel stimulus, manipulate an object, explore the environment, or play with peers served as reinforcers of behavior despite their lack of association with the reduction of drive tensions (e.g., Berlyne, 1950; Harlow et al., 1956; Terrell, 1959). And there is, of course, a classic Harlow (1958) study with surrogate mothers, demonstrating that infant monkeys become attached to terry cloth surrogate mothers despite the fact that it is wire surrogate mothers who provide food.

The secondary reinforcement account of the infant–mother bond is virtually identical in structure to the claim of Freudian theory that the infant becomes attached to the mother due to her association with drive reduction. Indeed, the convergence between Hullian and Freudian drive reduction made possible the 'translation' of Freudian concepts into Hullian behaviorist terms by Dollard and Miller (1941). It is interesting to note that Hull offered a seminar on the integration of conditioning and Freudian theory held at the Institute of Human Relations at Yale University (Gondra, 2002; see also Hilgard, 1957; McClelland, 1957). There is also convergence between Hullian and Freudian drive-reduction theory with regard to the nature of the critiques directed toward these theories. For example, as noted above, the classic Harlow (1958) study was intended to demonstrate that the infant monkey's attachment to its surrogate mother was based on 'contact comfort', not the provision of food. And one of the primary theoretical motivations for Bowlby's (1969) positing of an autonomous attachment system was an attempt to refute the Freudian version of the secondary reinforcement theory of infant–mother attachment. More and more ad hoc formulations defending the secondary reinforcement account were proposed by Hullian theorists. Eventually, the theory became too overloaded with ad hoc formulations and its influence markedly declined (See Lakatos, 1968, for a general philosophical account of the fate of theories in the light of contrary evidence). The relevance of the above findings to the issue of the role of consciousness and subjective experience lies in the consideration that it is difficult to understand how the opportunity to manipulate an object or to observe a novel stimulus can be rewarding without considering the conclusion that these activities are rewarding because they are *subjectively experienced as pleasurable* despite the absence of drive reduction. In short, the research findings on the reward value of non-drive-reducing cognitive motives served to puncture the behaviorist taboo against any direct or indirect allusion to subjective experience.

Although the dominance of behaviorism waned, it is important to recognize that its influence remains in many forms. For example, reflecting the continuing influence of behaviorism, virtually every introductory psychology textbook in the last 100 years defines psychology as the study of behavior. Psychology continues to be defined as the study of behavior, with little or no reference to consciousness and subjective experience. As Baars (2003) writes:

> Behaviorism and its radical rejection of personal experience was a major theme of the twentieth century, and continues even today. Rejection of consciousness became a core belief for academic psychologists and philosophers in the English-speaking world, justifying their claim to standing among the physical sciences

(p. 1)

Cognitive psychology: the cognitive revolution

The reduced influence of the behaviorism project is marked by the advent of the 'cognitive revolution'. As Miller (2003) writes, 'Psychology could not participate in the cognitive revolution until it freed itself from behaviorism …' (p. 141). Before embarking on a discussion of how cognitive psychology has dealt with the phenomenon of subjective experience, I want to comment on the important but overlooked role that E.C. Tolman's work played in the transition from behaviorism to cognitive psychology. The research and theorizing of Tolman and his colleagues stood out during an era in which American psychology was dominated by a Hullian stimulus–response drive-reduction form of behaviorism. According to that form of behaviorism, in order for learned behavior to take place, primary or secondary reinforcement needed to occur. This is where Tolman enters the picture.

Although Tolman viewed himself as a behaviorist, he referred to his form of behaviorism as 'purposive behaviorism'. Along with his students and colleagues, Tolman threatened behaviorist purity by distinguishing between behavior (performance) and learning; and by demonstrating that learning could occur and remain latent until it revealed itself in motivated performance. Thus, Tolman (1948) demonstrated that simply running a maze without any reward of food would result in the rat learning in the form of acquiring a 'cognitive map' of the maze. However, such learning would only become apparent in performance, as evidenced by such indices as more efficient performance when the rat ran the maze under conditions of reward.

By placing the adjective 'purposive' before behaviorism, and by insisting that psychology study 'molar' behavior rather than molecular elements of behavior, Tolman was essentially stating that the proper subject matter of psychology, including animal psychology, is purposive actions rather than simply behavior or elements of behavior. And by taking this position as well as introducing concepts such as 'cognitive maps' as intervening variables, Tolman was allowing some form of mentalistic concepts – purposes and intentions – as well as cognitive structures as proper objects of psychological study. Thus, in an important sense, Tolman can be seen as an early progenitor of the transition from the dominance of behaviorism to the emergence of the 'cognitive revolution'. Additionally, the strategy of positing the intervening variable of cognitive maps as a cognitive structure that is not directly observable in overt behavior and yet, has explanatory value, bears a strong family resemblance to what has been a basic strategy of cognitive psychology.

Although Tolman introduced mentalistic concepts, such as 'cognitive maps', into his explanatory accounts, he nevertheless wrote that '"Mental processes" are for the behaviorist, naught but inferred determinants of behavior, which ultimately are deducible from behavior' (Tolman, 1932, p. 3). However, if these mental processes are entirely deducible from behavior, that is, if they are 'exhaustively defined operationally' (Greenwood, 1999, p. 7) – as specific behaviors, it is not clear what explanatory value the intervening variable of 'mental processes' would have. Why not simply report the functional relations between stimulus inputs and specific behaviors in the manner of Skinner, Hull and other behaviorists? Inserting intervening variables – mental processes – which are exhaustedly operationally defined in terms of behaviors – would not seem to contribute much to explanation. Indeed, this was precisely the ground on which Skinner dismissed intervening variables in his argument that they possess no real explanatory value.

As MacCorquodale and Meehl (1948) noted, in their concept of 'hypothetical construct', if the positing of a variable or processes between stimulus input and response is to have explanatory value, that variable must have 'surplus meaning' beyond its behavioral operational definition. However, surplus meaning is precisely what strict behaviorists ruled out in stating that 'the only meaning possessed by intervening variable is their relationship to both independent and dependent variables' (Kendler, 1952, p. 271). One way of understanding 'surplus meaning' is to recognize that in order for a variable inserted between stimulus and response to have any explanatory value, it must point to a substantive process that furthers one's explanatory account. Consider Tolman's concept of cognitive map. Despite his use of the term 'intervening variable', as Greenwood (1999) notes, Tolman never attempted to provide an exhaustive operational definition for it. This suggests, as Greenwood (1999) notes, that the concept of a 'cognitive map' may have been intended to refer to a substantive representational structure, something like a map that has an explanatory role in accounting for certain phenomena. Indeed, following O'Keefe's (1971) later discovery of 'place cells' in the hippocampus that encode spatial location. O'Keefe and Nadel (1978) developed a cognitive map theory in which hippocampal function 'can be used to map and navigate the world' (Nadel, 2020, p. 1196).

In his brief history of the emergence of cognitive psychology, Miller (2003) writes that the cognitive revolution 'brought the mind back into experimental psychology' (p. 142)[9] (see also Mandler, 2002). The aspects of the mind that are brought back into experimental psychology are its 'representational and computational capacities' (p. 144). Miller cites a 1956 symposium on information theory at the Massachusetts Institute of Technology as marking the beginning of the cognitive revolution. What is important about Miller's observation is not the date, but the link between the origin of cognitive psychology and the increasing interest in information theory.[10] A basic strategy of cognitive researchers and theorists is to infer mentalistic cognitive processes and structures that underlie various cognitive behaviors and capacities being investigated (e.g., perception, memory, language). However, the mentalistic cognitive processes and structures that are primarily computational in nature are inaccessible to consciousness and subjective experience. Hence, it is not clear in what sense they are mentalistic concepts. This issue already arose prior to the advent of cognitive psychology. Consider the mentalistic concept of 'unconscious inference', which Helmholtz (1867) invoked as a means of accounting for the perceptual phenomenon of size constancy (i.e., perceiving an object as generally the same size at different distances despite different retinal images). The experience of size constancy is made possible by seemingly 'intelligent' inference-like computational brain processes that appear to entail a calculation of the relation between the distance and size of the retinal image. However, these inference-like and computation-like are inherently inaccessible to conscious experience. (Nor, one can add, are they observable in the brain as inferential and computational processes). Rather, one experiences the *product* of the neural processes which are metaphorically referred to as computational and inferential. That is, despite the term 'unconscious inference', one will not find inferences either in subjective experience or in assemblies of activated neurons. Rather, one employs cognitive metaphors such as unconscious inference or computation or some other intervening cognitive processes as 'bridges' to describe the relationship between subjective experience and brain processes. This has been a basic strategy of cognitive psychology. This strategy triggers the kind of question posed by Penrose (1994), who asks: 'Might we be doing something with our brain that cannot be described in computational terms at all? How do our feelings of conscious awareness – of happiness, pain, love, aesthetic sensibility, will, understanding, etc. – fit into such a computational picture?' (p. 12).

John Searle (e.g., 1990) has been a severe critic of the strategy of invoking mentalistic processes that are inherently inaccessible to conscious experience. Searle's objection to the positing of cognitive structures and processes between subjective experience and brain processes is that it implies a new ontology that is neither accessible to consciousness nor neurophysiological, that is, neither mental (i.e., potentially accessible to consciousness) nor neurophysiological, but something in between. He suggests that the cognitive structures and processes posited by cognitive psychology constitute 'descriptions of functional aspects of systems, which will have to be explained by underlying neurophysiological mechanisms. In such cases, what looks like mentalistic psychology is sometimes better construed as speculative neurophysiology' (p. 585).

Consider once again the phenomenon of size constancy. If I understand Searle correctly, his account of this phenomenon would be likely to be something like the following: our immediate subjective experience is of seeing objects at different distances as approximately the same size. An explanatory account of this experiential phenomenon will include a set of neurophysiological mechanisms that can be described in terms of a functional system that can be described in terms of computational features (i.e., can be described functionally as computing the relation between size and distance). However, there are no substantive computational or inferential cognitive processes accessible to consciousness that intervene between the subjective experience and the neurophysiological mechanism.

According to Searle (1990) (and others), intentionality in the Brentano sense of aboutness or directedness toward something is a criterion of the mental. Searle also writes that because 'we have no notion of intrinsic intentionality except in terms of its accessibility to consciousness' (p. 585), to view a process or state as a *mental* process or state, it must in principle be potentially accessible to consciousness. However, although described in mentalistic terms, the processes invoked by cognitive psychologists are not potentially accessible to consciousness. Hence, it is not clear in what way they can be viewed as mental processes. Implicit in Searle's criticism, and especially pertinent in the present context, is his overall critique that, as reflected in the mentalistic concepts it employs, cognitive psychology's conception of the mental totally neglects its essential property of access to consciousness and subjective experience. One can add – and this is, I think, also implicit in Searle's critique of cognitive psychology is that its conception of the mental is more appropriate to a view of the individual as an information-processing robot than as a living, experiencing human being.

As noted above, Searle (1990) writes that 'what looks like mentalistic psychology is *sometimes* [my emphasis] better construed as speculative neurophysiology' (p. 595). Thus, he allows that his critique does not apply to some mentalistic processes and structures posited in cognitive psychology. For example, whereas the computational processes underlying various perceptual experiences may not be accessible to conscious experience, the representational structure of cognitive maps posited by Tolman may, indeed, be accessible to consciousness. If Tolman's rat could speak, it could, in principle, report on some features of the maze it has learned. However, humans can speak and can tell you something of what they have learned. For example, in the course of walking around a new neighborhood, they may, in fact, refer to something like a map inside one's head.

Potential accessibility to consciousness and subjective experience is also a property of other cognitive structures inferred in cognitive psychology. Consider the concept of a 'working model' (also referred to as a 'internal working model' or IWM) as another example of a mentalistic concept that refers to mental contents potentially accessible to subjective experience. Although Craik (1943) and Young (1964) employed the term 'working model' to refer to a model of the external environment, Bowlby extended the concept to refer to models of prototypic interactions between the child and attachment figure.[11,12] Bowlby (1969) conceptualized IWMs as representations of one's attachment figure, of oneself in relation to the attachment figure, and of the prototypic interaction between oneself and one's attachment figure. Bowlby (1969) writes that it is one's brain that constructs working models, but also that

> although it is certainly not necessary for all such processes always to be conscious, it is probably necessary that some should be so sometimes. In particular, it seems likely that revising, extending, and checking of models are ill done or done not at all unless a model is subjected from time to time to whatever special benefits accrue from becoming conscious.
>
> (p. 82)

Recall that the aspects of the mind that, according to Miller (2003), are brought back into experimental psychology by the cognitive revolution are 'representational and computational capacities' (p. 585). I would suggest that whereas the computational processes entailed in perceptual phenomena such as size or color constancy are, so to speak, 'purely' neurophysiological – that is, they are inherently inaccessible to consciousness – as Bowlby suggests, representational processes may be accessible to consciousness. For example, repeated early experiences of rejection and consequent expectations of rejection in new relationships characteristic of an IWM associated with an avoidant attachment pattern may, in certain circumstances, be accessible to consciousness.

Is one's experience of agency an illusion?

I turn now to the issue of how some influential cognitive researchers and theorists have dealt with a sense of agency, a central aspect of subjective experience, that is, an experience of choice and of acting on the basis of motives, desires, intentions, goals, and aims to which one has experiential access. Agency is experienced in the simple sequence of, say, intending to get something and lifting one's arm in order to get it. As R. Eagle (2007) notes, in observing infants and toddlers, 'there appears to be an innate predisposition *to take great joy in the exercise of agency* [emphasis in original] – that is, in making things happen with their own body or with objects' (pp. 168–169). Despite the centrality of a sense of agency to one's sense of oneself as a person, a dominant claim in much of the cognitive psychology literature is that our sense of agency and choice is illusory.[13] It is one thing to be informed that we do not have conscious experiential access to neural processes underlying our perceptual experiences. That is relatively easy to accept and does not constitute a threat to one's sense of personal agency. We are also not necessarily expected to have introspective access to the external influences on one's behavior. It is another thing, however, to be informed that we do not have conscious access to the reasons and motives for our behaviors and decisions; and that when we think we are providing reasons and motives, we are, in fact, producing socially plausible causal theories. Such claims *do* constitute a threat to essential aspects of one's sense of agency, including the sense that we generally know why we do things.[14] There is a body of work in cognitive psychology of which the Nisbett and Wilson paper is representative, however, that makes precisely such claims.

In a widely cited and influential paper, Nisbett and Wilson (1977) claim that people have 'little or no direct introspective access to [higher] order cognitive processes' (p. 231). Rather, according to them, one's reports regarding the effects of a stimulus on one's behavior or of the reasons and motives for one's behavior are based not on introspection, but on 'implicit causal theories' (p. 231). Nisbett and Wilson (1977) summarize a number of studies the findings of which, according to them, suggest not only that we are often unaware of the external stimuli that influence our behavior, but also demonstrate that we do not have introspective access to the reasons and motives for our behaviors. An example of a study demonstrating a lack of awareness of external priming cues cited by Nisbett and Wilson (1977) is Maier's (1931) classic problem-solving experiment in which the task was to tie the ends of hanging from the ceiling cords that were too far apart to hold one cord while reaching for the other. After the subject was stumped, Maier casually set one of the cords in motion. Within a very short period after, the subject tied a weight to one of the cords and set it swinging like a pendulum, which enabled a solution to the problem. When asked how they solved the problem, subjects failed to refer to the pendulum cue Maier provided and instead referred to a useless cue. Nisbett and Wilson conclude that the subjects were not aware of the stimulus cue that primed their solution to the problem.

In another study, participants were asked to select which pair of four identical pairs of nylon stockings presented from left to right was the best quality. The right-most pair of stockings were selected by almost 80% of the subjects. When asked about the reasons for their choice, no subject mentioned position and, indeed, denied that position played any part in their choice.

The findings are interpreted by Nisbett and Wilson as providing support for their claim regarding lack of introspective access to the reasons and motives for one's behavior (Nisbett and Wilson do not report the reasons the subjects did offer; nor do they report the reasons given by the 20% of the subjects who did not select the right-most pair of stockings). Nisbett and Wilson write:

> Precisely why the position effect occurs is not obvious. It is possible that subjects carried into the judgment task the consumer's habit of 'shopping around', holding off on the choice of early-seen garments on the left in favor of later-seen garments on the right.
>
> (p. 244)

Let us take a closer look at the context and arrangements of the study. The participants in the study were being deceived in that they were led to believe that there were differences among the different pairs of stockings; that is, they were placed in a situation in which any choice could not really be justified. As Jack (2013) puts it, '… the subject is in a situation where they are likely to have nothing sensible to say, but where the social expectations are engineered to make them think they should have something to say' (p. 671). If one places oneself in the situation in which the subjects were placed, one can plausibly imagine the following taking place: after examining the first and second pairs of stockings and unable to detect any obvious difference in quality, one then goes from the second to the third pair, also detecting no obvious difference in quality; and then from the third pair to the right-most last pair, again not detecting any obvious difference in quality. An easy thing to do at this point is simply select the last pair. Thus, the 'shopping around' explanation that Nisbett and Wilson tentatively offer may be relevant, but not in the way they suggest, namely, that the subjects resorted to a causal theory to account for their choice. Rather, after 'shopping around' and finding no evident differences among the pairs of stockings in the different bins, why not simply select the last pair rather than go back and re-examine all the different pairs.

Given the demand characteristics of the experiment, trust in the experimenter's statement that there were differences in quality in the pairs of stockings, and perhaps the feeling that they were not skillful enough to detect the difference, the subjects would be unlikely to admit that position was the basis for their choice. However, this does not mean that under the proper conditions, including probing questioning, the subjects would not have introspective access to the reason for their choice. Indeed, Petitmengin et al. (2013) found that following an 'elicitation interview', most subjects were able to report the basis for their choice (See also Hurlburt & Heavey, 2001, on the use of 'Descriptive Experience Sampling'; and Howe's (1991) defense of introspection)

One also needs to raise the question of ecological validity. Would the subjects show the same behavior in ordinary situations? How generalizable are the findings in this contrived experimental situation to behavior in real-life situations? Nisbett and Wilson do not address these questions. Indeed, the strategy of the study seems to be to contrive experimental situations in which it will be quite likely that subjects will not have ready introspective access to the reasons and motives for their behavior. It is as if the role of the researcher is that of debunker of generally accepted commonsense assumptions, which presumably enhances the scientific status of the research.

As another example of presumed evidence that one does have access to the reasons and motives for one's behavior, Nisbett and Wilson refer to a classic study by Latane and Darley (1970), who reported not only that the greater the number of bystanders, the less likely that we will help others in distress, but also that we are unaware of the influence of the number of bystanders on one's behavior. Indeed, Latane and Darley reported that when asked, people deny such influence, which Nisbett and Wilson interpret as buttressing their claim that people are unaware of the reasons for their behavior. However, as in the case of the previously cited study on the choice of stockings, there is no evidence that careful 'elicitation interviews' were conducted.

The most plausible explanation for the relationship between the presence of bystanders and failing to help someone in distress is the implicit rationale to the effect that if other people are present, I do not need to get involved. This less than admirable reason is one that subjects are not likely to readily acknowledge to someone else or perhaps even to themselves. However, this hardly means that people do not have introspective access to the reason for their behavior. It is highly likely that under certain circumstances (e.g., an eliciting interview; or talking to a trusted friend), people will be aware of and acknowledge their reason. One should add that later studies on the bystander phenomenon demonstrate its complexity. The likelihood of helping behavior varies with a variety of factors other than the number of bystanders. For example, it varies with the in-group versus out-group status of the one who needs help (Levine et al., 2005) and whether or not a camera is present (van Bommel, 2013). This latter finding is especially interesting insofar as it suggests that non-helping behavior is accompanied by some degree of shame or guilt, which would make one less likely to report the reasons for the non-helping behavior.

Although Nisbett and Wilson (1977) acknowledge that 'subjective reports about higher mental processes are sometimes correct', they go on to say that 'even the instances of correct report are not due to direct introspective awareness', but rather are due to 'the incidentally correct employment of a priori causal theories' (p. 233). According to Nisbett and Wilson's reasoning, even when subjects do seem to be aware of their reasons and motives, their behavior should nevertheless be viewed as prompted by mini-causal theories. As Smith and Miller (1978) write: 'Nisbett and Wilson regard both correct and incorrect reports as illustrating this position. This means that their hypothesis cannot be falsified simply by demonstrating that there are occasions when peoples' verbal self-reports on their mental processes are correct' (p. 356).

Smith and Miller (1978) also argue convincingly that in a number of studies cited by Nisbett and Wilson, inappropriate statistical tests were employed; and that at least in one study, a reanalysis of the data 'demonstrates clear evidence for subjects' access to their mental processes contrary to the original author's interpretations'. As Smith and Miller (1978) comment, social psychology 'values counterintuitive findings' (p. 355). The zeal with which cognitive psychology attempts to debunk the commonsense view that we generally have experiential access to the reasons and motives for our behavior suggests to some (e.g., Jack, 2013) that a function of such efforts is to enhance the scientific status of research by demonstrating its superiority over commonsense thinking.

In a recent paper entitled 'Why bad science is sometimes more appealing than good science', Oreskes (2021), an historian of science, makes the point that surprising and novel results are cited more frequently than papers that provide modest and incremental knowledge. She also writes that 'surprising results are surprising because they go against what experience has led us to believe so far, which means that there's a good chance that they're wrong' (p. 83). The paper by Nisbet and Wilson (1977) represents an instance of the phenomenon to which Oreskes is referring. They report findings that are surprising, that contradict our everyday experiences, and that are cited with great frequency. However, as noted earlier, they are also based on limited and contrived experimental conditions. Thus, despite the fact that the studies cited by Nisbett and Wilson, at best, may demonstrate that under certain limited circumstances we may not be able to access the reasons and reasons for our decisions, they conclude that we are *virtually always not capable* of accessing our reasons and motives.

Continuing the frontal attack on one's sense of agency, in particular, on the commonsense belief that we can rely on our conscious experience, in a series of publications, Wegner (e.g., 2002, 2003, 2008) has asserted that the belief that one's actions are caused by a conscious will is illusory. In an attempt to provide empirical support for his claim that the experience of free will is an illusion, Wegner (2002) cites phenomena in which we think we have acted when in fact we have not, and when we have acted, but think we have not. Such phenomena include 'automatisms', such as the alien-hand syndrome where the person experiences his or her hand as having a mind of its own, post-hypnotic movements, and other behavior where we can be wrong as to whether or not we performed an action. Based largely on such findings, Wegner concludes that we do not have privileged access to our feelings and beliefs regarding the relation between our intentions and actions.

Similar to Nisbett and Wilson, Wegner cites contrived situations demonstrating that our sense of consciously willing an action can be mistaken, and then concludes that we are *always* mistaken in that regard. That this can occur under certain contrived experimental conditions and on rare occasions such as the occurrence of 'automatisms', in Moore's (2020) words, 'hardly supports the metaphysical claim that wills *never* [emphasis in original] cause bodily movements' (p. 241). The findings reported by Wegner simply do not support his sweeping conclusions. As Moore (2020) observes,

> One might read Wegner as not so much denying that we are always right in our beliefs about our own mental states and their causation of our behavior, but as asserting that we are always wrong about whether we have exercised voluntary agency in our overt behaviors.
>
> (p. 239)

It is worth noting that whatever the philosophical issues, from a psychological or experiential point of view, an individual's *sense* of free will rather than a sense of being compelled is a marker of mental health (Rapaport, 1956).

A much-discussed finding reported by Libet (1983) purports to show that one's sense that one's will or intentions play a causal role in one's action is illusory. However, insofar as this finding has been discussed primarily in terms of their philosophical implications, I defer discussion of them to Chapter 3. Suffice it to say for now that the conclusion one would reach based on the work of Nisbett and Wilson, Wegner, and Libet, which are cited here as representative of a view shared by others, is that, in many respects, ordinary, everyday experience is illusory and confabulatory. It takes the psychological scientist to reveal the many illusory aspects of our beliefs and experiences. As we will see in Chapter 2, the role assigned to the scientific investigator is similar to the role of the psychoanalyst as *Menschenkenner* who reveals the illusory and dissimulating nature of much of subjective experience and who informs us regarding what is really going on behind surface appearances; and in Chapter 3, the similar role assigned to the neuroscientifically informed philosopher of mind who informs us that our subjective experiences are nothing but neural processes.

Subjective experience in other psychological approaches

Research and theory in the discipline of psychology are characterized not only by a de-emphasis on subjective experience seen in the above contributions, but also by approaches to human behavior (particularly in clinical and social psychology) in which the individual's subjective perspective is viewed as a critical variable in understanding and explaining human behavior. The leading figure representing this perspective in social psychology was Kurt Lewin (e.g., 1935, 1936); and in clinical psychology, Carl Rogers (e.g., 1961). Although Lewin's theorizing was quite complex, a central feature of it was the proposition that psychology is 'the study of behavior in the psychological field' (Bronfenbrenner, 1977, p. 199) or life-space (Wong, 2002). What Lewin meant by life-space was not the individual's geographical environment or his or her early psychological environment, but his or her current environment as personally construed by him or her.

A similar distinction was made by the Gestalt psychologist Koffka (1935), who distinguished between the geographical and behavioral environment. He recounts the following old German legend to make the distinction dramatically patent:

> One winter evening amidst a driving snowstorm a man on horseback arrived at an inn, happy to have reached a shelter after hours of riding over the wind-swept plain on which the blanket of snow had covered all paths and land-marks. The landlord who came to the door viewed the stranger with surprised and asked him whence he came. The man pointed in the direction straight away from the inn, whereupon the landlord, in a tone of awe and wonder, said: 'Do you know that you have ridden across the Lake of Constance?' At which point the rider dropped stone dead at his feet
>
> (Koffka, 1935; as cited in Holahan, 1978)

Lewin's and Koffka's fundamental distinction between the role of the geographic and the psychological environment in psychological life stands in marked contrast to the later eagerness of cognitive and social psychology to demonstrate the explanatory irrelevance of appeal to subjective experience.

Other personality and social psychology theorists, among them Snygg and Combs, argued for the centrality of a subjective perspective in explaining behavior, and for a redefinition of psychology as the study of persons from an experiential perspective (e.g., Snygg & Combs, 1949). In this last paper, given in connection with his receipt of the Charlotte and Karl Buhler Award presented by the Division of Humanistic Psychology, Combs (1997) wrote: 'I turned to humanistic thinking because I was frustrated and disappointed with behaviorism' (p. 239). He also writes that he was enormously influenced by a 'pamphlet' given to him by Snygg entitled 'The need for a phenomenological system in psychology', as well as his experiences as a client of Rogers. For Combs (1997), at the center of 'perceptual-humanistic psychology' (p. 242) is the recognition 'that behavior is a consequence, not of the stimulus *per se*, but the person's perception of the stimulus' (p. 242).

Snygg published a paper in 1941 in *Psychological Review* entitled 'The need for a phenomenological system of psychology'. He writes in that paper that 'behavior is completely determined by and pertinent to the phenomenal field of the behavior of the organism' (p. 411), which he defines as the 'world of naïve, immediate experience' (p. 414). He refers to Lewin in passing (he is not included in the References), and although he writes approvingly of Gestalt psychology, he is critical of its presumed departure from phenomenology to objectivity (it is not entirely clear what that means). Finally, unlike other phenomenal psychologists (such as Giorgi, whose work I will briefly discuss), Snygg writes that the phenomenal approach is concerned not only with description, but also with 'prediction and control of behavior' (p. 421).

Despite differences in language and in affiliation with one or another school, there is a red thread running through the writings of Snygg and Combs, Lewin, and Rogers, which can be broadly characterized as phenomenological, however, not in the sense of Titchener's structuralism or, as will see, of Husserl's phenomenology but in the sense of according primacy to immediate subjective experience and to viewing the subject matter of psychology in terms of the individual's *subjective construal* of stimuli and events.

There is little evidence that the work of Snygg and Combs, and also perhaps the work of Lewin, have had much lasting influence. If anything, cognitive social psychology has moved away from a concern with subjective experience and away from studies of individuals in their 'life-space' and toward an increasing emphasis on the experimental laboratory as the primary setting for research. As for Rogers, his influence was always more pronounced in the context of psychotherapy rather than personality theory. And even in the context of psychotherapy, although many Rogerian concepts have been assimilated by other approaches, there is a great deal of emphasis in the contemporary psychotherapy literature on CBT and very little on client-centered therapy.

Phenomenology in psychological theory and research

A number of psychological theorists have developed an approach to psychological research based on the phenomenology of Husserl. I will discuss a paper by Giorgi as illustrative of work in this area. Giorgi (2014) locates his method in 'the continental phenomenological philosophy developed by Husserl ...' (p. 543). He writes that

> phenomenological work is done with the attitude of reduction, which means that all that is given to consciousness is taken to be a certain presence to consciousness, but no claim is made about the actual existence of what is given. The existential claim is withheld ...
>
> (p. 593)

As is the case in Titchenerian introspection, the focus is on experience itself rather than on the external object being experienced. As Giorgi (2014) writes, 'I am dealing with presences, not existences, which is precisely what a phenomenon is: how an object or situation is experienced, precisely how it is experienced; how an object or state of affairs presents itself to an observing consciousness' (p. 546). This is generally what Husserl meant by suspension of the natural attitude and what Titchener means by avoidance of the stimulus error. Giorgi (2014) also writes that 'the phenomenological researcher must *not* [emphasis in original] bring into the method a non-given factor [such as a theoretical assumption or hypothesis] to help render the phenomenon comprehensible' (p. 546). In short, the phenomenological method of Girogi, as well as the introspection method of Titchener, are purely descriptive. Indeed, Giorgi cites Titchener's (1901) statement in his manual for qualitative research: 'The object of the qualitative experiment in psychology is – if we may sum it up in a single word – to *describe*' (p. xiii) (as cited in Giorgi, 2014, p. 545). However, Giorgi does not refer to Titchener's (1910) position that explanation of mental phenomena (which, he believed, would take the form of identifying underlying physiological underpinnings of mental phenomena) would follow upon completion of the description project.

Giorgi (2014) argues that his phenomenological descriptive method is a legitimate 'way of conducting science' (p. 547). The question is the yield of this way of conducting science. Titchener (1912) wrote that adequate systematic description of the elements of consciousness (as instantiated in his introspective approach) needed to precede explanation. As we know from the history of structuralism, the explanation component remained a promissory note. This appears to be also the case with regard to a good deal of phenomenological research, including Giorgi's. The literature of phenomenological psychology literature has been heavy on descriptions of the phenomenological method and pronouncements on the method as an alternative to current scientific approaches, and light on significant findings and important insights, including insights regarding the nature of subjective experience. Much of that literature, including Giorgi's publications, is taken up with explications of the phenomenological method, critiques of misunderstandings and misuses of a true, Husserl-based, phenomenological method rather than presentations of significant products of that method. In a recent publication Applebaum (2011) provides a lengthy account of Giorgi's contributions in which there is not a single sentence pointing to a significant finding generated by the phenomenological approach favored by Giorgi. Instead, there are references to the importance of the 'phenomenological attitude', to phenomenology as 'a way of seeing ... a way of relating to the other ...' (p. 524), and virtually as a way of life.

Although accurate description is certainly a critically important aspect of a systematic approach to any class of phenomena, one may wonder what the bracketed description of experience of Husserlian phenomenology or the description yielded by the introspectionism of structuralism is actually describing. It does not seem to be a description of lived experience in the real world. That is, the ecological validity of these descriptions is far from clear. The irony here is that despite the phenomenological criticism that much of the research in experimental psychology does not do justice to experience, the question of ecological validity is as much an issue in the phenomenological research of Giorgio as it is in the contrived experimental situations understandably criticized by phenomenologists. As is the case with structuralism, it is also far from clear that much of great interest regarding human experience and behavior has emerged from phenomenological research.

Although a refreshing contrast from behaviorism, this approach is incomplete and limited. While it is true that a critical factor in understanding behavior is understanding how the external stimulus is construed by the individual, surely, the individual's construal has its own etiological history, one that goes beyond the discourse of personal construals.[15] An adequate explanatory account would include not only the individual's personal construal of an event, but also identification of the factors that influence one's personal construal. Surely, an explanatory account is far from complete or adequate without addressing this question. As the philosopher Max Black (1967) has commented, after providing the reasons and motives for one's behavior (which surely entails personal construals), an inquiring mind will want to go on to address 'the provenance and etiology' of these reasons and motives.

Phenomenology in the study of schizophrenia

There is one area, a description of psychotic experience, in which a phenomenological approach has been quite productive. Because schizophrenia is characterized by anomalies in the very structure of experience, there is a long history of a phenomenological approach to the investigation of the nature of these experiences exemplified by, among others, the writings of Jaspers, Laing, and Binswanger. The focus on subjective experience in this area stands in sharp contrast to, on the one hand, a strictly biological perspective, which largely ignores subjective experience, and, on the other hand, a psychoanalytic approach that focuses on the unconscious meanings of schizophrenic and psychotic thought, as reflected in Freud's (1911) analysis of the Schreber case, as well as in the writings of Klein and Bion and the neo-Kleinians.

A phenomenological descriptive approach has been more fruitful in the study of schizophrenia than it has been in other areas because unlike other approaches, which have relied on trained observers and have attempted to analyze the elements of experience, a phenomenological perspective in the study of schizophrenia focuses attention on the schizophrenic patient's lived subjective experience, with the aim of attempting to comprehend his or her experiential world.[16] This ecologically valid account of the schizophrenic patient's subjective experience can be fruitful not only in the therapeutic context, but also in the context of linking the core experiential impairments of schizophrenia to biological and neural processes. That is, an accurate description of the schizophrenic's subjective experiences can guide the investigator in identifying specific physiological and neural processes that underlie these experiences (see Sass et al., 2011). Indeed, a good deal of such work has emerged.

Investigators have identified anomalies in the subjective experience of schizophrenic individuals and have attempted to link them to neurophysiological correlates. For example, Kapur (2003) notes that 'aberrant salience', that is, experiential salience of certain elements of one's experience, is a common feature of schizophrenia, and hypothesizes that dopamine dysregulation underlies this experience. Kapur also hypothesizes that 'delusions are a cognitive effort by the patient to make sense of these aberrantly salient experiences ...' (p. 2). Ardizza et al. (2016) have shown that interoceptive accuracy (e.g., heartbeat perception) is significantly lower in schizophrenic patients than in healthy controls.[17] Some schizophrenic patients also report the experience of an invisible barrier between oneself and the world. As one patient put it, 'it is like living in a fog'; an impaired sense thing and hearing one's voice as if through a tape recorder; voices being heard as robotized (Cermolacce et al., 2007). Also prominent in accounts of experience by schizophrenic patients are impairments in one's sense of agency, as expressed in the breakdown between an intention to think or act and thinking and acting; and breakdown of boundaries between oneself and others, as seen, for example, in the same intensity of experience whether a touch is self-produced or one is touched on the palm of one's hand by someone else (Blakemore et al., 2000).

One set of experiences that stands out is, on the one hand, experiencing people as de-animated automatons, and, on the other hand, experiencing inanimate events as animate. For example, Renee, a schizophrenic girl, experiences the wind as alive, howling, moaning, and crying, and a chair making fun of her (Sechahaye, 1951). Renee's disturbing experiences are not limited to perceptual anomalies.

She also experiences such extraordinary guilt that she feels that she has no right to eat or live Renee's sense of loss of reality fluctuated with her emotional experiences with her therapist, for example, with experiences of feelings of being in contact with and being understood by her therapist. That the vicissitudes of Renee's feelings of loss of reality varied with her emotional relationship with her therapist is a phenomenon that should not be minimized; it is perhaps as important as understanding the neurophysiological processes underlying Renee's anomalous experiences.

Let me reiterate the reasons that a phenomenological approach shows more strength in the investigation of schizophrenia than in other areas. This is so because the focus is on the lived experience of the schizophrenic individual. Given the nature of schizophrenia, the issue of trained introspection or suspension of the natural attitude does not arise. Indeed, the former is totally inappropriate. And, as for the latter, certain features of schizophrenic experience already reflect not so much a suspension, but as impairment of the natural attitude. In short, a focus on the subjective experience of the schizophrenic individual not only accords greater ecological validity to the investigation; it also directs the research for the processes, including neural processes, that are associated with these experiences.

Gestalt psychology and subjective experience

A focus on immediate subjective experience is a central feature of Gestalt psychology. In that sense, one can describe Gestalt psychology as phenomenological in its approach. Indeed, because of their common focus on subjective experience, Spiegelberg (1972), an important phenomenological theorist, has linked Gestalt psychology and Husserl's phenomenology. However, in important respects, the phenomenological approach of Gestalt psychology to experience is the polar opposite of Husserl's phenomenology. I will have more to say about this issue in Chapter 3. However, for now, it is important to note that in its emphasis on immediate phenomenal experience, Gestalt psychology is thoroughly opposed to the atomistic approach of breaking up experiences into their presumed elements characteristic of structuralism as well as of the Husserlian approach of bracketing the natural attitude. As Koffka (1935) puts it, the aim of Gestalt psychology is to obtain 'as naïve and full a description of direct experiences as possible' (p. 73). It is worth citing Köhler's (1938, p. vii) description of Gestalt psychology's approach to subjective experience in full, not only because it provides a description of the perspective of Gestalt psychology, but also because it also provides an excellent description of a scientific approach to the study of subjective experience:

> There seems to be a single starting point for psychology exactly as for all the other sciences: the world as we find it, naively and uncritically. The naivete may be lost as we proceed. Problems may be found which were at first completely hidden from our eyes. For their solution, it may be necessary to devise concepts which seem to have little contact with direct primary experience. Nevertheless, the whole development must begin with a naïve picture of the world. This origin is necessary because there is no other basis from which a science can arise.
>
> (Köhler, 1947, p. 3)

Gestalt psychology is often described as holistic, the main proposition of which is that the whole is greater than the sum of its parts. However, the emphasis of Gestalt psychology on wholes largely derives from the fact that phenomenal experience is of whole meaningful objects and configurations, not elements such as sensations. For Gestalt psychology, the seams of the experiential world are placed at boundaries between and relations among objects, not the presumed elements of objects, such as redness or curved lines that are the product of trained introspection or suspension of the natural attitude. Although brain processes underlying perception organize various elements, we experience the *products* of these processes – whole objects – not the elements that are organized by brain processes (I will have more to say about this issue in other chapters). This is the case not only with regard to perception of objects, but also with regard to experience of meaningful action. Although the elements of meaningful actions are specific movements, we normally experience the actions, not the specific movements making up the action. As we have seen in the case of Renee (Sechahaye, 1951), it is only in severe pathology that we see the break-up of meaningful action into disconnected movements.

Notes

1 Note the equation of scientific status with experimental method (see Danziger, 1990).
2 Kant's (1781) 'transcendental unity of apperception' essentially constitutes a recognition of the binding phenomenon.
3 Interestingly, Schlick (1938) wrote that it is a study of the relations between experiences, not of experience itself, that yields scientific knowledge.

4 Angell's (1906) description of the functions of consciousness is similar to Freud's account of the functions of the ego in terms of mediation between the demands of drives and reality.

5 There is an interesting personal connection between Functionalism and Behaviorism. Baldwin, an important contributor to functionalism, hired Watson, one of the fathers of behaviorism, who then replaced Baldwin in the Psychology Department at John Hopkins University.

6 As we will see, this stance bears a family resemblance to Freud's position on consciousness.

7 In writing about the history of the increasing secularization of mind, Makari (2015) notes that 'whereas the body could be viewed as a mechanism – matter in motion, in Hobbes' (1651) words, religion was the province of the soul. Physicians and scientists were free to study the mechanics of the body so long as it did not violate the 'impass-able boundary' (p. 21) of soul and mind which belonged to God and religion. There is a parallel between this 17th and 18th century division of labor and the behaviorist doctrine of limiting the subject matter of science to behavior, and relegating mind and subjective experience to non-scientific enterprises.

8 Early on, Lovaas also employed aversive consequences for undesirable behavior, which after much criticism, was dropped as a technique. However, as far as I am aware, this technique was dropped, not only for ethical reasons, but rather because it was deemed to be ineffective.

9 Miller suggests here that the mind was already at the center of other areas of psychology.

10 It is worth noting in this context that neither Miller nor Mandler mention Neisser, who made seminal contributions to the advent of cognitive psychology and whose book *Cognitive Psychology* had a great influence on the emergence of the new field. Unlike other cognitive psychologists, whose work was more closely aligned with information processing and artificial intelligence, Neisser was concerned with ecological validity, that is, with relevance to everyday life, of this new field.

11 Interestingly, Bowlby initially used the term 'cognitive map' to refer to the knowledge the animal must have of its environment to achieve its goals. However, Bowlby (1969) writes that because the word 'map' 'conjures up merely a static representation of topog-raphy' (p. 80), he preferred the more dynamic term 'working model'. Bowlby makes no mention of Tolman, who first used the term 'cognitive map'.

12 Stern's (1985) concept of Representations of Interactions Generalized (RIG's) is virtu-ally identical to IWM's.

13 Interestingly, neurologists and neurosurgeons have little difficulty distinguishing between behavior and experiences associated with agency and behavior and experi-ences associated with *loss of agency* due to certain forms of brain damage. For example, Goldstein (1952) writes about stimulus boundedness (i.e., the compulsion to attend to every external stimulus) and the loss of the abstract attitude, which includes loss of the ability to engage in as-if and pretend behavior in brain damaged patients. And Lhermitte et al. (1986) write about the compulsion of certain brain damaged patients to imitate everything they hear.

14 I am leaving for Chapter 2, a discussion of this issue in the context of psychoanalytic theory.

15 The same issue arises with regard to the psychoanalytic concept of *psychic reality*, that is, the idea that we are influenced not by physical (or physiological) reality, but by the psychical construal of that reality.

16 This approach can be contrasted with an emphasis on ego impairments rather than sym-bolic meanings, as reflected, for example in the work of Federn (e.g., 1952). However, although Federn was a renowned psychoanalyst, his work has been largely ignored in the psychoanalytic literature.

17 Interestingly, Ardizza et al. (2016) note that whereas low interoceptive accuracy has also been found in anorexia nervosa, major depressive disorder, and depersonalization-derealization, abnormally high interoceptive accuracy has been found in anxiety disorders. There is some evidence that deficits in interoceptive accuracy have been associated with alterations of the insular cortex (e.g., Frank, 2015; Kerr et al., 2015).

References

Angell, J. (1907). The province of functional psychology. *Psychological Review*, *14*(2), 61–91.

Applebaum, M. H. (2011). Amedeo Giorgi and psychology as a human science. *NeuroQuantology*, *9*(3). https://doi.org/10.14704/NQ.2011.9.3.463

Ardizzi, M., Ambrosecchia, M., Buratta, L., Ferri, F., Peciccia, M., Donnari, S., ... Gallese, V. (2016). Interoception and positive symptoms in schizophrenia. *Frontiers in Human Neuroscience*, *10*, 379. https://doi.org/10.3389/fnhum.2016.00379

Baars, B. J. (2003). The double life of B. F. Skinner: Inner conflict, dissociation and the scientific taboo against consciousness. *Journal of Consciousness Studies*, *10*(1), 5–25.

Berlyne, D. E. (1950). Novelty and curiosity as determinants of exploratory behavior. *British Journal of Psychology*, *41*, 68–80.

Black, M. (1967). Review of A. R. Louch's "explanation & human action". *American Journal of Psychology*, *80*, 655–656. https://doi.org/10.2307/1421209

Blakemore, S. J., Wolpert, D., & Frith, C. (2000). Why can't you tickle yourself? *NeuroReport*, *11*(11), 11–16. https://doi.org/10.1097/00001756-200008030-00002

Boring, E. G. (1950). *A history of experimental psychology*. Prentice-Hall.

Bowlby, J. (1969). *Attachment and loss* (Vol. 1). Basic Books.

Bronfenbrenner, U. (1977). Lewinian space and ecological substance. *Journal of Social Issues*, *33*(4), 199–212. https://doi.org/10.1111/j.1540-4560.1977.tb02533.x

Cermolacce, M., Naudin, J., & Parnas, J. (2007). The minimal self in psychopathology: Re-examining the self-disorders in the schizophrenia spectrum. *Consciousness and Cognition*, *16*(3), 703–714. https://doi.org/10.1016/j.concog.2007.05.013

Chomsky, N. (1980). A review of B F Skinner's verbal behavior. *Readings in Philosophy of Psychology*, *1*, 48–63.

Combs, A. (1997). Being and becoming: A field approach to psychology. *Humanistic Psychologist*, *25*(3), 237–243. https://doi.org/10.1080/08873267.1997.9986884

Craik, K. J. W. (1943). *The nature of explanation*. Cambridge University Press.

Danziger, K. (1990). *Constructing the subject: Historical origins of psychological research*. Cambridge University Press. https://doi.org/10.1017/CBO9780511524059

Davison, G. C. (1968). Systematic desensitization as a counterconditioning process. *Journal of Abnormal Psychology*, *73*(2), 91–99. https://doi.org/10.1037/h0025501

Dewey, J. (1944). Letter to Arthur F. Bentley. In J. Dewey & A. F. Bentley (Eds.), *A philosophical correspondence 1932–1951*. Rutgers University Press.

Dollard, J., & Miller, N. E. (1941). *Social learning and imitation*. Yale University Press.

Eagle, R. (2007). *Help him make you smile: The development of intersubjectivity in the atypical child*. Rowman & Littlefield.

Field, A. P. (2000). I like it, but I'm not sure why: Can evaluative conditioning occur without conscious awareness? *Consciousness and Cognition*, *9*(1), 13–36. https://doi.org/10.1006/ccog.1999.0402

Frank, G. K. (2015). Advances from neuroimaging studies in eating disorders. *CNS Spectrums, 20*(4), 391–400. https://doi.org/10.1017/S1092852915000012

Freud, S. (1911). Notes on autobiographical account case of paranoia (dementia paranoides). In *Standard edition* (Vol. 12, pp. 9–82). Hogarth Press.

Giorgi, A. (2014). An affirmation of the phenomenological psychological descriptive method: A response to Rennie (2012). *Psychological Methods, 19*(4), 542–551. https://doi.org/10.1037/met0000015

Gondra, J. M. (2002). Clark L. Hull y elpsicoanálisis [Hull and psychoanalysis]. *Revista de Historia de la Psicología, 23*(3–4), 371–379.

Greenwood, J. D. (1999). Understanding the "cognitive revolution" in psychology. *Journal of the History of the Behavioral Sciences, 35*(1), 1–22.

Hamm, A. O., & Vaitl, D. (1996). Affective learning: Awareness and aversion. *Psychophysiology, 33*(6), 698–710.

Harlow, H. F. (1958). The nature of love. *American Psychologist, 13*(12), 673–685. https://doi.org/10.1037/h004788

Harlow, H. F., Blazer, N. C., & McClearn, G. E. (1956). Manipulatory motivation in infant rhesus monkey. *Journal of Comparative and Physiological Psychological, 49*, 444–448.

Helmholtz, H. (1867). *Handbuch der physiologischenOptik.* Voss.

Hilgard, E. R. (1957). Freud and experimental psychology. *Systems Research, 2*(1), 74–79. https://doi.org/10.1002/bs.3830020109

Hobbes, T. (1651). *Leviathan, or, the matter, form, and power of a common-wealth ecclesiastical and civil.* Printed for Andrew Crooke.

Holahan, C. (1978). *Environment and behavior: A dynamic perspective* (The Plenum Social Ecology Series). https://doi.org/10.1007/978-1-4684-2430-0

Howe, R. B. K. (1991). Introspection: A reassessment. *New Ideas in Psychology, 9*(1), 25–44.

Hull, C. L. (1943). *Principles of behavior.* Appleton-Century-Crofts.

Hur, J., Iordan, A. D., Berenbaum, H., & Dolcos, F. (2016). Emotion-attention interactions in fear conditioning: Moderation by executive load, neuroticism, and awareness. *Biological Psychology, 121*(B), 213–220. https://doi.org/10.1016/j.biopsycho.2015.10.007

Hurlburt, R. T., & Heavey, C. L. (2001). Telling what we know: Describing inner experience. *Trends in Cognitive Sciences, 5*(9), 400–403. https://doi.org/10.1016/s1364-6613(00)01724-1

Jack, A. I. (2013). Introspection: The tipping point. *Consciousness and Cognition, 22*(2), 670–671. https://doi.org/10.1016/J.CONCOG.2013.03.005

James, W. (1890). *The principles of psychology* (Vol. 1–2). Holt.

Kapur, S. (2003). Psychosis as a state of aberrant salience: A framework linking biology, phenomenology, and pharmacology in schizophrenia. *American Journal of Psychiatry, 160*(1), 13–23. https://doi.org/10.1176/appi.ajp.160.1.13

Kendler, H. H. (1952). What is learned?—A theoretical blind alley. *Psychological Review, 59*(4), 269–277. https://doi.org/10.1037/h0057469

Kerr, K. L., Moseman, S. E., Avery, J. A., Bodurka, J., Zucker, N. L., & Simmons, W. K. (2015). Altered insula activity during visceral interoception in weight-restored patients with anorexia nervosa. *Neuropsychopharmacology, 41*(2), 521–528. https://doi.org/10.1038/npp.2015.174

Koffka, K. (1935). *Principles of Gestalt psychology.* Harcourt Brace.

Köhler, W. (1938). *The place of value in a world of facts*. Kegan, Paul, Trench, Trubner, and Company.

Köhler, W. (1947). *Gestalt psychology; an introduction to new concepts in modern psychology* (Rev. edn.). Liveright.

La Mettrie, J. (1747). *L'homme machine (Man a Machine)*.

Lakatos, I. (1968). Criticism and the methodology of scientific research programmes. *Proceedings of the Aristotelian Society, 69*(1), 149–186.

Latane, B., & Darley, J. M. (1970). *The unresponsive bystander: Why doesn't he help?* Appleton-Century-Crofts.

Levine, M., Prosser, A., Evans, D., & Reicher, S. (2005). Identity and emergency intervention: How social group membership and inclusiveness of group boundaries shape helping behavior. *Personality and Social Psychology Bulletin, 31*(4), 443–453. https://doi.org/10.1177/0146167204271651

Lewin, K. (1935). *A dynamic theory of personality*. McGraw-Hill.

Lewin, K. (1936). *Principles of topological psychology*. McGraw-Hill.

Lhermitte, F., Pillon, B., &Serdaru, M. (1986). Human autonomy and the frontal lobes. Part I: Imitation and utilization behavior: A neuropsychological study of 75 patients. *Annals of Neurology, 19*(4), 326–334. https://doi.org/10.1002/ana.410190404

Libet, B., Gleason, C. A., Wright, E. W., & Pearl, D. K. (1983). Time of conscious intention to act in relation to onset of cerebral activity (readiness-potential). The unconscious initiation of a freely voluntary act. *Brain: A Journal of Neurology, 106*(3), 623–642. https://doi.org/10.1093/brain/106.3.623

Lovaas, O. I. (1987). Behavioral treatment and normal educational and intellectual functioning in young autistic children. *Journal of Consulting and Clinical Psychology, 55*(1), 3–9. https://doi.org/10.1037/0022-006X.55.1.3

MacCorquodale, K., & Meehl, P. E. (1948). On a distinction between hypothetical constructs and intervening variables. *Psychological Review, 55*(2), 95–107. https://doi.org/10.1037/h0056029

Maier, N. R. F. (1931). Reasoning in humans: The solution of a problem and its appearance in consciousness. *Journal of Comparative Psychology, 12*(2), 181–194. https://doi.org/10.1037/h0071361\

Makari, G. (2015). *Soul machine: The invention of the modern mind*. W. W. Norton & Company.

Mandler, G. (2002). Origins of the cognitive (r)evolution. *Journal of the History of the Behavioral Sciences, 38*(4), 339–353. https://doi.org/10.1002/jhbs.10066

McClelland, D. C. (1957). Conscience and the will rediscovered. *Contemporary Psychology: A Journal of Reviews, 2*(7), 177–179. https://doi.org/10.1037/005536,0.036.

Miller, G. A. (2003). The cognitive revolution: A historical perspective. *Trends in Cognitive Sciences, 7*(3), 141–144. https://doi.org/10.1016/S1364-6613(03)00029-9

Moore, M. S. (2020). *Mechanical choices: The responsibility of the human machine*. Oxford University Press.

Muller, J. P. (1840). *Handbuch der physiologie des menschen* (2 vols.). J. Holscher.

Nisbett, R. E., & Wilson, T. D. (1977). The halo effect: Evidence for unconscious alteration of judgments. *Journal of Personality and Social Psychology, 35*(4), 250–256. https://doi.org/10.1037/0022-3514.35.4.250

O'Keefe, J., & Dostrovsky, J. (1971). The hippocampus as a spatial map: Preliminary evidence from unit activity in the freely-moving rat. *Brain Research, 34*(1), 171–175. https://doi.org/10.1016/0006-8993(71)90358-1

O'Keefe, J., & Nadel, L. (1978). *The hippocampus as a cognitive map.* Oxford University Press.

Oreskes, N. (2021). Why bad science is sometimes more appealing than good science. *Scientific American.*

Pavlov, I. P. (1927). *Conditioned reflexes: An investigation of the physiological activity of the cerebral cortex.* Oxford University Press.

Penrose, R. (1994). *Shadows of the mind: A search for the missing science of consciousness.* Oxford University Press.

Petitmengin, C., Remillieux, A., Cahour, B., & Carter-Thomas, S. (2013). A gap in Nisbett and Wilson's findings? A first-person access to our cognitive processes. *Consciousness and Cognition, 22*(2), 654–669. https://doi.org/10.1016/j.concog.2013.02.004

Rachman, S. (1967). Systematic desensitization. *Psychological Bulletin, 67*(2), 93–103. https://doi.org/10.1037/h0024212

Rapaport, D. (1956). The theory of ego autonomy: A generalization. In M. Gill (Ed.), *The collected papers of David Rapaport* (pp. 722–744). Basic Books.

Rogers, C. (1961). *On becoming a person: A therapist's view of psychotherapy.* Constable.

Salter, A. (1949). *Conditioned reflex therapy, the direct approach to the reconstruction of personality.* Creative Age Press.

Sass, L., Parnas, J., & Zahavi, D. (2011). Phenomenological psychopathology and schizophrenia: Contemporary approaches and misunderstandings. *Philosophy, Psychiatry, and Psychology, 18*(1), 1–23. https://doi.org/10.1353/ppp.2011.0008

Schlick, M. (1938). *Gesammelte Aufsatze 1926–1936.* Gerold.

Searle, J. R. (1990). Consciousness, explanatory inversion and cognitive science. *Behavioral and Brain Sciences, 13*(1), 585–642.

Sechehaye, M. (1951). *Autobiography of a schizophrenic girl: Reality lost and gained, with analytic interpretation* (G. Rubin-Rabson, Trans.). Grune and Stratton.

Sechenov, I. M. (1863). Reflexes of the brain. In I. M. Sechenov (Ed.), *Selected works* (pp. 263–336). State Publishing House for Biological and Medical Literature.

Skinner, B. F. (1953). *Science and human behavior.* Macmillan.

Smith, E. R., & Miller, F. D. (1978). Limits on perception of cognitive processes: A reply to Nisbett and Wilson. *Psychological Review, 85*(4), 355–362. https://doi.org/10.1037/0033-295X.85.4.355

Snygg, D., & Combs, A. W. (1949). *Individual behavior: A new frame of reference for psychology.* Harper & Brothers Publishers.

Spiegelberg, H. (1972). *Phenomenology in psychology and psychiatry: An historical introduction.* Northwestern University Press.

Stern, D. N. (1985). *The interpersonal world of the infant: A view from psychoanalysis and developmental psychology.* Routledge. https://doi.org/10.4324/9780429482137

Terrell, J. (1959). Invisibility of the Lorenz contraction. *Physical Review, 116*(4), 1041. https://doi.org/10.1103/PhysRev.116.1041

Titchener, E. B. (1901). *Experimental psychology* (4 Vols.). Macmillan.

Titchener, E. B. (1910). *A textbook of psychology.* Macmillan.

Titchener, E. B. (1912). The schema of introspection. *American Journal of Psychology*, *23*(4), 485–508. https://doi.org/10.2307/1413058

Tolman, E. C. (1948). Cognitive maps in rats and men. *Psychological Review*, *55*(4), 189.

van Bommel, M., van Prooijen, J.-W., Elffers, H., & van Lange, P. A. M. (2013). Intervene to be seen: The power of a camera in attenuating the bystander effect. *Social Psychological and Personality Science*, *5*(4), 459–466. https://doi.org/10.1177/1948550613507958

Walther, E., & Nagengast, B. (2006). Evaluative conditioning and the awareness issue: Assessing contingency awareness with the four-picture recognition test. *Journal of Experimental Psychology: Animal Behavior Processes*, *32*(4), 454–459. https://doi.org /10.1037/0097-7403.32.4.454

Watson, J. B. (1913). Psychology as the behaviorist views it. *Psychological Review*, *20*(2), 158–177. https://doi.org/10.1037/h0074428

Watson, J. B. (1925). *Behaviorism*. W. W. Norton.

Weber, E. H. (1834). *De pulsu, resorptione, auditu et tactu. Anatationesanatomicae et physiologicae*. Koehler.

Wegner, D. M. (2002). *The illusion of conscious will*. MIT Press.

Wegner, D. M. (2003). The mind's best trick: How we experience conscious will. *Trends in Cognitive Science*, *7*(2), 65–69.

Wegner, D. M. (2008). Self is magic. In J. Baer, J. C. Kaufman, & R. F. Baumeister (Eds.), *Are we free? Psychology and free will* (pp. 226–247). Oxford University Press.

Wolpe, J. (1961). The systematic desensitization treatment of neuroses. *Journal of Nervous and Mental Disease*, *132*, 189–203. https://doi.org/10.1097/00005053-196103000 -00001

Wolpe, J. (1968). Psychotherapy by reciprocal inhibition. *Conditional Reflex*, *3*(4), 234–240. https://doi.org/10.1007/BF03000093

Wong, D. W. S. (2002). Modeling local segregation: A spatial interaction approach. *Geographic and Environmental Modeling*, *6*(1), 81–97.

Yerkes, R. M., & Morgulis, S. (1909). The method of Pawlow in animal psychology. *Psychological Bulletin*, *6*(8), 257–273. https://doi.org/10.1037/h0070886

Young, J. Z. (1964). *A model for the brain*. Oxford University Press.

Chapter 2

Consciousness and subjective experience in psychoanalysis

Given the very definition of psychoanalysis as a study of the unconscious (Freud, 1923; Laplanche & Pontalis, 1973), we are confronted right from the start with the question of the role of consciousness and subjective experience in a psychoanalytic theory of the mind as well as in psychoanalytic practice.[1] We have seen the eclipse of consciousness and experience in the form of behaviorism in the previous chapter. According to Thompson (2000), this is also the case with regard to psychoanalysis. He has lamented the 'singular absence [of subjective experience] in psychoanalytic theory and the gradual, if unwitting, decline of experience in its literature over the course of the century' (p. 30). I think Thompson is right, at least in regard to Freudian and Kleinian theory. As will be shown in this chapter, with a few exceptions, the marginalization of consciousness and conscious experience also characterizes psychoanalytic theory. The evidence for the 'singular absence' of subjective experience in psychoanalytic theory referred to by Thompson (2000) is provided by its following core features:

One, the marked emphasis on third-person self-knowledge (i.e., based on observation and inference) in contrast to first-person subjective experience.

Two, the view of consciousness as 'false consciousness', that is, as dissimulating and hiding and disguising latent unconscious meaning that expresses one's 'true' desires and motives.

Three, the assumption of unconscious subjectivity in the context of repressed unconscious contents.

Four, the conception of consciousness and subjective experience as epiphenomenal, that is, as having no causal powers.

Five, and particularly characteristic of Kleinian and Bionian theory, the relatively frequent resort to 'deep' interpretations of repressed mental contents not accessible to conscious experience.

Definition of terms

Before addressing each of these issues, I want to clarify how I understand and use key terms and concepts in this chapter. It is generally agreed that the emotional system comprises three components: neurophysiological processes, behavior, and

DOI: 10.4324/9781032686967-3

feelings or affects (Damasio, 1999). It is feelings and affects that are the experiential component of the emotional system. This is also the case with regard to other systems, including the perceptual system, which comprise neurophysiological, behavioral, and experiential components. In both cases, the neurophysiological and behavioral components of the system can be present without the experiential component. Thus, the neurophysiological and behavioral components of the emotional system can be present without the feeling component. This is seen, for example, in the 'repressive style' pattern (e.g., Weinberger et al., 1979). To describe such phenomena, one can perhaps refer to 'unconscious emotion' so long as one recognizes that one is referring to non-experiential neurophysiological and behavioral components of the emotional system, not to feelings and affects, which are inherently experiential.

Similarly, with regard to the perceptual system, which includes neural registration, discrimination, and encoding, behaviors, and perceptual experiences. As is the case with emotion, aspects of the perceptual system can operate without the experiential component. This is the case with regard to subliminal stimuli, which can be encoded and can influence behavior without the experiential component. In that sense, one can perhaps refer to' unconscious perception' so long as one recognizes that one is using the term 'perception' in an unusual way that does not imply experience. It would be less confusing if, in these cases, one used such terms as 'unconscious discrimination' or 'unconscious encoding' rather than 'perception', which normally implies a perceptual experience.

It is worth noting that whereas both for the emotional and perceptual systems, the neurophysiological and behavioral components can be present without the experiential component, it is not possible to experience an affect or a perception without the underlying neurophysiological component. In that sense, the neurophysiological component is fundamental. This should be no surprise in so far as we are not disembodied creatures. However, it is important to caution that whereas the neurophysiological is fundamental from the perspective of the operation of various biological and psychological systems, what is fundamental from the perspective of the living individual or person is the existence, nature, and quality of one's lived experience.

With what I hope are general clarifications, I turn to my use of specific terms in this chapter. There are two properties that are necessary aspects of subjectivity: accessibility to consciousness and a sense of personal ownership. These two properties are not simply idiosyncratic and arbitrary personal definitions, but reflect how the term is normally understood. With regard to the first property, the first definition of subjectivity in the authoritative *Compact Edition of the Oxford Dictionary* is 'Consciousness of one's perceived states'. Similarly, in *Encyclopedia.com*, subjectivity is defined as 'Primarily an aspect of consciousness'. The link between subjectivity and consciousness is also reflected in the centrality of *qualia* in conscious experience. That is, it is 'something it is like' (Nagel, 1974, p. 436) to consciously experience, for example, redness or pain or an emotional feeling. As Searle (1992) observes,

Consciousness, by definition, consists of states ... that are *qualitative* and *subjective*. Consciousness is qualitative in the sense that for any conscious state there is a certain qualitative character, a what-it-is-like or what-it-feels-like aspect. For example, the qualitative character of drinking beer is different from the qualitative character of listening to Beethoven's Ninth Symphony. These states are subjective in the ontological sense that they only exist as experienced by a human or animal subject.

(p. 98)

That is, these states are inherently from a first-person perspective. This leads us to the second property of subjectivity, its link to personal ownership.

As noted in the Introduction, I use the term 'subjective experience' as virtually (but, as we will see, not entirely) synonymous with 'conscious experience' on the grounds that experience necessarily means conscious experience. Although one can discriminate and encode unconscious stimuli, the concept of 'unconscious experience' is an oxymoron. I assume that with the exception of dissociated, ego-alien, 'not me' states, consciousness and subjective experience have the quality of *my-ness*. That is, consciousness is *my* consciousness and subjective experience is *my* experience. Similarly, I assume that the term 'subjectivity' always refers to *my* subjectivity; and that unbidden, ego-alien, not me mental contents that enter consciousness have the peculiar status of being part of my consciousness (what other consciousness could they be part of?) and yet, not part of one's subjectivity. Thus, whereas unbidden, ego-alien mental contents possess one aspect of subjectivity – they are conscious – they lack the property of being experienced as *my* experience. Indeed, it is this lack that gives dissociated experiences their peculiar and troubling quality. And finally, I assume that although repressed unconscious mental contents are part of one's personality and may possess *potential* subjectivity, so long as they remain repressed and ego-alien, they are not aspects of one's subjectivity. That is so because so long as they are repressed, they lack both the properties of consciousness as well as *my-ness*. It will be important to keep these definitional issues in mind in the later discussion of the conception of psychoanalysis as a 'science of subjectivity'.

The dissimulating nature of consciousness

As Ricoeur (1970) astutely observes, according to Freudian theory, consciousness is 'dissimulating' and 'false' in the sense that it hides and disguises one's 'real' underlying motives and desires.[2] Indeed, Ricoeur (1970) employs the terms 'school of suspicion' and 'hermeneutics of suspicion' to describe Freudian theory. As Strenger (1989) writes,

Freud rarely accepts what the patient says at face value. Excessive altruism is often nothing but a reaction against sadistic wishes; shrill moralism a defense against threatening sexual desire; much of what looks sublime is really covert fulfillment of infantile wishes.

(p. 598)

An example of what Strenger (1989) is referring to is Freud's (1912) statement that

... all the emotional relations of sympathy, friendship, trust, and the like, which can be turned to good account in our lives, are genetically linked with sexuality and have developed from purely sexual desires through a softening of their sexual aim, however pure and unsensual they may appear to our conscious self-perception.

(p. 105)[3]

The following passage by Le Bon, which Freud (1921) approvingly cites, captures Freud's view of the dissimulating nature of conscious experience almost better than Freud's own writings do

... unconscious phenomena play an altogether preponderant part not only in organic life, but also in the operations of the intelligence. The conscious life of the mind is of small importance in comparison with its unconscious life. The most subtle analyst, the most acute observer, is scarcely successful in discovering more than a very small number of the unconscious motives that determine his conduct ... Behind the avowed causes of our acts there undoubtedly lie secret causes that we do not avow, but behind these secret causes there are many others more secret still, of which we ourselves are ignorant. The greater part of our daily actions is the result of hidden motives which escape our observation.

(as cited in Freud, 1921, pp. 73–74)

As the above passage makes clear, according to Freud, consciousness and subjective are deceptive; they hide and disguise our real underlying motives and desires. Further, it is the enlightening psychoanalytic process that will enable us to overcome our self-deception and set us free. Thus, as Strenger (1989) observes, the intentions behind the hermeneutics of suspicion are Enlightenment and self-knowledge, removal of the shroud in order to reveal unpalatable truths. However, if one is to uncover these assiduously defended against self-truths, one must go beyond the surface of conscious experience to the depths of unconscious mental contents and processes. Strenger (1989) writes: 'Psychoanalysis, for Freud is the relentless pursuit of the truth about ourselves, the penetration beyond appearances to reality which was once too threatening to face' (Strenger, 1989, p. 598). For many psychoanalysts, the clinical psychoanalytic situation represents one's main hope for confronting and coming to terms with these self-truths. Indeed, Lear (1990) writes that

the only way to get at ... deeper meanings is through a peculiar human interaction, the likes of which never before existed in the world. It is in the structured setting of a psychoanalytic therapy that the deeper strata of a person's
subjectivity emerge.

(pp. 4–5)

Let me summarize the main points regarding the place of consciousness and subjective experience in Freudian theory. At least for those who are unanalyzed,
consciousness and subjective experience are unreliable and deceptive with regard
to our inner world and the nature of our 'real' desires and wishes. Conscious
experience should be viewed as essentially manifest content that hides and disguises latent unconscious meanings that we resist confronting. Thus, in an important sense, we are estranged from the major part of our unconscious mental life.
Like other manifest content, such as dreams, slips, and symptoms, conscious
experience of our inner world needs to be *interpreted* in order to uncover and
reveal its latent meaning. Psychoanalysis constitutes the main hope – the only
hope, according to Lear (1998) – of ameliorating that estrangement. In short,
there appears to be a remarkable and perhaps too good to be true convergence
between Enlightenment values of self-knowledge and truth-seeking and the road
to clinical cure.

A basic assumption of Freudian psychoanalysis, embedded in the Enlightenment
vision, is that self-knowledge and discovering the truth about oneself will set one
free. What some see as psychoanalysis' privileging of largely intellectual self-
knowledge over affective experience was decried as early as 1924 by Ferenczi
and Rank who criticized the overly intellectualized and fossilized nature of psychoanalysis and psychoanalytic treatment. An example *par excellence* of the
kind of approach Ferenczi and Rank criticized is Sterba's (1934) emphasis on
the importance of the patient developing 'a new point of view of intellectual contemplation' (p. 121). Perhaps partly in reaction to such excessive intellectualization, in his classic paper published the same year as the Sterba paper, Strachey
(1934) emphasized the importance of transference and transference interpretations because of their here-and-now emotional immediacy. That is, the patient's
reaction would be more likely to include not only intellectual understanding, but
also – and perhaps most important – a direct first-person immediate experience.
In that regard, Strachey's perspective stands in sharp contrast to Sterba's 'point
of view of intellectual comprehension'. Loewald (1952), too, reacted against the
excessive intellectualization of some psychoanalytic formulations. He wrote that
these formulations read like a description of the obsessive character's experience
and functioning. (I will return to this issue in discussing intellectual versus emotional insight).

Much of classical psychoanalytic theory and practice, as well as many psychoanalytic concepts and formulations, are concerned with various expressions and
forms of dissimulations as well as the means to deal with them. They include the
concepts of defense and resistance, transference and transference interpretations,

defense analysis, making the unconscious conscious, and working-through. I begin with the concept of resistance.

Resistance

As Freud repeatedly emphasizes, the achievement of self-truths does not come easily; we are strongly invested in avoiding confrontation with unpalatable self-knowledge and unacceptable self-truths. Given the hermeneutics of suspicion, it is understandable that transference and resistance are placed at the center of attention in the clinical situation in the struggle to attain self-knowledge. As Freud (1912a) wrote, if the therapist gives primacy to transference and resistance, s/he is carrying out psychoanalysis. The concept of resistance is embedded in the assumption that the patient's conscious experience, including experience of the analyst, is replete with distortion and disguise. Although the patient may consciously experience the analyst as someone to whom s/he is coming for relief from suffering, at an unconscious level, the analyst is experienced as a parental figure; and correspondingly, the unconscious motives for coming to treatment are embedded in the unconscious fantasy that his or her infantile wishes will be gratified by the analyst-parental figure. Indeed, it is this assumption that led Freud (1925) to view transference as the expression *par excellence* of resistance.

The very term 'resistance', so utterly congruent with a hermeneutics of suspicion, suggests a conflict of aims between patient and therapist, that is, an adversarial relationship. As Felski (2011) observes in a more general context, the hermeneutics of suspicion requires 'an adversarial sensibility to probe for concealed, repressed, or disavowed meanings' and 'an attitude that surface appearances [are] not only misleading, but deliberatively deceptive' (p. 221). The likelihood of an adversarial relationship is further heightened in the context of the analyst as a remote, silent, figure who gives nothing away of his or her personal reactions. There is little wonder that an analogy has been drawn between the analyst as the detective and the analysand as suspect (e.g., Felski, 2011). Both the analyst and the detective are in the business of tracking down and uncovering hidden motives that the suspect-analysand resists revealing. The guilty suspect hides criminal actions; the guilt-ridden analysand hides 'criminal' impulses and desires (e.g., anti-social, infantile incestuous, and death wishes). As Strenger (1989) writes, 'What will be discovered in the painstaking detective work of the analysis is another perverse wish, another infantile sexual theory and more murderous wishes towards those whom the patient consciously loves' (p. 598).

Freud (1912) was aware of the risk of an adversarial relationship between patient and analyst. He writes that 'It is certainly possible to forfeit ... success [in treatment] if ... one takes up any standpoint other than one of sympathetic understanding ... or if one behaves like are presentative or advocate of some contending party' (p. 140). However, this statement hardly jibes with his recommendation that the analyst's attitude should be that of a surgeon who 'puts aside all his feelings, even his human sympathy, and concentrates his mental forces on the single aim of performing the operation as skillfully as possible' (p. 115).[4] Nor does it jibe with Freud's (1912) warning to the analyst to be 'prepared for a perpetual struggle with his patient to keep in the psychical sphere all the impulses which the patient would like to direct into the motor sphere [i.e., into action]' (p. 153).

Psychoanalysis as a 'science of subjectivity'

Although, as noted, psychoanalysis is defined as a study of the unconscious (Laplanche & Pontalis), it has also been described as a discipline the primary subject matter of which is subjectivity. (e.g., Coburn, 1999; Giampieri-Deutsch, 2012; Harris, 1987; Layton, 2008; Meissner, 1999; Stolorow & Atwood, 1984). Indeed, Lear (1998) defines psychoanalysis as 'a science of subjectivity' (p. 3), while at the same time referring to the 'deeper strata' of subjectivity, and writing that 'a person, *by his nature* [my emphasis], is out of touch with his subjectivity' (p. 4). Lear's conception of subjectivity raises a host of questions. One such question is how psychoanalysis can be defined as a study of the unconscious as well as a science of subjectivity when, as we have seen, subjectivity is generally understood as entailing consciousness and personal ownership, neither of which characterizes unconscious repressed mental contents and states. If one adopts the generally accepted definition of psychoanalysis as a study of unconscious mental states, and at the same time defines it as a 'science of subjectivity', it would seem to follow that one locates subjectivity in unconscious states and processes, with the consequence that subjectivity is severed from consciousness and subjective experience – an odd and idiosyncratic conception of subjectivity. As Kriegel (2006) writes, 'a mental state beyond my awareness, and not for me, is not subjectivity' (see also Neisser, 2006, 2015, p. 7).[5]

Similar to Kriegel, Rubenstein (1977a) writes: 'From a critical point of view … it seems odd to regard the person as a subject or agent of an activity, or part of an activity, of which he is unaware' (p. 426). A similar point is made by Nagel (1995) who writes that mentalistic descriptions and explanations 'have to be understood by taking up, so far as it is possible, the point of view of the subject of the mental states and processes referred to' (p. 23). In his discussion of the crisis of experience, Jay (1998) asks: '*Who* can be said to experience something if there is no one to *whom* such experience can be assigned' (as cited in Thompson, 2000, p. 43). As Thompson (2000) observes, 'this question is prompted by the disappearance of the traditional *subject who experiences* [emphasis in original] in favor of a decentered subject that is reduced to an "effect" of invisible forces", including unconscious factors' (p. 43). In short, given the inextricable link between subjectivity and both accessibility to consciousness and personal ownership, it is not clear in what way mental contents that are not only inaccessible to conscious experience, but are also disavowed as ego-alien and, in Sullivanian language, 'not me', can nevertheless be viewed as central aspects of an individual's subjectivity. This is the crux of the difficulty in fully understanding Lear's (1990) positing of 'deeper strata' of subjectivity and in asserting that 'a person, by his nature, is out of touch with his subjectivity' (p. 4).[6,7]

What Lear means by 'deeper strata' is, of course, unconscious psychological life. There is little doubt that, as Freud posited, there is much more going on in mental life than is represented in consciousness and subjective experience. This is the case even if one puts aside the issue of repressed mental contents. For example, we harbor many beliefs, plans, goals, desires, etc., which, although not present in experience at a given time, are nevertheless aspects of one's subjectivity. That is so because they are readily accessible to consciousness and are experienced as *my* desires, beliefs, etc. However, this is not what Lear appears to have in mind when he refers to the 'deeper strata' of subjectivity and when he states that by one's nature, one is out of touch with one's subjectivity.

Perhaps one can understand Lear to be saying that insofar as any mental process or state of an individual, conscious or unconscious, ego-alien or ego-syntonic, it is part of that individual's personality structure and mental life, it should be viewed as an aspect of his or her subjectivity. However, although in an important sense, for a given individual, all mental states and processes 'belong' to him or her, it does not mean that they are all aspects of the individual's subjectivity, as conventionally understood – namely, as that which is readily available to consciousness and accompanied by a sense of personal ownership.

A perhaps plausible way of reading Lear's 'deeper strata' of subjectivity with which, by one's nature is out of touch, is that, although not readily accessible to consciousness, repressed mental contents can, in principle, become accessible under certain circumstances (e.g., when defenses are lifted). This view is congruent with Freud's (1915b) claim that unconscious wishes and desires are no different from conscious wishes and desires save for the property of consciousness. In this view, insofar as conscious and unconscious wishes are not essentially different from each other, and insofar as conscious wishes and desires are aspects of one's subjectivity, it would follow that whether conscious or unconscious, wishes and desires are aspects of one's subjectivity; unconscious wishes and desires simply represent 'deeper strata' of one's subjectivity that are unacknowledged and not permitted to gain access to consciousness.

In this view, when the unconscious is made conscious, repressed mental contents that were, in some sense, in the patient's unconscious 'all along' emerge in consciousness and are experienced in their original form. As Mitchell (2005) puts it, it is as if after one has lifted a rock, one sees the ants that were there all along. Understood this way, it would appear to follow that the patient's unconscious desires were always part of his or her subjectivity, but not acknowledged as such. I suspect that this formulation constitutes the basis for Lear's (1990) claim that disavowed repressed unconscious desires are nevertheless aspects of one's subjectivity.

There are a number of problems with this view. One problem is the questionable tenability of the formulation that fully formed repressed desires, no different from conscious desires, stored somewhere in a place called the unconscious, pressing for discharge and waiting to emerge into consciousness. Another problem has to do with the question of whether this description constitutes a realistic picture of the clinical process. It is important to keep in mind that in the clinical psychoanalytic situation, it is an outside observer, the analyst, who attributes repressed mental contents to the patient. That is, it is the analyst who makes the judgment that whether or not the patient acknowledges or is aware of them, repressed mental contents are aspects of the patient's subjectivity. The analyst's attributions reflect his or her judgment (based on the patient's free associations, dreams, transference reactions, etc.) that despite the non-representation of mental contents in consciousness and the patient's subjective experience, and despite the patient's disavowal of these mental contents, in *some way*, the attributed mental contents 'belong' to the patient; they are part of his or her 'deeper strata' of his or her subjectivity. However, quite often, the mental contents associated with the 'deeper strata' of subjectivity that are attributed to the patient have much to do with the analyst's theoretical affiliation. For example, for some analysts, the 'deeper strata' of subjectivity will inevitably center on oedipal wishes and conflicts. For other analysts, they will center on the patient's wishes to be empathically mirrored, and for other analysts, the 'deeper strata' of subjectivity will have to do with the patient's affective bond to the 'bad' alluring and rejecting internal object. All are candidates for representing the patient's 'deeper strata' of subjectivity.

As for the patient's experiences, it is highly unlikely that, following the analyst's attributions and the lifting of repression, the patient will now simply consciously experience the hitherto unconscious desires. For example, it is highly unlikely that following oedipal interpretations and attributions and the lifting of repression, the patient will consciously experience fully formed incestuous desires that had been stored all along in a location called the unconscious. It is more likely that even when the patient acknowledges the validity of the attribution, his or her perspective will be, similar to the analyst's perspective, namely, a third-person one, that is, something like 'it makes sense' or, at best, what Freud (1937) referred to as an 'assured conviction' (p. 266). Freud (1915b) writes that

> Psychoanalysis demands nothing more than that we should apply this process of inference to ourselves – a proceeding, to which, it is true, we are not constitutionally inclined. If we do this, we must say: all the acts and manifestations which I notice in myself and do not know how to link up with the rest of my mental life must be judged as if they belonged to someone else: they are to be explained by a mental life ascribed to this other person.

> (p. 169)[8]

This is as clear a prescription for taking a third-person perspective toward one's unconscious life as one can find (see Moran, 2001). Further, it is not entirely compatible with the idea that one's unconscious mental life is best understood as a form of subjectivity.

It seems to me that the most reasonable way to think of repressed unconscious mental contents is that of having *potential* subjectivity in the sense that under certain circumstances, and after much working-through, they may be both accessible to conscious experience and possess the property of *my-ness*. What remains unclear is why, *by one's nature*, one is out of touch with such mental contents. What Lear may have in mind here is not that there are certain aspects of oneself that are *inherently* inaccessible, but that, by one's nature, one is reluctant to confront and acknowledge them as aspects of oneself. Finally, what also remains unclear is why and in what way(s) aspects of oneself with which one is out of touch are 'deeper'. Are they more profound?

Are they more significant? In what ways? (See Wachtel, 2003 for an excellent discussion of the metaphors of surface and depth.)

Let us imagine the case in which the patient's reaction to the analyst's interpretation is not limited to agreement and third-person self-knowledge, but includes, following the lifting of repression, the patient's conscious experience and avowal as his or her own of precisely those mental contents attributed to him or her by the analyst. In this scenario, I would suggest, the attributed wish or desire now has the status of being part of the patient's subjectivity. Let us leave aside for the present the issues of suggestibility and the patient's compliance and desire to please the analyst. Would the patient's conscious experience of the attributed wish or desire mean that the analyst had uncovered the patient's 'deeper strata' of subjectivity? I think a more accurate and useful description is that the analyst had helped the patient transform non-subjectivity or potential subjectivity to actual subjectivity rather than that s/he had uncovered wishes and desires that were deeply buried in the unconscious all along.

The issue of what is meant by subjectivity is not simply a matter of semantics, but speaks to core issues of psychoanalytic theory and practice. To ban mental contents from one's consciousness and to view them as ego-alien and 'not me' is more accurately described as an *avoidance* of subjectivity than a representation of the 'deeper strata' of one's subjectivity. They become part of one's subjectivity when they are transformed from an ego-alien 'not me' status to the experience of 'I wish' or 'I desire'. They become aspects of one's sense of who one is. The view that repressed mental contents are, nevertheless, aspects of one's subjectivity would seem to be incompatible with the overriding psychoanalytic goal of where id was, there shall ego be, which can be understood as rendering the hitherto non-subjective 'it' so that it can be experienced as the subjective 'I' – more specifically, to render unconscious, disowned, and not me aspects of oneself accessible to consciousness and capable of being experienced as *my* mental contents. Indeed, one can understand psychoanalysis as a discipline that is primarily concerned with the individual's *avoidance* of subjectivity in regard to certain mental contents, as well as through the psychoanalytic process, making possible and facilitating the transformation of the non-subjective to the subjective, that is, from repressed unconscious to consciousness and from non-ownership to ownership.

Prior to that transformation, when the agent has no experiential access to what is attributed to him or her and, indeed, disavows the attributions, it is not clear who is the subject that is doing the wishing and desiring. It is also not clear how wishes and desires themselves are capable of pressing for representation in consciousness and for discharge in the form of action, properties Freud (1950) attributes to unconscious instinctual wishes and desires. Is it a homunculus separate from a person wishing and desiring? I think Rubinstein (1997) is correct in arguing that an unconscious mental content, such as a wish or desire, should be understood not as a wish or desire that, due to repression, one does not and cannot consciously experience as wishing or desiring, but rather as a 'protoneurological' concept, that is, as a neurophysiological predisposition that can be consciously experienced under certain conditions. It may be acceptable, for the sake of theory building, to divide the personality into the different structures of id, ego, and superego. However, it is of questionable legitimacy to view these different structures as mini-agents – homunculi – that are capable of engaging in wishing, desiring, punishing, pressing for discharge, and so on. This is still another reason for understanding repressed mental contents as possessing *potential* subjectivity rather than some special form of subjectivity or 'deeper strata' of subjectivity.

Rubinstein's position is quite similar, in the psychoanalytic context, to Searles' earlier noted criticism of cognitive psychology's tendency to posit mental processes that are essentially 'speculative neurophysiology'. Despite this similarity, there is, however, an important difference between the two contexts. It is the *inherent* inaccessibility of the cognitive structures posited by cognitive psychology that is at the core of Searle's critique. Unconscious desires and wishes, however, *are*, in principle, accessible to conscious experience. Hence, whereas the cognitive structures of cognitive psychology are, in Searle's (1990) simply 'speculative neurophysiology', insofar as unconscious wishes and desire are potentially available to consciousness, they can be viewed as mental processes that possess '*potential*' *subjectivity*. (I will return to this issue in Chapter 3).

Disjunction between behavior and experience

Freud's formulation to the effect that we gain knowledge of ourselves through third-person observation and inference suggests the possibility of disjunctions between subjective experience and aspects of our behavior. A phenomenon called 'repressive style' is an example of such a disjunction. 'Repressive style' refers to a pattern in a group of individuals who, despite reporting the experience of a relatively low level of anxiety in mildly to moderately stressful conditions, nevertheless show a high level of *physiological* arousal. They also tend to be conventional, socially conforming and not introspective (Weinberger, 1995). Thus, they show a disjunction or dissociation among subjective experience, overt behavior, and physiological response – the three components of the emotional system (Damasio, 2000). That is, despite the high level of physiological arousal normally associated with the experience of anxiety, the individual's subjective experience is of a low level of an anxiety. I do not think one would want to say that the individual's high level of physiological arousal represents the individual's deeper strata of subjectivity. Indeed, the primary feature of 'repressive style' that makes it interesting and worthy of investigation is that the individual's high level of anxiety is *unrepresented* in his or her subjectivity. I would add that the psychological factors to which the high level of physiological arousal point possess *potential* subjectivity.

Superego, internal objects, and subjectivity

The complexity of subjectivity in psychoanalytic theory is also evident in the concept of the superego, understood as a structure that represents the internalization of early parental prohibitions. Fairbairn (1952) noted that the concept of an internal object was based on Freud's description of the superego, which is often depicted as a little man or woman perched on one's shoulder issuing do's and mainly, don't's. As Fairbairn observes, an internal object is both part of oneself and not part of oneself. One can think of the analogy of swallowing a piece of plastic that is part of oneself in the sense that it is inside one's body and yet not part of oneself in that it is experienced as a foreign body that cannot be digested.[9] Fairbairn's concept of an internal object is similar to Schafer's (1976) description of an archaic introject, which is experienced as a 'presence', similar in the context of folk legends, to being inhabited by an alien agent such as a devil or dybbuk. The metaphor of being inhabited by a foreign body in these different contexts captures the strange experience of something being inside oneself and yet, not part of one's subjectivity. Indeed, Fairbairn (1952) writes that a goal of psychoanalytic treatment is to exorcise the anti-libidinal internal object, which functions as an 'internal saboteur' in the personality. The central point here is that there can be aspects of one's personality structure, such as internal objects and introjects, that are, in an important sense, part of oneself, and yet are not experienced as aspects of one's subjectivity in any straightforward way. Indeed, they are experienced as foreign bodies inhabiting one's mind.[10]

The 'deeper strata' of subjectivity

What remains unclear in Lear's (1998) formulation is the question of why *by one's nature*, one is out of touch with one's subjectivity, which seems to suggest that there are forms of subjectivity that are *inherently* inaccessible to subjective experience. The only structure of the personality that could possibly fit this description is the id. We are left with the odd conclusion that id impulses, which, by definition, we cannot directly experience, represent the deeper strata of one's subjectivity. This conclusion is compatible with Freud's (1923) statement that the id represents the true purpose of life and his approving citation of Groddeck's (1923) comment that we are 'lived by our id' (p. 23). However, given Freud's (1923) and A. Freud's (1936) assumption that the id is the natural enemy of the ego – A. Freud (1936) refers to the 'primary antagonism' between the ego and the id (p. 172), it is not clear how id related mental contents could ever achieve the status of subjectivity. That is, if there is a primary antagonism between the id and the ego, it is not clear how ego could ever be where id was.

Emphasis on self-knowledge versus subjective experience

Tension between an emphasis on self-knowledge acquired via analytic interpretations versus an emphasis on direct lived experiences in the therapeutic relationship has existed throughout the history of psychoanalysis. It also existed in debates in German philosophy during the period in which Freud formulated many of his main ideas. It would be useful to describe certain aspects of this debate insofar as they constitute a general intellectual milieu during the development of psychoanalysis and also parallel debates in the psychoanalytic context.

A German word for 'experience' is *Erlebnis*, which, with its obvious root in *leben* – living – focuses on immediate lived experience. However, there is another German word for 'experience': *Erfahrung*, which his linked to journey (*Fahrt*) and is associated with acquiring knowledge through experience, reason and rationality, an emphasis on the mediated nature of experience, and a relative distance from immediate experience. The debate in 19th-century German philosophy concerned which aspect of experience to emphasize in accounts of human behavior. The choice of one term over the other appeared to reflect one's position on what one takes to be central to the nature of human experience. *Erleben* is linked to life (*Leben*), is often translated as immediate 'lived experience' and suggests 'pre-reflective, holistic immediacy' (Jay, 2005, p. 66).[11] In contrast, *Erfahrung* carries the connotation of knowledge gained in the course of life's journey.

The distinction between *Erlebnis* and *Erfahrung* parallels Russell's (1910) famous distinction between knowledge by acquaintance, which is immediate and privileged, and knowledge by description, which is derivative and more susceptible to error. It also parallels Schlick's (1925) distinction between *Erlebnis* and *Erkennen*. (knowing). One should also note Schlick's observation that experience itself is not equivalent to knowledge; it is the examination of the *relations* between experiences that yields knowledge.

Jay (2005) observes that the philosophical writings of Kant, Locke, and Hume were seen as placing a greater emphasis on *Erfahrung* than on *Erlebnis*. As he puts it with regard to Kant, 'always *Erfahrung* ... never *Erlebnis*' (p. 66). Opposed to this view were those who objected to, in Jay's (2005) characterization of Schliermacher's perspective, 'the mortifying implications, rationalizations, impersonal legalism, and mechanical causality' (p. 95) as opposed to the concern with 'prereflective immediacy, intuitive holism, and intensity of feeling'. Dilthey (1883), the originator of the distinction between *Naturwissenschaften* (physical sciences) and *Geisteswissenschaften*,(humanities or human sciences) took a position similar to Schlierermacher. He wrote: 'there is no real blood flowing in the veins of the knowing subject fabricated by Locke, Hume, and Kant, but only the diluted juice of reason as mere intellectual activity' (p. 71). This characterization parallels Ferenczi and Rank's (1924) criticism that psychoanalysis 'had become overly scholastic' and 'that psychoanalytic method had fossilized ... and become an overly intellectualized process of educating patients about the content of their unconscious' (as cited in Makari, 2008, p. 352)

In the century following Schlierermacher and Dilthey's passionate pronouncements, the debate between *Erlebnis* and *Erfahrung* was continued by German Jewish philosophers in the context of discussing the nature of Judaism. There had long been tension in Judaism between *Halakah*, which emphasized restraint, duty, and law, and *Hasidism*, which placed emphasis on vitality and joy in pious lived experience. The German Jewish philosopher Martin Buber was drawn to what he felt was the vitality of *Hasidism*. As Jay (2005) puts it, 'Buber came to his Hasidic infatuation already imbued with a passion for *Erlebnis*' (p. 124). In contrast to Buber, another German Jewish philosopher, Walter Benjamin (e.g., 1913) rejected what he viewed as Buber's cult of *Erlebnis*, in favor of an emphasis on *Erfahrung*, or, at least, his modification of that concept.

Attempts to link Freud and Freudian theory to Jewish mysticism (e.g., Bakan, 1958) notwithstanding, both in regard to Freud's personal history and Freudian theory, the links to the more rational side of Judaism are unmistakable. With regard to the former, although Freud's father Jacob was raised in a Jewish orthodox tradition, and although he retained a strong Jewish identity, observed Jewish high holidays, and made sure that Sigmund received a Jewish education, he dissociated himself from Jewish orthodox religion. Sigmund's Jewish education was taught by 'enlightened' rather than orthodox teachers. This was made possible by Jacob's move from Galicia to a cosmopolitan city. In short, Freud viewed himself as an enlightened German Jew who had little personal contact with, and even less personal interest in, Eastern European shtetl Hasidism.

As for Freudian theory, the central role it accorded to rationality and reason, its emphasis on the importance of ego control over drives, its view of religion as a 'mass psychosis', its valuing of science as representing the pinnacle of thought, and so on, make crystal clear Freud's valuing of *Erfahrung* over *Erlebnis*. Indeed, there is little doubt that if Freud were forced to choose between Halakah, with its emphasis on restraints and duties, and either the mysticism of the Kabbalah or the emotionality of Hasidism, he would opt for the former.

Some controversies in psychoanalysis, such as experience-near versus experience-distant emphasis, and interpretation versus the therapeutic relationship and corrective emotional experience can be, at least in part, understood from the perspective of a continuing debate between *Erlebni* and *Erfahrung*. As noted above, Ferenczi and Rank (1924) expressed their disaffection with what they viewed as the over-intellectualized character of the former perspective. The tension between the two perspectives is also evident in the different conceptions of the role of the therapeutic relationship. Whereas, according to classical theory, the therapeutic relationship is mainly a vehicle for the truly therapeutic ingredients of interpretations leading to insight and self-knowledge to operate, from a contrasting perspective, it is the direct experience of the patient–therapist relationship that is therapeutic. Perhaps the clearest expression of the latter conception of treatment is the primacy accorded to 'corrective emotional experience' by Alexander and French (1946).[12] This conception of treatment is also reflected in the greater emphasis in self-psychology on *feeling understood* as contrasted with understanding. Indeed, Kohut (1984) writes: 'if an ill-disposed critic gleefully told me that ... I ... believe in the curative effect of corrective emotional experience and equate such an experience with analysis, I could only reply: so be it' (p. 78).

In a certain sense, the tension between self-knowledge and experience is also present within Freudian theory itself. That is, there are two ways in which one can understand the psychoanalytic goal of making the unconscious conscious: one, enhanced self-knowledge of repressed mental contents without necessarily consciously experiencing them; and two, conscious experience of these hitherto repressed mental contents (e.g., wishes and desires). According to the former understanding, the patient may agree that the analyst's interpretations make sense and that they seem to apply to him or her. Indeed, some observers argue that the patient's acceptance of the analyst's interpretation of contents attributed to him or her that should serve as a criterion for its veridicality. For example, Mischel (1963) writes that: '... if the interpretation is correct, it is expected that the patient will at least ideally, come to agree with it in the end' (p. 590). However, such agreement may be forthcoming without the patient ever consciously experiencing the mental contents attributed to him or her. For example, a patient may agree that an oedipal interpretation adds to his or her self-knowledge without ever experiencing an incestuous wish. One must also keep in mind the possibility that the patient's agreement may reflect little more than compliance and the patient's desire to please the analyst.

Showing a strong family resemblance to the distinction between the psychoanalytic goal of enhancing self-knowledge versus the goal of enriching the range of experience, in a recent paper, Ogden (2019) contrasts what he refers to as epistemological psychoanalysis, which refers to enhanced self-knowledge, and which, according to him, is represented by Freudian and Kleinian theories, and ontological psychoanalysis, which is primarily concerned with 'the struggle ... to more fully come into being as a person whose experience feels real and alive to himself or herself' (p. 663), and which, according to him) is represented by the work of Winnicott and Bion.[13,14] As the terms suggest, whereas epistemological psychoanalysis is primarily concerned with knowing and understanding (of unconscious meanings, wishes, and fantasies) mainly through interpretation, is facilitated by the withholding of interpretation and instead *waiting* for the patient, in Winnicott's (1969) words, 'arrive(s) at understanding creatively and with immense joy ...' (p. 86). Although the reason that the work of Winnicott is taken as representative of ontological psychoanalysis is quite clear, it is not entirely clear on what basis Bion's work is viewed as an expression of this perspective. Ogden's descriptions of Bion's work all have to do with the *analyst's* experiences, not the patient's experiences. For example, Ogden refers to Bion's insistence that the analyst needs to 'cultivate a watchful avoidance of memory' (Bion, 1967, p. 137); the analyst's 'reverie'; his or her need to renounce 'desire for results, "cure", or even understanding' (p. 137); the need for the analyst to be fully present at the moment and to have the 'experience of being with the patient' (Ogden, 2019, p. 270). In short, although Ogden informs us that ontological psychoanalysis has mainly to do with the issue of what kind of person the *patient* (not the analyst) wants to be – the emphasis in Bion's work cited by him is virtually entirely on the analyst's, not the patient's, experiences!

Strikingly, and reflecting the hermetic nature of much of the psychoanalytic literature, Ogden's discussion of the contrast between epistemological and onto-logical perspectives through the lens of the therapist's theoretical orientation and therapeutic stance makes no reference to the work of Carl Rogers whose emphasis on the goal of self-actualization certainly reflects more of an ontological than an epistemological perspective; and whose emphasis on the therapist's acceptance and empathic availability predates by many years Ogden's identification of the importance of the 'experience of being with the patient'. There is also no mention of the empirical finding that patients who experienced a high level of 'Rogerian conditions' showed more rapid positive therapeutic outcomes (Zuroff et al., 2010; Zuroff et al., 2016). Similarly, Curtis et al. (2004) found that psychoanalysts who reported on their own experiences in analysis rated as most helpful their analysts' qualities of 'genuineness and openness' (p. 183).

Intellectual versus emotional insight

The knowledge versus experience debate also appears in the form of the distinction between intellectual and emotional insight in the psychoanalytic literature. The patient's mere agreement that the analyst's interpretations apply to him or her has often been referred to in the psychoanalytic literature as intellectual insight, and is generally contrasted with emotional insight. The received wisdom in the psy-choanalytic literature is that the former is less likely to be robustly associated with therapeutic change than the latter. There is little systematic investigation in the literature as to why this should be the case. Indeed, much of the discussion on this topic is circular in its reasoning. Thus, lack of therapeutic change despite seeming insight is attributed to the merely intellectual nature of the insight. And the answer to the question of how one knows that the insight was merely intellectual is that it did not lead to therapeutic change. As far as I know, there are few studies in which intellectual versus emotional insight has been assessed independently of therapeu-tic change. A likely explanation of the failure of 'mere' intellectual insight to lead to therapeutic change – if, indeed, this turns out to be a reliable finding – is that such self-knowledge has not been integrated into one's subjectivity, that is, has not been experienced in the form of 'I wish', 'I feel', or 'I desire'.

As Richfield (1954) noted quite some time ago, 'The contrast of "intel-lectual" and "emotional" insight is made repeatedly, but never with adequate clarity' (p. 394). As Richfield (1954) puts it, emotional insight often means 'some kind of understanding accompanied by an emotional reaction' (p. 394). However, why should understanding accompanied by an emotional reaction be more likely to be associated with therapeutic change – if, indeed, it is? The answer to that question is not self-evident (Moran, personal communication). However, I think there is something valid in the intuition that compared to intellectual insight, insight accompanied by a visceral emotional reaction is more likely to be associated with therapeutic change. There is an important distinction between a coherent and even convincing interpretation or narrative that elicits, to cite Freud (1937), assured conviction and one that has 'hit home'. The latter is far more likely to be accompanied by the patient's affect. However, the association between experienced affect and therapeutic change is not, I believe, due to the experience of affect *per se*. Rather, the affect is a marker of the personal significance of the insight, one that contributes to one's sense of who one is. Insight with little or no experience of affect is an indication that it has not been assimilated and integrated into one's subjectivity, one's sense of who one is. Indeed, one may wonder whether insight unaccompanied by affect constitutes insight of any kind. It may be more accurately described as intellectualized self-knowledge (see Greenberg, 2014, for a discussion of the role of emotional experience in therapeutic change).[15]

It is important to note that although emotional insight is generally discussed in the context of positive change, precisely because affect is always a marker of the personal, it can also be associated with negative change. Consider O'Neill's (1946) *The Iceman Cometh*. The characters in the café are all sustained by their 'pipe dreams' that somehow their lives will turn around; someday they will take the necessary steps (e.g., look for a job) to change their lives. At some level, just below the surface of consciousness, the characters in the play know that their expectations and 'plans' are no more than pipe dreams and illusions. However, with the help of whiskey, and so long as they do not look inward and do not engage in much self-reflection, their lives remain stable and sustainable, even if at a marginal level. But along comes Hickey, the Iceman, whose motivation is to employ the truth as a destructive weapon, to destroy others as he himself is destroyed, who aggressively confronts them with the unbearable truth that their plans and expectations are nothing but pipe dreams. At a deeply personal and emotional level, the denizens of the know that Hickey is right. The emotional insight generated by this powerful confrontation is deeply destructive; without the pipe dreams, life is not sustainable. It is only after Hickey is discredited and destroyed that the pipe dreams are re-instituted and that life, however miserable it has been, is once more sustainable. A profound insight of *The Iceman Cometh* is that the psychological impact of imparting the truth to someone is strongly influenced by the motivation of the truth-imparter, and the context and manner in which the truth is imparted. All these factors are likely to influence the subjective experience of the individual to whom the truth is imparted and therefore, the psychological impact of imparting the truth. This insight is as valid in the psychoanalytic situation as it is in O'Neill's play.

The O'Neill play points to the distinction to be made between the stance of a truth-imparter and what Loewald (1952) describes as the ideal stance of the analyst as a 'truth-seeker'. Implicit in this distinction is the issue of motivation and intention, conscious and unconscious. The primary motive of the truth-imparter is to impart to the other the truth s/he has discovered. As illustrated by the character Hickey, it can take the form of attempting to enlighten the other through confrontation with self-truths the other has avoided. The motivation of the truth-seeker is primarily to search for the truth; the imparting of the truth is a somewhat separate matter. If I understand Loewald correctly, the ideal stance of the truth-seeker is not to impart the truth s/he has discovered, but rather to model truth-seeking and to engage the patient in becoming a truth-seeker. Implicit in this stance is a reduced emphasis on interpretations provided by the analyst and an increased emphasis on self-discovery and mutual truth-seeking. The contrast between the two stances can be instantiated by comparing an approach that focuses on 'deep' interpretations with the approach of Gray (1998) whose main focus is to invite the patient's attention to his or her behaviors that are more readily available to conscious experience.

Third-person versus first-person self-knowledge

In a seminal book, Moran (2001) makes an important distinction between third- and first-person self-knowledge. Insofar as third-person self-knowledge entails inference based on viewing oneself as an object of observation, it is not essentially different from the processes involved in gaining knowledge of another person. This form of self-knowledge lacks a critical aspect of subjectivity, namely, first-person privileged access. It also does not sufficiently partake of a first-person subjective experience and avowal that entails standing behind one's beliefs and desires (Moran, 2001). In contrast, according to Moran, first-person self-knowledge is immediate, unmediated, and entails privileged access to one's direct phenomenal experience.[16] To take a simple example, in contrast to observing someone scratching his arm and inferring that s/he has an itch, I do not observe myself scratching my arm and then infer that I have an itch. I simply have the phenomenal experience of an itch.

Consider Sartre's (1943) hypothetical example of the akratic gambler discussed by Moran (2001). The gambler resolves that he will stop gambling. Upon self-reflection or by having this pointed out by someone else, the gambler recognizes that s/he has made similar resolutions in the past, only to repeatedly fail to keep them. As Moran (2001) observes, in taking this objective attitude toward himself, the gambler's best prediction is that he will again once again fail to honor his resolution just as s/he has many times in the past. Moran (2001) notes that this third-person perspective as well as the prediction it engenders can serve to undermine the gambler's resolution in the form of: 'I have broken my resolution so many times in the past. The best bet is that I will also do the same this time too; so why bother to try to keep to my resolution this time'. Thus, as

Moran (2001) also notes, the gambler is using his third-person objective stance toward himself to weaken his resolution; that is, he is in bad faith. Moran notes that relying entirely on his subjective sense of the strength of his resolution and ignoring personal history is also a form of self-deception and bad faith. In other words, in order to avoid bad faith, the gambler needs to give voice both to past history as well as to his or her current resolution, that is, to both objective and subjective perspectives.

Consider some examples of taking an exclusive third-person objective stance toward oneself when what is wanted is a first-person commitment: A asks B to lend him a sum of money. B responds: 'Are you sure that you will pay me back by such and such a date'? A replies: 'I predict that I will'. This reply to the question is disconcerting, and B would be well advised to refuse the loan because what is wanted from A here is a simple first-person intention and a commitment to stand behind that intention.

Before leaving the topic of different forms of self-knowledge, I want to note that there is a form of self-knowledge that is neither first-person nor third-person self-knowledge, but what one may call second-person self-knowledge. I refer to an especially challenging form of self-knowledge that is gained from attempting to view oneself as others see you. This requires the ability to take the perspective of the other in relation to oneself, an ability that is not abundantly available.

Working-through

The concept of working-through was invoked by Freud (1914) in order to account for the patient's failure to change despite enhanced self-knowledge and insight (e.g., despite the unconscious having been made conscious). Freud (1926) writes that becoming conscious of repressed unconscious impulses does not 'cover(s) the whole state of affairs in analysis' (p. 159), and attributes the patient's failure to change to the fact that even after 'the ego has decided to relinquish its resistances, it still has difficulty in undoing the repressions. He refers to the period of strenuous effort which follows insight and the ego's praiseworthy decision to relinquish its resistances to the phase of "working-through"' (p. 159). He suggests that the need for working-through is due to the fact that despite the unconscious becoming conscious, persistence of id forces, the 'resistance of the unconscious' (p. 160), and the compulsion to repeat, need to be dealt with if the analysis is to proceed in a positive direction.

Despite stating that working-through 'is a part of the work which effects the greatest change in the patient and which distinguishes analytic treatment from treatment by suggestion' (Freud, 1914, p. 155), Freud devotes a total of about two and a half pages in his entire 24 volumes to the concept. The brief discussion of working-through is a rather thin reed on which to place so much weight. Freud's appeal to working-through to account for lack of significant therapeutic change despite enhanced self-knowledge and insight raises more questions than it answers. It tells us little regarding the specific nature of working-through, that is, what the patient experiences and does in the course of working-through. For example, what is the nature of the 'strenuous effort' that is required in working-through? What, precisely, do 'resistance of the unconscious' and 'persistence of id forces' mean; and how do they prevent therapeutic change? And if the ego has decided to relinquish its resistances, why does it continue to have 'difficulty in undoing repressions'?[17]

It seems to me that Freud's account of working-through in terms of resistances of the unconscious and of the ego's decision to relinquish its resistances has little explanatory value. I think, particularly from a clinical perspective, that working-through is best understood as a complex process through which third-person self-knowledge becomes increasingly transformed into a first-person sense of who one is. There are a number of discussions of the concept of working-through that capture this central aspect of it.

In an excellent review of the concept of working-through, Aron (1991) observes that the way in which the concept of working-through is understood varies with psychoanalytic theoretical developments. For example, Fenichel (1941) emphasized the need to integrate instinctual components into the total personality, a conception of working-through that hardly suggests renunciation. Schafer (1983) viewed working-through in terms of the patient viewing himself or herself as an agent who owns and takes responsibility for hitherto disowned material. This rendering of the meaning of working-through also hardly suggests renunciation. Similar to Freud, Waelder (1960) placed emphasis on renunciation or condemnation of instinctual impulses and conscious denial of their gratification. However, in contrast to Freud, he adds that after repeated denial of gratification over time, the impulse will be 'given up'; that is, like the process of dieting or attempting to give up smoking, patients will 'lose their craving' (p. 226). It should be noted that Waelder writes about renunciation of instinctual impulses in the language of persons doing and experiencing things – as if he were describing giving up a bad habit – rather than in the language of unconscious resistances and the ego deciding to relinquish resistances.

Drawing on concepts from cognitive psychology (see also Polanyi & Prosch, 1976), Rosenblatt (2004) writes that working-through can be understood in terms of (1) transforming procedural knowledge (implicit skills or knowledge), which is more resistant to change into declarative knowledge (explicit knowledge), which can be thought of as including insight; (2) repeated practice of translating one's insights into action, including outside the therapeutic situation; and (3) transformation of declarative knowledge into a new form of procedural knowledge; that is, the insight gained becomes an implicit aspect of oneself. As Poland (1988) puts it, the deepest level of understanding is integration 'without having to resort to conscious thought' (pp. 347–348). Valenstein (1983), too, emphasizes the need for action and for 'taking chances' (p. 362). He writes: 'Ultimately, the working through of insight is pivotally related to the function of action and to definitive changes in action patterns as they are consolidated into the action system' (p. 371).

In a somewhat different theoretical context, like Rosenblatt and Poland, Kohut (1984) also addresses the issue of deliberation and declarative knowledge versus procedural knowledge and implicit change in functioning in therapeutic outcome. He writes that

> Just as the optimum experience of self-object responsiveness in childhood lays down silently functioning regulatory structures which in adult life function outside awareness – that is, without the need to recall the personified imagoes of the self-objects of childhood … [so similarly, one should expect that] the experience of self-object responsiveness in analysis [will] lay(s) down regulatory structures which post-analytically function outside of awareness – that is, without the need to reinstate the functions of the self-object analyst in the form of a conscious exercise of self-analysis …
>
> (p. 170)

He refers to the former as a process of 'transmuting internalization' and accretions of psychic structure in psychoanalytic treatment. What Kohut is saying here is that in an ideal therapeutic outcome the patient will acquire structures that function silently and implicitly without the need for conscious control or the invocation of particular personified figures. In short, the changes have become an integral part of oneself, part of who one is. Although the procedural processes may be brought to consciousness if that is necessary, they need not be when functioning smoothly. In effect, Kohut is formulating a version of the nature of working-through in which whatever one has learned about oneself becomes transformed into who one has become, that is, into an integrated aspect of one's experiences and actions.

A number of commentators have noted that the relinquishment of instinctual impulses in the course of working-though often involves a loss and a mourning process, which Waelder (1960) compares to the process of weaning. Placing the emphasis on the mourning process suggests that working-through is more a matter of altering experience than gaining self-knowledge. In mourning, one ends up being a person for whom loss is now an aspect of one's life, of who one is.

In a paper entitled 'Working Through', Cooper (1989) also observes that how that concept is understood varies with different theories and different approaches to treatment. According to him, the successful outcome of working-through is the learning of new ways of being and relating to others. As Cooper puts it, there is an enhanced capacity to *have* as well as learn from new experiences. Cooper is one of the few commentators on the concept of working-through who places an explicit emphasis on the enhanced capacity for having new experiences as a central aspect of positive therapeutic outcome.

It may be useful to further examine the concept of working-through in the context of concrete clinical material. One of my patients described a pattern in which she was repeatedly attracted to the 'wrong man', to the 'party animal', as she described him. Her relationships with these men invariably ended with the experience of disappointment and much distress. However, despite repeated unhappiness, the attraction to these men – the 'chemistry' – persisted. This pattern continued even after the patient gained some awareness and insight into some underlying motives. As Freud would put it, 'the id forces persisted'. At one point in the treatment, my patient stated that despite the continued attraction and 'chemistry', she would no longer date the 'party animal' – the inevitable outcome of such dating was just too painful and destructive. It was clear that this decision was based on control and deliberation; the attraction and temptation remained.

My patient's resolution can perhaps be understood as an instance of what Freud (1926) referred to as the patient's 'strenuous effort' that is entailed in working-through. Perhaps it can just as readily be described in terms of will power or enhanced ability to delay gratification in the service of long-term benefits or even 'renunciation' of instinctual impulses (Freud, 1930[1929], p. 97). Despite my patient's resolution and consequent change in dating pattern, it does not seem accurate to conclude that she had worked through her 'compulsion to repeat' so long as her conflictual impulses and temptations remained with a significant degree of intensity. It would be more accurate to say that my patient had become more able to exert greater control over impulses and temptations that she continued to experience with considerable intensity rather than that she had worked them through. It may be, as Waelder (1960) suggests, that over time the temptations and impulses would weaken – she would lose her 'craving' – and that what was initially the product of deliberation and control would become implicit and relatively automatic. That is, there would be a weakening or perhaps disappearance of the attraction and 'chemistry' in relation to the 'wrong man'. This more ideal outcome would indicate a successful working-through, as I and, I think, many others, understand the term. I think that most observers would agree that without some alteration in the spontaneous impulses and temptations associated with much past distress, treatment outcome would not be an ideal one.

Let me now describe what actually happened with my patient in the course of treatment. She began to date men to whom she was not immediately sexually attracted. In the past, when this happened, the first date was the last one. However, at one point in the treatment, she met a man to whom she was not especially attracted, but who she found somewhat interesting and who was supportive and seemed to want the same things she wanted. On this occasion, she agreed to a second and third date. Although she did not feel the level of attraction she regularly felt for the 'party animal', there was a sufficient degree of attraction for her to want to continue to see him. The sexual attraction continued to grow and after a few months of dating, they became engaged and set a marriage date. Issues of temptation in relation to the 'wrong man' played less and less of a role in my patient's life. Thus, there seemed to be a genuine change in regard to the nature of her desires and impulses and correspondingly, less and less need for deliberation and ego control.

There is, of course, much more that can be reported about this case. The main point I want to make in the present context, however, is the difference between the outcome of enhanced knowledge and ego control over presumably immutable infantile instinctual impulses and an outcome characterized by changes in spontaneous experience, that is, in the desires and impulses themselves. Although the former may be a good enough outcome, the latter is an ideal one in which to paraphrase Confucius (1999, Analects 2.4), the dictates of one's heart and one's sense of right and wrong are one and the same. This outcome is characterized by less of a need to exert control over desires and impulses that are at odds with central aspects of oneself. In an important sense, this outcome entails subtle changes in one's identity.

Consider the difference between two erstwhile smokers both of whom have given up smoking: although no longer smoking, one person continues to crave for a cigarette, the other no longer has a desire to smoke. Whereas in an important sense, the former person remains a smoker who controls his or her temptation to smoke, the latter person is no longer a smoker. There is a subtle change in the latter's personal identity and nature of subjective experience – from someone who continues to want to smoke to someone who no longer has the identity of a smoker.

The ideal outcome, however, does not always occur in treatment. There may be few changes in patients' fantasies and spontaneous desires or in what Freud (1923) refers to as their 'unconscious prototype' (p. 15). Rather, therapeutic change may consist in a 'good enough' outcome limited to an enhanced capacity to reflect, to delay gratification in the service of long-term goals, and to exert greater ego control over destructive impulses and desires. This, I believe, is a more likely outcome with patients whom, what Freud (1916–1917) referred to as 'adhesiveness of the libido' (p. 348), is especially prominent. These patients experience unyielding attachment to early objects and wishes and fantasies linked to such objects. The concept of 'adhesiveness of the libido' bears a strong family resemblance to Fairbairn's (1952) formulation regarding the individual's persistent emotional attachment to the 'bad' object that is both alluring and rejecting. Both Freud's concept of 'adhesiveness of the libido' and Fairbairn's formulation of attachment to early 'bad' objects refer to the inability of some patients to give up attachments to early objects despite much suffering and distress.

I worked with a woman in treatment who could not give up her long-term relationship with a destructive, abusive man. Any serious effort or even serious thought of leaving the relationship was inevitably followed by severe, debilitating depression and thoughts of suicide, as was giving up the fantasy that someday he would love her and they would live happily ever after. She reported that without that fantasy, life had no meaning and suicide was the only option. In short, despite insight, she was never able to relinquish or work through what for her, was a life-sustaining fantasy. I have observed a similar dynamic as co-director of a project to develop and assess a therapeutic program for domestic violence survivors. The most frequent reason abused women give for returning to the abusive relationship is 'I love him'. Some of the women in our program were able to leave the abusive relationship (this was not the explicit goal of the program). However, the attachment to the 'bad' object remained and a significant number of women returned to the relationship. In one case, with the help of other women in the group, one of the women was able to safely exit the relationship. However, in a very short time, she became extremely depressed and dysfunctional, unable to work or even to get out of bed. Unsurprisingly, she returned to the relationship and to some sort of homeostatic balance.

There were other women who were able to leave the abusive relationship and did not return to it. However, they frequently reported that the men they met, some of whom seemed kind and supportive and were very unlikely to be abusive, were 'boring' – no excitement. It was as if they were addicted to an abusive relationship. That is, similar to the drug-dependent addict who becomes dysregulated in the absence of the drug, some women in our group became dysregulated after leaving the abusive relationship. It is important to note that my description is much less applicable to the women in the program who remained in the abusive relationship largely due to such issues as financial needs, presence of children, and getting caught in nightmarish legal complexities.

An important issue raised by the above clinical material is the degree to which the theoretical perspective of Freudian theory allows for the possibility of change in the patient's fundamental desires and aims rooted in unconscious instinctual wishes. Apfelbaun (1966) addresses this question in a classic paper. He observes that according to the id–ego model, repressed instinctual aims are timeless and not subject to modification. A. Freud (1936) refers to their 'immutability' (p. 140). In this view, perhaps the best outcome one can expect even in successful treatment is more effective ego control over these timeless and presumably immutable instinctual aims. Consider the concept of 'structural change', which is often viewed as the ideal treatment outcome. As understood in the psychoanalytic literature, it refers to changes in ego and superego structures of the personality. It would hardly make sense to talk about structural change in the id given its timelessness and immutability. Thus, 'structural change' does not appear to include changes in repressed instinctual aims and impulses. Rather it refers to positive changes in functioning of ego and superego structures, that is, the ways in which these structures deal with immutable id impulses. As we have seen, these changes in functioning focus on enhanced ego control, what Freud (1930[1929]) refers to as a 'condemning judgment' directed toward instinctual impulses (p. 53).

Freud (e.g., 1930[1929]) also refers to sublimation of infantile instinctual impulses, which is the closest he comes to entertaining the possibility of some modification of instinctual aims. However, as Freud (1930[1929]) notes, a robust capacity for sublimation is not that frequently encountered. And I would add, even if sublimation were readily achievable, it does not adequately address the clinical issues faced by many patients. For example, the primary problem faced by my patient was not one easily resolvable by sublimation, that is, diverting her sexual attraction to the 'wrong man' to a higher social aim.

Self-knowledge, veridicality, and assured conviction

In contrasting the emphasis on enhanced self-knowledge with an emphasis on enhanced experience as psychoanalytic goals, the implicit assumption is made that self-knowledge is in fact enhanced in the psychoanalytic situation, more specifically, that the analyst's interpretations tally with what is real in the patient. However, how does one determine whether an interpretation does in fact tally with what is real in the patient? As discussed earlier, Freud appeared to assume that once defenses are lifted and the unconscious becomes conscious, a hitherto repressed wish or desire becomes accessible to conscious experience. This would presumably constitute evidence that the analyst's attribution of particular unconscious mental content attributed to the patient is accurate. The problem of suggestion, however, looms large here (Meehl, 1994). That is, compliance may be at work in the patient's report of conscious experience of a hitherto repressed mental content. However, putting that issue aside, it is not clear how frequently patients actually report conscious subjective experience of a hitherto repressed wish or desire attributed to him or her by the analyst. For example, how frequently is the lifting of defenses followed by the patient's subjective experience of, say, incestuous wishes?

In his late writings, Freud himself appeared to harbor doubts regarding the frequency with which patients report direct experience of the unconscious wishes, fantasies, and early experiences attributed to the patient by the analyst. In one of his last papers, Freud (1937) wrote that although ideally, the analyst's interpretations – what Freud refers to as 'constructions' – regarding the patient's early experiences should result in the patient's recollections of what has been repressed, this does not always occur.[18] Instead, the patient will have 'an assured conviction of the truth of the construction' (p. 266). Furthermore, according to Freud, the patient's assured conviction 'achieves the same therapeutic result as a recaptured memory' (pp. 265–266).

Although Freud's (1937) focus is on recollection of repressed early events and experiences related to instinctual wishes and desires, given the assumptions of persistence of infantile instinctual impulses and the timelessness of the unconscious, these early wishes and desires – what Freud (1937) refers to as 'the affective impulses' (p. 257) – presumably remain active in adult life. Hence, in this view, the sufficiency of the patient's 'assured conviction' of the truth of the analyst's constructions to bring about a therapeutic result would apply not only to the analyst's constructions of historical events, but also to the constructions of the patient's *currently active* wishes and desires. In short, it would follow that just as a therapeutic result may not require the patient's actual recollection of repressed memories of early experiences attributed to him or her by the analyst, so similarly, it may also not require the patient's actual experience of the presumably currently active repressed wishes and desires attributed to him or her by the analyst. In both instances, the patient's assured conviction of the truth of the analyst's construction does not necessarily constitute self-knowledge.

In view of the fact there may be only a loose connection between assured conviction and self-knowledge, Freud's shift to the sufficiency of the former is a momentous one. It allows the possibility that the degree to which an interpretation elicits assured conviction of its truth may be therapeutically more important than whether or not it tallies with what is real in the patient. If there is no one-to-one correspondence between the patient's assured conviction of the truth of interpretations and the degree to which they tally with what is real in the patient, one can no longer claim, at least in any straightforward way, that either enhanced self-knowledge or the experience of hitherto repressed mental contents are primary factors of the psychoanalytic process.

It should also be added that the patient's assured conviction of the truth of the analyst's constructions regarding his or her mental contents is not essentially different in form from an assured conviction of the truth of attributions made to a third person. This is so insofar as attributed mental contents regarding which one has an assured conviction have not necessarily achieved the status of subjectivity in the sense that they are not necessarily experienced as 'I wish' or 'I desire' or 'I remember'.

Freud's (1937) allowance for 'assured conviction' rather than actual recollection opened the door to the possibility that the veridicality of the analyst's interpretations, that is, how well it tallies with what is real in the patient, may not be a necessary component of psychoanalytic treatment or a condition for therapeutic effectiveness. Spence (1983) enters the opened door and widens it further with his argument that because we cannot provide 'historical truth', that is, what really happened in regard to the patient's early experiences and early events, the best the analyst can do is construct narratives that elicit the patient's assured conviction of their truth. According to Spence (1983), these narratives possess 'narrative truth'. It turns out, however, that what Spence means by 'narrative truth' has little to do with truth of any kind, historical or narrative, but rather with the *persuasiveness* to the patient of the analyst's construction. He writes: 'To the extent that a narrative is persuasive and compelling, it acquires features of what might be called *narrative truth*' [emphasis in the original] (Spence, 1983, p. 465). Spence also observes that familiarity and repetition may also contribute to the persuasiveness of a narrative. He writes that a narrative 'may gain support by virtue of repetition quite apart from its evidential value' (Spence, 1983, p. 462). Spence appears to recognize here that with sufficient repetition a falsehood may come to be believed as the truth. And surely, it is disturbingly clear, in the light of historical and contemporary events that many constructions that are plausible and that elicit assured conviction of their truth may nevertheless be false. In short, what Spence inadvertantly does is 1) lay bare the untenability of Freud's assumption that assured conviction of the truth and the actual truth are in a one-to-one relationship; and 2) allow for the possibility that the patient's assured conviction of the truth of the analyst's interpretations may have far more to with their persuasiveness than their veridicality. However, in referring to narrative *truth* rather than narrative *persuasiveness*, Spence obscures this conclusion by suggesting that some kind of truth is still at work.

Spence (1983) provides an example of so-called 'narrative truth', which has striking contemporary relevance in demonstrating the serious problems attending that concept. The example taken from Singer (1971) is one in which in a

> politician who wants to win the next election and who, in support of that claim, makes the statement that he *will* win the election; Spence writes that the politician makes the statement in the hope that it will acquire narrative truth and thereby influence the outcome of the election. By making the statement he hopes to influence its truth value.
>
> (p. 467)

The politician's statement that he will win the election cannot possibly be true or false at the time that he makes the statement because the election has not yet taken place. All that one can legitimately say is that the politician *expects* to win the election and that his confident assertion that he will win the election may play a role in his actually winning the election. Introducing the idea that the politician's statement will acquire narrative truth adds nothing other than confusion. As we have seen, an overwhelming number of Trump loyalists believe the narrative that Trump won the election and was denied re-election through fraud and conspiracy. Does this narrative acquire narrative truth by virtue of its persuasiveness to a large number of people?[19,20]

It is not clear why a concept like narrative truth has gained traction in the psychoanalytic literature. I wonder if at least one of the reasons is it allows one to avoid confrontation with the stark possibility that it may be the sheer persuasiveness of the analyst's interpretation – quite apart from any issue of veridicality – that may be a primary therapeutic factor in the therapeutic situation – a claim made some time ago by Frank (1974) in his book *Persuasion and healing* as well as by others. The term 'narrative truth' creates the illusion that sheer persuasiveness entails some special kind of truth even if its relationship to what one normally thinks of as truth is far from clear. 'Narrative persuasiveness' would be a far more accurate description of what Spence has in mind than the term 'narrative truth'. The illusion generated by narrative *truth* may provide some comfort to those who want to retain the belief, one central to the embeddedness of the psychoanalytic project in the Enlightenment vision, that the truth will set one free (see Eagle, 2011, 2011a).

The door to severing the relation between interpretation and the nature of the patient's inner world, approached either epistemologically (self-knowledge) or as subjectively experienced, has been opened even wider by a number of analysts who have taken a position that explicitly eliminates any semblance of the idea that they are engaged in seeking and uncovering truths of any kind. Rather, they propose that analytic narratives and constructions should be viewed not as veridical accounts, that is, accounts that tally with what is real in the patient, but rather as 'aesthetic fictions' (Geha, 1984; see Eagle, 1984, for response to Geha); as 'inventions' that 'are imagined, not discovered' (Viderman, 1979, p. 265); and as internally coherent accounts (Sherwood, 1969; see Eagle, 1973), or as 'master narratives', each narrative incommensurate with the other and each no more valid than the other Schafer, 1992).

An implication of the above position is that a patient in analysis with two analysts of different theoretical persuasions would emerge from the analyses with two different incommensurate master narratives, each equally valid (Schafer, 1992). In this view, the patient's productions (i.e., free associations, dreams, reports of subjective experience) are primarily data to be interpreted in accord with the analyst's master narrative. Any patient who naively entered analysis with the aim of discovering truths about himself or herself or the aim of, in Winnicott's (1960) term, his or her 'true self' would need to disabuse himself or herself of this essentialist idea (see Eagle, 1984a; Sass, 1987, for a further discussion of this issue).

Let us say that one patient enters an analysis with a classical Freudian analyst and another patient enters an analysis with a self-psychology analyst. I think that there would be general agreement that the former's master narrative would include, among other ideas, the centrality of the Oedipus complex; it would, therefore, be highly likely that the analyst would find oedipal derivatives in the patient's free associations, dreams, and so on. For this analyst, oedipal interpretations would be viewed as interpretations that tally with what is real in the patient. In contrast, a self-psychology analyst would be likely to find evidence of issues having to do with self-cohesiveness. This phenomenon is not entirely hypothetical. Gedo (1980) observed that whereas the 1978 self-psychology casebook edited by Goldberg was replete with references to self-defects and hardly mentions oedipal issues; a classically oriented casebook published in the same year (Firestein, 1978) dealing with seemingly similar clinical material has not a word about self-defects, but a great deal about oedipal issues. Both analysts are likely to claim that their interpretations tally with what is real in the patient. This, of course, is not a new observation. The point I want to highlight in the present context is that if assured conviction or persuasiveness or aesthetic quality or coherence of narrative are the critical properties of analytic interpretations, the claim that psychoanalysis enhances self-knowledge is essentially relinquished. It is replaced by the patient's adoption of a new perspective about himself or herself that is more coherent, aesthetic, etc., a perspective that tallies with the analyst's theoretical position.

Let me share a personal experience of many years ago. I had joined a study group on self-psychology at a psychoanalytic institute with which I was affiliated at the time. Each of the members of the group was expected to present clinical material to be discussed. During one meeting, the following clinical material was presented: a male analytic patient, age 38, living with a female partner, who he described as supportive and loving, felt that he could never be as successful as his father. The words he used to express that feeling were: 'I could never measure up to him'. The patient was also troubled by the fact that he had difficulty feeling sexual toward his girlfriend. In the session presented, the patient reported that he frequently went to strip clubs – behavior that troubled him – where he had the fantasy that the stripper was looking directly at him throughout her performance. One of the members of the group interpreted this fantasy as an expression of the patient's need for self-affirmation due to his lack of self-cohesiveness. There was general agreement with this interpretation. I commented that much of the oedipally tinged clinical material presented regarding the patient's relationship with his father and his difficulty experiencing sexual desire for his girlfriend was being ignored. I also raised the question of why the patient would need to look to the stripper for self-affirmation rather than to his supportive and loving girlfriend. The response to my comments was that the function of the study group was to provide interpretations and understandings from the perspective of self-psychology theory, not from other theoretical perspectives. Strikingly, the full range of the patient's actual experiences seemed secondary to the importance of generating an interpretation congruent with a self-psychology perspective.[21]

One could argue, as Pine (1985) does, that different theoretical perspectives focus on different aspects of the patient's personality and experiences and are all relevant in the clinical situation. However, analysts of different theoretical persuasions tend not to take this position. Rather, like the blind men and the elephant, each theoretical school takes the position that its perspective accounts for every aspect of the individual. Thus, each theoretical school tends to reduce different aspects of the personality to the one dimension that is at its theoretical center. For example, for Freudian drive theory, all behavior, directly or indirectly, is motivated by instinctual drives. For self-psychology, virtually all behavior can be understood in terms of the pursuit of self-cohesiveness. The same pattern is present with regard to other psychoanalytic schools. The point here is the patient's reports of his or her subjective experience is heard from a preset particular theoretical perspective.

Spence's emphasis on persuasiveness, whatever its problems, at least possesses the virtue of entailing a reference to the patient's experience and reaction to the analyst's interpretations (i.e., being persuaded). In contrast, a conception of the analyst's narratives as aesthetic fictions, imaginative inventions, and internally coherent master narratives all refer to *internal* properties of the narratives. The sole consideration that would link these properties to something external to the narrative itself, namely, the patient, would be the assumption that when communicated to the patient, narratives with these properties are associated with positive therapeutic change. Without this assumption, it is not at all clear why one should be especially interested in the question of how aesthetic, how coherent, and how imaginative, inventive and clever the analyst's narratives are. That is, without the assumption that these narrative properties are associated with therapeutic change, preoccupation with them – and for that matter, preoccupation with any analytic activities – smack of self-absorption. Strikingly, with the exception of Spence's work, little is said regarding issues of therapeutic effectiveness and of the patient's experience of and reaction to the analyst's narratives, let alone citing evidence that 'aesthetic fictions' or 'master narratives' are systematically associated with therapeutic outcome.

The ideas that the analyst's interpretations are essentially aesthetic fictions, imaginative inventions, and persuasive narratives, and that these properties are sufficient for therapeutic change, essentially sound the death knell for the fundamental assumptions of psychoanalytic theory embedded in the Enlightenment vision that psychoanalysis uncovers truths about the patient and enhances self-knowledge, and that greater access to self-truths and self-knowledge is the primary ingredient of therapeutic action. If the persuasiveness, aesthetic qualities, and inventiveness of interpretations are mainly what matters in treatment, the large literature dealing with the criteria for the accuracy of interpretations is virtually irrelevant, at least as far as the nature of therapeutic action is concerned. This is the case not only in regard to historical narratives, but also with regard to interpretations in which *currently* active unconscious wishes and desires are attributed to the patient. One would need to modify Freud's (1917) claim that only interpretations that tally with what is real in the patient are conducive to therapeutic change with the proposition that only interpretations that are aesthetic, inventive and that the patient finds persuasive are conducive to therapeutic change.

If enhancement of self-knowledge through interpretation is no longer viewed as the overriding process goal of psychoanalytic treatment, what replaces it? Alternatives offered in the psychoanalytic literature such as acquiring new perspectives (e.g., Renik, 1996, 1998), replacing experiences of meaninglessness with experience of meaning (e.g., Curtis, 1991), and enhancement of 'implicit relational knowing' (Lyons-Ruth et al., 1999) share a greater emphasis on more experiential factors that are embedded in the therapeutic relationship. However, the most explicit expression of the centrality of experience in psychoanalytic treatment is Alexander and French's (1946) concept of 'corrective emotional experience'.

Corrective emotional experience

Although the concept of 'corrective emotional experience' was rejected by the psychoanalytic establishment at the time it was introduced – Alexander and French were viewed as pariahs by the psychoanalytic establishment – it has re-emerged and has exerted a strong influence on post-Freudian psychodynamic approaches that are marked by a shift in emphasis from knowledge to experience. This shift is seen in the writings of Guntrip (e.g., 1968), Winnicott (1969), Kohut (1984), and others. Hand in hand with the shift in emphasis from knowledge to experience is a relative de-emphasis on interpretation and an enhanced emphasis on the therapeutic relationship. The very title of one of Winnicott's books – *The Maturational Process and the Facilitating Environment* – reflects his view that therapeutic change is largely a product of growth-inducing experiences in a therapeutic environment rather than self-knowledge-enhancing interpretation. However, one need not rely on the title of his book to identify Winnicott's attitude toward interpretation. Winnicott (1969) writes that the patient needs not an interpretation, but a new experience. He also writes: 'It appalls me to think how much deep change I have prevented or delayed in patients in a certain classification by my personal need to interpret' and adds 'If only we can wait, the patient arrives at understanding creatively and with immense joy, and I can now enjoy this joy more than I used to enjoy the sense of being clever' (Winnicott, 1971, p. 356). As is apparent in this last sentence, from Winnicott's perspective, ideally, the patient's self-understanding is not simply a matter of the enhancement of self-knowledge, but also includes a strong affective subjective experience. For Winnicott, a facilitating therapeutic environment is a safe environment, that is, one that is non-impinging and non-intrusive. It seems clear that in Winnicott's view, too often interpretation is experienced as impingement by the patient. If one were to sum up Winnicott's conception of treatment in relatively few words, one would say that its goal is developmental growth rather than enhanced self-knowledge; and that the primary means of achieving such growth is the facilitating environment provided by the therapeutic relationship rather than interpretation and insight. The template for a facilitating environment for Winnicott is the provision of holding, literal holding in the infant-mother relationship and psychological holding in the therapeutic relationship.

At the center of Kohut's (1984) approach to treatment is a lessened focus on the patient's understanding accompanied by an enhanced focus on the vital importance of the patient's *experience of feeling empathically understood* by the analyst, which, for Kohut, is essentially a corrective emotional experience. He writes that if an ill-disposed critic wants to criticize the self-psychology approach to treatment on the ground that its focus is on corrective emotional experiences, his response is 'so be it' (Kohut, 1984, p. 86). Kohut makes it clear that in his view, the goal of treatment is not enhanced awareness and insight through interpretation, but rather 'accretions of psychic structure' through experiences of feeling empathically understood.

Corrective emotional experience is often implicitly understood in terms of the therapist's behavior (e.g., behaving differently than parental figures; being empathic). However, a central issue that arises in treatment is the patient's often powerful tendency to assimilate potentially new experiences into old schemas and thus experience them in the same, repetitive rigid way. This raises the question of how an experience can be emotionally corrective if it is assimilated into pre-existing schemas and therefore *subjectively experienced* as a version of old experiences. Of course, this issue is at the core of transference analysis. Thus, corrective emotional experiences cannot be meaningfully defined primarily from the perspective of the analyst's behaviors or intentions; the concept needs to be understood from the perspective of the patient's subjective experience. As Aron (1991) writes, 'the central problem for the analyst in the clinical situation is to find a way into which to enter the patient's subjective world without being transformed or assimilated into an old object schema' (p. 104). Aron asks: 'If whatever the analyst says or does, the patient … takes in (or assimilates) only that which conforms to the preformed patterns of their inner representational world, then how does the internal world ever change?' (p. 104).

Aron (1991) appeals to Piaget's (1954) conceptualizations of the processes of assimilation and accommodation as 'a useful conceptual strategy for approaching this dilemma' (p. 104). He states that although there may be a great deal of assimilation, 'some accommodation to the actual interpersonal experience must also occur' (p. 104). This may well be true. But how does such accommodation occur? Aron's answer is that 'the analyst needs to work his or her way out of the transformation and articulate this event in the form of an interpretation' (p. 105), which, I assume, refers to transference interpretation. However, especially with patients who show little capacity for accommodation, this leaves us with the very same problem that the patient may assimilate the very interpretation that attempts to deal with his or her tendency to assimilate.

There is no easy way out of this dilemma. Indeed, much of therapeutic work particularly transference interpretations, consists precisely in trying to deal constructively with this dilemma. The therapist's ability to deal with this dilemma as well as the patient's capacity for accommodation, which can be understood as the individual's ability to modify his or her representational world or internal working model, are likely to be critical variables associated with therapeutic outcome. Although not discussed specifically in this context, Control-Mastery Theory (CMT) essentially addresses this issue in its central proposal that the modification of unconscious pathogenic beliefs is associated with the therapist passing certain tests that betoken conditions of safety (Silberschatz, 2005: Weiss & Sampson, 1986).

Interpretation and corrective emotional experience

As we have seen in previous discussions, there has been an ongoing tension in the history of psychoanalysis between the roles of interpretation and insight and corrective emotional experience inherent in the therapeutic relationship. I noted at the beginning of this chapter Laplanche and Pontalis' (1973) definition of psychoanalysis as a study of the unconscious. However, they also write that 'Interpretation is at the heart of Freudian doctrine and technique. Psychoanalysis itself might be defined in terms of it, as the latent meaning of given material' (p. 277). The last phrase is especially important. If consciousness is dissimulating, that is, if we are self-deceiving creatures, then only interpretation can uncover the latent meanings that consciousness hides and disguises. This is at the core of the psychoanalytic project. For classical psychoanalytic theorists and clinicians, it is this core that was believed to be threatened by too much emphasis on corrective emotional experiences and the therapeutic relationship.

The dichotomy between interpretation and corrective emotional experience rests on the assumption that whereas interpretation serves mainly to enhance the patient's self-knowledge and insight, the therapeutic relationship provides corrective emotional experiences. However, this contrast is often far from clear for a number of reasons. The most obvious reason is that because in the clinical situation interpretations are given in the context of an ongoing relationship, how they are experienced by the patient as well as the effects they will have are likely to be influenced by the nature of the relationship. Another related reason is that the affective tone of an interpretation, which often reflects the nature of the relationship, may have as great an effect as its semantic content. Still another reason, one mentioned earlier, is that the therapeutic effects of an interpretation may lie as much in the patient's experience of feeling understood as by understanding and gaining insight. Ideally, both occur.

There is not just one kind of interpretation. There are many different kinds of interpretations; and the experiences they elicit and the effects they have are likely to vary with the kind of interpretation offered. One distinction that I think is important is whether the interpretation has to do with mental states and contents that are readily accessible to conscious experience, or is a 'deep' interpretation concerned with mental states and contents largely inaccessible to conscious experience. The analysis of defensive processes just below the surface of consciousness, exemplified by Gray's (1994) 'close process monitoring' is illustrative of the former kind of interpretation, whereas interpretations of 'deeply' repressed instinctual wishes are illustrative of the latter. Whereas the former is directed at *showing*, the latter is concerned with *revealing* or *uncovering* (Heaton, 1972). Although it is an empirical question, one would expect that whereas the former kind of interpretation can readily elicit what Moran (2001) refers to as first-person self-knowledge, the effects of the latter kind of interpretation would seem to be limited to third-person self-knowledge.

There is a kind of corrective emotional experience that is not described as such in the psychoanalytic literature, perhaps partly because it is not simply a corrective experience, but also entails elements of enhanced self-knowledge. I refer to a common clinical experience, namely, the anxiety-allaying effect of interpretations that bring meaning to hitherto meaningless symptomatic experiences. Let me provide some clinical vignettes that illustrate the transformation of meaninglessness into meaning. In one case, the patient, a successful businessman, became dysfunctional following the death of his wife. He could not leave his home and did so only to come for treatment. During one session, he reported that although he felt encouraged by his emerging ability to leave the house to shop for food, he felt 'worse than ever' when he returned home. He described this experience as one foot forward and two steps backward, which filled him with hopelessness and despair. In the course of our discussion of this disturbing experience, what emerged was that getting better, as expressed in leaving the house, meant accepting the intolerable reality of the loss of his wife. My patient's experience of his feeling 'worse than ever' upon returning home as meaningful rather than meaningless had a marked positive effect.

In another case, the patient reported a sense of failure, depression, and the conviction that his colleagues would view him as a failure in reaction to a business deal that did not live up to his expectations – although the deal was very profitable. He also had reported earlier in the treatment that he felt 'puny' as an adolescent and young man and that the dominant feeling his parents had toward

him was 'pity'. I brought his attention to these early feelings which he then connected to his current feelings regarding failure despite the profitability of the
business deal. Again, the sense of meaningfulness, in this case in relation to his
symptom of feelings of failure, was very helpful for him. In this and the previous
vignette, whatever else was going on, the interpretations were not directed toward
uncovering repressed impulses or wishes and thereby enhancing self-knowledge,
although they may succeed in doing so. Rather, they helped the patient experience
the meaningfulness of his symptoms rather than experience a continued sense of
meaninglessness. In short, the experience of meaningfulness can itself be therapeutic (see Curtis, 1991; Frankl, 1967).[22]

Interpretation and construction of experience

Due to its social constructivist perspective, relational psychoanalysis places primary emphasis on the role of interpretation in the very *construction and co-con-
struction* of the patient's experiences. Rather than viewing subjective experience
as immediately 'given', relational psychoanalysis views it as 'interpretively constructed'. Mitchell (1998) writes that 'Consciousness comes into being through
acts of construction either by others or, through self-reflection by oneself' (p.
16). When one engages in self-reflection, one is reflecting on already experienced
mental contents. What could self-reflection possibly be prior to consciousness?
What would one reflect on? And although one may infer through observation
what someone else is experiencing, one does not infer one's own subjective experience. As discussed above, one does not infer one's own subjective experience as
a product of observation and inference; it is simply 'given'. That is what is meant
by first-person subjective experience (Moran, 2001).

Reflecting the influence of Sullivan's (1953) position that there is no such thing
as an individual personality, only an interpersonal field, Mitchell (2000) writes
that 'the individual mind is an oxymoron' (p. 57). If, indeed, there is no such thing
as an individual personality and if the individual mind is an oxymoron, the interpersonal field cannot be understood as two individual personalities in interaction
creating an interpersonal field, or as Chodorow (1999) puts it, two subjectivities
interacting. This leaves one puzzled as to what the interpersonal field is meant to
be. As Cannon (2016) observes, relational psychoanalysis 'defines intersubjectivity in terms of a vague field that includes a merging of subjectivities in the "relational unconscious"' (p. 21). In short, relational psychoanalysis de-emphasizes
individual subjective experience in favor of an emphasis on social construction
and an interpersonal field.

In his discussion of ego autonomy, Rapaport (1957/1967) proposed that the
relative autonomy of ego functioning from the excessive influence of the inner
world of drives is supported by the availability of stimulus input from the external, including the social, world; and conversely, that the relative autonomy of
ego functioning from the excessive influence of the external world is supported
by the availability of input from one's inner world. According to the logic of this

formulation, the unavailability or the severe restriction of input from the external world (as in sensory deprivation or solitary confinement or social exclusion) leaves one at the mercy of one's inner world; and conversely, the unavailability or severe restriction of input from one's inner world (as in the case of an impoverished cognitive and affective inner world) leaves one at the mercy of excessive influence by one's external environment. In ordinary discourse, we describe the latter in terms of the individual lacking inner resources.

I bring up Rapaport's formulation in the present context in order to articulate some of the implications of a thoroughgoing social construction perspective on the nature of mind. Such a perspective leaves little room for an inner world that is preserved and protected from social influence, and is disturbingly redolent of a social state of affairs in which there is complete social control over the nature of experience. Rapaport (1957/1967) cites Orwell's (1949) *Nineteen Eighty-Four*, although fictional, as a compelling instantiation of a social condition in which 'the individual is robbed of his privacy, the environment invades it' (p. 730). He also writes that

> the individual rebellion which Orwell describes has its roots in a yearning for tenderness, love, and sex, which … are *ultimate* guarantees of the ego's autonomy from the environment. In the society depicted by Orwell, private and personal experiences such as sexual love, that belong to one's inner world, are a threat to the social order. As I have noted elsewhere (Eagle, 2011), the word 'totalitarian' … is intended to convey the idea of … the total dominance of the social over the personal and the inner … the Winnicottian idea of an inviolable inner private aspect of the self cannot be tolerated.
>
> (p. 139)

Of course, I am not suggesting that relational psychoanalysis is totalitarian in its perspective. What I am suggesting is that a thoroughgoing social constructivist point of view is uncomfortably compatible with a totalitarian worldview depicted in *Nineteen Eighty-Four*. In the context of psychotherapy, at the level of patient–therapist relationship, the idea that the analyst constructs or co-constructs the analysand's mind smacks too much of a domination of the social at the expense of one's inner world – all becomes social. One of the criticisms directed toward classical psychoanalysis is, a warranted one, I believe, lies in the danger that the patient may emerge from treatment with certain convictions, for example, that s/he harbors a particular set of unconscious wishes and desires, that are the product of suggestion rather than constituting an account that tallies with what is real in him or her. In certain respects, this outcome could be seen as the development of a false self. However, a similar or perhaps greater danger is present in a therapeutic approach that takes the position that the patient's ongoing subjective experiences and the very organization of his or her mind are entirely the products of social construction.[23]

Notes

1 This definition is not limited to Freudian theory. As Hirsch and Roth (1995) note, although 'changes in the conception of unconscious' are linked to 'shifts in psycho-analytic theorizing', 'inherent in anything called psychoanalysis is some notion of unconscious processes' (p. 263). In the course of writing a book on core concepts in psychoanalytic theory (Eagle, 2018a, 2018b), I asked a group of psychoanalysts from different psychoanalytic perspectives to identify the four or five core concepts of psy-choanalytic theory. The concept of unconscious processes was by far the most frequent choice. However, it is important to point out that when Laplanche and Pontalis define psychoanalysis as a study of the unconscious, they, along with all Freudian theorists, are referring to the *dynamic* unconscious, not the computational or cognitive uncon-scious. It is far from clear that this definition would be accepted by non-Freudian psy-choanalytic theorists.

2 The term 'false consciousness' was first used by Engels (1949) in a letter to Mehring. What Engels and later, what Marxists meant, by 'false consciousness' is the tendency of the working class to experience and act against their own interests. Although the term 'false consciousness' may refer to different aspects of behavior in the contexts of Marxist theory and psychoanalysis, the common meaning shared in both contexts is the failure of consciousness to inform and guide us to experience and act in accord with our true interests, in the context of Marxist theory, our economic interests, and in the context of Freudian theory, with our psychological interests. In the context of Marxist theory, this failure is the result of internalization of the values and interest of the ruling classes; and in the context of psychoanalysis, this failure is due to the internalization of the values and restraints of (Victorian) society. In the former case, the consequence is acquiescence to oppression; and in the latter case, it is neurosis and failure to experi-ence gratification of our vital sexual needs and interests.

Another point of convergence between Marxist theory and psychoanalysis is the promise of liberation, through education and revolution in the former; and through the analytic process in the latter. In both cases, liberation consists in the restructuring of consciousness so that it more adequately represents the nature of reality and of one's true interests. Whereas Marxist theory focuses on that aspect of reality that has to do with the means of production and distribution and the oppression of the working class, psychoanalysis focuses on unconscious processes which, according to Freud (1900), are the true psychic reality. In both cases, liberation from false consciousness consists in consciousness more faithfully representing fundamental aspects of reality. In short, Marxist theory and psychoanalysis each has its own version of the reality principle; and experiencing and acting in accord with that principle are central aspects of the libera-tion and restructuring of false consciousness.

Many of the early followers of Freudian theory were also Marxists or at least sympathetic to Marxism (See Fenichel's *Rundbriefe*; also see Jacoby, 1971; Marcuse, 1955; Reich, 1953).For many of these early followers, economic and social *oppression* were not independent of personal, particularly sexual, oppression. Hence, economic and social not independent of sexual liberation. This link is most clearly seen in the writings of Reich (e.g., 1953). Interestingly, Trotsky made many supportive comments about Freudian theory in his writings (see Trotsky, 1925). Indeed, until about 1930, when Stalin banned psychoanalysis in the Soviet Union, there was much enthusiasm for psychoanalysis following the Russian revolution. This is not surprising insofar as the early Marxist psychoanalysts and the early leaders of the Russian revolution shared the vision that under ideal conditions – economic and social conditions in the case of Marxist beliefs and psychological transformation in the case of psychoanalysis – the human being could achieve his or her greatest potential.

3 Although consciousness is seen as dissimulating in regard to one's inner world, it is viewed in Freudian theory as generally reliable and veridical in regard to perceptual experience of one's external world. I will have more to say about this issue in Chapter 3 (also see Eagle, 2022).

4 Most contemporary psychoanalysts, I believe, would reject this description as an appropriate analytic stance.

5 Kriegel's point is perhaps clearer if it restated as: 'If a mental state is beyond my awareness, although it can be viewed as mental state by an outside observer, it is not a mental state "for me" and hence, it does not have the property of subjectivity'.

6 Notably, however, Lear's conception of subjectivity can be viewed as compatible with a view of consciousness and subjective experience as dissimulating. On this view, consciousness and subjective experience generally falsify the 'deeper strata' of subjectivity.

7 For a perspective that allows for the possibility of 'unconscious subjectivity', see Mills (1999) and Neisser (2015).

8 It is important to keep in mind that in the analytic situation, the patient is often reflecting on the *analyst's construal* of the patient's unconscious mental contents.

9 Similar to Fairbairn's 'excorcism' of the internal object, Freud (1927[1930]) refers to the need to renounce and repudiate the infantile instinctual wish. However, in a number of contexts, the most important one being the goal of 'where id was, there shall ego be' (Freud, 1933, p. 106), he also emphasizes the importance of *integrating* hitherto unintegrated wishes. This shift occurs in the context of the advent of drive theory. That is, insofar as instinctual wishes are embedded in one's psychobiological make-up, one cannot simply nullify their demands by removing them from the personality; one must find ways to integrate them in one way or another.

10 Recall Freud's (1894) description of repressed wishes as 'a sort of parasite', 'which finds a lodgment in consciousness' (p. 49).

11 I rely heavily on Jay's (2005) encyclopedic *Songs of Experience* in discussing this debate between *Erlebnis* and *Erfahrung*.

12 As we know, they virtually became pariahs in the psychoanalytic community for this position as well for as other heresies.

13 As Ogden writes, there is no inherent opposition between self-knowledge and experience nor, as he notes, is there a pure form of epistemological psychoanalysis and ontological psychoanalysis.

14 Ogden writes that it is beyond the scope of his paper to discuss the contributions of the existential analyst contributors (except for Laing) or the work of Kohut to 'the ontological' (approach).

15 Interestingly, Freud (1915b) wrote with regard to repression, that one can allow an unacceptable idea to remain conscious as long as its connection to affective feelings is severed.

16 Although Moran (2001) refers to first-person knowledge, he makes it clear that he does not view it primarily as epistemological. Rather, his emphasis is on its properties of experiential immediacy, privileged access, and moral commitment. Hence, what Moran refers to as first-person self-knowledge can just as readily be understood as first-person direct experience combined with the property of moral commitment. The kind of self-knowledge entailed is reflected in such statements as 'I know what I feel'.

17 Freud (1919) also writes that 'patients need to be persuaded by the analyst to renounce infantile impulses [which presumably means renounce attempts to gratify them] and accept that one cannot live according to the pleasure principle' (p. 159).According to the Freudian formulation of the timelessness of the unconscious, – in A. Freud's (1936) words, 'the immutability of the id' (p. 141), one cannot eliminate or substantially alter instinctual impulses; the best one can do is renounce or sublimate them. That is, in so far as infantile impulses are timeless and immutable, the best one can do is renounce or

sublimate them. However, it is not clear how one would renounce powerful id impulses. It would seem to entail constant effort to exert ego control – what Freud (1915a) refers to as a 'constant expenditure of force' (p. 151) – over attempts to gratify these impulses. This hardly seems to be a desirable outcome. As for sublimation, that avenue only makes sense in the context of a tension or excitation reduction model in which the tensions associated with drive impulses (e.g., sexual drives) can be discharged through 'higher' social aims. Just how this would take place is unclear. In any case, there is widespread agreement that Freud's (1923) model of the mind as a discharge apparatus, on which the concept of sublimation rests, is not a tenable one.

18 It is interesting to observe that as late as 1937 Freud continues to maintain that recollection of repressed early memories is a key ingredient of positive therapeutic outcome.

19 There is a good deal of work in social-cognitive psychology on self-fulfilling prophecy phenomena which indicates that through their influence on one's own behavior and others' reaction to that behavior, a prophecy or expectation can contribute to the fulfillment of that prophecy or expectation. This is likely to be equally true of the expectation that one will lose an election as of the expectation that one will win an election.

20 Although, as the above example of the politician makes clear, Spence (1983) intends his concept of 'narrative truth' to apply not only to biographical historical accounts, but to *all* constructions and narratives having to do with the present as well as the past.

21 Keep in mind that one of Kohut's (1984) important claims is that in contrast to a classical perspective, self-psychology is more experience-near, makes greater use of empathic understanding, and is less influenced by experience-distant metapsychological formulations.

22 In replacing meaninglessness with meaning, the treatment follows the course of the emergence of psychoanalysis – from viewing symptomatology as a product of constitutional weakness to viewing it as the product of motives, wishes, and conflicts.

23 It is important to distinguish between, on the one hand, recognition that the relational and the social are the milieu in which the capacity for subjective experience develops and that these factors have an enormous influence on shaping the nature of subjective experience and, on the other hand, claiming that the individual's ongoing experiences are socially constructed, that is, is entirely constructed through social interaction.

References

Alexander, F., & French, T. M. (1946). *Psychoanalytic therapy; Principles and application.* Ronald Press.

Aron, L. (1991). Working through the past—Working toward the future. *Contemporary Psychoanalysis, 27*(1), 81–109. https://doi.org/10.1080/00107530.1991.10746694

Apfelbaum, B. (1966). On ego psychology: A critique of the structural approach to psychoanalytic theory. *The International Journal of Psychoanalysis, 47*(4), 451–475.

Bakan, D. (1958). *Sigmund Freud and the Jewish mystical tradition.* D. Van Nostrand. https://doi.org/10.1037/11509-000

Benjamin, W. (1913). Experience. In M. Bullock & M. W. Jenning (Eds.), *Walter Benjamin's selected writing* (Vol. 1, pp. 3–6). Harvard University Press.

Bion, W. R. (1967). Notes on memory and desire. In R. Lang (Ed.), *Classics in psychoanalytic technique.* Jason Aronson.

Cannon, B. (2016). What would I do with Lacan today? Thoughts on Sartre, Lacan, and contemporary psychoanalysis. *Sartre Studies International, 22*(2), 13–38. http://www.jstor.org/stable/44652888

Chodorow, N. (1999). *The power of feelings: Personal meaning in psychoanalysis, gender, and culture.* Yale University Press.

Coburn, W. J. (1999). Attitudes of embeddedness and transcendence in psychoanalysis: Subjectivity, self-experience and countertransference. *Journal of the American Academy of Psychoanalysis, 26*(2).

Cooper, A. M. (1989). Working through. *Contemporary Psychoanalysis, 25*(1), 34–62. https://doi.org/10.1080/00107530.1989.10746280

Curtis, R. (1991). How people change. In R. C. Curtis & G. Stricker (Eds.), *How people change* (The Springer Series in Social /Clinical Psychology). https://doi.org/10.1007/978-1-4899-0741-7_1

Curtis, R., Field, C., Knaan-Kostman, I., & Mannix, K. (2004). What 75 psychoanalysts found helpful and hurtful in their own analyses. *Psychoanalytic Psychology, 21*(2), 183–202. https://doi.org/10.1037/0736-9735.21.2.183

Damasio, A. R. (1999). *The feeling of what happens: Body and emotion in the making of consciousness.* Harcourt Brace.

Damasio, A. R. (2000). A second chance for emotion. In R. D. Lane & L. Nadel (Eds.), *Cognitive neuroscience of emotion* (pp. 12–23). Oxford University Press.

Dilthey, W. (1883). *Introduction to the human sciences.* Princeton University Press.

Eagle, M. N. (1973). Sherwood on the logic of explanation in psychoanalysis. In B. B. Rubenstein (Ed.), *Psychoanalysis and contemporary science* (pp. 331–337). MacMillan and Co.

Eagle, M. N. (1984). Psychoanalytic theory and modern psychodynamic theories. In N. S. Endler & J. McV Hunt (Eds.), *Personality and the behavior disorders* (Rev. ed.). Wiley.

Eagle, M. N. (2011). *From classical to contemporary psychoanalysis: A critique and integration.* Routledge.

Eagle, M. N. (2018a). *Core concepts in classical psychoanalysis: Clinical, research evidence and conceptual critiques.* Routledge.

Eagle, M. N. (2018b). *Core concepts in contemporary psychoanalysis: Clinical, research evidence and conceptual critiques.* Routledge.

Eagle, M. N. (2022). *Toward a unified psychoanalytic theory: Foundation in a revised and expanded ego psychology.* Routledge.

Engels, F. (1949). Letter to F. Mehring. In K. Marx & F. Engels (Eds.), *Selected works in two volumes* (Vol. II). Foreign Languages Publishing House.

Fairbairn, W. R. (1952). *Psychoanalytic studies of the personality.* Tavistock, Routledge & Kegan Paul.

Felski, R. (2011). Suspicious minds. *Poetics Today, 32*(2), 215–234.

Fenichel, O. (1941). *Problems of psychoanalytic technique.* Psychoanalytic Quarterly.

Fenichel, O. (1998). *119 Rundbriefe (1934-1945), Bd. I, Bd. II. [Otto Fenichel: 119 circular letters (1934-1945), Vols 1 and 2]* (J. Reichmayr & E. Mühlleitner, Eds.). Stroemfeld Publications.

Ferenczi, S., & Rank, O. (1924). *The development of psychoanalysis* (C. Newton, Trans.). Nervous and Mental Disease Publishing Company.

Firestein, S. K. (1978). *Termination in psychoanalysis.* International Universities Press.

Frank, J. D. (1974). *Persuasion and healing: A comparative study of psychotherapy.* Schocken Books.

Frankl, V. E. (1967). *Psychotherapy and existentialism.* Simon and Schuster.

Freud, A. (1966). *The ego and the mechanisms of defense*. International Universities Press. https://doi.org/10.1017/S1092852915000012. (Original work published 1936).

Freud, S. (1894). The neuro-psychoses of defense. In *Standard edition* (Vol. 3, pp. 45–61). Hogarth Press.

Freud, S. (1900). The interpretation of dreams. Part I. In *Standard edition* (Vol. 4, pp. 1–338). Hogarth Press.

Freud, S. (1912a). Recommendations to physicians practicing psycho-analysis. In *Standard edition* (Vol. 12, pp. 111–120). Hogarth Press.

Freud, S. (1912b). The dynamics of transference. In *Standard edition* (Vol. 12, pp. 97–108). Hogarth Press.

Freud, S. (1914). Remembering, repeating and working-through (further recommendations on the technique of psycho-analysis II). In *Standard edition* (Vol. 12, pp. 145–156). Hogarth Press.

Freud, S. (1915a). Repression. In *Standard edition* (Vol. 14, pp. 141–158). Hogarth Press.

Freud, S. (1915b). The unconscious. In *Standard edition* (Vol. 14, pp.166–204). Hogarth Press.

Freud, S. (1916–1917). Introductory lectures on psycho-analysis. In *Standard edition* (Vol. 15–16, pp. 1–482). Hogarth Press.

Freud, S. (1919). Lines of advance in psycho-analytic therapy. In *Standard edition* (Vol. 17, pp. 159–168). Hogarth Press.

Freud, S. (1921). Group psychology and the analysis of the ego. In *Standard edition* (Vol. 18, pp. 69–143). Hogarth Press.

Freud, S. (1923). The ego and the id. In *Standard edition* (Vol. 19, pp. 12–66). Hogarth Press.

Freud, S. (1925). The occult significance of dreams. In *Standard edition* (Vol. 19, pp. 125–138). Hogarth Press.

Freud, S. (1926). Inhibitions, symptoms, and anxiety. In *Standard edition* (Vol. 20, pp. 77–174). Hogarth Press.

Freud, S. (1927). The future of an illusion. In *Standard edition* (Vol. 21, pp. 5–56). Hogarth Press.

Freud, S. (1929). Civilization and its discontents. In *Standard edition* (Vol. 21, pp. 64–145). Hogarth Press.

Freud, S. (1933). New introductory lectures on psycho-analysis. In *Standard edition* (Vol. 22, pp. 5–182). Hogarth Press.

Freud, S. (1936). *Inhibitions, symptoms and anxiety* (Standard Edition, Vol. 20, pp. 77–174). Hogarth Press.

Freud, S. (1937). Constructions in analysis. In *Standard edition* (Vol. 23, pp. 257–269). Hogarth Press.

Freud, S. (1950 [1895]). *Project for a scientific psychology* (Standard Edition, Vol. 1, pp. 283–397). Hogartth Press.

Gedo, J. E. (1980). Reflections on some current controversies in psychoanalysis. *Journal of the American Psychoanalytic Association, 28*(2), 363–383. https://doi.org/10.1177/000306518002800205

Geha, R. E. (1984). On psychoanalytic history and the "real" story of fictitious lives. *International Forum for Psychoanalysis, 1*(3/4), 221–291.

Giampieri-Deutsch, P. (2012). Perception, conscious and unconscious processes. In F. G. Barth, P. Giampieri-Deutsch, & H.-D. Klein (Eds.), *Sensory perception: Mind and matter* (pp. 245–264). Springer Science + Business Media/SpringerWien.

Gray, P. (1994). *The ego and the analysis of defense*. Jason Aronson.

Gray, R. E. (1998). Four perspectives on unconventional therapies. *Health, 2*(1), 55–74. https://doi.org/10.1177/136345939800200104

Greenberg, L. (2014). The therapeutic relationship in emotion-focused therapy. *Psychotherapy, 51*(3), 350–357. https://doi.org/10.1037/a0037336

Groddeck, G. (2015). *The book of the it*. Martino Fine Books. (Original work published 1923).

Guntrip, H. (1968). *Schizoid phenomena, object relations and the self*. International Universities Press.

Harris, H. (1987). Subjectivity and symbolization. *Psychoanalytic Review, 74*(1), 1–17.

Heaton, J. M. (1972). *The eye: Phenomenology and psychology of function and disorder*. Tavistock Publications.

Hirsch, I., & Roth, J. (1995). Changing conceptions of unconscious. *Contemporary Psychoanalysis, 31*(2), 263–276. https://doi.org/10.1080/00107530.1995.10746910

Jacoby, R. (1971). Towards a critique of automatic Marxism: The politics of philosophy from Lukács to the Frankfurt School. *Telos: Critical Theory of the Contemporary, 10*, 119.

Jay, M. (1998, November 14). *The crisis of experience in a post-subjective age* [Public lecture]. University of California Press.

Jay, M. (2005). *Songs of experience: Modern American and European variations on a universal theme*. University of California Press.

Kohut, H. (1984). *How does analysis cure?* University of Chicago Press. http://doi.org/10.7208/chicago/9780226006147.001.0001

Kriegel, U. (2006). The concept of consciousness in the cognitive sciences: Phenomenal consciousness, access consciousness, and scientific practice. In P. Thagard (Ed.), *Handbook of the philosophy of psychology and cognitive science*. North-Holland.

Laplanche, J., & Pontalis, J.-B. (1973). *The language of psycho-analysis*. Hogarth Press.

Layton, L. (2008). What divides the subject? Psychoanalytic reflections on subjectivity, subjection and resistance. *Subjectivity, 22*(1), 60–72. https://doi.org/10.1057/sub.2008.3

Lear, J. (1990). *Love and its place in nature: A philosophical interpretation of Freudian psychoanalysis*. Yale University Press.

Lear, J. (1995). The shrink is in. *The New Republic, 213*(26).

Lear, J. (1998). *Open minded: Working out the logic of the soul*. Harvard University Press.

Loewald, H. W. (1952). The problem of defense and the neurotic interpretation of reality. *International Journal of Psychoanalysis, 33*(4), 444–449.

Lyons-Ruth, K. (1999). The two-person unconscious: Intersubjective dialogue, enactive relational representation, and the emergence of new forms of relational organization. *Psychoanalytic Inquiry, 19*(4), 576–617. https://doi.org/10.1080/07351699909534267

Makari, G. (2008). *Revolution in mind: The creation of psychoanalysis*. HarperCollins Publishers.

Marcuse, H. (1955). *Eros and civilization: A philosophical inquiry into Freud*. Beacon Press.

Meehl, P. (1994). Subjectivity in psychoanalytic inference: The nagging persistence of Wilhelm Fliess's Achensee question. *Psychoanalysis and Contemporary Thought, 17*(1), 3–82.

Meissner, W. W. (1999). The dynamic principle in psychoanalysis: I. The classic theory reconsidered. *Psychoanalysis & Contemporary Thought, 22*(1), 3–40.

Mills, J. (1999). Unconscious subjectivity. *Contemporary Psychoanalysis*, *35*(2), 342–347. https://doi.org/10.1080/00107530.1999.10747040

Mischel, T. (1963). Psychology and explanations of human behavior. *Philosophy and Phenomenological Research*, *23*(4), 578–594.

Mitchell, M. (2005). Self-awareness and control in decentralized systems. Working Papers of the AAAI 2005 Spring Symposium on Metacognitionin Computation.

Mitchell, S. A. (1998). The analyst's knowledge authority. *Psychoanalytic Quarterly*, *67*(1), 1–31.

Mitchell, S. A. (2000). *Relationality: From attachment to intersubjectivity.* Analytic Press.

Moran, R. A. (2001). *Authority and estrangement: An essay on self-knowledge.* Princeton University Press.

Nagel, T. (1974). What is it like to be a bat? *The Philosophical Review*, *83*(4), 435–450.

Nagel, T. (1995). *Other minds: Critical essays, 1969–1994.* Oxford University Press.

Neisser, J. U. (2006). Unconscious subjectivity. *Psyche: An Interdisciplinary Journal of Research on Consciousness*, *12*.

Neisser, J. U. (2015). *The Science of subjectivity.* Palgrave Macmillan.

Ogden, T. H. (2019). Ontological psychoanalysis or "what do you want to be when you grow up?" *The Psychoanalytic Quarterly*, *88*(4), 661–684. https://doi.org/10.1080/00332828.2019.1656928

O'Neill, E. (1946). *The iceman cometh.* Random House.

Orwell, G. (1949). *1984.* Harcourt Brace.

Piaget, J. (1954). *The construction of reality in the child* (M. Cook, Trans.). Basic Books. https://doi.org/10.1037/11168-000

Pine, F. (1985). *Developmental theory and clinical process.* Yale University Press.

Poland, W. S. (1988). Insight and the analytic dyad. *The Psychoanalytic Quarterly*, *57*(3), 341–369. https://doi.org/10.1080/00332828.1988.12021932

Polanyi, M., & Prosch, H. (1975). Meaning. *Philosophy and Rhetoric*, *10*(2), 123–125.

Polanyi, M., & Prosch, H. (1976). *Meaning.* University of Chicago Press.

Rapaport, D. (1967). The theory of ego autonomy: A generalization. In M. Gill (Ed.), *The collected papers of David Rapaport* (pp. 722–744). Basic Books. (Original work published 1957).

Reich, W. (1953). *People in trouble.* Macmillan.

Renik, O. (1996). The perils of neutrality. *The Psychoanalytic Quarterly*, *65*(3), 495–517.

Renik, O. (1998). The analyst's subjectivity and the analyst's objectivity. *International Journal of Psychoanalysis*, *79*(3), 487–498.

Richfield, J. (1954). An analysis of the concept of insight. *Psychoanalytic Quarterly*, *23*(3), 390–408.

Ricoeur, P. (1970). *Freud and philosophy: An essay on interpretation.* Yale University Press.

Rosenblatt, A. (2004). Insight, working through, and practice: The role of procedural knowledge. *Journal of the American Psychoanalytic Association*, *52*(1), 189–207. https://doi.org/10.1177/00030651040520011901

Rubinstein, B. B. (1997). *Psychoanalysis and the philosophy of science: Collected papers of Benjamin B. Rubinstein* (R. R. Holt, Ed.). International Universities Press.

Russell, B. A. W. (1910). Knowledge by acquaintance and knowledge by description. *Proceedings of the Aristotelian Society*, *11*(1), 108–128.

Sartre, J. (1956 [1943]). *Being and nothingness* (H. Barnes, Trans.). Philosophical Library. (Original work published 1943).

Sass, L. A. (1987). Introspection, schizophrenia, and the fragmentation of self. *Representations, 19*(1), 1–34. https://doi.org/10.2307/2928529.

Schafer, R. (1976). *A new language for psychoanalysis.* Yale University Press.

Schafer, R. (1983). *The analytic attitude.* Basic Books.

Schafer, R. (1992). *Retelling a life: Narration and dialogue in psychoanalysis.* Basic Books.

Schlick, M. (1985). *General theory of knowledge* (A. E. Blumberg, Trans.). Open Court. (Original work published 1925).

Searle, J. R. (1990). Consciousness, explanatory inversion and cognitive science. *Behavioral and Brain Sciences, 13*(1), 585–642.

Searle, J. R. (1992). *The rediscovery of the mind.* MIT Press.

Sherwood, M. (1969). *The logic of explanation in psychoanalysis.* Academic Press.

Silberschatz, G. (2005). The control-mastery theory. In G. Silberschatz (Ed.), *Transformative relationships: The control-mastery theory of psychotherapy* (pp. 3–23). Routledge.

Singer, M. G. (1971). The pragmatic use of language and the will to believe. *American Philosophical Quarterly, 8*, 24–34.

Spence, D. P. (1983). Narrative persuasion. *Psychoanalysis and Contemporary Thought, 6*, 457–481.

Sterba, R. (1934). The fate of the ego in analytic therapy. *International Journal of Psychoanalysis, 15*, 117–126.

Stolorow, R. D., & Atwood, G. E. (1984). Psychoanalytic phenomenology: Toward a science of human experience. *Psychoanalytic Inquiry, 4*(1), 87–105. https://doi.org/10.1080/07351698409533532

Strachey, J. (1934). The nature of the therapeutic action of psychoanalysis. *The International Journal of Psychoanalysis, 15*, 127–159.

Strenger, C. (1989). The classic and the romantic vision in psychoanalysis. *The International Journal of Psycho-Analysis, 70*(4), 593–610.

Sullivan, H. S. (1953). *The interpersonal theory of psychiatry.* Routledge. https://doi.org/10.4324/9781315014029

Thompson, M. G. (2000). The crisis of experience in contemporary psychoanalysis. *Contemporary Psychoanalysis, 36*(1), 29–56.

Trotsky, L. (1925). *Literature and revolution.* International Publishers.

Valenstein, A. F. (1983). Working through and resistance to change: Insight and the action system. *Journal of the American Psychoanalytic Association, 31*(1), 353–373.

Viderman, S. (1979). The analytic space: Meaning and problems. *The Psychoanalytic Quarterly, 48*(2), 257–291.

Wachtel, P. L. (2003). The surface and the depths: The metaphor of depth in psychoanalysis and the ways in which it can mislead. *Contemporary Psychoanalysis, 39*(1), 5–26. https://doi.org/10.1080/00107530.2003.10747197

Waelder, R. (1960). *Basic theory of psychoanalysis.* International University Press.

Weinberger, D. A. (1995). The construct validity of the repressive coping style. In J. L. Singer (Ed.), *Repression and dissociation: Implications for personality theory, psychopathology, and health* (pp. 337–386). University of Chicago Press.

Weinberger, D. A., Schwartz, G. E., & Davidson, R. J. (1979). Low-anxious, high-anxious, and repressive coping styles: Psychometric patterns and behavioral and physiological responses to stress. *Journal of Abnormal Psychology, 88*(4), 369–380.

Weiss, J., Sampson, H., Zion, Mt., & Psychotherapy Research Group. (1986). *The psychoanalytic process: Theory, clinical observations, and empirical research.* Guilford Press.

Winnicott, D. W. (1960). Ego distortion in terms of true and false self. In D. W. Winnicott (Ed.), *The maturational processes and the facilitating environment* (pp. 140–152). International Universities Press.

Winnicott, D. W. (1969). The use of an object. *International Journal of Psycho-analyses, 50,* 711–716.

Winnicott, D. W. (1971). *Playing and reality.* Penguin.

Zuroff, D. C., Kelly, A. C., Leybman, M. J., Blatt, S. J., & Wampold, B. E. (2010). Between-therapist and within-therapist differences in the quality of the therapeutic relationship: Effects on maladjustment and self-critical perfectionism. *Journal of Clinical Psychology, 66*(7), 681–697. https://doi.org/10.1002/jclp.20683

Zuroff, D. C., Shahar, G., Blatt, S. J., Kelly, A. C., &Leybman, M. J. (2016). Predictors and moderators of between-therapists and within-therapist differences in depressed outpatients' experiences of the Rogerian conditions. *Journal of Counseling Psychology, 63*(2), 162–172. https://doi.org/10.1037/cou0000139

Chapter 3

Consciousness and subjective experience in philosophy of mind

I will discuss in this chapter a number of different philosophical approaches to consciousness and subjective experience which belong to one of three categories: one, a phenomenological approach, exemplified by the work of Husserl and his followers; two, different forms of reductionism, which, as we will see, include Freud's philosophical writings on the nature of the mind, exemplified by the writings of Crick, Chater, and Dennett[1]; and three, a philosophical perspective, which can be referred to as biological naturalism or some form of realism associated with the writings of Searle and others at the center of which is the assumption that consciousness and subjective experience are natural phenomena in the world on a par with neural processes.

Consciousness and subjective experience in philosophical phenomenology

Phenomenology has been defined as 'the study of structures of consciousness from the first-person point of view' (Smith, 2018). It has also been described as the direct investigation of phenomena as consciously experienced and free of suppositions. At the core of the philosophical phenomenology project is the assumption that 'what I experience and how my experiences are structured are prior to what can infer about the external world, including scientific laws' In that sense, 'consciousness is prior to physics' (Koch, 2019, p. 2). The Romanized Greek root of the term 'phenomenology' is *phainomenon*, which is translated as 'that which appears' or 'thing appearing to view'. In other words, phenomenology is concerned, not with what is, but what is experienced. According to Husserl, the founder of phenomenology as a philosophical discipline, phenomenology is foundational in the sense that scientific knowledge can be understood only if we first understand the *Lebenswelt*, our lived world. One implication of this claim is that the primary task of phenomenology is *description*, which needs to precede any attempt at explanation. (See discussion in Chapter 1 of Titchener's descriptive approach to the study of consciousness).

DOI: 10.4324/9781032686967-4

Husserl's presumed concern with the *Lebenswelt* notwithstanding, his approach to the investigation of the structure of consciousness does not, in fact, focus on spontaneous lived experience. Rather, in the effort to reach the presumed essence of experience, Husserl's approach employs methods such as 'bracketing' reality, and the suspension of the natural attitude. According to Husserl, we can describe objects as phenomena only after we have 'bracketed existence' or 'suspended our belief in the existence of objects'. Husserl calls this the 'phenomenological epoche' or the 'phenomenological reduction' (Schmitt, 1967, p. 140). As Husserl (1913/1983, p. XIX) writes, '*a new style of attitude* is needed which is entirely altered in contrast to the natural attitude in experiencing and the natural attitude in thinking'.[2]

Back to the things themselves[3]

A central aim of Husserl's phenomenological methodology (i.e., bracketing, epoche, reduction and suspension of the natural attitude) is to direct experience 'back to the things themselves' (*zuruck du den sachenselbst*), rather than, based on socialization and commonsense assumptions, to how we assume they must be (Husserl, 2001, p. 168). That is, the aim of back to the things themselves is to capture the structure of experience 'in as raw and unelaborated a way as possible' (Willis, 2001, p. 1), before it is shaped by language and thus relatively free of descriptions of the physical object out there. Thus, Willis (2001) writes that '… the act of naming stands between the knower and the "things themselves"' (p. 4). As Husserl (1973, p. 5) puts it,

> The universal *epoche* of the world as it becomes conscious (putting it in brackets) has the effect of shutting out from the phenomenological field the world as it simply exists; its place however, is taken by the world as it is given in consciousness (perceived, remembered, judged, thought, valued, etc.).

An implicit assumption underlying the Husserlian phenomenological project, including its call to 'back to the things themselves', is that prior to and underlying our linguistic, cognitive, and socially saturated perceptual experience of objects in the world is a primordial 'pure' level of experience that can be revealed through phenomenological methodology. It is this presumably fundamental level of experience that the Husserlian project attempts to reach and describe. (As we have seen, it is also this level of experience that Titchener tried to reach in the search for the presumed elements of consciousness). Ironically, however, although the central aim of Husserlian phenomenology is to describe the structure of experience, its methodology of suspension of the natural attitude, reduction, and bracketing, that is, suspension of belief in the existence of objects, artificializes spontaneous lived experience, a consideration, as we will see, that distinguishes it from the phenomenological approach of Gestalt psychology.

Phenomenology and the sensation–perception distinction

A long-held assumption of philosophers and psychologists is that 'perceiving consists in the synthesis and interpretation of sensations' (Hirst, 1967, p. 407). An example of that position is Blanshard's (1939) formulation that 'perceptual consciousness consists in sensing a datum and judging and inferring that it belongs to a material object' (as cited in Hirst, 1967, p. 410). In this view, sensations or sense-data are the primary units of experience that are synthesized, interpreted, and subjected to language and social convention in the process of yielding ordinary perception. This view seems evident in Titchener's search for the elements of consciousness and avoidance of the stimulus error. It also represents a way of understanding the Husserlian phenomenological project is in terms of a search to capture the presumed sensations or sensa underlying ordinary perception. The distinction between a primordial 'pure' level of experience entailing bracketing and suspension of the natural attitude and ordinary experience bears a strong family resemblance to the distinction between sensation and perception that has a long history in the psychological and philosophical literature.

Although Ben-Zeev (1984) argues that 'the sensation-perception distinction did not appear before the seventeenth century' (p. 327), some version of this distinction is already seen in the writings of the pre-Socratic Protagoras, who proposed that whereas perception entails interpretation, sensation does not; it is immediately given (Alexander, 1967). A similar formulation is also found in Aquinas' distinction between, on the one hand, passively received sensory input and, on the other hand, judgment, a necessary ingredient of perception. The distinction between sensation and perception is most fully articulated by the British empiricists' conception of perception as the product of *associations of sensations*, or in James Mills' words, as 'clusters of sensations' (as cited in Alexander, 1967, p. 417). The distinction between sensation and perception continues into the modern era.[4]

A claim one finds in the sensation–perception literature is that error is possible only with regard to perception (Alexander, 1967). That is, sense-data themselves are not subject to error, only the judgments, inferences, and interpretations made about them that result in perception. The reasoning is that in contrast to perception, sensation is immunized against 'cognitive, emotional and evaluative contributions of the agent' (Ben-Zeev, 1984, p. 327). That is, in a version of Descartes' thinking, the argument is that although one can be mistaken regarding objects in the world, one cannot be mistaken in relation to one's own inner experiences. Another way to put it is to note that whereas one's experiences may represent only appearances that can be mistaken in regard to external reality, one cannot be mistaken regarding the experience of these appearances. In short, in contrast to perception, sensations or sense-data, represent a pure, primordial level of experience 'unspoiled' by the influences of socialization and convention regarding the nature of the world. Thus, not only does the concept of sensation or sense-data entail a form of bracketing, but as such, also does not adequately represent the nature of lived experience.

In a rejection of the claim of a family resemblance between the sensation–perception distinction and the Husserlian phenomenological project, Schmitt (1967) writes that by 'immediate experience', phenomenological philosophers

> do not mean sensory observation which are not interpreted or classified under general concepts ('raw sense-data') ... the phenomenologists are not at all sure that there are for us any sensory observations which are not interpreted or classified under general concepts. The appeal to phenomena or to immediate experience is therefore not an appeal to simple, uninterpreted data of sensory experience ... The phenomenologists do not claim to have discovered that besides all kinds of entities found in this world (physical objects, thoughts, numbers, feelings, poems, etc.), there is another class, phenomena. Any object is a phenomenon if looked at or considered in a particular way.
>
> (p. 137)

Schmitt (1967) also notes that the slogan *Zu den Sachen* admonishes one "to get down to the proper business of the philosopher by examining and describing all kinds of objects in the particular way that reveals them as phenomena' (p. 137).

As we can see, the gist of Schmitt's (1967) comments regarding the phenomenological perspective is that it asks us to approach "'objects of all kinds', not as things that exist in the world, but to take a stance – suspension of the natural attitude, bracketing or suspension of belief in the existence of objects in the external world, which allows one to experience stimuli in the particular way that reveals them as phenomena". However, if one suspends belief in the existence of the object through attending to and reporting, not the object as it exists in the world, but rather the subjective experiences that occupy one's consciousness, what will be left to experience and report? Presumably, it will be something like, say, 'red patch' or 'roundness' rather than the object 'apple'. However, 'red patch' and 'roundness' turn out to be, in the context of the sensation–perception distinction, precisely the sense-data units that, when synthesized, generate the perception 'apple'. Further, in the contexts of both phenomenological methodology and the sensation–perception distinction, contents such as 'red patch' and 'roundness' are seen as somehow fundamental in the sense of being prior to and constitutive of experience of the object ('apple') as it exists in the external world. In short, when one brackets belief in the existence of objects and suspends one's natural attitude, what emerges in experience are precisely the phenomena that, in the context of the sensation–perception distinction, are seen as sensation units that are synthesized to yield perceptions. Although the assumption that a particular stance will reveal the sense-data units of perceptual experience is relatively explicit in Titchener's reference to *elements* of consciousness, it is implicit in Husserl's discussion of the phenomena revealed by bracketing and suspension of the natural attitude.

Common to the various versions of the sensation–perception distinction area number of implicit and explicit assumptions. One such assumption is that there are two sets and stages of experience, one the passive experience of sensations or sense-data, and the other, ordinary perceptual experience, the product of active interpretive, inferential, and binding processes in relation to the sense-data. Another assumption made is that under the proper conditions and with the appropriate methodology, one can experience (as well as report) the sense-data prior to their subjection to the interpretive, inferential, and binding processes that generate ordinary perception.

I think there is a fundamental confusion of levels of discourse in the various expressions of the sensation–perception distinction. There is little doubt that our perceptual experience of objects in the world is the product of complex processes that encode stimulus inputs (in terms of specific features such as color, shape, contour, etc.) and also synthesize these specific features into unified percepts, with the result that we perceive unified objects rather than a disconnected array of separate features. (As we have seen, this has been referred to as the *binding problem*.) However, – and this is the critical point – these synthesizing processes take place at the neural level and are neither represented in nor accessible to subjective experience.[5] That is, as Lashley (1958) writes, we experience the *products* of these processes, not the processes themselves. Miller (1962, p. 72) makes the same point when he writes that we have no awareness of the processes leading to perception.

Equally important, when, say, in Titchener's experimental or Husserl's phenomenological laboratory, we are instructed to avoid the 'stimulus error' or to suspend one's natural attitude and report our experience from that stance, *what we experience are nevertheless perceptions*, not sensations that constitute the raw data that are organized to yield the perceptions. For example, experiencing a patch of red rather than an apple is nevertheless a perceptual experience, namely, of a patch of red, which is generated by a particular stance toward the stimulus with which one is presented. The experience of a red patch or roundness does not exist at a different ontological or epistemological level than the experience of apple – they are both perceptual experiences under different conditions. Or to put it another way, the experience of a particular feature of an apple – its redness, for example – is the result of a particular deployment of attention (brought about through compliance with instructions), is no less a perceptual experience than the experience of the unified object 'apple'.

The search for the primordial level or sensory elements of experience is essentially chimerical mainly because there are no such 'raw' or primordial elements in ordinary perceptual experience. The perceptual experiences that emerge in the application of phenomenological methodology (whether generated by Titchenerian introspection or Husserlian suspension of the natural attitude) are no more primordial or fundamental than any other experience. Rather, they are simply perceptual experiences under certain conditions. When one investigates ordinary experience, one does not find 'two states of mind', a sensing state and a perceiving state (Hirst, 1967, p. 410). As Hirst (1967) puts it, 'sensing is seeing under another name or a myth' (p. 412). One does not find any evidence of an *experiential* process of interpretation or inference from sense-data to percepts of objects. Rather, one observes an individual's immediate perception of an object. Whatever interpretive-like, inferential-like, or binding processes are involved in perception of an object *take place at the level of neural activity*. As noted, we experience the *products* of such processes, not the processes themselves. Confusion of the level of discourse is facilitated by the conflation of an abstract and logical level of task analysis with the nature of lived experience. Thus, whereas constructing, say, a robot, may require the inclusion of a component that is something like sense-data, it does not follow that in human beings such a component is expressed or realized in any experiential form.

Although not formulated in those terms, a version of the sensation-perception issue was debated with regard to Helmholtz's (1867) concept of 'unconscious inference' in accounting for such experiential phenomena as size and color constancy. Despite explanatory appeal to the mentalistic concept of 'unconscious inference', there is no evidence of inferential processes potentially accessible to consciousness. Rather, an accurate and useful explanatory account took the following form: cues from the retinal image of the object (e.g., a square) plus cues regarding the distance of the object from oneself would constitute the sensations or sense-data; unconscious computational inferences based on the cues from these sources would then result in the perceptual experience of size constancy, that is, perceiving the square at different distances as the same size despite differences in retinal images. The debate regarding unconscious inference was essentially resolved through the recognition that whatever inferential or computational processes were involved in producing size constancy were taking place at a *neural level*. Further, only the product of these computational processes – perception of size – are represented in experience, not the neural processes that underlie the experience. There is no evidence of any experience corresponding to either retinal image sense-data or of experiences corresponding to computational or inferential processes that synthesize information from retinal images and distance cues and produce the perceptual experience of a square of a certain size.

What made the concept of 'unconscious inference' seem so plausible is the fact that the perceptual product of experience of the constant size of objects despite different distances is just what one would experience if one consciously engaged in certain inferences and computations. This allowed one to say that the brain processes that underlie size and color constancy function *as if* one were engaged in inference and calculation (see Rock, 1983, for a similar account of other perceptual phenomena, such as induced movement). However, the *as if*, metaphoric meaning of unconscious inference got lost, with the result that it came to be understood as a person making inferences, albeit at an unconscious level. This completed the conceptual confusion of levels of discourse.

The problems inherent in the sensation–perception distinction are especially apparent in the context of the perception of intentional action. Unlike the perception of inanimate objects, where different features of the object such as color, shape, etc., are neurally encoded and bound to generate the perception of a unified object, there is little evidence that separate movements are encoded and bound together to generate the experience of intentional actions. As Gallese and his colleagues (Gallese, 2001; Rizzolatti et al., 2006) have reported, mirror neurons respond to different motor acts so long as they serve the same goal or intention. Sheer movements without intention or goal do not trigger mirror neurons; it is only when they are part of intentional action that motor behaviors trigger mirror neurons. Thus, even at the neural level, encoding of motor acts appears to take into account intentions and goals.

Let me sum up by returning to the context of the phenomenological project of reaching the fundamental structure of experience. The assumption of Husserlian phenomenology is that the application of phenomenological methods – bracketing, reduction, *epoche*, and suspension of the natural attitude – will make possible the emergence of a primordial form of experience freed from language and social convention. However, as I have tried to show, I think this is a myth. What emerges in consciousness in the phenomenological laboratory, just as what emerged in consciousness in Titchener's experimental laboratory, are not sense-data or fundamental units of experience or experience freed from language and social convention, but rather simply experience in particular circumstances.[6] Ironically, although a motive for phenomenology is to rescue lived subjective experience from its denial and objectification in the sciences, its treatment of subjective experience results in a version of subjective experience that bears little ecological resemblance to everyday experience. That is so because instead of capturing lived experience, the phenomenological methodology produces an artificial product.

Phenomenology, sensation–perception, and Gestalt psychology

Nowhere is the chimerical nature of the search for sensations as units of experience made clearer than in the research and theoretical writings of Gestalt psychologists. Because of their common emphasis on subjective experience, some phenomenological theorists (e.g., Spiegelberg, 1972) have linked Gestalt psychology and Husserl's phenomenology. Given the sharp differences in their perspectives on the nature of subjective experience, this is unwarranted and unconvincing. As Kohler (1938) writes, 'There seems to be a single starting point for psychology as for all other sciences: the world as we find it naively and uncritically' (p. 3).

Making clear his differences with Husserl's phenomenological approach, Kohler (1944) also writes:

> I do not believe that we are justified in putting certain phases of experience in brackets. A first account of experience ought to be given and carefully studied without selections of any kind. It is otherwise to be expected that even if

the brackets are introduced as mere methodological tools, they will sooner or later turn out to be weapons of anontological prejudice.

(Kohler, 1944, p. 203, fn. 2)

Further, as Henle (1979) observes, 'Kohler regards Husserl's phenomenology as a retreat before the advance of science ...' (p. 5). It is also inaccurate to characterize Gestalt psychology, as Gurwitsch (1964) does, as limited to a descriptive orientation. Although they insisted on accurate description, Gestalt theorists were equally concerned with scientific explanation of the phenomena being described. As Kohler (1938) writes with regard to the purpose of explanation, 'it may be necessary to devise concepts which seem to have little contact with direct primary experience' (p. 3). For example, as reflected in the concept of isomorphism, Gestalt psychologists were very much concerned with explanatory accounts in the form of formulating hypotheses regarding the relationship between phenomenal experience and brain states.

Merleau-Ponty and the sensation–perception distinction

In contrast to Husserl, whose concept of *hyle* seems to represent his version of sensation, Merleau-Ponty rejects the concept of sensation as constituting the units or building blocks of perception. Indeed, his *Phenomenology of Perception* opens with a critique of the philosophical notion of sensation, which he views as confused. Reflecting the influence of Gestalt psychology, Merleau-Ponty rejects any atomistic or associationist account of perception as the product of association among sensations. Relatedly, he also rejects an intellectualist conception of perception as entailing the 'addition' of cognitive processes such as judgment to the 'raw feels' of sensation. For Merleau-Ponty, as for the Gestalt psychologists, perceptual experiences always entail spontaneous organization (e.g., figure-ground). Also reflecting the influence of Gestalt psychology, Merleau-Ponty's criticisms of the concept of sensation are also based on findings that in both human and sub-human animals, perception is a response to *relations*, not the absolute value of stimulus inputs. In other words, perceptual experience is contextual. As Tae-Chang (2009) writes in summing up Merleau-Ponty's position, sensation 'has no place in the analysis of perception' (p. 50). There is much more that can be said regarding Merleau-Ponty's complex and rich writings. Before moving on, I want to note that whether or not acknowledged, Merleau-Ponty's emphasis on the role of the body in perceptual experience has had much influence on current work on embodied cognition.

Sensation and perception in post-Freudian psychoanalytic theory

The attempt to reach the pre-socialized 'raw' elements of experience brings to mind Bion's (1962a, 1962b) concepts of beta- and alpha-elements, which can be understood as the sensation-perception distinction applied to thought and thinking.[7] That is, paralleling the formulation that sense-data are synthesized to generate perception, Bion's (1962a, 1962b) proposed that through a process he refers to as alpha functioning, fragmentary beta-elements, which can be understood as fragmentary and 'unmentalized' elements of experience, are 'digested' to generate alpha elements available for thoughts and thinking. This is all murky and vague. However the distinction between beta and alpha elements parallels the sensation–perception distinction in the context of stimulus input, not from objects in the external world, but from stimulus input from one's inner world of inchoate feelings and fragmented elements of thought. Continuing the parallel, just as sensations from external stimuli are synthesized to generate perceptions, so similarly inchoate and fragmentary feelings and thought elements are structured to generate emotions and thoughts.

Neurophenomenology: naturalizing phenomenology

Whether or not explicitly acknowledged, the problems and limitations of a Husserlian phenomenological approach to experience have been recognized within the phenomenological literature. In a 1996 paper entitled 'Neurophenomenology', Varela called for an integration between Husserlian phenomenology and cognitive science, including cognitive neuroscience. In effect, Varela proposes that phenomenology turns to the program outlined by Ladd in 1887 and Titchener in 1910: to the effect explanation, which follows description, takes the form of appeal to physiological processes. The term 'neurophenomenology' suggests a systematic investigation of the relationship between first-person phenomenological data and underlying cognitive and neural processes. Understood this way, neurophenomenology does not seem essentially different from the 'standard' approach in many psychological studies of the neural correlates of reports of experience. Whatever differences there are between the two would seem to consist mainly of a greater emphasis on first-person experience than is currently the case in some cognitive science studies. As Roy et al. (1999) write, current cognitive science is 'a theory of mind without being a theory of consciousness' (p. 7).

Lutz (2004) refers to the need to 'obtain richer first-person data through disciplined phenomenological exploration of experience' (p. 328), which suggests the use of trained subjects. The problem with this requirement is that it runs the risk of repeating the problems encountered by structuralism, that is, the compromised ecological validity of the data obtained. As Zahavi (2004) recognizes, the practice of using trained subjects in phenomenological investigations would need to be relinquished in the project of neurophenomenology. The goal of psychological investigations, after all, is to shed light on ordinary experience, not the experience of those trained to report on experience in a particular way. If one drops the requirement of trained subjects, one is left with an approach to psychological studies that is not very different from ongoing current research on the neural processes underlying subjective experience. As noted, the only difference is greater emphasis on the importance of 'obtain[ing] richer first-person data'.

In short, the presumed new project of 'neurophenomenology' is hardly anything new. Rather, it seems to reflect the recognition that, for the most part, phenomenological research has not been especially productive as well as an attempt of phenomenology to 'catch up' with the findings of cognitive science, while at the same time, pressing for the importance of obtaining richer first-person data in cognitive science and neuroscience.

One of the issues raised by the 'neurophenomenology' project is the recognition that it would require *Naturalizing Phenomenology*, the title of a 1999 book edited by Petitot, Varela, Pachoud, and Roy. What is essentially meant by naturalizing phenomenology is that a phenomenological perspective will need to be integrated into a scientific explanatory framework. This presents a challenge to Husserlian phenomenology insofar as Husserl viewed the phenomenological perspective as prior to a scientific view of consciousness. As Zahavi (2004) notes, the more fundamentally philosophical challenge to the naturalizing project is the threat it represents to the very philosophical core of Husserlian phenomenology. From a Husserlian perspective, phenomenology is not simply another way of acquiring scientific facts about the nature of consciousness and experience; rather, it questions and investigates the very foundation of experience and the presuppositions that make scientific thought possible. It is this philosophical ambition that must be relinquished in the project of naturalizing phenomenology (Zahavi, 2004). Whether or not explicitly acknowledged, it would seem that the 'neurophenomenology' project reflects the inadequacies of Husserlian phenomenology, at least as far as providing insights into the nature of subjective experience.

The fate of consciousness and subjective experience in a scientific world view

There are various philosophical positions on the place of consciousness and subjective experience in the context of a scientific world view. These positions range from hopelessness and skepticism as to whether it is possible for science to accommodate consciousness and subjective experience to forms of reductionism to eliminative materialism to the position that as natural phenomena in the world, science must make room for consciousness and subjective experience.

As an expression of hopelessness and skepticism, Fodor (1990) writes that '... that the problem of consciousness is *probably* hopeless' (p. 128), and that 'the problem of consciousness ... does not look to be tractable' (Fodor, 1994, p. 82). Similarly, Milliken (1984) writes:

> Of course, human purposes are in large part conscious purposes, and this is fundamental to their nature. What consciousness consists in from a naturalist's point of view, if it consists in *anything* [emphasis in original] from a naturalist's point of view, I have nothing to say about.

(p. 48)[8]

It should be clear that Fodor's judgment of intractability and Milliken's silence regarding consciousness have to do with the question of whether consciousness and subjective experience can be accounted for in a physicalist scientific context.

A not uncommon philosophical position is that although consciousness and subjective experience are aspects of the natural world, because science deals only with observable physical phenomena and processes, any scientific theory of the mind cannot take consciousness and subjective experience as its primary subject matter. The proscription against consciousness and subjective experience as subject matter for science was central to methodological behaviorism, and, as we will see, is also central to the Freudian theory of the mind. Another perspective, which can be referred to as 'nothing but' reductionism, fueled by the fear of dualism, makes the *ontological* claim that consciousness and subjective experience are nothing but physical (i.e., behavioral and neural) phenomena.[9] This position is essentially the same as what has been referred to as 'eliminative materialism' in so far as it essentially denies the reality of consciousness and subjective experience (Moore, 2020).

Nothing but reductionism

As Searle (1990) writes, 'since Descartes, we have, for the most part, thought that consciousness was not an appropriate subject for a serious science or a scientific philosophy of mind' (p. 585). And as Baars (2003) similarly writes, an important reason for the rejection of personal experience as a worthy topic among philosophers and psychologists in the English-speaking world is the need to justify their claim to 'standing among the physical sciences' (p. 1). As Searle (1997) observes, the difficulty the natural sciences have had in granting full existential status to consciousness and subjective experience on a par with other natural phenomena in the universe may be largely motivated by the fear that such status to consciousness would constitute acceptance of two kinds of phenomena in the world and would thus entail acceptance of Cartesian dualism between *res extensa* and *res inextensa*.

In order to avoid this danger, mental states need to be 'naturalized' in order to be assimilated into a scientific physicalist world view. An appealing 'solution' to the seemingly intractable difficulty of finding a place for consciousness and subjective experience in a scientific world view is to reduce them to neural processes. Thus, Crick's (1994) 'astonishing hypothesis' that

> You, your joys and sorrows, your memories and ambitions, your sense of personal identity and free will are, in fact, no more than the behavior of a vast assembly of nerve cells and their molecules. As Lewis Carrol's Alice might have phrased it: 'You are nothing but a pack of neurons'.
>
> (p. 3)

However, unlike the fruitful reductionism of the sciences, for example, the reduction of heat to molecular movements, consciousness and conscious experience are not reducible to neural firing without eliminating the very phenomena one is attempting to investigate and understand.

That the 'astonishing hypothesis', however, is largely eye-catching hyperbole is evident throughout the book. For example, in the very first paragraph of the Preface, Crick (1994) writes: 'What I want to know is exactly going on in my brain when I see something' (p. xii) There is no 'nothing but' talk here. Rather, Crick makes a clear distinction between the subjective experience of seeing something and what is going on in the brain. This is also the case with regard to Crick's (1994) comment that the book deals with 'various possible experimental approaches to the problem of visual awareness' (p. xiii), and to his reference to 'the visual correlate of seeing red' (p. 9). In short, what Crick wants to know is what every neuropsychologist and neuroscientist wants to know in carrying out their ordinary scientific studies. There is nothing astonishing about the fact that all our experiences, including our joys and sorrows, are underlain by neural processes. If our joys and sorrows 'are, in fact, *no more than* the behavior of a vast assembly of nerve cells', that would indeed be astonishing. However, in that case, it would make no sense to refer to neural correlates. Neural correlates of what?

As Crick's comments regarding neural correlates indicate, he is clearly aware that the very choice of which assembly of nerve cells to be investigated is not random, but guided by the attempt to identify the neural correlates of subjective experiences, including our joys and sorrows. Thus, the starting point for the investigation is subjective experience of one kind or another, not assemblies of neural cells. In short, the 'astonishing hypothesis' notwithstanding, as Crick's book itself illustrates, the legitimate function of neuroscientific investigations is not to reduce subjective experience to neural activity, but rather to broaden our understanding of the underlying neural foundations of subjective experience.

Taking a more extreme position than Crick, Chater (2018) writes that

> no one, at any point in human history, has ever been guided by inner beliefs or desires, any more than any human being has been possessed by evil spirits or watched over by a guardian angel. Beliefs, motives, and other imagined inhabitants of our 'inner world' are entirely a figment of our imaginations. The stories we tell to justify our own and others' behavior aren't just wrong in detail – they are a thoroughgoing fabrication from start to finish.
>
> (p. 6)

Chater also writes that 'we will explore the psychological evidence that talk of beliefs, desires, hopes and fears is pure fiction' (p. 7). Thus, going much further than Nisbett and Wilson (1977) who try to demonstrate that we do not necessarily have access to our reasons and motives, Chater (2018) informs us that there are no such real things as reasons and motives – they are only fabrications. And as a final example, as a number of critics have noted, despite its title, a more accurate title for Dennett's (1991) *Consciousness Explained* is 'Consciousness Eliminated'.

At the risk of appearing too dismissive, it seems to me that despite the cleverness and perhaps even brilliance of some philosophical arguments in this area, it is downright silly to deny the existence of consciousness and/or reduce it to nothing but neuronal firings. It makes little sense to deny that the many books and papers on the proposition that consciousness, subjective experience, reasons, and motives are nothing but neural processes or are illusory require a conscious subject who spells out his or her evidence and reasoning processes and whose motive is to convince the reader of the soundness of his or her arguments. Thus, the paradox, noted by Baars (2003), of conscious human beings writing articles and books denying the existence of consciousness. Presenting evidence, fashioning arguments, and having motives are not anything neurons do (see Hacker, 2018). They are things that persons do.[10]

There is little doubt that in their ordinary daily lives, like everyone else, Crick, Chater, and other 'nothing but' theorists function and relate to others as intentional beings whose behavior can be understood in terms of motives, desires, aims, etc. Indeed, if one came across someone who experienced and reacted to another person's expressions of his or her joys and sorrows as nothing but assemblies of neural cells; or who experienced oneself and others without motives and reasons in relation to feelings and actions; or who, in relating to others, ceased all talk (and presumably all thought) of mental states, it would be clear that that individual was very likely experiencing a psychotic episode.[11] And yet, this view is presented as a serious philosophical position. One should add that the task of science is to account for phenomena that exist in the world, not to transform or deform them so that they fit a particular philosophical ideology. Surely, Chater had reasons and motives for writing his book as well as expectations that his arguments would convince readers. As for Crick's *Astonishing Hypothesis*, if all our joys and sorrows – and one might add, motives, aims, and goals – are no more than assemblies of neural cells, one would have to wonder how and why the book was written and who wrote the book. Was the Crick book written by assemblies of neural cells or by a person? I am reminded of a recent letter to the *New York Times Book Review*, a reader writes the following: in his review of 'Himalaya', by Ed Douglas (January 10), Jeffrey Gettleman approvingly quotes Douglas' statement: 'It's easy to see why a philosophy stressing the illusory nature of an individual consciousness, as Buddhism does, might prosper here. But it's even easier to see that it takes an individual consciousness to believe that individual consciousness is illusory' (Ackerman, 2021, p. 5).

I used the term 'silly' above to describe the 'nothing but' approach to consciousness and subjective experience. It appears that I am not alone in this view. In a paper entitled 'The Consciousness Deniers', Strawson (2018) refers to the 'nothing but' and eliminative philosophical positions as the 'Great Silliness' (p. 1); and also notes that in 1925, C.D. Broad also employed the term 'silly' to characterize the denial of consciousness by philosophical behaviorism. Strawson also observes that the argument that conscious experience is an illusion is a deficient argument insofar as having an illusion is itself an instance of conscious experience. As Strawson (2018) puts it, 'the trouble with this [argument] is that any such illusion is already and necessarily an actual instance of the thing said to be an illusion' (p. 1).

Some reductionist philosophers who maintain that their form of reductionism is not equivalent to eliminative materialism, argue that they are not eliminating consciousness, but rather reducing it or rendering it equivalent to something else (i.e., something that can be assimilated into a physicalist world view). For example, in response to Strawson, Dennett (2018), whose writings are one of the targets of Strawson's criticisms, writes: 'I don't deny consciousness; *of course*, consciousness exists; it just isn't what most people think it is ...' (p. 1). However, it is not always clear what Dennett thinks consciousness might be. Below are some passages from Dennett's writings on consciousness cited by Strawson:

> A philosopher's zombie [essentially an automaton] is behaviorally indistinguishable from a normal human being, but is not conscious. There is nothing it is like to be a zombie; it just seems that way to observers.
>
> We are all zombies.
>
> In regard to the argument that to *seem* to have 'qualia', such as pain, a visual experience, and so on, is necessarily already to have such qualia, Dennett (2007) writes: 'There are no *real seemings* ... judgments are about the qualia of experiences in the same way novels are about their characters ... If materialism is true, there are no real seemings.
>
> If two organisms are behaviorally exactly alike, they are psychologically exactly alike.
>
> Nature contains 'any number of stupendous organization and sensitivity and discrimination ... The idea that, in addition to all of those, there's this extra special something – subjectivity – what distinguishes us from the zombie – that's an illusion.

Dennett (2013) writes:

> When I squint just right it *does* sort of seem that consciousness must be something in addition to all the things it does for us and to us, some kind of special private glow or *here-I-am-ness* [Dennett is obviously referring here, in a somewhat derisive way, to subjectivity and subjective experience] that would be absent in any robot. But I've learned not to credit the hunch. I think it is a flat-out mistake.

We may be able to build robots that do things that human beings do. But that has little to do with the issue of consciousness and subjective experience. Indeed, as Searle (1997) writes:

To try to create consciousness by creating a machine which behaves as if it were conscious is simply irrelevant. Behavior is important to the study of consciousness only to the extent that we take the behavior as an expression of, as an effect of, the inner conscious processes.

(p. 204)

Behavior that is the effect of inner conscious processes is what we normally think of as action. That is the distinction between sheer movement or behavior and action. The normal structure of action follows the belief-desire practical syllogism. For example, I have a desire to get a particular book, the belief that a particular library has the book, and therefore go to the library. The practical syllogism does not apply to sheer behavior.

The bottom line, as Strawson notes, is that Dennett's claim that he is not denying the existence of consciousness notwithstanding, his writings suggest that his approach to consciousness constitutes a form of 'nothing but' eliminative materialism. Strictly speaking, to say that consciousness is nothing but neural processes or behavior is not to deny consciousness, but to claim that it is something else. However, as Strawson notes, '… to reduce consciousness to behavior and dispositions to behavior is to eliminate it. To say that consciousness is nothing more than (dispositions to) behavior is to say that it doesn't exist'. (See Moore, 2018, for a similar argument that so-called 'nonreductionist physicalism' is essentially equivalent to eliminating consciousness). Strawson (2018) cites Block's remark that the way Dennett attempts to account for consciousness and 'qualia' 'has the relation to qualia that the US Air Force had to so many Vietnamese villages: he destroys qualia in order to save them'.

Nothing but reductionism and related perspectives can be contrasted with what seems to me the far more defensible philosophical position that insofar as consciousness and subjective experience are natural phenomena in the world, they do not need to be reduced to something else in order to be assimilated into a scientific worldview. Rather, science needs to find a way to accommodate these vital phenomena. not for the phenomena to be deformed or reduced to 'nothing but' other phenomena. As Searle (1998) has argued, if phenomena that are so clearly part of the natural world cannot be accommodated by current science, the challenge for science is to find ways to deal with these vital aspects of the world. The challenge is to confront the earlier noted question posed by Penrose (1994): 'How do our feeling of conscious awareness – of happiness, pain, love, aesthetic sensibility, will, understanding, etc. – fit into such a … picture?' (p. 12).

Of course, it may be the case, as Edelman (as cited in Searle, 1997) has argued, that science cannot tell us why warm feels warm and we shouldn't ask it to. In that case, science should go about its task, in which it has been so remarkably successful, of explaining what it can explain rather than deforming phenomena so that they can be accommodated by a particular view regarding what can be and cannot be investigated by science, with the consequence that what is being investigated has little ecological validity. There is much for science to do in such areas as shedding light on the structure of experience and elucidating the relations between the factors that make possible and influence first-person subjective experience.

It should be clear that in emphasizing the centrality of subjective experience, Searle is not suggesting a turn to phenomenology. We have already seen the sterility of approaches that attempt to investigate the decontextualized elements of 'pure' experience, just as we have seen, in the work of the Gestalt psychologists, the fruitfulness of relating spontaneous first-person perceptual experiences to environmental patterns. As Searle (1997) writes: 'There is no reason why an objective science cannot study subjective experiences' (p. 123). As he observes, neurologists do this all the time. For Searle, whatever difficulties the sciences may have in dealing with subjective experience, the solution lies in the further development of the scientific method rather than the denial of first-person experience or its reduction to processes the current sciences can more readily accommodate. Indeed, the development of new technologies has led to an extension of research on experience.

One of the assumptions made by many philosophers, including Freud as philosopher, is that because science has a firm grasp on the nature of the physical and because the 'mystery' of consciousness cannot be accommodated by a physicalist world view, in investigating the nature of the mind, one must focus on the physical even if that means reducing consciousness to 'workable' physical processes such as behavior or neural events. However, conceptions of the nature of the physical have changed over time and, in many respects, is itself the real mystery. Consider quantum phenomena or the strange phenomenon of entanglement. Strawson (2016) cites the remark of the great physicist Richard Feynman that 'I think I can safely say that nobody understands quantum mechanics'. Consider also Russell's (1948) comments that

> the physical world is only known as regards certain abstract features of its space-time structure ... we know nothing about the events that make the world, except their space-time structure. We know nothing about the intrinsic quality of physical events except when these are mental events that we directly experience.
>
> (p. 240)

The basic point here is that consciousness and subjective experience are as much natural categories of the physical (including the biological) as stones and trees. As aspects of the world, they are certainly neither unnatural nor supernatural. This is not a new idea. Darwin (1838) had already raised the question of 'Why is thought [consciousness] being a secretion of the brain more wonderful than gravity, a property of matter?' (as cited in Strawson, 2018). There are also the following remarkable passages from the 1827 Notebooks of Giacomo Leopardi, an Italian poet and philosopher:

... we should have taken it to be indubitable that matter can think; that matter thinks and feels.

I see bodies that think and feel. I mean bodies: that is, men and animals that I do not see, do not feel, do not know, and cannot know, to be other than bodies. Therefore I say: matter can think and feel ... No sir, you should rather say: matter can never think and feel in any way – Why? 'Because we do not understand how it can do it' – Fantastic!

Leopardi goes on to note that although we do not know how many physical phenomena work, we do not deny that they are part of the physical world.

Implicit in the above passage from Leopardi, as well as the views of others, including those of Russell (1948) and Searle (1997), is the position that if the current conception of the physical world cannot find a place for consciousness and subjective experience, it is the conception of the nature of the physical that is wanting and that needs to change. In short, although it may seem jarring, from a scientific perspective, the phenomena we think of as mental, including consciousness and subjective experience, are best understood as particular aspects of the physical world. This, perhaps, should be no more jarring than what we have learned – and likely, will continue to learn about the nature of the physical.

Behaviorists allowed consciousness and subjective experience into behaviorism through the back door of referring to reports of experience as 'verbal behavior'. Some contemporary neuroscientists and philosophers engage in a similar tactic through the odd linguistic usage of statements of brains and brain parts having intentions, beliefs and desires, and doing and experiencing things. Some passages from Dennett (2007) are illustrative:

> We don't attribute *fully fledged* [original emphasis] belief (or decision or desire – or pain, heaven knows) to the brain parts – that *would* [emphasis in original] be a fallacy. No, we attribute an attenuated sort of beliefs and desires to these parts, belief and desire stripped of many of their everyday connotations (about responsibility and comprehension, for instance).
>
> (p. 87)

It is not clear why attribution of *attenuated* [my emphasis] beliefs and desires to brain parts is any more defensible than attribution of fully fledged beliefs and desires – unless attenuated means using language loosely and/or metaphorically. Dennett (2007) also writes that 'The reason for regarding an individual neuron (or a thermostat) as an intentional system are unimpressive, but not zero ...' (p. 88). In what conceivable way would there be any non-zero reason for attributing intentionality to a single neuron or even more so to a thermostat unless one employed an idiosyncratic meaning of 'intentionality'?

Robinson (2007) wittily confronts us with a sentence such as 'Breakfast was a delight to the hypothalamus, for witness how its electrical behavior was sated as the meal progresses' (p. 186). He also reminds us of the silliness of proposing that the Deep Blue computer engages in the activity of actually 'playing' chess as well as of the locution that the microwave 'cooks soup'. As Wittgenstein (1953) remarks 'Only of a human being and what resembles (behaves like) a living human being can one say it has sensations; it sees, is blind; hears, is deaf; is conscious or unconscious' (p. 281). And long before Wittgenstein, the fallacy of attributing the feelings of a human being to body parts was already recognized by Aristotle who wrote that

> to say that the soul [psyche] is angry is as if one were to say that the soul weaves or builds. For it is surely better not to say that the soul pities, learns or thinks, but that a man does these with his soul.
>
> (as cited in Bennett & Hacker, 2007, p. 131)

One must also keep in mind that, as Locke (1689/1894) noted, we view a human as a *person*, with all the forensic implications that bestowing personhood entails. Such a forensic perspective cannot be assigned to brains or brain parts.

To the extent that Dennett allows for an attenuated form of intentionality in single neurons and thermostats, he would perhaps not view the locutions of a hypothalamus having a delightful breakfast, a computer playing chess, and a microwave cooking soup as patent confusions of levels of discourse. That this is likely the case is suggested by Dennett's (1986) calm acceptance of what he sees as the implications of eliminative materialism. He writes:

> the triumph of neuroscience and its 'cerebroscopes' would – and should – lead to the demise of mentalistic language and we would all cease talking *as if* there were minds and mental events, a clear improvement in our conceptual scheme from the perspective of Occam's Razor.
>
> (p. 4)

It is not at all clear in what way the replacement of 'mentalistic language' a language that reflects and captures the richness of lived experience with talk about brain events would be a clear improvement. As for Occam's Razor, it is a relevant consideration in the context of explanation and competing theories; it is not intended to impoverish the phenomena under investigation.

Free will and reductionism

As we have seen in the above discussions, we are informed by psychologists, neuroscientists, and philosophers of mind that our joys and sorrows are nothing but brain processes, that we are inevitably mistaken regarding the reasons we give for our behavior, and more radically, that the belief that reasons and motives underlie behavior is an illusion. We have also been informed by Freudian theory that consciousness is dissimulating, including our conscious sense of the reasons we do and feel things. Thus, skepticism toward the role of consciousness and subjective experience is extended to the belief in one's agency, that is, to the belief that one's conscious intentions and what Moore (2018) calls 'willings', play a causal role in one's decisions and actions. Recall that Crick's 'astonishing hypothesis' also includes the assertion that 'one's sense of free will' is illusory.

This claim, of course, is a hallowed philosophical one, frequently based on the arguments against the dualism it implies as well as the incompatibility between free will and at least, 'hard' determinism and the nature of causality. For example, Wegner's (2002) claim that the commonsense belief that one's actions are caused by one's will is illusory is partly based on the arguments one, that this belief constitutes a form of dualism insofar as it implies mental causation of physical events; and two, on the implicit (but mistaken) assumption that free will implies the existence of 'uncaused causes' as constituting the origin of our behavior. As Moore (2020) notes, the argument seems to be that if intentions and willings are themselves causally determined, they cannot be free because only uncaused causes can be seen as free. Thus, according to the 'hard determinate world, free will is impossible – end of discussion'.[12]

What has emerged in the last number of years are additional arguments against the possibility of free will, but also the additional claim that there is empirical evidence supporting the illusory nature of one's sense of free will (Wegner, 2002, 2003, 2008). The empirical evidence most frequently cited are findings from research by Libet and his colleagues (e.g., Libet et al., 1983), which have been hailed as having major philosophical implications (Haggard et al., 1999).

I turn now to the work of Libet and his colleagues, whose 1983 paper (Libet et al., 1983) was hailed as 'one of the most philosophically challenging papers in modern scientific psychology' (Haggard et al., 1999, p. 291). In the 1983 study, subjects were asked to move the fingers of their right hand whenever they wanted to do so. They were also instructed to indicate the precise time that they decided to move their fingers. A major finding was that a slow negative shift in electrical potential in the supplemental motor area of the brain (SMA), which is referred to as readiness potential (RP), was detected at 550 msec. prior to the finger movements. Also, the time at which subjects made the decision to move their fingers was 350 msec after RP detection. Hence, the subjects' decision to move their fingers came 200 msec. *after* detection of RP (and 200 msec before actual movement). Thus, it appears that brain processes caused the decision to move one's fingers.[13] According to Haggard and Libet (2001), these findings 'deeply undermine the concept of conscious free will: preparatory brain activity causes our conscious intentions ... if the moment of conscious intention followed the onset of the readiness potential, then free will cannot exist' (Haggard & Libet, 2001, pp. 47–48). In other words, if brain activity causes intentions or what Moore (2020) calls 'willings', the latter cannot be free.

In the context of considering the implications of these and similar findings for questions of legal and moral responsibility, Moore (2020) brilliantly examines their philosophical interpretations. I will discuss only limited aspects of Moore's extended discussion. As he writes, there are subtle differences in the arguments against free will based on the Libet study (as well as similar findings). One argument is that intentions or willings are epiphenomenal, that is, have no causal properties. In this argument, the causal chain goes straight from brain events to behavior; the notion that intention or will is a part of that chain is an illusion. The other argument, associated with Wegner's (2002) writings, allows that intentions or willings can play a role in the causal chain, but because they are themselves caused by brain events, they cannot be free willings or intentions. As noted above, the implicit assumption here is that free will implies the existence of 'uncaused causes' as constituting the origin of our behavior. The argument seems to be that if intentions and willings are themselves causally determined, they cannot be free because only uncaused causes can be seen as free. Therefore, because there can be no uncaused causes in a determinate world, there is no such thing as free will. As Moore (2020) notes, all that the concept of free will requires is not that one's will or intention is uncaused, but that it is part of a causal chain. As he writes, 'just because brain events both cause bodily movements and precede willings does not count as evidence against the possibility that such brain events cause bodily movements *through* such willings' (p. 235).

As for the fear that the concept of free will implies acceptance of dualism, if one thinks of as intentions as cut off from the brain, it is, of course, a form of (untenable) dualism. However, one can avoid dualism by recognizing that conscious intention 'has its own distinctive brain correlates ...' (Moore, 2020, p. 239). (See Nahmias, 2002 for an excellent critique of Wegner's, 2002 *The illusion of conscious will*.)

Let me add some comments to Moore's (2020) cogent discussion of the import of the Libet findings. What seems to be overlooked in considering the philosophical implications of the Libet findings is the sheer fact that had the subjects not intended, in compliance with the experimenter's instructions, to move their fingers, there would be no such movements. This stark fact stands out independently of other issues, including the issue of the relation between time of decision, of neural activity, and of finger movement. Thus, if one defines cause as something necessary for a particular event to occur, then, of course, the subject's intentions (including their intentions to comply with the experimental instructions) played a causal role.[14]

How well do the above contra free will arguments work in contexts outside the experimental situation of the Libet study? Let us say that I have general intention or plan to go to the movies at some point during this week. There surely must be some brain processes that are part of this dispositional intention or plan. Let us also say that at a particular time, I decide to see a particular movie and go ahead and do so. Let us further say that RP neural activity preceded in time my awareness of my decision and, of course, my action of going to the movies. Could one reasonably conclude that the RP neural activity caused both my decision to go to the movie as well as my going to the movie action? What is the role in this scenario of other causal determinants, such as wanting to see this particular movie, feeling bored, wanting to be entertained, memories of being taken to the movies as a child, and so on? Without addressing the relation between the Libet findings and these questions, the meaningfulness and ecological validity of these findings are far from clear.

Let me describe some important empirical research on the relation between conscious intentions and action that speaks to the claim that intentions are epiphenomenal. Ordinarily – the Libet (1983) study notwithstanding – a conscious intention to raise one's arm is followed by raising one's arm. However, this sequence is not possible for some paralyzed individuals. A number of investigators have been able to partly overcome this limitation with a paralyzed man.

The paralyzed individual's imaginal intention to write by hand, is decoded and translated into text on a computer screen (Willett et al., 2021). With extensive training, the paralyzed individual achieved typing speeds of 90 characters per minute. In effect, the decoding and translating device carries out what would be achieved by the individual's muscular movements.

What is the role of the individual's subjective intention and imagining in the 'typing' of words that appear on the screen? Of course, without the neural activity accompanying the subjective imagining (of writing by hand) and the intention to 'type' specific words, there would be no story to tell. However, it is also clear that the starting point of the above narrative is the individual's subjective imagining of writing specific words; and that without that starting point, there would also be no story to tell. Thus, it is accurate to say that the paralyzed man's imagining and intention played a vital causal role in the appearance of words on the computer screen.

The relation between the paralyzed individual's intention and the appearance of the intended word on the computer screen parallels the ordinary relation between one's intentions and actions. The device that codes neural signals and transforms them into words on a screen essentially does the work that would be normally carried out by sets of muscles. My intention to raise my arm is accompanied by neural activity that sends signals to muscles in my arm that result in my raising my arm. Just as without the paralyzed individual's intention there would be no word printed on the computer screen, so similarly, without my intention to raise my arm, there would be no arm-raising action. In short, as noted by Moore (2020), what he refers to as one's 'willings' play an integral role in a causal chain.[15]

As noted earlier, reluctance to accept the fact that intentions or 'willings' play a causal role in action is fueled by the fear of dualism; hence, some philosophers would be more comfortable stating that it is the neural activity – a respectable physical factor – accompanying the imagining that played the causal role in the appearance of the words on the screen. Thus, it is mainly a metaphysical conviction that leads to the conclusion that insofar as intentions are not physical, they can only be viewed as epiphenomenal, with no causal powers. Rather than viewing causal chains through the metaphysically neutral lens of a particular factor's contribution to the occurrence of an event, a metaphysical requirement is now imposed on the concept of cause. From the former perspective, the individual's imaginings and intentions are part of a causal chain that plays an explanatory role in accounting for the appearance of words on a screen.

Let us say that in one's desire to keep all causal properties at the level of physical processes, one argues, in accord with the way Libet's (1983) findings were largely interpreted, that the individual's imaginings and intentions were caused by immediately prior neural activities. Hence, the argument continues, the imaginings and intentions are epiphenomena playing no causal role. Let us also say for the sake of argument that the first claim is valid. Would the second part of the argument follow, namely, that the imaginings and intentions are epiphenomena? To take the position that because imaginings and intentions themselves have a causal history, they cannot play a causal role is, as Moore (2020) notes, to make the untenable claim that only uncaused events can play a causal role.

The investigators who carry out the kind of research discussed above are unlikely to spend much time wondering whether they are espousing dualism in their investigations of the effects of imaginings and intentions on behavior. Rather, they carry out fruitful research on such matters as variations in behavior and neural patterns as a function of variations in experiential variables such as culturally conditioned attitudes, perceptions, feelings, and so on. They also have little hesitance in formulating explanatory accounts at the appropriate level of discourse. There would simply be no possibility of the above kinds of studies if one took seriously the claim that all our joys and sorrows are nothing but assemblies of neural cells. Nor would such studies be possible were it the case that, as Dennett (1991) maintains, consciousness and subjective experience are 'uninvestigatable'. I turn to that issue in the next chapter.

Forensic and moral implications of 'nothing but' eliminative materialism

The forensic and moral implications of 'nothing but' reductionism and eliminative materialism is a topic that merits its own full treatment, something that cannot be accomplished in this book. However, let me make a few comments. Although neural processes underlie and are necessary for consciousness and the experience of joys and sorrows or any other feelings, the very idea of experience is tied up with being a human being (or a non-human animal), and in the case of the former, having a forensic status as a person. One of the issues at play here is the question of one's particular perspective on what it means to be a human being. Aristotle writes that

> A physicist would define an affection of the soul differently from a dialectician; the latter would define e.g., anger as the appétit for returning pain for pain ... while the former would define it as a boiling of the blood or warm substance surrounding the heart.
>
> (as cited in Bennett & Hacker, 2007, p. 187)

Rubinstein (1997a) makes a similar point in his distinction between the perspectives of viewing the other as an organism versus as a person. It is only in the context of the latter perspective that forensic and moral issues of responsibility arise. Or to put it another way, the view of the human being as 'nothing but' assemblies of neural cells carries important implications for issues of legal and moral responsibility.

In a superb and magisterial work, the eminent philosopher of law Michael Moore (2020) brilliantly discusses the implications of different philosophical positions and neuroscientific findings on the question of legal responsibility. According to Moore (2020), the general attitude of neuroscience toward issues of responsibility is that 'there can be no such thing as moral desert because neuroscience has shown that human agency needed to sustain such a thing, does not exist' (p. 3). And as Dretske (1988) observes, on that view, we might ultimately have to 'relinquish a conception of ourselves as human agents' (p. x). For some, the conception of the human being absent agency and responsibility would constitute a disaster. For example, Fodor (1987) writes that 'if commonsense intentional psychology really were to collapse, that would be, beyond comprehension, the greatest intellectual catastrophe in the history of our species' (p. xii). In contrast, Dennett is not especially concerned about the legal and moral implications of replacing statements about our beliefs, desires, thoughts, and sensations with reference to brain states. It is not only Dennett, but also Stich (1992) who is somewhat dismissive of the reactions of Fodor and Dretske. Stich introduces Fodor's above-cited passage by saying: 'Jerry Fodor, who is rarely accused of understating the case ...' (p. 243); and describes Dretske's statement as 'similarly apocalyptic' (p. 243).

Here we have a fundamental difference that goes beyond intellectual disagreement and validity of argumentation, and has much to do with values and with individual reactions to the prospect of living in a radically different social and psychological world. I think Dennett (2001) is correct when he writes that

> one of the most fascinating bifurcations in the intellectual world today is between those to whom it is obvious – *obvious* – that a theory that leaves out the Subject [and, I would add, subjective experience] is therefore disqualified as a theory of consciousness ... and those to whom it is just as obvious that any theory that *doesn't* leave out the subject is disqualified.
>
> (p. 6)

Where Dennett (2005) stands in regard to this bifurcation is evident. He writes: 'I submit that the former have to be wrong, but they certainly don't lack for conviction as these recent declarations eloquently attest' (p. 6). That general statement is supplemented by more specific statements such as the following one:

> ... just as the heart is basically a pump, and could in principle be made of anything so long as it did the requisite pumping without damaging the blood, so a mind is fundamentally a control system implemented in fact by the organic

brain, but anything else that could *compute the same control functions* would serve as well.

(Dennett, 2001, p. 9)

As noted above, Dennett seems to have little interest in the forensic and moral implications of his position. He writes that 'arguments about whether a robot could ever be conscious have been conducted in the factually impoverished arena of what is "possible in principle"' (p. 1). He goes on to say that 'A team at MIT, of which I am part, is now embarking on a long-term project to design and build a humanoid robot …' (Dennett, 1994, p. 133). Dennett goes on to note that 'the aim of the project is not to make a conscious robot'. If this is so, in what way does the robot project reduce the presumed factual impoverishment regarding the question of whether a robot could ever be conscious? That the MIT robot project is irrelevant to the issue raised by Dennett, even by his own reasoning, is indicated by his later statement that 'the best reason for believing that robots might some-day become conscious is that we human beings are conscious, and we are sort of robots ourselves' (Dennett, 1997, p. 17)

Not only, according to Dennett, are we 'sort of robots', but we are also not essentially different from 'zombies'. He writes:

> Why should a zombie's crushed hopes matter less than a conscious person's crushed hopes? There is a trick with mirrors here that should be exposed and discarded. Consciousness, you say, is what matters, but then you cling to doctrines about consciousness that systematically prevent us from getting any purchase on why it matters. Postulating inner qualities that are not only private and intrinsically valuable, but also unconfirmable and uninvestigatable is just obscurantism.

(Dennett, 1991, p. 450)

Dennett entirely misses the point here. As Searle (1997) observes, the reason that a conscious person's crushed hopes matter more than a 'zombie's' crushed hopes is that *zombies have no crushed hopes or feelings of any kind.* And, he goes on to ask, when you pinch yourself and feel pain, are 'you postulating inner qualities that are unconfirmable and uninvestigatable?' And are you being 'obscurantist'? (pp. 107–108).

Whereas for Dennett, human beings are essentially information processors, for Searle, although, of course, recognizing the information capacity of human beings, most important about being alive are consciousness and subjective experience. He takes it for granted that in so far as it is at the center of one's life consciousness is 'intrinsically valuable'. For Searle, 'Behavior is important to the study of consciousness only to the extent that we take the behavior as an expression, as an effect of, the inner conscious processes' (p. 204). Thus, unlike Dennett, Searle is not especially impressed by demonstrations of computers or robots doing things that human beings do. He writes:

We could build a computer that prints out 'OUCH' every time you hit the keyboard hard enough. Would this give us any reason at all to suppose that we had created pains in the computer? None whatever. This point keeps coming up over and over in these debates so let me emphasize: *where the ontology of consciousness is concerned, behavior is irrelevant* [emphasis in original]. At best, behavior is epistemically relevant – we can typically tell when other people are conscious by their behavior.

(Searle, 1997, p. 204)[16]

Although you can have a complete causal account of pain at the level of neuronal patterns, this will tell you nothing about what the pain feels like (Searle, 1997). To have a subjective experience like pain is to feel something qualitatively (Nagel, 1974). Neuronal firings do not feel, only beings capable of conscious experience do. The great challenge, of course, is how to understand the process by which neuronal firings can generate qualitative feelings and experiences. 'Nothing but' reductionist theories essentially bypass that challenge, and do so at a great cost of eliminating the phenomena that are at the core of one's existence and one's sense of being as a person.

Consciousness and heterophenomenology

Dennett (2005) labels his approach to phenomenology 'heterophenomenolgy', which is specifically designed to be a '*third-person* [emphasis in original] approach to consciousness' (p. 246). He writes:

Heterophenomenology is explicitly not a first-person methodology (as its name makes clear) but it is also not directly about 'brain processes and the like'; it is a reasoned, objective extrapolation from patterns discernible in the behavior of subjects, including especially their test-producing or communicative behavior, and as such it is *about* [emphasis in original] precisely the higher-level dispositions, both cognitive and emotional, that convince us that our fellow human beings are conscious.

(p. 231)

Dennett (2005) also writes: 'The third-person approach is not antithetical to, or eager to ignore, the subjective nuances of experience; it simply insists on anchoring these subjective nuances to *something* [emphasis in original] – anything, really – that can be detected and confirmed in replicable experiments' (p. 149).

It is not clear what kind of anchoring Dennett requires. As I will discuss in the next chapter, there is a long history of replicable studies of the relationship between nuances in subjective experiences and variations in physical stimuli – that field is referred to as psychophysics. And ironically, the reemergence of interest in consciousness and conscious experience in the psychological and philosophical literature is at least partly due to the availability of more sophisticated technology, such as fMRI techniques, that enable systematic investigations of the relationship between brain processes and replicable subjective experiences. Indeed, the project of cognitive and affective neurosciences consists of a systematic investigation of the neural underpinnings of replicable subjective experiences. Further, the disciplines of cognitive and affective neuroscience would not be possible were there no replicable subjective experiences.

Dennett's description of heterophenomenology is redolent of early functionalism in which, based on observation of behavior, one inferred conscious states. However, as Boring (1950) observes, figures such as Watson, soon concluded that 'a functional psychology could get along without consciousness' (p. 556). The result was that functionalism was soon replaced by the more radical behaviorist position that one can do without any reference to inferred conscious states and simply chart functional relations between environmental stimuli and behavioral responses. Some form of this behaviorist program seems to be implicit in Dennett's position – the phenomenology drops out and the third-person hetero remains. That is, any focus on first-person experiences and conscious states is replaced by a focus on functional relations between stimulus and behavioral response.

In so far as one cannot get inside another's skin, to some extent, investigations of another's first-person experiences are necessarily heterophenomenological. That is, based on observation of behavior, one infers certain conscious states in the other. But that is not the only way one gets to understand another's conscious states. There is a large literature, for example, on the mirror neuron system, intentional attunement, and embodied simulation, at least with regard to motor actions and facial expressions of emotions (Gallese, 2005; Eagle, 2021). However, most important in the present context, as is evident in his writings, Dennett is not especially concerned with first-person conscious states as phenomena to be investigated, but primarily with observing the behaviors that enable one to infer subjective conscious states in others. As noted earlier, in much of his writing, Dennett is saying something like: 'I am not denying the existence of subjective conscious states. My position leaves room for inferring their existence based on observation of behavior'.

However, as some commentators have remarked, it is difficult to pin down what Dennett is saying regarding consciousness and subjective experience.). At times, Dennett's investment in cleverness interferes with clarity of meaning. As Crick (1994) writes, Dennett '… appears to be overpersuaded by his own eloquence' (p. 282). The net result is, as Wright (2000) puts it, 'Of course, the problem here is with the claim that consciousness is 'identical to brain states. The more Dennett al try to explain to me, the more convinced I become is what they really mean is that consciousness doesn't exist' (as cited in Dennett, 2001). Wright's assessment is similar to Koch's (2019), who writes that a more accurate title for Dennett's book *Consciousness Explained* would be 'Consciousness Explained Away' (p. 176, fn. 5). One thing is clear, however: for Dennett, subjective conscious states do not constitute data for science and cannot be accommodated by the scientific method – which, of course, is precisely the position taken by at least methodological behaviorism.

In a 1970 paper on incorrigibility and the mental Rorty writes that

> if it came to pass that people found that they could explain behavior at least as well by reference to brain states as by reference to beliefs, desires, thoughts, and sensations, then reference to the latter might simply disappear from the language.
>
> (p. 421)

In his discussion of Rorty's paper, Dennett (1986) refers to a 'very sophisticated machine' (Cog) being built at the AI lab at MIT and suggests the possibility that Cog might be 'a plausible candidate … for elevation to first-person status' (p. 6), by which he presumably means that Cog's reports of its experiences are granted the first-person privilege of incorrigibility. Dennett (1997) writes that one need not worry that in blurring the distinction between robots and humans one is de-humanizing humans; rather, he argues, one is humanizing robots, elevating them to first-person status. However, a much more plausible argument can be made that in humanizing robots and in blurring the distinction between robots and humans, one is, indeed, de-humanizing humans. Recall Moore's (2020) description of the general attitude of neuroscience toward issues of responsibility: 'there can be no such thing as moral desert because neuroscience has shown that human agency needed to sustain such a thing, does not exist' (p. 3). Thus, from this perspective, as far as agency and responsibility are concerned, we are already robots or 'zombies'.

In a number of recent papers, there has been much discussion of implementing *self-awareness* in robots. For example, in a recent paper, Chella et al. (2020) propose that one can implement 'a form of robot self-awareness by developing inner speech in the robot' (p. 1).[17] They write that 'inner speech is known to importantly participate in the development and maintenance of human self-awareness (Morin, 2018); thus, self-talk in robots is an essential behavioral capability of robot self-awareness' (p. 1). Whether they believe that 'robot self-awareness' is the same as human self-awareness is not clear. On the one hand, they write as if robot self-awareness is the same as human self-awareness. On the other hand, they also write as if they do not equate them.

For example, they often put self-awareness in quotes; they refer to 'the anthropomorphism of the robot'; and they argue that such anthropomorphism would 'enhance trust in human-robot.

Cooperation' (p. 2). In other words, designing the robot with such features as being able to report 'inner speech' would enhance anthropomorphism, that is, enhance the human's experience *as if* the robot were human. One is led to wonder whether the authors themselves have been seduced by their own anthropomorphism. But of course, this *as if* anthropomorphic feeling has nothing to do with the substantive issue of self-awareness in the robot.

Emergentism

Before leaving the topic of reductionism it is important to note that the issues raised by that philosophical position arise not only in regard to the relation between psychology and the so-called physical sciences, but also, as Mayr (1988) observes, in the relation between biology and the physical sciences. He writes that 'attempts to "reduce" biological systems to the level of simple physio-chemical processes have failed because during the reduction the systems lost their specific biological properties. Living systems ... have numerous properties that are simply not found in the inanimate world' (p. 1). Of course, this does not mean that biological phenomena are not subject to physical and chemical laws. What it does mean is that 'new properties and capacities *emerge* at higher hierarchical levels and can be explained only in terms of the constituents at this level' (p. 11). This is also the case with regard to the relation between psychological phenomena and physio-chemical processes. The philosophical position represented by Mayr's comments has been referred to as *emergentism*, a term coined by G.H. Lewes in 1875. A relatively simple and clear definition of emergence is provided by Mayr (1961): 'When two entities are combined at a higher level of integration, not all the properties of the new entity are not necessarily a logical or predictable consequence of the properties of the components' (p. 34). The perspective of emergentism has a long history that goes back to Aristotle's distinction between matter and form as well as between matter and function, includes the writings of J.S. Mill and C.D. Broad, and continues to the present day in the writings of, for example, Mayr (1982), Searle (2017) who coins the term 'biological naturalism', Cartwright (1994, 1999), and Rumbaugh et al. (1996). Emergentism bears a family resemblance to functionalism in its emphasis on functional organization.

As noted above, Mayr (1961) writes that biological processes are emergent phenomena that possess properties that are not possessed by the constituents of these processes. Life itself is an emergent phenomenon in so far as the chemical constituents of life do not themselves possess the property of life. It is only in the organization of these constituents that biological systems with new properties, such as homeostasis and metabolic exchange of energy, emerge. Although biological systems that emerge are subject to physio-chemical laws, new lawful regularities emerge that cannot be derived from these lower-level physio-chemical laws.

Each of the above statements is applicable not only to biological, but also to psychological phenomena. In an important sense, the mind–body problem is preceded by the life–matter problem. That is, life is a property that emerges from the organization of chemical elements that alone do not have that property. And similarly, the properties of consciousness and subjective experience emerge from the organization of physio-chemical elements that, themselves, do not have those properties. Further, as Rumbaugh et al. (1996) put it, the subject matter of psychology is 'generated only by life – the human animal life of the world' (p. 114). Of course, these statements regarding emergence have little explanatory value in accounting for the processes and mechanisms that make possible the emergence of life and consciousness. That extraordinarily difficult challenge remains for the nitty-gritty work of scientific investigation.

The clearest expression of an overriding theoretical that is relevant primarily to biological emergent phenomena is, of course, evolutionary theory. As Mayr (1988) writes, 'there is nothing in the physical sciences that corresponds to the biology of ultimate causations' (p. 17). What Mayr is referring to here is the fact that a relatively complete account of any biological phenomenon needs to include both proximate causes (e.g., a cause of eating is feeling hungry) and ultimate causes or what has also been referred to as 'ultimate functions', that is, its adaptive function and basis for natural selection.

Although there is no psychological theory comparable in its breadth to evolutionary theory, one can identify limited and domain-specific psychological theories that are relevant and operational only at the level of emergent psychological phenomena. Examples include Helson's (1964) level of adaptation theory; the Yerkes-Dodge law; the Weber-Fechner law; and Kulpe's (1893/1895/1999, 1902) work on attention and perception span. What these formulations have in common is not their immunity to 'lower-level' laws governing physical-chemical processes – they have no such immunity – but the fact that they arise only in the context of the emergence of the phenomena of consciousness and subjective experience.

Emergentism has been subject to a variety of critiques, including the specific criticisms that it is mysterian, constitutes a form of vitalism, explains little or nothing regarding the processes and mechanisms involved in emergence (e.g., what are the processes involved in the emergence of consciousness from the interaction and organization of neural cells), and can be invoked in regard to virtually all interactional and organized phenomena. It seems to me that, for the most part, these are unwarranted criticisms. For example, in referring to emergent phenomena, neither Mayr nor Searle is invoking a mysterian *elan vital*. Further, the recognition of the emergent nature of certain phenomena does not preclude the scientific search for the processes involved in the emergence of these phenomena. Finally, I think the philosophical importance of emergentism lies not in its explanatory power in regard to specific phenomena, but rather as a stand against reductionism and eliminativism, as an insistence that vital phenomena in the world cannot be reduced away because they (presumably) cannot be accommodated in a physicalist world view. To repeat Mayr's (1988) comments, 'reducing biological systems to the level of simple physio-chemical processes has failed because during the reduction the system lost their specific biological properties. Living systems … have numerous properties that are simply not found in the inanimate world' (p. 1).[18]

Consciousness and subjective experience in Freudian theory

It may seem odd to include an account of the Freudian theory of the mind in a discussion of different philosophical perspectives on consciousness and subjective experience. Although at one point in his life, Freud intended to study philosophy, he did not view himself as a philosopher – indeed, at times, he denigrated philosophy – as we will see, his writings on the role of consciousness and subjective experience in psychological life are essentially philosophical arguments in the service of developing a scientific psychoanalytic theory of the mind. Indeed, the eminent philosopher of science, Clark Glymour (1991), writes that

> Freud's writings contain … a philosophy of mind that addresses many of the issues about the mental that nowadays concern philosophers and ought to concern psychologists. Freud's thinking about the issues in the philosophy of mind is better than much of what goes on in contemporary philosophy …
>
> (p. 46)[19]

(See also Wakefield, 2018 for an excellent account of Freud as philosopher.) In short, the focus in this section is not on Freud as psychoanalyst, but on Freud as philosopher of mind. For a long period of time, both in the arena of common sense as well as in philosophical conceptions of mind, there was a general consensus that mind equals conscious, that is, that mental states are inherently conscious. Hence, the concept of unconscious mental states was viewed by many as an oxymoron. As Descartes (1641) wrote, 'the fact that nothing can exist in the mind, insofar as it is a thinking thing, of which it is not conscious seems to me self-evident' (p. 115). In accord with this view, Locke (1689) stated that 'to be happy or miserable without being conscious of it, seems to me to be utterly inconsistent and impossible' (para. 2.1.12). Similarly, Hume (1739) wrote: 'Since all actions and sensation of the mind are known to us by consciousness, they must necessarily appear in every particular what they are, and be what they appear' (p. 190). And Brentano (1874), one of Freud's teachers, also firmly rejected the idea of unconscious mental states – although, as we will see, Brentano's identification of intentionality as the marker of the mental paved the way for Freud's conception of unconscious mental states. The equation of mental with conscious, and the concomitant rejection of the idea of unconscious mental states were dominant not only in philosophy, but also in psychology. James (1890) referred to the idea of unconscious mental states as 'pure mythology'. Similarly, Titchener (1909) relegated the idea of unconscious mental states to 'the sphere of fiction' (p. 40). In a paper entitled 'Is the conception of the unconscious of value in psychology?', Field et al. (1922) was a resounding 'No'.

Unlike 'nothing but' reductionists, Freud never denied the reality of consciousness. Indeed, he wrote that 'consciousness is one of the fundamental facts of our life' (Freud, 1938, p. 283).

However, he argued that because consciousness is too 'mysterious', too unstable and occasional an aspect of the mental, it cannot constitute the subject matter of a scientific theory of the mind. Most important in a philosophical context, from his earliest to his late writings, Freud repeatedly maintained that mental processes are inherently unconscious. Thus, in 1900, he writes that 'The unconscious is the true psychical reality' (p. 613); in 1924, he writes that 'Mental processes are in themselves unconscious' (p. 198); and in 1940 he writes that 'The psychical is unconscious in itself' (p. 158). Thus, it is not mere semantic happenstance that psychoanalysis came to be known as a 'depth psychology' (a *Tiefenpsychologie*) of unconscious processes, which contrasted it with the surface nature of consciousness and conscious experience.

The most fundamental claims of the Freudian theory of the mind are: one, the existence of unconscious mental states; two, that the major part of mental life goes on outside of conscious awareness; three, that the essence of the mental is not consciousness, but intentionality in Brentano's sense of aboutness, that is, directedness toward something; four, that unconscious mental states possess the property of intentionality; five, that unconscious processes are similar in kind to all the other natural processes, suggesting that like all natural processes, the mental is essentially physical in nature;[20] six, that as for the specific nature of these physical processes, 'no physiological concept or chemical process can give us any notion of their nature' (Freud, 1915b, p. 168); seven, that consciousness is only an incomplete, occasional, and 'unstable quality' of the mental (Freud, 1938, p. 283); eight, that the 'gaps' in the succession of conscious mental states require the assumption of the existence of unconscious mental states in order to provide continuity in accounts of mental life (Freud, 1915b); and nine, and perhaps most important in the present context, that because of the incompleteness and instability of conscious mental states, as well as the mysterious and explanation defying nature of consciousness, it cannot serve as a basis for the scientific study of the nature of the mind.[21]

Following are some passages from Freud's writings in which the above claims are stated: 'The psychical, whatever its nature may be, is in itself unconscious and probably similar in kind to all other natural processes of which we have knowledge' (Freud, 1938, p. 283). 'The ... view, which held that the psychical is unconscious in itself, enabled psychology to take its place as natural science like any other' (Freud, 1940, p. 158).

> Consciousness is one of the fundamental facts of our life and our researches come up against it like a blank wall and can find no path beyond it. Moreover, the equation of what is mental with what is conscious had the unwelcome result of divorcing mental processes from the general context of events in the universe and of setting them in complete contrast to all others.
>
> (Freud, 1938, p. 283)

Freud is clearly suggesting here that consciousness is divorced 'from the general context of events in the universe'; and therefore, to equate the mental with consciousness is to separate the mental from the general context of events in the universe. Although he does not state it explicitly, it is the physical that constitutes the general context of events in the universe.

Brentano's (1874) concept of intentionality exerted a pivotal influence on Freud's understanding of the nature of the mind and his formulation of unconscious mental states. As noted, Brentano proposed that the essence of the mental is intentionality, by which he meant the property of directedness or aboutness in relation to some object. As Brentano (1874) put it: 'Every mental phenomenon is characterized by ... reference to a content, direction toward an object' (p. 68). Brentano maintained that only conscious mental states have intentionality. However, although Freud agreed with Brentano that intentionality is the essence of the mental, he rejected his view that intentionality is limited to conscious mental states. (Wakefield, 2018). Rather, at the core of Freud's conception of the nature of the mind, is the central idea that unconscious states can possess intentionality and can therefore be understood as mental states. In short, according to Brentano, intentionality = consciousness = the mental (Wakefield, 2018, p. 350). What Freud does is simply eliminate consciousness from the equation.

In contrast to Brentano's Cartesian position, Freud tried to 'naturalize' intentionality by severing its necessary connection to consciousness. He does so through the following argument: one, the property of intentionality is the essence of the mental; two, the psychical is itself unconscious; and three, therefore, all unconscious mental states are characterized by intentionality. This allows one to bypass the 'mystery' of consciousness, or at least limit its function to a perceptual-epistemological one, and get on with the business of developing a scientific theory of the mind, that is, providing a scientific account of the mental in terms of what Freud (1938) referred to as 'natural processes' (p. 283).

Similar to some contemporary philosophers of mind, Freud believed that because the phenomenon of consciousness is a mystery that cannot be penetrated, a scientific world view cannot accommodate consciousness and subjective experience; therefore, these phenomena cannot be the focus of a scientific project on the nature of the mind. Late in his writings, Freud (1940) wrote that consciousness 'defies all explanation' (p. 158). Hence, according to Freud's reasoning, if psychology is to be a science, it cannot be based on the centrality of conscious experience, a mysterious phenomenon that defies all explanation. If, however, one recognized 'that the psychical is unconscious itself ... psychology ... [could] take its place as a natural science like any other' (p. 158). That is, mental phenomena can be subject to scientific investigation, rather than stand as a mysterious thing apart when one's conception of mental life is limited to consciousness and conscious experience. As Wakefield (2018) puts it, 'it is not obvious to Freud whether consciousness can ultimately be reducible to naturalized theories – it appears that his immediate reaction is to suspect that it can't be ...' (p. 350).

It needs to be noted again that, unlike other philosophical perspectives, Freud's position does not reduce consciousness to other processes (e.g., neural processes). He does not deny that consciousness exists. Rather, he argues against taking consciousness as the subject matter of psychology based on the methodological requirements of scientific investigation. In that sense, Freud's position bears a family resemblance to methodological rather than ontological behaviorism.

Freud not only challenged the assumption that the mental and physical are distinct and opposing ontological categories, but according to Wakefield and supported by textual references, essentially postulated 'a form of intrinsic intentionality that is nonetheless physical and possesses its content independently of consciousness' (p. 221). For example, Freud (1940) writes that

It of course becomes plausible to lay the stress in psychology on these somatic processes, to see in them the true essence of what is psychical … [Psychoanalysis] explains the supposedly somatic concomitant phenomena as being what is truly psychical …

(pp. 157–158)

Freud's reasoning is that because science has a firm grasp on the nature of the physical and because the 'mystery' of consciousness cannot be accommodated by a physicalist world view, in investigating the nature of the mind, one must focus on the physical in investigating the nature of the mind. Given Freud's hints in the above passages to the effect that unconscious mental processes are essentially somatic in nature, a focus on the physical is, in effect, a focus on unconscious mental processes.

The idea that some physical processes (e.g., brain states) possess essential mental properties such as intentionality and representationality may be conceptually jarring (see Wakefield, 2018 for an elaboration of this view). However, as noted above, there are properties of the physical that we do not understand. It is also worth noting Chomsky's (1968) comment to the effect that we need not be overly troubled by this idea because what we come to view as physical in the light of new discoveries and new knowledge will be very different from our current conception of the physical. As Chomsky (1968) writes,

We can … be fairly sure that there will be a physical explanation for the phenomena in question [i.e., human mentality], if they can be explained at all, for an uninteresting terminological reason, namely, that the concept of 'physical explanation' will no doubt be extended to incorporate whatever is discovered in this domain, exactly as it was extended to accommodate gravitational and electromagnetic force, massless particles, and numerous other entities and processes that would have offended the common sense of earlier generations.

(p. 84)[22]

In any case, whatever one's conception of the physical and the mental, as Koch (2019) puts it, 'Consciousness belongs to the natural realm' (p. xi). And he adds, 'Just like mass and charge, it has causal powers' (p.xi).

Conceptions of the nature of the physical have changed over time and, in many respects, the nature of the physical is perhaps as much a mystery as the nature of consciousness. As Sellars (1962) writes, '… the scientific image is not yet complete; we have not yet penetrated all the secrets of nature' (p. 37). He also writes that

> Sensa are not 'material' as 'matter' is construed in the context of a physics with a particulate paradigm. But, then, as has often been pointed out, the more seriously this paradigm is taken, and the more classically it is construed, the less 'matter' there seems to be.
>
> (Sellars, 1971, p. 446)

And finally, he writes: 'The important thing is not to let our reflections on the developing Scientific Image of man-in-the-world be tied too closely to the current institutional and methodological structure of science, or, above all, to its current categorical structure' (Sellars, 1971, p. 440). Sellars' comments are especially prescient in the light of the discovery of such strange phenomena as quantum entanglement. As John Clauser, one of the 2022 Nobel Prize laureates, states, 'Why it happens I haven't the foggiest. I have no understanding of how it works, but entanglement appears to be very real' (as quoted in Borenstein et al., October 5, 2022).

Perceptual model of consciousness

After describing the functions of the 'system *Pcs*', Freud (1900) asks 'what part is there left to be played in our scheme by consciousness'? His answer is 'Only that of a sense-organ for the perception of psychical qualities' (Freud, 1900, p. 615).[23] He also writes in a later paper that 'In psychoanalysis there is no choice for us to assert that mental processes are in themselves unconscious, and liken the perception of them by means of consciousness to the perception of the external world by means of the sense-organs …' (Freud, 1915, p. 171). Thus, like a flashlight, consciousness lights up a sampling of unconscious mental life that is subjectively experienced.

Freud (1915) follows the above statement with the comment that

> Just as Kant warned us not to overlook the fact that our perceptions are sub-jectively conditioned and must not regarded as identical with what is per-ceived and unknowable, so psychoanalysis warns us not to equate perception by means of consciousness with the unconscious mental processes which are their object. Like the physical, the psychical is not necessarily in reality what it appears to us to be.
>
> (Freud, 1915, p. 171)

In alluding to Kant's warning, Freud is stating that in our perception of the exter-nal world we do not subjectively experience the object as it is, which is unknow-able (Kant's *noumena*), but as it is 'subjectively conditioned', that is, as the object appears to us through the inborn subjective categories through which we experi-ence the world.

If one combines Freud's reference to Kant's warning with his statements that 'the psychical ... is itself unconscious' (Freud, 1938, p. 283), that it is 'similar in kind to all other natural processes of which we have knowledge' (Freud, 1938, p. 283), and that 'the true essence of what is psychical' is to be seen in 'somatic processes' (Freud, 1940, pp. 157–158), we would need to conclude that Freud's position is that in perceiving the external object, we are experiencing in consciousness the brain states activated by the external object. As Wakefield (2018) observes '... Freud's perceptual model of consciousness ... reduces consciousness to the perception of what is going on at the brain level and leaves it no direct causal function of its own' (p. 287); that is, consciousness is essentially an epiphenomenon.

Freud (1915b) also warns us in regard to our experience of our inner world. He cautions us not to 'equate perceptions by means of consciousness with the unconscious mental processes which are their object' (p. 171). Stating that unconscious mental processes are the objects of consciousness is another way of saying that what is experienced in consciousness is a sampling of unconscious mental processes. However, insofar as Freud views unconscious mental processes as essentially brain states, he is saying that consciousness in regard to our inner world – what Freud refers to as 'internal perception' – is essentially the experience of one's brain states activated by internal stimuli (e.g., drives). From this perspective, an unconscious mental state such as an unconscious desire is essentially a brain state that may, under certain conditions, be consciously experienced (See Rubinstein, 1997b, who views unconscious mental states as 'proto-neurological' terms). As Wakefield (2018) puts it,

> The conscious experience of one's desire is a perception of that brain state. Thus, being consciously aware of one's desire by perceiving the desire (i.e., perceiving the brain state) is exactly analogous to being aware of the tomato by perceiving the tomato.
>
> (p. 214)

Although in both our external and internal words, we are bombarded by a flow of external and internal stimuli which activate a wide range of brain states, we consciously experience or 'read' only a selected sample of these activated brain states. Further, the sample of brain states linked to both inner and outer stimuli, but especially inner stimuli, that gains access to conscious experience is not random, but influenced by motivational forces, including the avoidance of unpleasure and the protection of one's self-image. In short, according to Freud, consciousness is primarily a perceptual tool that brings to conscious experience only a sample of the unconscious mental states and processes that constitute a major part of one's mental life.

There is a myriad of issues generated by the perceptual model of consciousness, particularly by the specific conception of consciousness in terms of perception of brain states. Every perceptual system is subject to the possibility of error. In the case of consciousness as perception of brain states, there are at least two possible sources of error: one, there may be error at the level of the brain state itself. That is, the brain states activated by the external or internal stimuli may not accurately reflect them. For example, with regard to external stimuli, under certain circumstances, the external object 'apple' may activate a brain state representative of a pear, with the consequence that one consciously perceives a pear. It is only upon re-examination, say in better lighting, that one discovers that the object is an apple. Another source of possible error is that the perception of the brain state may be faulty; that is, conscious experience may not accurately reflect the brain state. Thus, although the brain state representation is that of an apple, consciousness may misperceive the brain state, due, say, to the strong expectation that a pear would be presented. Or to put it more accurately, one should say that the neural processes underlying the conscious experience of pear 'misread' the brain state representation of apple. Still another possibility is that the strong expectations of seeing a pear exerted a top-down influence on the formation of the brain state such that despite the fact that the external stimulus was an apple, the brain state it activated was a representation of a pear.

As noted above, Freud views consciousness as a sense-organ both in regard to external and internal perception. In the case of the external world, the subjective experience is that of an external object – e.g., 'I see an apple'. In the case of one's inner world and internal perception, one subjectively experiences, desires, feelings, thoughts, reasoning, and so on. On this view, my current conscious desiring, intending, thinking and reasoning in which I am now engaged in writing this passage should be understood as a perceptual sampling of unconscious mental states, which are no different from conscious mental states save for the fact that they lack consciousness. In this view, consciousness is entirely passive, exerting no influence on the mental states that have been read.

The epistemological function of consciousness: the issue of veridicality

Like any perceptual tool, a primary function of consciousness is to provide information and knowledge regarding one's external and inner worlds. A question that immediately arises is the veridicality of the information provided by that perceptual tool.[24] It is clear from Freud's writings that whereas he views perception of external objects as relatively immune to at least motivated distortion, perception of one's inner world of desires, wishes, and motives is regularly subject to the dissimulating influences of defense and self-deception (Eagle, 2022). Indeed, Freud (1924) makes it clear that it is only in psychosis that the experience of the external world is markedly disturbed by the influence of motivational influences. He writes that 'We call behavior "normal" or "healthy" … if it disavows [external] reality as little as does a neurosis …' (Freud, 1924, p. 185), and also writes that '*neurosis is the result of a conflict between the ego and the id, whereas psychosis is the analogous outcome of a similar disturbance in the relations between the ego and the external world*' [emphasis in original] (Freud, 1924, p. 149).

In the perception of an external object, I and others can check on the veridical-ity of my perception by examining the external object. I may examine the object in a better light and learn that my perception was inaccurate. How to examine the accuracy of my experience of a desire is not as clear. What 'object' would I reexamine? Given that there is no external object against which to check, how do I know whether the sense-organ of consciousness has perceived my unconscious wishes and desires accurately? Given the primary emphasis of a psychoanalytic theory of the mind on one's inner world, this is an especially germane question.

Before addressing that question, I want to return to the observation that, according to Freudian theory, perception of external objects is relatively immune to the influence of motivational factors. There is an early body of early research on 'perceptual defense' on the effects of motives, taboos, conflict, and accom-panying emotional reactions on perception which seems to run counter to this claim. However, research findings in this area were largely limited to demon-strations of delayed recognition thresholds for presumably conflict-laden, taboo words (Erikse, 1954; see also Eagle & Wolitzky, 1977; Erdelyi, 1974). These findings were interpreted as indicating the operation of defense against experience of anxiety-laden material – hence, the term 'perceptual defense'. More broadly, these findings were taken to demonstrate the influence of psychodynamic factors, such as conflict, need, and defense, on perceptual processes, a domain dominated by experimental psychologists, who largely ignored such influences as irrelevant to their research. The 'perceptual defense' findings presumably demonstrated the relevance of psychodynamic factors to phenomena that were assumed to be rela-tively immune to the influence of such factors.

At a superficial level, the findings of perceptual defense appear to contra-dict this claim of the relative autonomy of perceptual functioning. However, these findings, virtually exclusively, have to do not with the effects of dynamic factors on the *formation* of the content of the percept formed or its veridical-ity, but rather with subtle processes such as recognition threshold. That is, the 'perceptual defense' findings did not show that psychodynamic factors influ-ence the content of what is perceived. Nor did they demonstrate an influence on the veridicality of the perception. In short, these findings provided no basis for skepticism regarding the proposition that central aspects of perceptual experi-ence show a good deal of autonomy from conflict, need and defense. They cast little doubt on Freud's position to the effect that in normal functioning, per-ceptual functioning in relation to the external world is relatively *autonomous*, that is, relatively resistant to the influences of conflict, need, and defense. This position was more fully elaborated in Hartmann's (1939) formulation of ego autonomy, that is, the idea that from an adaptive point of view, and seemingly paradoxical, reality-testing ego functions, including perception, must be able to operate independently of the pressures of need and drive, if they are to be capable of facilitating need and drive satisfaction.

There are two additional considerations that it is important to note. One con-sideration is that even the relatively subtle effects on recognition thresholds reported required contrived experimental conditions such as stachistoscopic rapid exposure, raising the question of the degree of ecological validity of the findings. The other consideration is that plausible alternative interpretations of the findings of the 'perceptual findings' were proposed. For example, delayed recognition threshold was attributed to the fact that taboo words were less frequently used and encountered than non-taboo words (e.g., Wiener, 1955).

I think one can conclude that overall, as Freud proposed, perception, in particular, the percept that is formed, is relatively immune to influence by motivational factors. However, there is evidence that perception is also relatively immune to influence by propositional knowledge. As Rock (1985) writes that

> Knowledge concerning the object, scene, or event in a propositional form generally does not affect perception. By and large, perception is autonomous with respect to thought ... Exceptions to this generalization can occur if the stimulus is ambiguous and can support a cued or suggested interpretation or in line with what is known to be present as well as it can support the interpretation that occurs spontaneously.
>
> (p. 3)

That knowledge does not easily influence perception is also noted by Fodor (1983), as exemplified by the failure of explicit knowledge to influence one's perception in the Muller-Lyon illusion. As another example, given the knowledge that the Ames room is trapezoidal rather than rectangular has no effect on the perceptual illusion in which a person looks markedly tall in one corner of the room and markedly small in another corner of the room (see Gregory, 1987). The resistance of perceptual illusions to the influence of explicit knowledge leads Fodor to propose a modular theory of mind characterized by modules carrying out their specific functions relatively free of influence from other modules.

Let me return to the issue of the differences between the perception of outer and inner worlds. When an external object I perceive is occluded, I no longer perceive it – although I know that it is still there; and when the occlusion is removed, I perceive the object once again. The analogy to occlusion in regard to one's inner world is a repressive defense that bars an unconscious mental content from being consciously experienced. Were the analogy complete, I would consciously experience the repressed mental content once defense is lifted. This outcome would be predicted by a perceptual model of consciousness that applies equally to perception in regard to one's inner and outer worlds. However, this is not the case in any simple way. Indeed, the rationale for psychoanalysis as a form of treatment rests on the assumption that consciousness is dissimulating in relation to one's inner world, as well as on the claim that a psychoanalytic approach is uniquely able to uncover and alter dissimulation. However, as discussed in the previous chapter, following the lifting of repression, a direct experience of hitherto repressed mental contents is not what necessarily or even generally occurs. Rather, once defenses are lifted, the patient may have an 'assured conviction' that the unconscious desire is part of him or her in some way, without ever directly experiencing the desire. This state of affairs bears a greater similarity to a situation in which despite the external object remaining occluded, the individual *knows* it is still there than to a situation in which the removal of the occlusion leads to the direct perception of the object. This suggests an *epistemological* model of consciousness in regard to one's inner world, a conclusion also supported by Freud's (1915b) comment that in order to acquire knowledge about one's unconscious mental states, one must view oneself as one would view another.

Note that we have returned to the issue of relative emphasis on knowledge versus experience in psychoanalytic theory discussed in the previous chapter. However, here the context of the discussion is primarily philosophical rather than clinical. From the perspective of an epistemological model of consciousness, it is possible to have knowledge of one's unconscious mental states without directly experiencing them. For example, one can readily imagine the statement: 'Although I am not aware of having such and such a belief (or desire), I can observe that I act as if I had that particular belief (or desire). Judging from my behavior, I seem to believe (or desire) "such and such"' (Feyaerts & Vanheule, 2017). This is obviously a third-person perspective in which based on one's (or another's) observations, one makes certain inferences about one's mental state. 'I seem to believe' (or 'I seem to desire') is quite different from 'I believe' (or 'I desire').[25,26]

I have referred a number of times to Moran's (2001) distinction between what he refers to as third-person self-knowledge, based on observation and inference, versus first-person self-knowledge, which is non-inferential, immediate, and to which one has some sort of privileged access. However, despite referring to first-person *knowledge*, Moran's characterization of it suggests that what he means by that term is not primarily epistemological. Rather, what he refers to as first-person self-knowledge is accorded properties, such as a special authority, immediacy, and moral commitment that is not possessed by third-person self-knowledge. Moran (2001) writes that first-person authority is not a matter of being an 'expert witness' and that a discussion of first-person self-knowledge 'moves from the epistemology of introspection to a set of issues in the moral psychology of the first-person' (p. 4). Were first-person statements of one's mental states primarily an epistemological process, that is, an expression of knowledge of one's unconscious mental states, it would not be odd to say 'In all probability, I have a headache' or 'It is likely that I intend to go to the library'. Such statements, as Moran notes, reflect a third-person stance toward one's mental states. In contrast, from a first-person perspective, one *has* intentions, desires, goals, etc.; and one wills or resolves to do (or not to do) such and such.

Indeed, one may have knowledge about one's unconscious mental state without experiencing it and without any of the other properties that normally accompany first-person experiences.[27,28]

Do consciousness and subjective experience have any motivational properties in Freudian theory?

As we have seen, the sole functions of consciousness and subjective experience are perceptual and epistemological in the Freudian theory of the mind. Are they accorded any motivational properties? One might interpret Freud's concept of the pleasure principle as, in fact, according motivational properties to consciousness and subjective experience if one interprets it as asserting that, generally speaking, seeking the conscious experience or *feeling* of pleasure and avoiding the experience and *feeling* of unpleasure serve as central motives in guiding one's behavior. On this view, the function of consciousness would go beyond the perceptual and the epistemological and would extend to the motivational, which would appear to contradict the claim that consciousness is epiphenomenal. However, as articulated in Freudian metapsychology, the pleasure principle does not refer to the *experience* of pleasure and unpleasure, but to quantitative build-up and discharge of tension and excitation. As far as I know, there is only one place in his theoretical writings in which Freud discusses the relation between the pleasure principle and *subjective* experiences of pleasure and unpleasure. He writes that pleasurable and unpleasurable feelings

> cannot be referred to an increase or decrease in quantity [which we describe as tension due to a stimulus], although they have a great deal to with that factor. It appears that they depend, not on some characteristic of it which we can only describe as a qualitative one.
>
> (Freud, 1924, p. 160)

He then goes on to speculate that this 'qualitative characteristic' is 'perhaps [due to] the rhythm, the temporal sequence of changes, rises and falls in the quantity of stimulus. We do not know' (p. 160). However, Freud does not pursue the issue of the 'qualitative characteristic' any further. Had he done so, it might have led to a direct focus on the motivational function of conscious qualitative experiences. For example, it might have led to the idea that from an evolutionary perspective, subjective experiences of pleasure and unpleasure are linked to meeting one's vital needs.[29]

As Rapaport (1960) writes, Freud assigned motivational power entirely to unconscious id forces (see Eagle, 2022a for a further discussion of this issue). This is seen in Freud's (1923) approving citation of Groddeck's (1923) statement that 'we are lived by our id' as well as his own assertion that the true purpose of life is represented by the id (Freud, 1923). Given the conception of the id in Freudian theory as the unconscious representation of instinctual drives, and its psychological status as an impersonal 'it' (*Das Es*), the statements that we are lived by our id and that the id represents the true purpose of life essentially claim that infantile instinctual aims and impulses constitute the primary motivational factors that govern one's psychological life. That we are lived by our id also implies that the subjective experience that our conscious intentions and motives motivate our actions is an illusion, a conclusion, we have seen, also reached by, among others, Nisbett and Wilson (as well as Wegner). The difference is that whereas Nisbett and Wilson propose that our behavior is determined by mini causal theories, according to Freud, we are motivated by impersonal id forces. (Recall Freud's (1923) horse and rider metaphor.)

As Moore (2020) writes, however, it is entirely possible that impersonal forces, including neurophysiological brain states underlying instinctual drives, cause behavior, but do so *through* one's willings. This is an extremely important point. The claim that we are lived by our id suggests that there is a direct, unmediated pathway from id to behavior, as if we were programmed automatons, and that our conscious intentions are epiphenomenal. In this view, the feeling and belief that our conscious desires, intentions, etc. play a causal-motivational role in our actions are simply illusory. Further, given the presumed 'primary antagonism' between id and ego (A. Freud, 1936), and the inherent ego-alien, not-me status of id impulses, the forces by which we are lived are inherently alien to one's sense of who one is. Thus, just as the oft-noted observation that the Copernican revolution disabused us of the belief that we are at the center of the universe, so similarly, Freudian theory not only disabuses us of the belief that we are masters in our own house, but goes a step further in suggesting that the masters are unwelcome invaders of our house.

One can perhaps charitably understand the claim that we are lived by our id as the more plausible claim that our conscious motives and desires are themselves strongly influenced by unconscious instinctual drives. This formulation would be similar in form to the idea that distal evolutionary functions (or what Mayr, 1993, refers to as 'ultimate causes') strongly influence one's proximal motives. A firm believer in evolutionary theory, Freud would have been aware of this distinction, even if not in those precise terms. From this perspective, pursuing and gratifying one's proximal motives and desires would constitute the primary means of carrying out the distal evolutionary functions that enhance survival and inclusive fitness. A major problem with this interpretation, however, is that, as we have seen, according to Freud (1915b) and in A. Freud's (1966) words, there is a 'primary antagonism' (p. 149) between the id and the ego. This raises the question of how could fulfillment of instinctual aims be seen as serving distal evolutionary functions when the id is an implacable enemy of a vital aspect of one's personality. This would certainly not be possible were there a primary antagonism between the id and the ego, the latter representing the seat of one's conscious desires and wishes, that is, one's proximal motives. Were there an inherent antagonism between the id and the ego, distal functions and proximal motives would be, so to speak, at war. Therefore, the latter could not be the means through which the former are represented.

Let us assume that there is no primary antagonism between id and ego. In that context, the claim that we are lived by our id would seem entirely plausible when it is interpreted as stating that instinctual drives strongly influence our conscious aims and motives. In that view, instinctual drives do not influence behavior directly, but through influencing what we desire and want to do, just as distal functions do not influence behavior directly, but, as noted above, through influencing proximal motives, that is, by influencing what we want and desire. Further, to the extent that doing what we desire and want to do is associated with meeting vital biological needs, survival and inclusive fitness are enhanced. The point here is that quite contrary to Rapaport's (1960) claim that only the id possesses motivational power, it is the ego, that is, conscious desires, intentions, and aims, that are the seat of motivation. The narrative of unconscious id forces directing behavior rather than influencing behavior through one's desires and motives, is a description of severe pathology and an automaton rather than a functioning person.

To take an obvious example, we eat because it is pleasurable, not simply because it is necessary for survival. And similarly, although propagation of one's genes may be a distal function, it is made more likely by engaging in experiencing sex as pleasurable. Evolution works in a manner in which distal functions are served through the intervention of conscious subjective experiences of the form of I desire, I want, I am aim for. In short, although they are strongly shaped and influenced by our id, we are lived, not by our id, but by our conscious perceptions, desires, and aims.

Rapaport (1960) (as well as in Freud's and Hartmann's) seems to assume that because conscious desires and motives are themselves causally influenced by unconscious id forces, they cannot causally influence one's actions. The implicit assumption is that if something is itself caused, it cannot play a causal role, including a motivational form of a causal role. Thus, consciousness, as well as conscious desires and motives, are epiphenomenal. The 'real' causal-motivational factors are the id forces that cause the conscious desires and motives. However, as noted earlier, the requirement that only something that is itself uncaused can play a causal or motivational role in behavior makes little sense.

Being an 'I' who has personal desires and motives and is trying to fulfill them is a relatively efficient and compact way of representing the various needs of the individual and thereby achieving distal functions. That is, the subjective experience of willing, intending, and wanting as processes intervening between biological imperatives and behavior may be the most efficient way of dealing with these biological imperatives for a complex organism. It is not clear that consciousness and subjective experience would have evolved were it more efficient to go directly from biological program to behavior. This is something that James, Dewey, and other functionalists took into account in their assumption that given its evolutionary selection, consciousness had to have a vital function evolutionary function.

Inconsistencies between Freudian theoretical formulations and clinical context

Freud's scientific ambitions for psychoanalysis as a theory of the mind are not infrequently at odds with his clinical formulations. For example, the view that consciousness is epiphenomenal and merely samples unconscious mental states would seem to be incompatible with the clinical importance of making the unconscious conscious. Also, seemingly incompatible are, on the one hand, the proposition that conscious and unconscious mental states are no different save for the presence or absence of the property of consciousness and on the other hand, the proposition that whereas conscious thought is governed by secondary process, unconscious thought is governed by primary process. As still another example, despite viewing the id as the implacable enemy of the id in his metapsychological writings, Freud (1915) suggests that the threatening quality of id impulses is the *illusory consequence*, not the cause, of repression. He writes that the 'repressed instinct-presentation [which is unconscious] … develops in a more unchecked and luxurious fashion. It ramifies, like a fungus, so to speak, in the dark and takes on extreme forms of expression' that are ego-alien and terrifying because of 'the way in which they reflect an extraordinary strength of instinct. This *illusory* [my emphasis] strength of instinct is the result of an uninhibited development in phantasy and of the damming-up consequent on lack of real satisfaction' (Freud, 1915b, p. 149). In other words, contrary to the positing of an inherent 'primary antagonism' between the id and the ego (A. Freud, 1966, p. 166), Freud clearly suggests that because the mental content is repressed and relegated to the unconscious, and therefore not exposed to the light of reality, it takes on the illusory property of being a threat to the ego.

As another example, despite the view of conscious experience as epiphenomenal in the Freudian theory of the nature of the mind, and despite the claim that we are lived by our id, he nevertheless proposes as the overriding goals of psychoanalytic treatment making the unconscious conscious and where id was, there shall ego be.[30] These goals would make little sense if consciousness is truly epiphenomenal and if we are lived by our id. There are a number of other incompatibilities between Freud's metapsychological and clinical writings on unconscious mental states and their relation to consciousness. For example, in a theoretical context Freud (1933) describes the unconscious id as a 'cauldron, full of seething excitations' (p. 73) dominated by the non-rational mode of primary process thinking. However, in the more clinical writings, he states that repressed unconscious mental states are no different from conscious mental states save for the presence or absence of consciousness. However, as Wakefield (2018) writes the repressed mental states described by Freud 'are so radically different from anything found among conscious mental states that they would seem to pose a *prima facie* challenge to Freud's argument that these are specifically mental states' (p. 274). In short, in some of his writings, the property of being unconscious itself has an extraordinary influence on how the unconscious mental content is represented and the affective impact that it has. This hardly suggests that the sole difference between conscious and unconscious mental states is the property of being conscious.

Consciousness and motility

Freud, as well as other psychoanalytic theorists, have written relatively little on action – what Freud (1923) refers to as 'motility' (p. 55). This is largely so because of the psychoanalytic emphasis on intrapsychic phenomena. Indeed, a central concept in Freud's (1895/1950) theory of the mind is *inhibition*, that is, the capacity to not act (see Eagle, 2022). According to Freudian theory, the emergence of mind, particularly the structure of the ego, is marked by an increasing capacity for delay of motor discharge. The capacity to delay, in turn, allows the operation of such conscious ego functions as planning and assessment of the potential consequences of one's actions, as well as decisions regarding which specific actions to take.

Freud (1923) writes that 'the ego controls the approaches to motility' (p. 17) and therefore 'to the realization of mental desires' (Freud, 1916–1917, p. 359). In other words, the ego controls actions, including actions necessary to satisfy one's desires. Insofar as Freud (1923) proposed that at least some ego functions are unconscious, Freud's statement that the ego controls the approaches to motility is not necessarily equivalent to saying that consciousness controls motility. However, Freud (1923) writes that 'by interposing the process of thinking [the ego] secures a postponement of motor discharges and controls the access to motility' (Freud, 1923, p. 55). He also writes that 'judging ... decides the choice of motor action, which puts an end to the postponement due to thought and ... leaks over from thinking to action' (Freud, 1925, p. 238). Freud is obviously referring here to delay of gratification which allows the intervention of thinking, deciding and planning regarding the consequences of one's actions, mental activities highly likely to entail consciousness and conscious deliberation of some sort. Indeed, as Freud (1940/1938) writes, in sleep, when one is not conscious, motility is 'paralyzed', a state of affairs that allows the id 'a harmless amount of liberty' (p. 166), harmless because id impulses cannot be acted on during this state. Putting all these comments together, the reasonable conclusion is that according to Freud, conscious thought and judgment exert control not only over whether or not one will engage in action, but also over which actions to take. This is hardly a description of an epiphenomenal consciousness with no causal properties.

Before leaving the topic of the relation between consciousness and action, I want to address an issue that is rarely discussed, in the psychoanalytic literature namely, the relation between repression and action. Virtually all the discussions on repression are focused on its function of barring certain anxiety-inducing mental states from consciousness and thereby serving to regulate negative affect. However, if consciousness controls motility, including in the fundamental sense that one must be in a conscious state in order to be capable of acting, it would follow that by preventing a desire or impulse from reaching consciousness or by removing it from consciousness, one is also making less likely the carrying out of intentional and voluntary actions necessary to gratify the desire or impulse. What is left is the possibility of disguised, partial, and compromised gratification in the form of symptoms, parapraxes, and dreams, phenomena which one can view as purposive quasi-acts rather than what we normally think of as actions.

The important point I want to emphasize here is that on this view, repression protects one not only from the negative affect one would experience were the repressed impulse to reach consciousness, but perhaps more fundamentally, it also protects one from the potentially severe costs and dangers that would ensue were one to carry out the actions necessary to gratify the repressed desire. In short, repression is directed not only at the fear of having certain experiences, but also at the fantasied fear of carrying out potential actions that accompany these experiences. To put it very simply, to not experience a particular desire is to reduce the probability that one will carry out actions to gratify that desire. Despite the costs of repression, it may be a more economical course than facing the challenge of having to repudiate, renounce, or sublimate the desire.

Summing up view of consciousness and subjective experience in Freudian theory

What stands out clearly in the Freudian theory is the dethronement of the primacy of consciousness and conscious experience as constituting the essential nature of mind. This is expressed in various ways: one, the claim that the major part of mental life goes on outside awareness; two, the view that a focus on consciousness and conscious experience is incompatible with the possibility of a scientific investigation of the mind; three, the conception of consciousness as only an incomplete and 'unstable' aspect of mental life; four, the claim that 'we are lived by our id' and that the true purpose of life lies in the id, that is, that the unconscious id represents the true source of our motivations; five, the claim that the main functions of consciousness are perceptual and epistemological, that is, the perception and provision of knowledge in regard to one's unconscious mental life; six, the view of consciousness as dissimulating suggesting that the information it provides regarding one's inner world is frequently misleading; and seven, the primary function of free association not as a means of monitoring consciousness, but as a vehicle for identifying unconscious drive derivates that slip through ego controls. The dethronement of the primacy of consciousness and conscious experience is now complete.

Notes

1 Although Crick is a biologist and Chater is a neuroscientist, their claims regarding consciousness and subjective experience are philosophical in nature.
2 Note the parallel between Husserl's bracketing and Titchener's trained introspectionism. Insofar as both entail a suspension of the natural attitude, which is characterized by a report of the object one has perceived. Indeed, as we have seen earlier, to report the object rather than the elements of experience was termed a 'stimulus error' by Titchener. This parallel is not happenstance. Titchener was influenced by Husserl, as evidenced by a number of references to his work.
3 The relation between 'back to the things themselves' and Kant's (1781/1987) thing-in-itself (*ding ansich*) is a complex and interesting issue which obviously merits much further discussion. However, it can be noted that Husserl's conviction that one can reach the things themselves through phenomenological investigation would seem to imply an idealism that dissolves the Kantian distinction between our experience of the world and

the world as it is. This also appears to be the case in Merleau-Ponty's (1968) comment that 'We see the things themselves, the world is what we see' (pp. 3–4). Further discussion of these issue is beyond the scope of this book.

4 One can find a similar distinction in the psychoanalytic context in Bion's (1962b) concepts of beta and alpha elements, as well as Lacan's (1966/2002) concepts of the Real and the Imaginary I will discuss these concepts later in the chapter).

5 Note that sensation as a mentalistic concept is subject to Searle's (1990) critique that it is essentially speculative neurophysiology.

6 However, the parallel between Husserl and Titchener is not unqualified. Although, like Husserl, Titchener believe that adequate *description* of conscious experience via trained introspection was the proper approach to psychology, he was more detailed in his belief that explanation could begin when the descriptive project was complete. Further, he argued that explanation would take the form of identifying the physiological underpinnings of experience. In his *Textbook of Psychology*, Titchener (1910) wrote: '… it is by reference to the body, to the nervous system and the organs attached to it that we can explain mental phenomena' (p. 39). Similar to Titchener, Ladd (1894) defined psychology as 'the science of the facts or states of consciousness' (p. 7). Like Titchener, although, Ladd took the position that the subject matter of psychology is consciousness, he argued that the proper *explanation* for the phenomenon of conscious experience lay in underlying brain states. Thus, Ladd's 1887 book is entitled: *Elements of Physiological Psychology: A Treatise of the Activities and Nature of the Physical and Experimental View*.

7 Although less obvious, Lacan's (1966/2002) concepts of the Real and the Imaginary also bear a family resemblance to sensation and perception.

8 The phrases 'from the naturalist's point of view' as well as 'naturalizing phenomenology' seem to suggest that consciousness and subjective experience need to be *made* part of the natural world. We are left with the odd state of affairs in which if the phenomena in our lives that are at the very center of one's existence cannot be accommodated by current scientific theory, one must view them somehow as 'unnatural'.

9 In an important sense, Cartesian dualism furthered the work of science, which was permitted to carry out its investigations of physical reality so long as mental reality and the soul remained under control of religion (see Makari 2015). To some extent, a similar apportionment characterizes contemporary eliminativism and reduction of consciousness and conscious experience to brain processes. That is, brain processes, neurophysiology, and behavior belong to the sciences and whatever is, so to speak, left over can either be ignored or left to the humanities (see C.P. Snow, 1990, on the two cultures).

10 Fascinating findings are presented regarding the neural processes underlying vision and other psychological functions in both the Crick and Chater books. This material makes these books worth reading. However, the fascinating findings reported by Crick and Chater stand on their own. They do not require nor do they support the eliminative and nothing but philosophical positions of these authors.

11 Recall Renee's experience during her psychotic break of experiencing others as engaged in disconnected, mechanical movements rather than as carrying out intentional actions.

12 Wegner's position regarding free will belongs to a philosophical stance referred to as *incompatibilism*. In contrast, the *compatibilist* position is that determinism and freedom of will are compatible; that is, it makes little sense to require that in order for one to view an action as freely willed, the willing itself needs to be uncaused. `Debates regarding the possibility of freedom of the will have a long history. Indeed, Hume (1748/1975, p. 95). referred to it as 'the most contentious question of metaphysics'. However, it is worth noting that Hume took a straightforward compatibilist stance on that question. He understood free will as the 'power of acting or of not acting, according to the deter-

mination of the will; that is, if we choose to remain at rest, we may; if we choose to move, we also may … This hypothetical liberty is universally allowed to belong to everyone who is not a prisoner and in chains' (p. 103). He also wrote that all the freedom one needs is the ability to get what one desires. Similarly, Hobbes (1651/1968) wrote that 'A free agent is he that can do as he will, and forbear as he will, and that liberty is the absence of external impediments' (as cited in Peters, 1967, p. 41). One can see in the references to 'external impediments' and being 'in chains' that for Hume and Hobbes, the opposite of free will is external compulsion.

In contrast to Hume and Hobbes, Spinoza was skeptical regarding the possibility of free will. He emphasized the power of the passions, as well as of external events, to determine our actions. For example, with regard to the latter, Spinoza (1677/1985) wrote that 'we are in many ways driven about by external causes, and like the waves of the sea, driven by contending winds, we are swayed hither and thither, unconscious of the issue and our destiny'. And yet, Spinoza allowed for a certain form of freedom of action, namely, the freedom that is generated by becoming aware of and understanding the causes of our actions. He wrote: 'The mind has greater power over the passions, and is less subject to them, in so far as it understands all things as necessary' (Ethics, V, 4, Scholium). He also writes that 'An emotion which is a passion ceases to be a passion as soon as we form a clear and distinct idea of it' (Ethics, V, 3). (Note the congruence between Spinoza's and Freud's views).

13 Similar results have been found in which brain activity in the SMA has been detected prior to movement on the order of 2 to 3 seconds (Lau et al., 2004). Strikingly, a similar pattern has been found with regard to decisions as to whether one will add or subtract, that is, where no movement is involved (Haynes et al., 2007).

14 One could argue that because the subject's intention to move his or her fingers was caused by the experimenter's instructions, it was not free. But this argument is, once again, that for an intention to be relevant to free will, it must itself be uncaused.

15 Let us say that stimulating the appropriate neural area results in my arm being raised. But here arm raising is a movement, not an action. I may experience involuntary arm movements as part of a neurological illness. One would hardly want to refer to such movements as actions.

16 See Searle's (1980) Chinese Room argument.

17 It seems that little has been learned from the behaviorist ill-conceived attempt to equate thinking with implicit speech.

18 I recall one of my teachers, Hans Lukas-Teuber, distinguishing among different levels of explanation by noting that, in contrast to an inanimate object, a cat falling out the windows obeys not only the law of gravity, but also the law of righting reflexes, as well as whatever mini-laws might be available in accounting for the cat's motives in jumping out of the window.

19 One of the main reasons that Freud denigrated philosophy is that he found it too speculative and not sufficiently scientific.

20 Recall that, as Strachey (1893–1895) observes, 'Freud owed a fundamental allegiance to the school of Helmholtz, which held that all natural phenomena are ultimately explicable in terms of physical and chemical forces' (p. xxii).

21 It is worth noting that Hullian and neo-Hullian behaviorists were quite comfortable with Freud's emphasis on unconscious rather than conscious processes and phenomena. Indeed, in an influential book at the time, Dollard and Miller (1950), two neo-Hullians, published a book in which they translated Freudian concepts into behaviorist terms. And Hull himself offered seminars at the Human Relation Institute at Yale University in which he attempted to integrate conditioning theory with psychoanalysis (Gondra, J.M., 2002; McClelland, 1957).

22 It should be noted that physical explanation now includes gravitational and electromagnetic force and massless particles is hardly a matter of an uninteresting terminological reason.

23 Here Freud follows Locke (1689/1894), who defined consciousness as 'the perception of what passes in a man's own mind' (II, I, 19). He continues: it 'might properly enough be called "internal sense" because the understanding turns inward upon itself, reflects on its own operations, and makes them the object of its own contemplation' (II, I, 4 and 8). Damasio, 1999, 2000) takes a similar position in stating that affective feelings are essentially 'readings' of one's bodily state.

24 One should not confuse the issue of the veridicality of information with the issue of privileged access in relation to my immediate experience. Using the above example, although my immediate experience was 'apple', I was mistaken – the external object was a 'pear'. Hence, my privileged access to my experience of 'apple' does not extend to its accuracy.

25 Indeed, I suspect that many analysts would take the position that an analysis is not complete without the transformation from 'I seem to believe' (or 'I seem to desire') to 'I believe' (or 'I desire'), that is, the transformation from a third-person perspective based on observation and inference to a first-person experiential perspective.

26 As I have noted elsewhere (Eagle, 1982), the same Descartes who argued for the greater certainty of knowledge of mind also wrote: 'And in order to know what [people's] opinions really were, I needed to pay attention more so what they did, than to what they said, not only because ... there are few people who are willing to say everything which they believe, but also because many do not know themselves (Discourse, Part, III)' (p. 361).

27 There is another epistemological issue that I can only mention and will not pursue. It can be shown that there is an important distinction between your experience and the *report* of your experience. In a classic study, Sperling and Averbach (1961) demonstrated that due to the evanescence of short-term storage, your report of even immediate experience does not capture everything you have experienced and encoded. This does not threaten the first-person authority of your report. However, it does mean that in at least some circumstances your report of your experience is only a partial account of what you have experienced and encoded.

28 In an *expressivist* account of first-person authority, Wittgenstein (1981) argues that such authority issues from the fact that statements such as 'I am in pain' should not be understood as based on observation and report of one's mental state (i.e., should not be viewed as an epistemological statement), but rather as a *verbal expression* of one's mental state. In that sense, such statements are on a par with groans or saying 'ouch'. Although it is clear that the statement 'I am in pain' is not based on observation, it is not clear why it should not be viewed as a verbal report of one's experience of pain rather than simply an expression of being in pain equivalent to 'ouch'. A problem with the expressivist account is that it overlooks the communicative function of first-person statements. For example, if someone asks you why you are grimacing or how you feel, you are likely to reply 'I am in pain', not 'Ouch', which on the expressivist account is equivalent to 'I am in pain'. Also, although the expressivist account may work in the context of such relatively simple statements such as 'I am in pain', it becomes less plausible as first-person statements become more complex.

29 It is noteworthy that with the exception of Freud's (1900) early reference to hunger in the context of an account of the development of the reality principle, his discussion of the pleasure principle is primarily concerned not with vital needs, but virtually always, with infantile instinctual *wishes*, drives, impulses, and desires that need to be repudiated and renounced.

30 It is not clear that such integration would be possible were there an inherent antagonism between the id and the ego and were the id an inherent threat and danger to the ego.

References

Ackerman, F. N. (2021, January 22). Individual consciousness, lengthy biographies and other letters to the editor. *The New York Times*. https://www.nytimes.com/2021/01/22/books/review/individual-consciousness-lengthy-biographies-and-other-letters-to-the-editor.html

Alexander, P. (1967). Ernst Mach. In P. Edwards (Ed.), *The encyclopedia of philosophy* (Vol. 5, pp. 115–119). Macmillan.

Averbach, E., & Sperling, G. (1961). Short term storage of information in vision. In C. Cherry (Ed.), *Information theory* (pp. 196–211). Butterworth & Co.

Baars, B. J. (2003). The double life of B. F. Skinner: Inner conflict, dissociation and the scientific taboo against consciousness. *Journal of Consciousness Studies, 10*(1), 5–25.

Ben-Zeev, A. (1984, December). The passivity assumption of the sensation—Perception distinction. *British Journal for the Philosophy of Science, 35*, 327–343.

Bion, W. R. (1962a). *Learning from experience*. Maresfield Reprints/Karnac.

Bion, W. R. (1962b). A theory of thinking. *International Journal of Psychoanalyses, 43*, 306–310.

Blanshard, B. (1939). *The nature of thought*. George Allen and Unwin.

Borenstein, S., Burakoff, M., & Jordans, F. (2022, October 5). 3 scientists share Nobel Prize for work in 'totally crazy' quantum science. *WralTechWire News*. https://wraltechwire.com/2022/10/05/3-scientists-share-nobel-prize-for-work-in-totally-crazy-quantum-science/

Boring, E. G. (1950). *A history of experimental psychology*. Prentice-Hall.

Brentano, F. (1874). *Psychology from an empirical standpoint*. Routledge.

Broad, C. D. (1925). *The mind and its place in nature*. Routledge.

Cartwright, N. (1994). Fundamentalism vs. the patchwork of laws. *Proceedings of the Aristotelian Society, 94*(1), 279–292.

Cartwright, N. (1999). *The dappled world*. Cambridge University Press.

Chater, N. (2018). *The mind is flat: The remarkable shallowness of the improvising brain*. Yale University Press.

Chella, A., Pipitone, A., Morin, A., & Racy, F. (2020). Developing self-swareness in robots via inner speech. *Frontiers in Robotics and AI, 7*, 16. https://doi.org/10.3389/frobt.2020.00016

Chomsky, N. (1968). *Language and mind*. Harper and Row. https://doi.org/10.1037/e400082009-004

Crick, F. H. C. (1994). *The astonishing hypothesis: The scientific search for the soul*. Charles Scribner's Sons.

Damasio, A. R. (1999). *The feeling of what happens: Body and emotion in the making of consciousness*. Harcourt Brace.

Damasio, A. R. (2000). A second chance for emotion. In R. D. Lane & L. Nadel (Eds.), *Cognitive neuroscience of emotion* (pp. 12–23). Oxford University Press.

Darwin, C. (1987). Notebook C 166. In *Charles Darwin's notebooks 1836–1844*. Cambridge University Press (Original work published 1838).

Dennett, D. C. (1986). The case for rorts. In R. Brandom (Ed.), *Rorty and his critics*. Wiley-Blackwell.

Dennett, D. C. (1991). *Consciousness explained*. Penguin.

Dennett, D. C. (1994). The practical requirements for making a conscious robot [and discussion]. *Philosophical Transactions: Physical Sciences and Engineering, 349*(1689), 133–146. http://www.jstor.org/stable/54381

Dennett, D. C. (1997). Consciousness in human and robot minds. In M. Ito, Y. Miyashita, & E. T. Rolls (Eds.), *Cognition, computation, and consciousness* (pp. 17–29). Oxford University Press. https://doi.org/10.1037/10247-002

Dennett, D. C. (2001). Are we explaining consciousness yet? *Cognition, 79*(1–2), 221–237.

Dennett, D. C. (2005). *Sweet dreams: Philosophical obstacles to a science of consciousness.* MIT Press.

Dennett, D. C. (2007). Philosophy as naive anthropology: Comment on Bennett and Hacker. In M. Bennett, D. Dennett, P. Hacker, & J. Searle (Eds.), *Neuroscience and philosophy: Brain, mind, and language* (pp. 73–95). Columbia University Press.

Dennett, D. C. (2013). *Intuition pumps and other tools for thinking.* Penguin.

Dennett, D. C. (2018). Facing up to the hard question of consciousness. *Philosophical Transactions of the Royal Society of London Series B, Biological sciences, 373*(1755), 20170342. https://doi.org/10.1098/rstb.2017.0342

Descartes, R. (1911). Meditations on first philosophy. In E. S. Haldane (Trans.), *The philosophical works of Descartes.* Cambridge University Press (Original work published 1641).

Dollard, J. & Miller, N. E. (1950). *Personality & psychotherapy: An analysis in terms of learning, thinking, & culture.* New York: McGraw-Hill.

Dretske, F. I. (1988). *Explaining behavior: Reasons in a world of causes.* MIT Press.

Eagle, M. N. (2021). *Toward a unified psychoanalytic theory: Foundation in a revised and expanded ego psychology.* Routledge.

Eagle, M., & Wolitzky, D. L. (1997). Empathy: A psychoanalytic perspective. In A. C. Bohart & L. S. Greenberg (Eds.), *Empathy reconsidered: New directions in psychotherapy* (pp. 217–244). American Psychological Association. https://doi.org/10.1037/10226-009

Erdelyi, M. H. (1974). A new look at the new look: Perceptual defense and vigilance. *Psychological Review, 81*(1), 1–25. https://doi.org/10.1037/h0035852

Eriksen, C. W. (1954). Psychological defenses and "ego strength" in the recall of completed and incompleted tasks. *The Journal of Abnormal and Social Psychology, 49*(1), 45–50. https://doi.org/10.1037/h0061913

Feyaerts, J., &Vanheule, S. (2017). Expression and the unconscious. *Frontiers in Psychology, 8.* https://doi.org/10.3389/fpsyg.2017.02162

Field, G. C., Aveling, R., & Laird, J. (1922). Is the conception of the unconscious of value in psychology? *Mind, 31,* 413–442.

Fodor, J. A. (1983). *The modularity of mind.* MIT Press.

Fodor, J. A. (1987). *Psychosemantics: The problem of meaning in the philosophy of mind.* MIT Press.

Fodor, J. A. (1990). *A theory of content and other essays.* MIT Press.

Fodor, J. A. (1994). *The elm and the expert: Mentalese and its semantics.* MIT Press.

Freud, A. (1966). *The ego and the mechanisms of defense.* International Universities Press (Original work published 1936). https://doi.org/10.1017/S1092852915000012

Freud, S. (1900). The interpretation of dreams. Part I. *Standard edition* (Vol. 4, pp. 1–338). Hogarth Press.

Freud, S. (1915). Instincts and their vicissitudes. *Standard edition* (Vol. 14, pp. 117–140). Hogarth Press.

Freud, S. (1915b). The unconscious. *Standard edition.* Hogarth Press (Vol. 14, pp. 166–204).

Freud, S. (1924). Neurosis and psychosis. *Standard edition* (Vol. 19, pp.149–156). London: Hogarth Press.

Freud, S. (1925). Negation. *Standard edition* (Vol. 19, pp. 235–239). Hogarth Press.

Freud, S. (1933). New introductory lectures on psycho-analysis. *Standard edition* (Vol. 22, pp. 5–182). Hogarth Press.

Freud, S. (1938). Some elementary lessons in psycho-analysis. *Standard edition* (Vol. 23, pp. 279–286). Hogarth Press.

Freud, S. (1940 [1938]). An outline of psychoanalysis.*Standard edition* (Vol. 23, pp. 139–207). Hogarth Press.

Gallese, V. (2005). Embodied simulation: From neurons to phenomenal experience. *Phenomenology and the Cognitive Sciences, 4*(1), 23–48. https://doi.org/10.1007/s11097-005-4737-z.

Gettleman, J. (2021, January 5). Climbing the Himalayas with soldiers, spies, lamas and mountaineers. *The New York Times.* https://www.nytimes.com/2021/01/05/books/review/himalaya-a-human-history-ed-douglas.html

Glymour, C. (1991). Freud's androids. In J. Neu (Ed.), *The Cambridge, UK: Cambridge companion to Freud* (pp. 44–48). Cambridge University Press.

Gondra, J. M. (2002). Clark L. Hull y elpsicoanálisis [Hull and psychoanalysis]. *Revista de Historia de la Psicología, 23*(3–4), 371–379.

Gregory, R. (1987). Analogue. *Transactions of the with Adelbert Ames. Perception, 16*(3), 277–282.

Groddeck, G. (2015). *The book of the it.* Martino Fine Books (Original work published 1923).

Gurwitsch, A. (1964). *The Field of consciousness.* Duquesne University Press.

Hacker, P. M. S. (2018). *The passions: A study of human nature.* Wiley-Blackwell.

Hacker, P. M. S., & Bennett, M. R. (2007). The conceptual presuppositions of cognitive neuroscience: A reply to critics. In D. Robinson (Ed.), *Neuroscience & philosophy: Brain, mind, & language* (pp. 127–162). Columbia University Press.

Haggard, P., & Libet, B. (2001). Conscious intention and brain activity. *Journal of Consciousness Studies, 8*(11), 47–63.

Haggard, P., Newman, C., & Magno, E. (1999). On the perceived time of voluntary actions. *British Journal of Psychology, 90*(2), 291–303. https://doi.org/10.1348/000712699161413

Hartmann, H. (1958). *Ego psychology and the problem of adaptation* (D. Rapaport, Trans.). International Universities Press (Original work published 1939). https://doi.org/10.1037/13180-000

Haynes, J.-D., Sakai, K., Rees, G., Gilbert, S., Frith, C., & Passingham, R. E. (2007). Reading intentions in the human brain. *Current Biology, 17*, 323–328.

Helmholtz, H. (1867). *Handbuch der physiologischenOptik.* Voss.

Helson, H. (1964). *Adaptation-level theory: An experimental and systematic approach to behavior.* Harper & Row.

Henle, M. (1979). Phenomenology in Gestalt psychology. *Journal of Phenomenological Psychology, 10*(1), 1–17. https://doi.org/10.1163/156916279X00022

Hirst, R. J. (1967). Primary and secondary qualities. In P. Edwards (Ed.), *The encyclopedia of philosophy.* Macmillan.

Hobbes, T. (1968). *Leviathan.* Penguin (Original work published 1651).

Hume, D. (1975). An enquiry concerning human understanding. In L. A. Selby-Bigge & P. Niddich (Eds.), *Hume's enquiries.* Clarendon Press (Original work published 1748).

Husserl, E. (1983). *Ideas pertaining to a pure phenomenology and to a phenomenological philosophy* (F. Kersten, Trans.). Martinus Nijhoff (Original work published 1913).

Husserl, E. (2001). *Logical investigations* (Vol. 1). Routledge.

James, W. (1890). *The principles of psychology* (Vols. 1–2). Holt.

Kant, E. (1987). *Critique of pure reason* (P. Guyer & A. Wood, Trans.). Cambridge University Press (Original work published 1781).

Koch, C. (2019). *The feeling of life itself: Why consciousness is widespread but can't be computed*. MIT Press.

Köhler, W. (1938). *The place of value in a world of facts*. Kegan, Paul, Trench, Trubner, and Company.

Köhler, W. (1944). Value and fact. *Journal of Philosophy, 41*(8), 197–212.

Kulpe, O. (1895). *Outlines of psychology* (E. B. Titchener, Trans.). Sonnenschein.

Kulpe, O. (1902). The problem of attention. *Monist, 13*(1), 38–68. https://doi.org/10.5840/monist190213130

Lacan, J. (2002). *Ecrits* (B. Fink, Trans.). W. W. Norton. Original work published 1966.

Ladd, G. T. (1887). *Elements of physiological psychology: A treatise of the activities and nature of the mind from the physical and experimental point of view*. Charles Scribner's Sons. https://doi.org/10.1037/10862-000

Lashley, K. S. (1958). Cerebral organization and behavior. *Research Publications of the Association for Research in Nervous & Mental Disease, 36*, 1–18.

Lau, H. C., Rogers, R. D., Haggard, P., & Passingham, R. E. (2004). Attention to intention. *Science, 303*(5661), 1208–1210. https://doi.org/10.1126/science.1090973

Libet, B., Gleason, C. A., Wright, E. W., & Pearl, D. K. (1983). Time of conscious intention to act in relation to onset of cerebral activity (readiness-potential). The unconscious initiation of a freely voluntary act. *Brain: A Journal of Neurology, 106*(3), 623–642. https://doi.org/10.1093/brain/106.3.623

Locke, J. (1894). *Essay concerning human understanding*. Clarendon Press (Original work published 1689).

Makari, G. (2015). *Soul machine: The invention of the modern mind*. W. W. Norton & Company.

Mayr, E. (1961). Cause and effect in biology. *Science, 134*(3489), 1501–1506. https://doi.org/10.1126/science.134.3489.1501

Mayr, E. (1982). *The growth of biological thought*. Harvard University Press.

Mayr, E. (1988). *Toward a new philosophy of biology: Observations of an evolutionist*. Belknap Press of Harvard University Press.

Mayr, E. (1993). Proximate and ultimate causations. *Biology and Philosophy, 8*(1), 93–94.

McClelland, D. C. (1957). Conscience and the will rediscovered. *Contemporary Psychology: A Journal of Reviews, 2*(7), 177–179. https://doi.org/10.1037/005536,0.036.

Merleau-Ponty, M. (1968). *The visible and the invisible*. Northwestern University Press.

Miller, G. A. (1962). *Psychology: The science of mental life*. Harper & Row.

Millikan, R. G. (1984). *Language, thought, and other biological categories: New foundations for realism*. MIT Press.

Moore, M. S. (2018). "Nothing but a pack of neurons": The moral responsibility of the human machine. In *Neurolaw and responsibility for action: Concepts, crimes, and courts* (pp. 28–70). Cambridge University Press.

Moore, M. S. (2020). *Mechanical choices: The responsibility of the human machine*. Oxford University Press.

Moran, R. A. (2001). *Authority and estrangement: An essay on self-knowledge*. Princeton University Press.

Morin, A. (2018). The self-reflective function of inner speech: Thirteen years later. In P. Langland-Hassan & A. Vicente (Eds.), *Inner speech: New voices*. Oxford University Press.

Nagel, T. (1974). What is it like to be a bat? *The Philosophical Review*, *83*(4), 435–450.

Nahmias, E. (2002). When consciousness matters: A critical review of Daniel Wegner's The illusion of conscious will. *Philosophical Psychology*, *15*(4), 527–541. https://doi.org/10.1080/0951508021000042049

Nisbett, R. E., & Wilson, T. D. (1977). The halo effect: Evidence for unconscious alteration of judgments. *Journal of Personality and Social Psychology*, *35*(4), 250–256. https://doi.org/10.1037/0022-3514.35.4.250

Penrose, R. (1994). Shadows of the mind: A search for the missing science of consciousness. Oxford University Press.

Peters, R. (1967). *Hobbes*. Penguin.

Petitot, J., Varela, F. J., Pachoud, B., & Roy, J.-M. (Eds.). (1999). *Naturalizing phenomenology: Issues in contemporary phenomenology and cognitive science*. Stanford University Press.

Rapaport, D. (1960). On the psychoanalytic theory of motivation. In M. Gill (Ed.), *The collected papers of David Rapaport* (pp. 853–915). Basic Books.

Robinson, D. N. (2007). Theoretical psychology: What is it and who needs it? *Theory and Psychology*, *17*(2), 186–198. https://doi.org/10.1177/0959354307075042

Rock, I. (1983). *The logic of perception*. MIT Press.

Rorty, R. (1970). Incorrigibility as the mark of the mental. *Journal of Philosophy*, *67*(12), 399–424.

Roy, J.-M., Petitot, J., Pachoud, B., & Varela, F. J. (1999). Beyond the gap: An introduction to naturalizing phenomenology. In J. Petitot, F. J. Varela, B. Pacoud, & J.-M. Roy (Eds.), *Naturalizing phenomenology*. Stanford University Press.

Rubinstein, B. B. (1997a). Person, organism, and self: Their worlds and their psychoanalytically relevant relationships (1977 [1981] [1969]). *Psychological Issues (62-63)*, 415–445.

Rubinstein, B. B. (1997b). *Psychoanalysis and the philosophy of science: Collected papers of Benjamin B. Rubinstein* (R. R. Holt, Ed.). International Universities Press.

Rumbaugh, D. M., Savage-Rumbaugh, E. S., & Washburn, D. A. (1996). Toward a new outlook on primate learning and behavior: Complex learning and emergent processes in comparative perspective. *The Japanese Psychological Research*, *38*(3), 113–125. https://doi.org/10.1111/j.1468-5884.1996.tb00016.x

Russell, B. A. W. (1948). *Human knowledge: Its scope and limits*. Simon and Schuster.

Schmitt, R. (1967). Phenomenology. In P. Edwards (Ed.), *The encyclopedia of philosophy*, 6. Macmillan.

Searle, J. (2017). Biological naturalism. In S. Schneider & M. Velmans (Eds.), *The Blackwell companion to consciousness*. https://doi.org/10.1002/9781119132363.ch23

Searle, J. R. (1990). Consciousness, explanatory inversion and cognitive science. *Behavioral and Brain Sciences*, *13*(1), 585–642.

Searle, J. R. (1997). *The mystery of consciousness*. The New York Review of Books (Original work published 1990).

Searle, J. R. (1998). How to study consciousness scientifically. *Philosophical Transactions: Biological Sciences*, *353*(1377), 1935–1942. http://www.jstor.org/stable/56909

Sellars, W. S. (1962). Philosophy and the scientific image of man. In R. Colodny (Ed.), *Science, perception, and reality*. Humanities Press. Ridgeview.

Sellars, W. S. (1971). Science, sense impressions, and sensa: A reply to Cornman. *The Review of Metaphysics, 24*(3), 391–447. http://www.jstor.org/stable/20125810

Smith, D. W. (2018). Phenomenology. In *The Stanford Encyclopedia of Philosophy* (E. N. Zalta, Ed.). https://plato.stanford.edu/archives/sum2018/entries/phenomenology/

Snow, C. P. (1990). The two cultures. *Leonardo, 23*(2/3), 169–173. https://doi.org/10.2307/1578601

Spiegelberg, H. (1972). *Phenomenology in psychology and psychiatry: An historical introduction*. Northwestern University Press.

Spinoza, B. D. (1985). Ethics. In E. Curley (Ed. & Trans.), *The collected works of Spinoza*. Princeton University Press.

Stich, S. P. (1992). What is a theory of mental representation? *Mind, New Series, 101*(402), 243–261.

Strawson, G. (2016, May 16). Consciousness isn't a mystery. It's matter. *The New York Times*. https://www.nytimes.com/2016/05/16/opinion/consciousness-isnt-a-mystery-its-matter.html

Strawson, G. (2018, March 13). The consciousness deniers. *The New York Review of Books*. https://www.nybooks.com/daily/2018/03/13/the-consciousness-deniers/

Tae-Chang, J. (2009). Sensation in Merleau-Ponty and Husserl. The 3rd BESETO Conference of Philosophy, Session 2.

Titchener, E. B. (1909). *Lectures on the experimental psychology of the thought-processes*. Macmillan. https://doi.org/10.1037/10877-000

Titchener, E. B. (1910). *A textbook of psychology*. Macmillan.

Varela, F. (1996). Neurophenomenology: A methodological remedy for the hard problem. *Journal of Consciousness Studies, 3*(4), 330–349.

Wakefield, J. C. (2018). *Freud and philosophy of mind: Reconstructing the argument for unconscious mental states*. Springer International Publishing. https://doi.org/10.1007/978-3-319-96343-3

Wegner, D. M. (2002). *The illusion of conscious will*. MIT Press.

Wegner, D. M. (2003). The mind's best trick: How we experience conscious will. *Trends in Cognitive Science, 7*(2), 65–69.

Wegner, D. M. (2008). Self is magic. In J. Baer, J. C. Kaufman, & R. F. Baumeister (Eds.), *Are we free? Psychology and free will* (pp. 226–247). Oxford University Press.

Wiener, M. (1955). Word frequency or motivation in perceptual defense. *The Journal of Abnormal and Social Psychology, 51*(2), 214–218. https://doi.org/10.1037/h0046494

Willett, F. R., Avansino, D. T., Hochberg, L. R., Henderson, J. M., & Shenoy, K. V. (2021). High-performance brain-to-text communication via handwriting. *Nature, 593*(7858), 249–254. https://doi.org/10.1038/s41586-021-03506-2

Willis, P. (2001). The "things themselves" in phenomenology. *Indo-Pacific Journal of Phenomenology, 1*(1), 1–12. https://doi.org/10.1080/20797222.2001.11433860

Wittgenstein, L. (1953). *Philosophical investigations. PhilosophischeUntersuchungen*. Macmillan.

Wittgenstein, L. (1981). *Zettel* (G. E. M. Anscombe, Trans.). University of California Press (Original work published 1967).

Wright, R. (2000). *Nonzero: The logic of human destiny*. Pantheon.

Zahavi, D. (2004). Phenomenology and the project of naturalization. *Phenomenology and the Cognitive Sciences, 3*(4), 331–347.

Chapter 4

Are consciousness and subjective experience uninvestigatable?

Introduction

A familiar behaviorist position, one held by Dennett (1991), is that because it is private, subjective experience is 'uninvestigatable'. That is, one cannot have another's experience; only behavior is observable. Dennett (1991) writes: 'The idea at its simplest was that since you can never "see directly" into people's minds, but have to take their word for it, any such facts as there are about mental events are not among the data of science' (pp. 70–71)

> .....Consciousness, you say, is what matters, but then you cling to doctrines about consciousness that systematically prevent us from getting any purchase on why it matters. Postulating inner qualities that are not only private and intrinsically valuable, but also unconfirmable and uninvestigatable is just obscurantism.
>
> (p. 450)

Although it is, of course true, that one cannot get inside another's head, and cannot have another's experience, one can have an empathic sense of what another person is experiencing. There is a large literature on empathy, including its neural underpinnings (see Eagle, 2022b). However, leaving that issue aside, is it, in fact, the case that consciousness and subjective experience are uninvestigatable? That the presumed uninvestigatability of subjective experience is a pseudo-problem is suggested by the history of valuable research in psychology on the functional relations between reports of first-person experiences and external stimuli, as well as by the large number of studies on the neural correlates of subjective experiences being carried out – without, one might add, getting into debates about the existence of consciousness or whether scientific method is able to accommodate subjective experience.

I already noted the very productive research of psychophysics begun by Fechner (1860) in which the basic method is investigating the functional relations between first-person reports of one's experiences and differences in physical dimensions (e.g., weight, brightness). There is also Muller's (1840) discovery

DOI: 10.4324/9781032686967-5

of specific nerve energies through the investigation of the functional relations between first-person experiences and neural stimulation, as well as the body of research on color vision (e.g., Werner et al., 1998). Consider also the very fruitful work of Gestalt psychologists on the functional relations between external stimulus configurations and phenomenal experience. That even Behaviorism could not get very far in human research without reference to subjective experience is indicated by its need to resort to the evasion of allowing reports of first-person experiences, but referring to them as 'verbal behavior'. In short, the investigation of the lawful relations between replicable reports of first-person experiences and external stimuli as well as between reports of first-person experience and neural activation is well represented in the history of psychology as well as in contemporary research.

Historical empirical investigations of the structure of subjective experience

Psychophysics

As noted above, the early work of Weber and Fechner stands as an early and important example of systematic research on the relation between experience and external stimulus dimensions, the culmination of which resulted in the Weber–Fechner Law. One simple statement of this law is that one's report of a just noticeable difference (jnd) along a particular physical dimension (e.g., weight, brightness) is proportional to the intensity of the initial stimulus. Thus, if the initial stimulus weighs 100 grams and one reports a jnd at 105 grams, then the jnd for a 200-gram object will be 10 grams. Despite some limitations, for example, extreme points on a dimension, the Weber–Fechner Law generally holds for various dimensions. Also, further refinements of the law have been formulated (e.g., Stevens, 1957, 'Power Law'). The main point here is, claims of the uninvestigatability of subjective experience notwithstanding, psychophysics research on reports on subjective experience has not constituted a barrier to productive and important findings on the systematic relations between experience and external stimulus dimensions.

Mach and Gestalt psychology

Mach, who is viewed as a forerunner, if not one of the founders, of Gestalt psychology, was inspired by the psychophysics research of Fechner. His contributions to physics and philosophy are enormous. Indeed, with regard to the former, Einstein referred to 'Mach's Conjecture' in discussing rotational phenomena. However, what I want to take note of in the present context is Mach's emphasis on the primacy of sense experience in science, an emphasis that characterizes the fundamental perspective of Gestalt psychology.[1] The Gestalt psychologists made many important contributions to psychology, among them the formulation of laws (e.g., grouping, pregnanz) governing visual perception. Similar to psychophysics, the research of the Gestalt psychologists stands as a model for the systematic and unconscious mental states and their relation to consciousness.

Unlike the artificializing of experience in Titchener's Structuralism, in which experience is broken down into its presumed elements, as well as unlike Husserlian 'bracketing' and suspension of the natural attitude, the Gestalt psychologists investigated phenomenal experience as it is lived, a fact that accounts for the lasting ecological validity of its findings. It should be added that the Gestalt psychologists were also interested in the relations between experience and brain states, as reflected in their concept of *isomorphism* (more on that below).

Although Gestalt psychology is identified mainly with the investigation of perceptual phenomena, in its emphasis on the primacy of direct immediate experience and its careful use of both description and explanation, its approach can stand as a model for the systematic study of subjective experience. Unlike the research programs of those affiliated with phenomenological psychology, Gestalt psychology has yielded significant findings in our understanding of perceptual experience. Further, although these findings have been generated in the experimental laboratory, they are characterized by a robust ecological validity outside the experimental laboratory situation.

An example of an explanatory concept invoked by Kohler and Koffka that goes beyond phenomenal experience is that of *isomorphism*, which proposes structural similarities among experience, behavior, and brain states. Kohler and Koffka also invoke isomorphism in addressing the issue of knowledge of other minds. More specifically, they hypothesize that there are structural similarities between the state of the person being observed and the inner state of the observer. One can identify two forms of isomorphism in Gestalt theory: intrapersonal and external/interpersonal. Intrapersonal isomorphism refers to similarity in form among an experience (e.g., of an emotion), the expressive movement accompanying the experience, and the corresponding pattern of neural activation. External isomorphism refers to similarity in structure among the perceptual experience of the observer, the object observed, and the neural pattern accompanying the experience.

Of course, given the absence of technical tools (e.g., fMRIs), the hypothesis remained at the level of speculation. However, there is some evidence for intrapersonal isomorphism. Damasio (1994) cites research by Tootell, who

> has shown that when a monkey sees certain shapes, such as a cross or square, the activity of neurons in early visual cortices will be topographically organized in a pattern that conforms to the shape the monkey is viewing. In other words, an independent observer looking at the external stimulus and the brain activity recognizes structural similarity.
>
> (p. 103)

External isomorphism, which is also intended to apply to the perceptual experience of other people, refers to the structural similarity among processes in the observer and the one observed. That is, when one perceives another's expressive movements, neural processes are activated in the observer that are isomorphic with the neural processes accompanying the neural processes accompanying the observed person's expressive movements. As Koffka (1924) writes,

> ... every form of behavior has a certain articulation or phrasing. This articulation issues from a similar articulation of the central nervous processes of the acting individual. This central articulation in turn corresponds to the individual's experience, which is articulated in like manner. Thus, the perception in the mind of an onlooker, if it is so constituted as to embrace what is going on in the agent, must possess a similar articulation. And hence, the experience of Agent A and the observant B must resemble each other.
>
> (pp. 130–131)

As Eagle and Wakefield (2007) observe, the isomorphism hypothesis represents a remarkable anticipation of the mirror neuron discovery of Rizzolatti and Gallese (1996). (See also Gallese, 2016, for a discussion of the links between the concept of isomorphism and the mirror neuron discovery).

In summary, more than any other school of psychology, Gestalt psychology both grants primacy to phenomenal experience and at the same time recognizes the importance of searching for explanatory accounts that attempt to link variations in phenomenal experience to variations in external stimuli as well as to variations in neurophysiological processes. It avoids the extreme of 'pure' phenomenology, on the one hand, and, on the other hand, the extreme of focusing entirely on processes inaccessible to consciousness. In doing so, Gestalt psychology serves as a model for psychological research and theory.

Level of adaptation research and theory

I turn now to another historical example of research and theory on subjective experience that has not been given its adequate due: the important and productive research and theory on the level of adaptation associated with Harry Helson and his colleagues. What is remarkable about this body of work is its applicability to phenomena and processes that range from responses of nerve fibers and sensory and neural systems to perception of external stimuli to social and economic processes to affective processes and reports of satisfaction and happiness. For example, sensory and neural systems adapt to a repeated and constant stimulus and become re-activated when there is a shift in stimulus value – a departure from the current stimulus condition. In other words, the sensory and neural systems adapt to current stimulation and tend to respond to *differences* in stimulation rather – within limits – than absolute magnitude.

With regard to experiences of affect and pleasure, it is a common observation that over time people tend to become adapted to the condition in which they find themselves in various domains, including level of income, status, sexual interest, desirability of purchased objects, and so on. In all these instances, their current state can be viewed as the 'point of indifference'; it is discrepancies from this level that generate affective experience. It is this feature of the level of adaptation that generates what has been referred to as a 'hedonic treadmill' (Brickman & Campbell, 1971, p. 287), that is, a chronic sense of dissatisfaction that may be temporarily relieved by a departure from one's current level of adaptation, only to be reinstated when one adapts to this new level. In a well-known study by Brickman et al. (1978), lottery winners and accident victims – both of whom experienced an event that radically altered their life conditions – were asked to predict what their level of happiness would be no less than one month or no more than one year following, respectively, winning the lottery and being the victim of an accident. The basic finding was that the lottery winners were not as happy as they thought they would be, and the accident victims were not as unhappy as they thought they would be. Each group had adapted over time to the new circumstances in which they found themselves.

The level of adaptation phenomenon also holds for some interpersonal processes such as the trajectory of sexual desire in long-term relationships. There is a good deal of evidence, particularly among males, that the intensity of sexual feelings toward a partner wanes with time and familiarity and is enhanced with novelty (see Eagle, 2007, 2013). This is true for both humans and nonhuman animals. With regard to the latter, as Symons (1979) writes, 'while males of many species are indiscriminate in that they will copulate with any estrous female of their species, they are extremely discriminating in that they recognize females individually, and they are partial to variety and prejudiced against familiarity' (p. 210).

The level of adaptation phenomenon helps one understand certain clinical phenomena that are of much interest in the psychoanalytic context. Let us take another look at the study on lottery winners and accident victims reported by Brickman et al. (1978). Given the virtually inevitable discrepancy between fantasied and actual gratification, it is not surprising that disappointment is not an infrequent experience in regard to the latter. If one has become adapted to a fantasied and unrealistically high level of gratification, the discrepancy from that fantasied level of actual gratification is likely to include the experience of disappointment. Given the ubiquity of fantasy, the 'hedonic treadmill' is not a surprising phenomenon.

Although not immediately obvious, there is a family resemblance between level of adaptation theory and psychoanalytic formulations on the nature of desire associated mainly with Lacan and Freud. The point of convergence lies in the idea of the insatiability of desire. Freud (1920) writes '… it is in the difference in the amount between the pleasure of satisfaction [*lust befreudung*], which is demanded and that which is actually achieved that provides the driving factor which will permit of no holding of any position attained' (p. 42). What Freud is saying here is that due to the difference between the level of satisfaction demanded and anticipated – and one can add, fantasied – and the level of satisfaction actually experienced, the driving force of desire will continue to exert its influence – there will be no 'holding of any position attained'. This statement has a family resemblance to the thesis of level of adaptation theory to the effect that given our tendency to adapt to a given level of satisfaction, desire will never be satiated.

According to Lacan (1966/2002), the so to speak ur-desire is the desire for the lost object: the breast. Other versions of this formulation include Mahler's (1968) concept of the fantasy of symbiotic gratification; and Loewald's (2000) Mahlerian reinterpretation of the Oedipus complex as the conflict between symbiotic union and separation. The link to level of adaptation theory consists in the consideration that given the presumed universal fantasied desire for the lost object and for symbiotic unity, any actual satisfaction will inevitably fall short of the level of satisfaction associated with the fantasied unobtainable desire. There is another aspect of desire discussed by Lacan that carries the implication of its insatiability, namely, living in accord with the desire of the Other. The insatiability of one's desire to please or rescue or revivify the other lies in the likelihood that this desire, which is generally the residue of early experiences with parents, cannot be realistically gratified. This is generally an ungratifiable fantasy rather than a desire that can be fulfilled by particular actions.

To sum up, just as the findings of psychophysics and of the research of the Gestalt psychologists reveal aspects of the structure of experience in relation to external stimuli, the level of adaptation research sheds light on the structure of experience not only in relation to external stimuli, but also in relation to the experience of desire, expectation, pleasure, affect, and happiness. It should be noted that the research on psychophysics, the work of the Gestalt psychologists on perception, and the level of adaptation research constitute a very different way of thinking about the structure of experience from the Structuralist approach of Titchener and the bracketing and suspension of the natural attitude of Husserl's phenomenology.

Contemporary research on various aspects of subjective experience

The structure of experience: the binding problem

As noted in the earlier chapters, a fundamental quality of subjective experience is that we normally experience a coherent world of distinct and unified objects in specific locations rather than a jumble of disconnected features of objects (e.g., colors, shapes, locations). Although there is evidence that different features of an object are encoded by different brain modules, we nevertheless subjectively experience a unified object. How we 'bind' these different features of an object into the unified experience of a separate, delineated object that is different from other objects; how this fundamental structure of the unity of perceptual experience is achieved is the 'binding problem' (originally named by von der Malsburg, 1981). The binding problem is not limited to perception, but also includes memory and cognition. Insofar as we do not fully understand how binding comes about, it is referred to as the 'binding problem'. However, I will also refer to it as the 'binding phenomenon' insofar as it is a fundamental property of the structure of experience.[2,3]

There is a large and robust research and theoretical literature on various aspects of the binding phenomenon. There is evidence that figure-ground perception, which can be viewed as a form of binding is present at birth and that perception of a unified object is present at four months of age (Kellman & Spelke, 1983) and possibly as early as two months of age (Johnson, 2001). There is also evidence that newborn chicks are capable of binding color and shape features into integrated representations (Wood, 2014). A number of processes, for example, attentional mechanisms (e.g., Wolfe & Cave, 1999) and temporal synchrony (e.g., Gray, 1999) have been proposed to account for binding phenomena.

Investigation of the binding phenomenon, including identification of underlying neural processes, is a quintessential example of a research project, the starting point of which lies in an attempt to understand a fundamental property of the structure of experience. Were one to accept the proposition that our subjective experiences are nothing but assemblies of neural cells, the idea of an investigation of binding phenomena would never get off the ground. It is the existence of as well as the attempt to understand a phenomenal property of subjective experience that motivates and guides our search for identifying underlying neural processes. This kind of work should put to rest any claim that because they are private and not publicly accessible, subject experience is 'uninvestigatable' by scientific means.

Binding and the environment

Hubel and Wiesel (1959, 1962) demonstrated that there are neurons that encode distinct visual features such as the orientation of a line (e.g., horizontal or vertical). Based on their work, Blasdel et al. (1977) reported that compared to kittens raised in a normal visual environment, kittens raised in an environment that consisted of stripes at one of three orientations – horizontal, left oblique, or right oblique – showed 'a deficit in visual acuity for orientations that were not present in the early visual environment' (p. 615). These and other findings, which can be understood as a form of synaptic priming, suggest that the particular visual features that are encoded and 'bound' together are influenced by the early environment. In other words, it is not only that we bind features of the environment to 'construct' a unified object, but also that the nature of the environment to which one is exposed, particularly during critical periods in development, influences which features are available to be combined. Thus, it is not simply, as the philosopher Nelson Goodman suggests, that we construct objects by cutting the world at different seams, but also that the nature of the world to which we are exposed sets limits on the seams at which it can be cut. It is also worth noting that the seams at which the world is cut are different for different species. For example, what is an object for a bat, as well as the specific features that are combined to yield the experience of a unified object, are very different from the nature of the experienced object for human beings. Each species is adapting to its specific environmental niche of experienced objects.

Binding and psychopathology

We can observe the effects on subjective experience of impairments in binding neural processes in pathological conditions such as schizophrenia. For example, Burglen et al. (2004) reported that compared to healthy controls, schizophrenic individuals show disproportionate poorer memory performance when the task requires a form of binding (i.e., remembering the combined object and its location) compared to remembering individual features (i.e., an object or its location alone). Waters et al. (2004) showed that whereas healthy controls were able to identify both the source and the temporal context of events, schizophrenic individuals 'tended to have a more fractionated recollection of those events' (p. 119). In a review of the literature, Wallace and Stevenson (2014) reported that along with autistic and dyslexic individuals, schizophrenic patients show impairments in multisensory temporal binding, an ability, as the authors point out, that is critical in perception.[4]

According to Uhlhaas and Mishara (2007), phenomenological data suggest that a fundamental dysfunction in schizophrenia is a relative 'deficit in the ability to combine stimulus elements into coherent object representations' (p. 142), which in turn, is linked to altered self-experience and the emergence of delusions. One consequence of this basic dysfunction is the failure to perceive objects in meaningful relationships with each other. As one patient puts it, 'Everything I see is split up. It's like a photograph that's torn in bits and pieces' (p. 144). Uhlhaas and Mishara (2007) refer to Matussek's (1952/1987) emphasis on altered perceptual experiences that are 'the result of the accentuation of the object's *expressive* qualities' (p. 144) in schizophrenia. Expressive aspects of the object become salient independently of their natural contexts.

Other aspects of the experiential world of the schizophrenic individual noted by Uhlhaas and Mishara (2007) include loss of continuity of experiences, a sense of disconnection between oneself and the world, loss of experience of the *affordances* of objects, such as their use as tools, or obstacles, or objects of desire, hyper reflexive forms of awareness along with experience of aspects of oneself as if one were an external object. Uhlhaas and Mishara (2007) cite evidence of a relationship between impairments in perceptual organization and dysfunctional neural synchronization. They conclude that taking account of the nature of the schizophrenic individual's subjective experience can 'guide the search for the underlying cognitive and neurophysiological dysfunctions associated with this disorder' (p. 152).

Autobiographical accounts of recovered individuals are a rich source of information on the nature of subjective experience in schizophrenic individuals. One such classic account, written by Renee and noted earlier, is entitled *Autobiography of a Schizophrenic Girl* (1951), accompanied by an account by her therapist (Sechahaye, 1951). Renee's account includes breakdowns in perception itself, such as the experience of features of her friend's face as separate from each other, and the loss of perceptual perspective. Other experiential anomalies she reports include hearing voices as metallic, loss of the meaning of words, and external scenes having no coherent meaning. While some philosophers debate whether or not subjective experience can be accommodated by a physicalist scientific worldview, one can pick up virtually any current psychological journal and find empirical investigations a central feature of which includes the reporting of data on various aspects of subjective experience as well as the factors that influence experience. For example, just before sitting down to write this section, I received the latest issue of *Psychological Science, 32*(8). There are at least six articles in the issue dealing with subjective experience, including the experience of empathy; judgments of the relationship between expressions of anger and guilt or innocence; global variations in subjective well-being and their relation to altruism; timed and untimed experience of visual illusions; and size discrimination and size constancy.

Let me provide in somewhat greater detail a few specific examples of research on various aspects of subjective experience. These studies are not selected because they are representative of any particular approach. They are merely intended to provide the reader with some illustrations of ordinary empirical research that includes findings on different aspects of subjective experience. The studies I have selected have in common that they deal with the relation between different aspects of subjective experience (e.g., affective experiences; experience of meaning in life) and various other factors (e.g., health outcomes; mortality).

The effects of adversity on health outcomes

Much has been learned regarding the neurodevelopmental effects of various forms of childhood adversity. For example, childhood adversity is associated with disrupted functioning of the hypothalamic–pituitary–adrenal (HPAP) axis, the autonomic nervous system, and the immune system (Smith & Pollak, 2020). However, as Smith and Pollak (2020) observe, different forms of adversity may influence different aspects of development. Most important in the present context, they also note the possibility 'that the individual's perception of the event is more influential than the features of the event itself …'; and that 'perceived adversity, and its associated neurobiological responses, can occur in the absence of any specific identifiable event …' (p. 76). Their examples of such phenomena are 'rumination over previous experiences or events or anxiety about future events …' (p. 76). Of course, one would want to know what accounts for individual differences in perceived adversity of a given event. However, whatever the factors that account for such differences (e.g., temperament), the fact remains that subjective perceptions play a significant role in a causal chain.

There is a good deal of evidence that the experience of negative affect as a reaction to daily stressors is associated with mental and physical illness as well as mortality (Cacioppo, 1998; Charles et al., 2013; Mroczek et al., 2015). There is also evidence that rumination about the stressors is associated with negative health outcomes (Brosschot et al., 2006). In a ten-year longitudinal study involving a large community sample (N = 1,155), Leger et al. (2018) reported that lingering negative affect a day after the stressful experience was associated with negative health outcomes ten years later. As the authors note, ruminating and lingering negative affect is likely to activate the same physiological reactions as the stressors themselves. Thus, 'research has documented that the tendency to perseverate on stressful experiences with prolonged activation of the cardiovascular system (Brosschot et al., 2006; Glynn et al., 2002) and the hypothalamic–pituitary–adrenal axis Zoccola and Dickerson, 2012)' (p. 1288). Leger et al. (2018) note that poorer health outcomes associated with negative affect may also be attributable to poorer health behaviors (e.g., less physical activity, poor eating habits) that often accompany negative moods.

Complementing the above study, Stewart et al. (2019) reported that the experience of positive affect served as a buffer between the experience of chronic stress symptom severity of anxiety and depression. Whereas positive affect significantly moderated the effects of chronic interpersonal stress on subsequent social anxiety disorder (SAD) and major depressive disorder (MDD), it did not moderate the effects of noninterpersonal stress on symptom severity in SAD, MDD, or generalized anxiety disorder (GAD). However, in accord with the Leger et al. (2018) findings, negative affect enhanced the effects of noninterpersonal stress on MDD symptom severity. There is also evidence that positive affect reduces the physiological effects of negative emotion (Frederickson, 2004; Ong et al., 2006). Also, just as negative affect leads to poorer health behaviors, Stewart et al. (2019) suggest that one of the ways positive affect serves as a buffering effect is that it tends to generate more socially adaptive behaviors (e.g., seeking social support).

Relationship between sense of meaning in life and health outcomes

There are a large number of studies on the relationship between experienced meaning in life and a number of other variables, including reported well-being across different ages and cultures (e.g., McMahon & Renken, 2011; Ho et al., 2010; Scannell et al., 2002); Garcia-Alandete, 2015; Reker et al., 1987). There is evidence that the desire for symbolic immortality fully mediated the relationship between generativity and well-being. There is also evidence that diary reports of subjective well-being within an individual varied as a function of the degree of success in areas valued by the individual (Oishi et al., 1999; Huta & Zuroff, 2007). Schnell and Krampke (2020) reported that meaning in life and a sense of self-control served as buffers against stress related to COVID-19 as well as general anxiety and depression. There is also evidence of a significant association between meaning in life and mortality. In a longitudinal study with people aged 65 and older, Krause (2009) found that 'older people with a strong sense of meaning in life are less likely to die over the study follow-up period than those who do not have a strong sense of meaning' (p. 517).

There are a number of factors that mediate the relationship between meaning and mortality. For example, Krause (2007) has focused on the stress-buffering effects of meaning; and Park (2007) suggests that meaning is related to the likelihood of engaging in health behaviors. As Krause (2009) observes, if meaning affects health, it must be linked to physiological factors. There is some evidence that meaning is associated with increased immune functioning (Bower et al., 2003). After reviewing research in this area, Salovey et al. (2000) conclude that the beneficial effects of meaning on immune functioning is at least partly accounted for by the fact that positive affect is associated with meaning (see also Reker, 2000).

The important point to be noted in the present context is that in the above studies, experiential variables – positive and negative affect, a sense of meaning in life, experience of well-being – are critical in understanding some vital aspects of one's life, including dealing with stressors, health outcomes, and mortality. Without the inclusion of these experiential variables, our understanding of reactions to stress, health outcomes, and mortality would be more poorly understood. Further, it is clear in these studies that the effects of the experiential variables on health outcomes are mediated through physiological processes accompanying various experiences. If the researchers in this area ruminated over the problem that positing effects of experience on physiological processes constituted dualism, or over the impossibility of investigating subjective experience, or of the impossibility of obtaining reliable and valid reports of subjective experience, these investigations would never have been undertaken.

In the light of ordinary studies such as those summarized above, the discussion or such issues as the dissimulating and/or epiphenomenal nature of consciousness and subjective experience or the question of the differences between 'zombies' and human beings takes on a different hue. The above findings indicate that the experience of negative and positive affect is part of a complex causal chain related to health and illness outcomes, including life and death. Furthermore, insofar as the experience of affect is influenced not simply by events themselves, but also by the individual's *construal* of events (i.e., the individual's psychic reality), the sheer inadequacy of explanations limited to environmental stimuli and neural activity becomes evident.

Notes

1 What has been referred to as Mach's Sensationalism was not shared by the Gestalt psychologists, whose focus was on the perception of the object as a whole gestalt rather than on sensations as the presumed elements of perception (Mach, 1886). In this regard, Mach's perspective was more in line with Berkeley, Hume, & Locke. Another

way in which Mach's perspective differs from that of the Gestalt psychologists is his belief that precise description constitutes scientific explanation. As Alexander (1967) notes, this position reflects Mach's 'hostility to the metaphysical' (p. 118). This position also reflects the phenomenological bent of the Mach of the Vienna Circle. Indeed, Husserl commented approvingly of Mach's emphasis on experience.

2 In their attempt to lay bare the presumed elements of experience, Titchener's trained introspection and Husserl's bracketing and suspension of the natural attitude can be thought of as, in effect, constituting efforts at *unbinding* what is normally bound together in ordinary perception. Among the problems of such efforts noted earlier, one can add the confusion of levels of discourse. In ordinary perception of an external object, the presumed elements of experience, for example, color and shape, are not experienced separately and then combined to yield the perception of, say, a red ball. As the Gestalt psychologists recognized, one experiences a red ball as a unified object. Also, insofar as Titchener asked his subjects to report fragmented features of objects, he was asking them, in effect, to take on an attitude that is more representative of pathological rather than normal experience.

3 Di Lollo (2012) has argued that the binding problem is moot because brain modules assumed to be independent 'are now known to code jointly for multiple features' (p. 317). However, even if it could be definitively shown that joint coding occurs, one would nevertheless need to identify the processes involved in 'binding' the features together into a coherent object. Indeed, Di Lollo himself proposes a 'hierarchical reentrant system [that] explains the emergence of coherent visual objects from primitive features' (p. 317).

4 There is a family resemblance between fragmented experience in schizophrenia and the pre-binding 'raw' units of experience that Titchener and Husserl appear to want to capture.

References

Alexander, P. (1967). Ernst mach. In P. Edwards (Ed.), *The encyclopedia of philosophy* (Vol. 5, pp. 115–119). Macmillan.

Blasdel, G., Mitchell, D. E., Muir, D. W., & Pettigrew, J. D. (1977). A physiological and behavioural study in cats of the effect of early visual experience with contours of a single orientation. *Journal of Physiology, 265*(3), 615–636.

Bower, J. E., Kemeny, M. E., Taylor, S. E., & Fahey, J. L. (2003). Finding positive meaning and its association with natural killer cell cytotoxicity among participants in a bereavement-related disclosure intervention. *Annals of Behavioral Medicine, 25*(2), 146–155.

Brickman, P., & Campbell, D. T. (1971). Hedonic relativism and planning the good society. In M. H. Appley (Ed.), *Adaptation-level theory* (pp. 287–305). Academic Press.

Brickman, P., Coates, D., & Janoff-Bulman, R. (1978). Lottery winners and accident victims: Is happiness relative? *Journal of Personality and Social Psychology, 36*(8), 917–927. https://doi.org/10.1037/0022-3514.36.8.917

Brosschot, J. F., Gerin, W., & Thayer, J. F. (2006). The perseverative cognition hypothesis: A review of worry, prolonged stress-related physiological activation, and health. *Journal of Psychosomatic Research, 60*(2), 113–124. https://doi.org/10.1016/j.jpsychores.2005.06.074

Burglen, F., Marczewski, P., Mitchell, K. J., van der Linden, M., Johnson, M. K., Danion, J.-M., & Salamé, P. (2004). Impaired performance in a working memory binding task in patients with schizophrenia. *Psychiatry Research, 125*(3), 247–255. https://doi.org/10.1016/j.psychres.2003.12.014

Cacioppo, J. T., Ito, T. A., Larsen, J. T., & Smith, N. K. (1998). Negative information weighs more heavily on the brain: The negativity bias in evaluative categorizations. *Journal of Personality and Social Psychology, 75*(4), 887–900. https://doi.org/10.1037/0022-3514.75.4.887

Charles, S. T., Piazza, J. R., Mogle, J., Sliwinski, M. J., & Almeida, D. M. (2013). The wear and tear of daily stressors on mental health. *Psychological Science, 24*(5), 733–741. https://doi.org/10.1177/0956797612462222

Damasio, A. R. (1994). *Descartes' error: Emotion, reason, and the human brain*. Putnam.

Dennett, D. C. (1991). *Consciousness explained*. Penguin.

Di Lollo, V. (2012). The feature-binding problem is an ill-posed problem. *Trends in Cognitive Sciences, 16*(6), 317–321. https://doi.org/10.1016/j.tics.2012.04.007

Eagle, M. N. (2022). Two visions of psychoanalysis: An essay in memory of Carlo Strenger. *Psychoanalytic Psychology, 39*(1), 27–36. https://doi.org/10.1037/pap0000394

Eagle, M. N., & Wakefield, J. C. (2007). Gestalt psychology and the mirror neuron discovery. *Gestalt Theory, 29*(1), 59–64.

Fechner, G. T. (1860). *Elemente der Psychophysik [elements of psychophysics]* (Vol. 2). Breitkopf und Härtel.

Fredrickson, B. L. (2004). The broaden-and-build theory of positive emotions. *Philosophical Transactions of the Royal Society of London Series B, Biological sciences, 359*(1449), 1367–1378. https://doi.org/10.1098/rstb.2004.1512

Freud, S. (1920). Beyond the pleasure principle. In *Standard edition* (Vol. 18, pp. 7–64). Hogarth Press.

Gallese, V. (2016). The multimodal nature of visual perception: Facts and speculations. *Gestalt Theory, 38*(2/3), 127–140.

Gallese, V., & Goldman, A. (1998). Mirror neurons and the simulation theory of mind-reading. *Trends in Cognitive Sciences, 2*(12), 493–501. https://doi.org/10.1016/s1364-6613(98)01262-5

García-Alandete, J. (2015). Does meaning in life predict psychological well-being? An analysis using the Spanish versions of the purpose-in-life test and the Ryff's Scales. *The European Journal of Counselling Psychology, 3*(2), 89–98. https://doi.org/10.23668/psycharchives.2014

Glynn, L. M., Christenfeld, N., & Gerin, W. (2002). The role of rumination in recovery from reactivity: Cardiovascular consequences of emotional states. *Psychosomatic Medicine, 64*(5), 714–726. https://doi.org/10.1097/01.PSY.0000031574.42041.23

Gray, C. M. (1999). The temporal correlation hypothesis of visual feature integration. *Neuron, 24*(1), 31–47.

Ho, M. Y., Cheung, F. M., & Cheung, S. F. (2010). The role of meaning in life and optimism in promoting well-being. *Personality and Individual Differences, 48*(5), 658–663. https://doi.org/10.1016/j.paid.2010.01.008

Hubel, D. H., & Wiesel, T. N. (1959). Receptive fields of single neurons in the cat's striate cortex. *The Journal of Physiology, 148*(3), 574–591. https://doi.org/10.1113/jphysiol.1959.sp006308

Hubel, D. H., & Wiesel, T. N. (1962). Receptive fields, binocular interaction and functional architecture in the cat's visual cortex. *The Journal of Physiology, 160*(1), 106–154. https://doi.org/10.1113/jphysiol.1962.sp006837

Huta, V., & Zuroff, D. C. (2007). Examining mediators of the link between generativity and well-being. *Journal of Adult Development, 14*(1–2), 47–52. https://doi.org/10.1007/s10804-007-9030-7

Johnson, S. P. (2001). Visual development in human infants: Binding features, surfaces, and objects. *Visual Cognition, 8*(3–5), 565–578. https://doi.org/10.1080/13506280143000124

Kellman, P. J., & Spelke, E. S. (1983). Perception of partly occluded objects in infancy. *Cognitive Psychology, 15*(4), 483–524. https://doi.org/10.1016/0010-0285(83)90017-8

Koffka, K. (1924). *Growth of the mind*. Harcourt Brace.

Krause, N. (2007). Self-Expression and depressive symptoms in late life. *Research on Aging, 29*(3), 187–206. https://doi.org/10.1177/0164027506298226

Krause, N. (2009). Meaning in life and mortality. *The Journals of Gerontology: Series B: Psychological Sciences and Social Sciences, 64*(4), 517–527.

Lacan, J. (2002). *Ecrits* (B. Fink, Trans.). W. W. Norton. (Original work published 1966).

Leger, K. A., Charles, S. T., & Almeida, D. M. (2018). Let it go: Lingering negative affect in response to daily stressors is associated with physical health years later. *Psychological Science, 29*(8), 1283–1290. https://doi.org/10.1177/0956797618763097

Loewald, H. W. (2000). The waning of the Oedipus complex: Introduction. *The Journal of Psychotherapy Practice and Research, 9*(4), 238.

Mach, E. (1886). *Contributions to the analysis of the sensations. Classics in psychology, 1855–1914*. Thoemmes Continuum.

Mahler, M. (1968). *On human symbiosis and the vicissitudes of human individuation*. International Universities Press.

Matussek, P. (1987). Studies in delusional perception (translated and condensed). In J. Cutting & M. Sheppard (Eds.), *Clinical roots of the schizophrenia concept: Translations of seminal European contributions on schizophrenia*. Cambridge University Press. (Original work published 1952).

McMahan, E. A., & Renken, M. D. (2011). Eudaimonic conceptions of well-being, meaning in life, and self-reported well-being: Initial test of a mediational model. *Personality and Individual Differences, 51*(5). http://doi.org/10.1016/j.paid.2011.05.020

Mroczek, D. K., Stawski, R. S., Turiano, N. A., Chan, W., Almeida, D. M., Neupert, S. D., & Spiro, A. (2015). Emotional reactivity and mortality: Longitudinal findings from the VA normative aging study. *The Journals of Gerontology: Series B, Psychological Sciences and Social Sciences, 70*(3), 398–406. https://doi.org/10.1093/geronb/gbt107

Muller, J. P. (1840). *Handbuch der physiologie des menschen* (2 vols.). Bal42. J. Holscher.

Oishi, S., Diener, E. F., Lucas, R. E., & Suh, E. M. (1999). Cross-cultural variations in predictors of life satisfaction: Perspectives from needs and values. *Personality and Social Psychology Bulletin, 25*(8), 980–990. https://doi.org/10.1177/01461672992511006

Ong, A. D., Bergeman, C. S., Bisconti, T. L., & Wallace, K. A. (2006). Psychological resilience, positive emotions, and successful adaptation to stress in later life. *Journal of Personality and Social Psychology, 91*(4), 730–749. https://doi.org/10.1037/0022-3514.91.4.730

Park, N., & Peterson, C. (2007). Methodological issues in positive psychology and the assessment of character strengths. In A. D. Ong & M. H. M. van Dulmen (Eds.), *Oxford handbook of methods in positive psychology* (pp. 292–305). Oxford University Press.

Reker, G. T. (2000). Theoretical perspective, dimensions, and measurement of existential meaning. In G. T. Reker & K. Chamberlain (Eds.), *Exploring existential meaning: Optimizing human development across the life span* (pp. 39–58). Sage Publications.

Reker, G. T., Peacock, E. J., & Wong, P. T. (1987). Meaning and purpose in life and well-being: A life-span perspective. *Journal of Gerontology*, *42*(1), 44–49. https://doi.org/10.1093/geronj/42.1.44

Rizzolatti, G., Fadiga, L., Gallese, V., & Fogassi, L. (1996). Premotor cortex and the recognition of motor actions. *Brain Research. Cognitive Brain Research*, *3*(2), 131–141. https://doi.org/10.1016/0926-6410(95)00038-0

Salovey, P., Rothman, A. J., Detweiler, J. B., & Steward, W. T. (2000). Emotional states and physical health. *American Psychologist*, *55*(1), 110–121. https://doi.org/10.1037/0003-066X.55.1.110

Scannell, E. D., Allen, F. C. L., & Burton, J. (2002). Meaning in life and positive and negative well-being. *North American Journal of Psychology*, *4*(1), 93–112.

Schnell, T., & Krampe, H. (2020). Meaning in life and self-control buffer stress in times of COVID-19: Moderating and mediating effects with regard to mental distress. *Frontiers in Psychiatry*, *11*, 983. https://doi.org/10.3389/fpsyt.2020.582352

Sechehaye, M. (1951). *Autobiography of a schizophrenic girl: Reality lost and gained, with analytic interpretation* (G. Rubin-Rabson, Trans.). Grune & Stratton. https://doi.org/10.1037/11511-000

Sewart, A. R., Zbozinek, T. D., Hammen, C., Zinbarg, R. E., Mineka, S., & Craske, M. G. (2019). Positive affect as a buffer between chronic stress and symptom severity of emotional disorders. *Clinical Psychological Science*, *7*(5), 914–927. https://doi.org/10.1177/2167702619834576

Smith, K. E., & Pollak, S. D. (2020). Early life stress and development: Potential mechanisms for adverse outcomes. *Journal of Neurodevelopmental Disorders*, *12*(1), 34. https://doi.org/10.1186/s11689-020-09337-y

Stevens, S. S. (1957). On the psychophysical law. *Psychological Review*, *64*(3), 153–181. https://doi.org/10.1037/h0046162, PMID: 13441853.

Symons, D. (1979). *The evolution of human sexuality*. Oxford University Press.

Uhlhaas, P. J., & Mishara, A. L. (2007). Perceptual anomalies in schizophrenia: Integrating phenomenology and cognitive neuroscience. *Schizophrenia Bulletin*, *33*(1), 142–156. https://doi.org/10.1093/schbul/sbl047

von der Malsburg, C. (1981). *The correlation theory of brain function* (Internal Report) (Vol. 81, No. 2). Department of Neurobiology, Max Plank Institute of Biophysikal Chemistry.

Waters, F. A., Maybery, M. T., Badcock, J. C., & Michie, P. T. (2004). Context memory and binding in schizophrenia. *Schizophrenia Research*, *68*(2–3), 119–125. https://doi.org/10.1016/S0920-9964(03)00221-4

Weber, E. H. (1834). *De pulsu, resorptione, auditu et tactu. Anatationesanatomicae et physiologicae*. Koehler.

Wolfe, J. M., & Cave, K. R. (1999). The psychophysical evidence for a binding problem in human vision. *Neuron*, *24*(1), 11–125. https://doi.org/10.1016/s0896-6273(00)80818-1

Wood, J. N. (2014). Newly hatched chicks solve the visual binding problem. *Psychological Science*, *25*(7), 1475–1481. https://doi.org/10.1177/0956797614528955

Zoccola, P. M., & Dickerson, S. S. (2012). Assessing the relationship between rumination and cortisol: A review. *Journal of Psychosomatic Research*, *73*(1), 1–9. https://doi.org/10.1016/j.jpsychores.2012.03.007

Chapter 5

Intersubjective experience

Initially, I considered labeling this chapter 'Intersubjectivity', a topic that has exploded in the recent philosophical and psychoanalytic literature. However, the term 'intersubjectivity' is embedded – I am tempted to say mired – in complex and often obtuse debates as to what the term means. There is a bewildering array of different meanings in the literature (e.g., see Bohleber, 2013; Schwartz, 2012). Although it may be difficult to altogether avoid semantic debates, I can try to avoid becoming bogged down in them by using the simpler title 'Intersubjective experience', by which I refer mainly to the question of how one person experiences and understands another person, like oneself, as an intentional being whose actions are inextricably linked to his or her mental states, that is, intentions, desires, aims, emotions, and so on.

Whereas the previous chapters were largely taken up with a discussion of consciousness and subjective experience in the context of individual experience of external inanimate as well of one's inner world (of desires, wishes, intentions, and motives), this chapter is concerned with the question of how we experience and understand another person. We are social beings who live in a social world in which many, if not most, of our significant experiences in our daily lives take place in the context of interaction with others. No discussion of consciousness and subjective experience could be even remotely adequate if it did not devote at least some attention to intersubjective experience.

A set of readily observable facts stand out regarding intersubjective experience or, if one prefers, the nature of intersubjectivity. The default situation for most people is that one generally experiences the other person as, like oneself, an intentional being whose behavior is linked to his or her mental states (i.e., intentions, desires, and motives). Although there is much room for error, one routinely understands the mental states of the other person, a capacity vital for social interaction. There is much evidence that some early form of this capacity, a form of affective attunement, what Trevarthen (1979) refers to as 'primary intersubjectivity', is already present in infancy (see R. Eagle, 2007; Hobson, 1993; Stern, 1985). As R. Eagle (2007) notes, affective communication extends to the infant's '*making things happen in and by another person*' [emphasis in original] (p. 169). There is also some evidence that the mirror neuron system is operative in early infancy

DOI: 10.4324/9781032686967-6

(Simpson et al., 2014). How do the different disciplines discussed in the previous chapters deal with intersubjective experience, that is, with the issue of how we experience and understand others is the focus of this chapter.[1]

Intersubjective experience and reductionism

If, as Crick (1994) maintains, all our joys and sorrows are nothing but assemblies of neural cells; if, as Chater (2018) writes, motives and desires do not exist; and if, as proposed by Dennett (1986), we ceased all talk of minds and mental events, it would follow that not only are our experiences of ourselves as agents illusory, but also that our experiences of others as intentional beings, are illusory.[2] On a 'nothing but' reductionist view, social interaction and relations are replaced by one assembly of neural cells interacting with and relating to another assembly of neural cells. It is not at all clear as to what living in such a world would be like. However, it would certainly not be a world in which persons as intentional beings understand and relate to each other. Further, the empirical question of how such understanding and relating among persons comes about would disappear from view.

Intersubjective experience and phenomenology

Although Husserl (1931) appears to have coined the term 'intersubjectivity', a Husserlian phenomenological perspective fares no better in dealing with the question of how we experience and understand each other than nothing but reductionism. As noted in Chapter 3, the overriding aim of the Husserlian phenomenological project is to reach the (presumed) fundamental elements of consciousness through bracketing and suspension of the natural attitude. I have already discussed some problems with this approach in regard to the individual's experience of inanimate objects. It seems to me that the problems are magnified with regard to experiencing, and understanding another person. We know that in the context of intersubjective experience, the natural attitude is to experience the other as a person, that is, as an intentional being whose behaviors and actions are linked to and given meaning by reference to inner mental states of intentions, desires, and motives It is not clear what bracketing and suspension of the natural attitude would mean in the context of this spontaneous intersubjective experience. Would it entail, for example, the experience of fragmented, disconnected movements rather than of an integrated intentional action?

Grayling (2019), along with others, raises the question: 'How is intersubjectivity possible if the fundamental conditions of "lived experience" are so deep in subjectivity?' (p. 475). A similar question is raised by Hall (1976), who writes that

> Transcendental subjectivity, as the locus of all possible constituting acts and constituting meanings has no 'outside'. The phenomenologist encounters

nothing 'beyond' the (ideal) unities of meaning constituted within transcendental consciousness. Transcendental phenomenology is, in this sense, a transcendental idealism … But it is, in this same sense, a transcendental solipsism as well.

(p. 53) (see Zahavi, 2004, for a different view)

Late in his writings, particularly in his Fifth Cartesian Meditation, Husserl (1929/1960) (see also Husserl, 1929–1935) attempted to deal with the solipsistic implications of his phenomenological approach of bracketing and suspension of the natural attitude by asserting that consciousness, in Grayling's (2019) words, 'has an essential communal dimension' (p. 475). That is, prior to any theorizing about individual experience, we live in a 'life-world', 'a social, political, historical environment in which people interact with each other' (Grayling, 2019, p. 476). There is much more, of course, to be said about this topic. However, the point I want to make here is that statements such as consciousness has a communal dimension and that we live in an interactional 'life-world' do not, themselves, tell us very much regarding the fundamental question of how we routinely understand each other (see Carr, 1973, for a further discussion of Husserl's approach to intersubjectivity).

Intersubjective experience in psychoanalytic theories

One might expect that a psychoanalytic perspective would place a great deal of emphasis on intersubjective experience, including on the question of how we normally understand each other. As I have discussed elsewhere (Eagle, 2022), this is not the case in any straightforward way. Although perhaps exaggerated, I think Laing (1967) correctly identifies some serious concerns when he writes that

the metapsychology of Freud, Federn, Rapaport, Hartmann, Kris has no constructs for any social system generated by more than one person at a time … This theory has no category of 'you' … It has no way of expressing the meeting of an 'I' with 'another, and the impact of one person on another'.

(p. 149)

To the extent that Freudian theory deals with intersubjective experience, it does so in a problematic way. As Friedman (1995), the biographer of Buber notes,

the 'theory of ideology' which has become prominent through the influence of Marx, Nietzsche, and Freud – Ricoeur's (1970) three 'masters of suspicion' consists in seeing through and unmasking the other in terms of individual psychology or sociology. One assumes that the other dissembles of necessity and looks for the unconscious motive, 'complex', or group interest that clothes itself in his seemingly objective judgment.

(p. 125)

A conception of consciousness as dissimulating and therefore requiring unmasking inevitably results in, as Buber puts it, a mistrust between man and man that becomes existentially normative. Thus, as is implicit in Buber's reasoning, the source of the problems between man and man is not limited to an I–It relationship, but also includes a particular form of an I-Thou relationship, one saturated with mutual suspicion. That is, although one may experience another as a Thou rather than an It, the Thou that is experienced is a Thou with malevolent intentions and motives, including many to which he or she has no conscious access. Thus, ordinary interactions, including overtly benevolent ones, cannot be taken at face value by either the agent of the behavior or the other to whom the behavior is directed – unconscious intentions and motives that are anything but benevolent may be lurking and may represent what 'is really going on' in the interpersonal interaction.

Whatever explicit concern for interpersonal experience and understanding is shown in psychoanalytic theories, it is mainly limited to the clinical situation, and in particular, to the analyst's understanding of the patient. For example, as can be seen in Bolognini's (2004) documentation, virtually all references to empathy in the psychoanalytic literature are concerned with the analyst's understanding of the patient.[3] The few exceptions are concerned with mother-child interactions.

As for the patient, given the posited ubiquity of transference, the emphasis is on relative *failure* of understanding.[4] Outside the clinical context, although there are scattered comments here and there in the psychoanalytic literature, there is little or no systematic formulation on the question of how we normally and routinely understand each other. For example, to the extent that Freud comments on the issue at all, he writes 'that other people, too, possess a consciousness is an inference which we draw by analogy from their observable utterances and actions, in order to make this behavior of theirs intelligible to us' (Freud, 1915, p. 169).

There are a number of considerations that account for this relative lack of interest in the ordinary understanding of each other in everyday life. One consideration is apparent in the very definition of psychoanalysis as a study of the unconscious, and its subject matter as unconscious mental states. From the perspective of a discipline that views unconscious mental phenomena as the true psychic reality, truly understanding another person would entail understanding his or her *unconscious* mental states. Another consideration is that when one exits the clinical arena and looks to a systematic theory of intersubjective experience in the context of object relations theory, one finds, quite strikingly, that different psychoanalytic 'schools', each in its own way, tend to implicitly view the other, not as an intentional being with a separate center of existence, but as an instrumentality.

The other as an instrumentality

Not only do psychoanalytic theories fail to adequately address our capacity for routine, quotidian understanding of each other, but quite strikingly a core theoretical feature on which they all converge is an instrumental conception of the other. There is little in psychoanalytic theories that goes beyond this conception of the other and that speaks to the fundamental capacity to experience another person as a subject, as a separate center of existence with his or her own needs, desires, intentions, and goals. Without an adequate recognition of the capacity to experience the other as a subject, the issue of understanding the other is a non-starter. As the term '*object* relations' suggests, psychoanalytic theories tend to emphasize less an understanding of the other and more the *uses* of the other in intersubjective experience (Eagle, 2022b). As I will describe below, each psychoanalytic school has its own version of the other as an instrumentality.

Freudian theory

An instrumentalist conception of the other is especially evident in Freud's formulation of the nature of object relations. According to Freudian theory, a primary function of mind (the mental apparatus) is to discharge excitation, which protects the ego from being overwhelmed by excessive excitation, a major source of which lies in the demand of instinctual drives for gratification. In order to prevent excessive excitation from the drives an object must be found to facilitate discharge of excitation. Thus, the definition of the object as 'the thing in regard to which the instinct achieves its aim' (Freud, 1915, p. 122). Further, according to Freudian theory (1915), insofar as in the earliest stage of development, the infant experiences the object as disrupting its state of nirvana, the infant's initial reaction to objects is one of 'repulsion' and 'hate' (p. 137). However, according to Freud, in the course of development, including the development of reality-testing, the infant comes to recognize the necessity of objects for drive gratification. Hatred of the object is then replaced by love of the object due to the object's role in gratification.

The instrumental nature of objects in Freudian theory is also evident in the theoretical assumption that early in development, the drive and the object are separate. The drive is characterized by the tendency to blind discharge and will become connected to any object that is associated with discharge. It is only when the infant experiences the necessity of the object to drive gratification that the two become linked. In short, according to Freudian theory, our primary relation to the other is as an instrumentality for the discharge of excitation related to drives.

Freud's view of the object as an instrumentality is also evident in his 1914 essay 'On Narcissism'. Borrowing from a poem by Heine, Freud (1914) writes 'in the last restore we must begin to love if we are not to fall ill ...' (p. 85). However, there is little poetry in the immediately following elucidating passage in which he writes that the function of loving the object – now described in the metapsychological language of libidinal cathexis of the object – is to avoid the danger of the ego being inundated with excessive libido were it to remain invested in the self and not directed to the external object. Thus, just as the function of the object is to facilitate drive discharge and thereby prevent the ego from being overwhelmed by excessive excitation, so similarly, the primary function of libidinal investment in the object is to avoid a situation in which the ego is inundated with excessive libido. The importance of object love lies in its role in draining away excessive libido from the ego. In short, even in the context of love for the object, one's relation to the object is essentially instrumental. Nothing is written in 'On Narcissism' that speaks to a conception of the object as a separate center of existence.

Freud's formulations in 'On Narcissism' are reinforced in his very short essay written during World War I 'On Transcience' where he wonders why the evanescence of the beauty of nature or of a human face should interfere with one's appreciation of them. He attributes such interference to 'a revolt ... against mourning' and to their 'decease' (Freud, 1916[1915], p. 306). Freud then goes on to discuss the 'great riddle' of 'mourning over something we have lost or admired' (p. 306). Freud accounts for mourning as follows: 1) There is 'a certain amount of capacity for love – what we call libido – which in the earliest stages of development is directed towards our own ego' (p. 306); 2) Later in development, libido is 'diverted from the ego on to objects ...' (p. 306); 3) If the object is destroyed or lost, 'our capacity for love (our libido) is *once more liberated* [my emphasis]; and it can then either take other objects instead or can temporarily return to the ego' (p. 306). Freud then wonders:

> But why it is that this detachment of libido from its objects should be such a painful process is a mystery to us and we have hitherto not been able to frame any hypothesis to account for it. We only see that libido clings to its objects and will not renounce those that are lost even when a substitute lies ready to hand. Such then is mourning.
>
> (pp. 306–307)

Freud (1916 [1915]) continues the discussion in the context of the experience of destruction and losses in World War I. However, in the present context, one is struck with Freud's puzzlement as to why the loss of a loved one is so devastatingly painful. One is also struck with his statement, derived from a set of metapsychological assumptions, that when the object is destroyed or lost, 'our capacity for love' (our libido) is once more liberated, and we can then 'take other objects'. It is as if Freud does not seem to recognize that objects and object love are not interchangeable – another expression of a failure to fully appreciate the other, particularly one who is loved. as a separate and unique center of existence. One is also reminded here of Spitz's insistence that love is not possible when objects are interchangeable.

Ego psychology

One of Hartmann's major contributions to classical psychoanalytic theory is his positing of the relative autonomy of the ego from drives. Thus, in normal development, ego functioning, including reality-testing, can be relatively independent of the influence of drives. However, as I have noted elsewhere (Eagle, 2022), Hartmann does not extend autonomy of object relations from the influence of drives and drive gratification. Hence, he does not question Freud's conception of the object as the thing in regard to which the instinct achieves its aim, with the consequence that Hartmann's ego psychology does not leave much room for what one might refer to as intersubjective reality-testing, that is, recognition of the other as a separate center of existence and experience of the other for who he or she is.

Kleinian theory

In contrast to Freudian theory, according to Kleinian theory, there is no such thing as a drive without an object (just as, according to Sandler [1981], there is no such thing as a wish without a wished-for role of the other). Klein's insistence on the inherent link between drive and object marks the emergence of an explicit object relations perspective. However, the view of the object is no less instrumentalist in Kleinian theory than it is in Freudian theory. Kleinian theory, like Freudian theory, does not provide a conception of the object as a subject with a separate center of existence relatively independent of its role as the thing in regard to which the instinct achieves its aim. Further, according to Kleinian theory, we need good objects in order to temper and modulate one's hate and destructiveness associated with an inborn death instinct. Segal (1964, p. 12) writes that one needs objects on which to project one's destructiveness as a means of containing the death instinct. And Klein (1935) writes that 'preservation of the good object is regarded as synonymous with the survival of the ego' (p. 264).

One should also add that according to Kleinian theory, we construct the world, including the interpersonal world, through processes of projection, introjection, and projective identification. Insofar as, on this view, we essentially construct the other through projection and introjection, it would seem impossible to experience or understand another as a separate center of existence relatively independent of one's projections and introjections.

There is one potential opening in Kleinian theory to the concept of the other as a separate center of existence relatively independent of one's projections and introjections. I refer here to Klein's (1921/1975) concept of *reparation* accompanying the child's capacity for guilt due to his or her imagined or actual harm to the other (the mother in Kleinian theory). The idea that one feels a need to repair the harm one feels one has visited on another appears to imply that one has a sense of a separate other.

Self-psychology

The instrumentalist conception of the other is especially apparent in self-psychology theory, in particular, as reflected in the centrality of the concept of 'selfobject'. According to Kohut (1984), one relates to and experiences the other as a 'selfobject', a neologistic term employed by Kohut in order to convey the idea that we relate to others neither as part of oneself nor as a fully separate other, but rather in terms of the narcissistic function served by the other of enhancing the cohesiveness of one's self. As Wolf (1983) writes, selfobjects are 'neither self nor object; they are the subjective aspect of a function performed by a relationship' (p. 271). And as Fosshage (2017) writes, 'Kohut defined selfobject as the use of the other to provide certain functions pertaining to the development and maintenance of the self' (p. 129). As Bacal and Newman, themselves self-psychologists, have noted, self-psychology cannot rightly be viewed as an object relations theory in so far as it does not allow for the possibility of two independent subjects interacting with and relating to each other. (See Fosshage's [2017] attempt to integrate relational psychoanalysis and self-psychology.)

According to self-psychology theory, relating to another as a selfobject is a fundamental way of relating to the other whether expressed in mature or archaic ways. Accordingly, the primary goal of treatment from a self-psychology perspective is to enable the patient to relate to and make use of selfobjects in a more mature way. For example, Kohut (1984) writes that rather than demand perfect empathic mirroring, the ability of the patient to benefit from a friend putting a comforting arm on his or her shoulder is also relating to his or her friend as a selfobject, however, in a mature way. A question that Kohut does not address is the mode of the analyst's relation to the patient. If relating to another as a selfobject is a universal mode of relating, it would follow that the analyst relates to the patient as a selfobject. To his credit, Stolorow (1995) does address this question and takes the universalist claim that we relate to others as selfobjects to its logical conclusion. He writes: 'Not only does the patient turn to the analyst for selfobject experiences, but the analyst also turns to the patient for such experiences … and a parallel statement can be made about the child-caregiver system as well' (pp. 395–396).[5]

Kohut (1984) writes that the analyst understands the patient through an empathic process that he refers to as 'vicarious introspection' (p. 82). It is not clear whether he views vicarious introspection as a general means of interpersonal understanding or is limited to the analyst's understanding of the patient. However, in either case, the emphasis on 'vicarious introspection' as a primary means by which one understands another person seems incompatible with the claim that we generally relate to others as selfobjects, that is, in terms of the narcissistic function served by the other person. The question that arises is how one can empathically understand another, that is, take the perspective of the other, when the other is experienced and related to, not as a separate other, but primarily in terms of his or her narcissistic function of sustaining and enhancing one's self-cohesiveness? The answer to this question is that Kohut (1984) discusses 'vicarious introspection' or empathy only in relation to the analyst's experience of the patient, not the patient's experience of the analyst.

The theoretical starting point for self-psychology theory was Kohut's objections to Freud's (1914) insistence that in normal development one moves from narcissism to object love. In his early work, Kohut (1971, 1977) proposed that separate and parallel to the developmental line of object love, there is a separate and parallel line of development from archaic to mature narcissism. However, in his last book, Kohut's (1984) virtually exclusive focus is on narcissism with nary a word about object love. Further, and especially important in the present context, Kohut's account of object relations is formulated entirely in terms of self–selfobject relations. There is no account of self–other relations. It appears that Kohut was so intent on rejecting Freud's idea that in the course of normal development one must move from narcissism to object love and on insisting that narcissism is a separate line of development that he left little in his theorizing for the possibility of experiencing and relating to the other as a separate center of existence.[6]

Fairbairn and object relations theory

Fairbairn's (1952) theoretical formulations are perhaps the most fully articulated expression of a psychoanalytic object relations perspective. However, along with Freud, Klein, and Kohut, Fairbairn also appears to conceptualize the object as an instrumentality. Fairbairn clearly recognizes our inherent social nature and our need for others. As Mitchell (1988) puts it in characterizing Fairbairn's object relations theory, we are 'relational by design' (p. 21). A central claim of Fairbairn's (1944) object relations theory is expressed in the adage that 'libido is primarily object-seeking (rather than pleasure-seeking as in classic theory)' (p. 70). In the present context, a central question is: what is sought in object-seeking? Fairbairn's answer, summed up by Jones (1952) in his Preface to Fairbairn's book is as follows: 'Dr. Fairbairn starts at the center of the personality, the ego, and depicts its strivings and difficulties in its endeavor to reach an object where it may find support' (p. V). In other words, along with Freud, Klein, and Kohut, each in his or her own way, for Fairbairn too, the primary function of the object is to provide support for oneself. Indeed, according to Fairbairn, so vital is one's need for connection to the object that one clings to even bad objects in order to ward off the risk of the ultimate psychopathological disaster, namely, living in an empty, objectless inner world.

Similar to other psychoanalytic theorists, there is little or no discussion of mutuality or of one's support of the other. Indeed, there is little discussion of the other as a separate center of existence.

Rather, according to Fairbairn's version of object relations theory, we relate, not to the actual other, but to the other as a *stand-in for internal objects*, that is, to an *internalized representation of any early parental figure*.[7] Further, in so far as the internal object is conceptualized as a sub-structure within one's personality structure, in relating to another as a stand-in for an internal object, *one is relating not to another, but to an aspect of oneself*. There is one element of Fairbairn's theoretical formulations that appears to allow for the possibility of relating to another as a separate other. That element lies in his emphasis on the shift from absorption in fantasy to receptivity to the actual world as an overriding therapeutic goal. A specific fantasy that is frequently discussed by Fairbairn is that the 'bad' object will be loving if only one is good enough to earn it. Fairbairn also refers to 'exorcism of' the 'bad' internal object as a therapeutic goal. However, beyond writing that this requires the experience of the analyst as a 'good' object, there is no extended discussion of how that can be accomplished. In view of the fact that the internal object is presumably part of one's personality structure, this is an especially important issue.

Relational psychoanalysis

The American version of object relations theory, associated with the writings of Mitchell, Aron, and others, is referred to as relational psychoanalysis. Clearly influenced by Sullivan's (1953) claim that there is no such thing as an individual personality, but only an interpersonal field, Mitchell (1988) writes that 'the basic unit of study is not the individual as a separate entity ... but an in interactional field ...' (p. 3). Mitchell also (1988) writes that 'Mind has been redefined from a set of predetermined structures emerging from inside an individual organism to transactional patterns and internal structures from an interactional interpersonal field' (p. 17); that 'Human minds are fundamentally social phenomena that become focalized and secondarily elaborated by individuals' (Mitchell, 2000, p. xii); and that 'An individual mind is an oxymoron'. To say that an 'individual mind is oxymoronic is to say that no individual human mind can arise *sui generis* and sustain itself totally independent of other minds' (Mitchell, 2000, p. 57).[8]

It is difficult to address the question of how one experiences and understands another as a separate center of existence when the other is not seen as a separate entity. However, in a later paper, Mitchell acknowledges that 'individual psyches with subjectively experienced interior spaces' (p. 57) do, in fact, develop. Most important in the present context, which Mitchell does (1988) comment on the relations between 'individual psyches', much like Fairbairn and Kohut, his conception of the object is an instrumental one. For example, echoing Fairbairn, Mitchell (1988) writes that we need objects because of 'a powerful need to preserve an abiding sense of oneself' (p. 33). However, he does not address the issue of one's experience of the other apart from one's powerful need to preserve an abiding sense of oneself. Also, there appears to be an inconsistency between the assertion that the individual mind is an oxymoron and the idea that we need others due to a 'powerful need to preserve and abiding sense of oneself'.

Intersubjective-systems theory

According to Stolorow and his colleagues, the Freudian mind – as well as, to varying degrees, the mind in other psychoanalytic perspectives – is a Cartesian isolated mind (Stolorow et al., 2002) in which 'one isolated mind, the analyst, is claimed to make objective observation and interpretations of another isolated mind, the patient' (Stolorow, 2013). The isolated Cartesian mind of other psychoanalytic theories, Stolorow (2013) writes, is supplanted in a 'post-Cartesian "Intersubjective-Systems Theory", according to which, "intersubjective ...

refer(s) to any psychological field formed by interacting worlds of experience" (p. 384). Based on recurring intersubjective interactions, the child forms principles ... that unconsciously organize subsequent emotional and related experiences' (Stolorow, 2013, p. 383).[9] These organizing principles shape one's 'horizons of awareness'.

There is a great deal more one can say about intersubjective-systems theory. However, in the present context, the issues I want to address are: one, how that theory deals with the questions of how one person experiences and understands another; and two, to what extent, it allows for a non-instrumental conception of the object. With regard to the first issue, Stolorow (2013) writes:

> The patient's transference experience is co-constituted by the patient's pre-reflective organizing activity and whatever is coming from the analyst that is lending itself to being organized by them. A parallel statement can be made about the analyst's transference. The psychological field formed by the inter-play of the patient's transference and the analyst's transference is an example of what we call an *intersubjective system* [emphasis in original].

> (p. 383)

Stolorow's concluding statement is: 'Psychoanalysis is a dialogical method for bringing prereflective organizing activity into reflective self-awareness' (p. 383). Thus, his answer to the question of how we understand each other seems to be that through dialogue, one needs to reflect on the ways in which one's unconscious or implicit organizing principles influence one's experience of the other person. Thus, unlike other psychoanalytic theories, the intersubjective theory of Stolorow and his colleagues does seem to allow for the possibility of experiencing the other as a separate center of existence. However, it is not clear to what extent the theory is intended to be applicable beyond the clinical situation.

To sum up, with the possible exception of intersubjective-systems theory, as well as the inclusion of concepts that suggest recognition of the other as a separate center of experience, (e.g., the Kleinian concept of reparation) different psychoanalytic theories on the nature of intersubjective experience tend to view the object primarily as an instrumentality in the service of one's personal ends, whether these ends are understood as drive gratification, modulating the impact of the death instinct, enhancing one's self-cohesiveness, or providing ego support.

As we have seen, a serious problem with psychoanalytic accounts of inter-subjective experience is the inconsistency between, on the one hand, universalist formulations and, on the other hand, formulations of intersubjective experience in the clinical situation that appear to represent exceptions to universalist claims. In discussing self-psychology, I raised the question as to whether the presumed universality of the claim that we relate to others primarily as a selfobject is also applicable to the analyst's relation to the patient. A similar question can be raised with regard to other psychoanalytic theories of the nature of interpersonal experience and understanding. Thus, one can ask whether the analyst relates to the patient as 'the thing in regard to which the instinct achieves its aim'. And similarly with regard to Fairbairn's object relations theory, one can ask whether the analyst relates to the patient as a stand-in for an internal object. A negative answer to these questions leaves us with a situation in which universalist claims regarding the nature of intersubjective experience and formulations in the clinical context are, at the very least, inconsistent with each other.

A similar situation holds with regard to the caregiver's relation to the infant, which has frequently been viewed as analogous to the analyst–patient relationship. Does mother relate to her infant as selfobject or as the thing in regard to which the instinct achieves its aim or as a stand-in for an internal object? Although such modes of mother–infant interaction are possible, they are neither primary nor generally the case. Thus, there is the odd situation in which universalist claims are made about interpersonal experiences that somehow exempt certain classes of relationships (i.e., analyst–patient and mother–infant). The bottom line is that we are left with a contradiction between, on the one hand, universalist theories regarding the nature of the mind and of interpersonal relations and, on the other hand, formulations in the clinical situation that appear to represent exceptions to these universalist claims.

The other as a separate center of existence

Perhaps more than any other theorist in the psychoanalytic literature, Benjamin (e.g., 1988, 2000, 1995, 2013) has emphasized the importance of supplementing an object relations approach with what one may refer to as subject relations. Although much of Benjamin's work is written in the context of gender studies and discussions of 'the third' – a concept I have difficulty grasping – its importance extends beyond that area. For Benjamin, at the core of intersubjectivity are mutual recognition, recognition of differences, and, borrowing from Winnicott (1971), subjective versus objective understanding of the other. She understands intersubjectivity 'as the zone of experience in which the other is not merely the object of the ego's need/drive or cognition/perception, but has a separate and equivalent center of self' (p. 45).

Although, according to Benjamin, the potential for mutual recognition and the capacity to view the other as a subject is inborn, the realization of this potential is a developmental achievement. From Benjamin's perspective, a central goal of treatment is the enhancement of one's ability to relate to the other as a separate subject rather than as an instrumental object.[10] Benjamin's perspective is captured by her suggested replacement of 'where id was, there shall ego be' with 'where objects were, subjects must be' (Benjamin, 1990, p. 34). I have been able to find a few other papers in the psychoanalytic literature that discuss the issue of experiencing and understanding the other not simply as instrumental object, but as a separate center of existence. Bollas (2006) introduces the concept 'perceptive identification' (in contrast to projective identification), which he describes as 'based on the self's ability to perceive the object as a thing-in-itself' (p. 714). It entails one's appreciation of 'the integrity of the object' as well as the 'appreciation of the object's qualities', which allows one to 'love the object *for itself*, not for *oneself*' (p. 714). Bollas goes on to stress the object's separateness and distinctness from the self. However, he ends his paper with the comment that 'A theory of perceptive identification may enable us to think about the complex way that *we use objects*' [my emphasis] (p. 716), that is, as instrumentalities.

In experiencing the other as a subject, one is essentially recognizing the other as someone who, like oneself, has his or her own thoughts, feelings, desires, etc. that are different from one's own. Such recognition requires the capacity to experience the other both as someone who, just like me, has thoughts and feelings as well as someone who is not just like me in the sense of having specific thoughts and feelings that are different from the ones I have.[11] One needs to balance these two perspectives. That is, one needs to be able to take an intentional stance toward another without assuming an identity between one's own and the other's intentional world.[12]

In addressing the question of 'what is an outer object', Zachrisson (2013) writes 'The perception [of the other] will never be completely free of "distortions" from the internal object. Like Fairbairn', Zachrisson (2013) also identifies as a central goal of psychoanalytic treatment a more realistic perception of the other. Thus, Zachrisson suggests that although one's perception of another is always colored by one's transference, one can, nevertheless, experience the other as an 'independent existence' rather than as an instrumental object; and one can aspire to understand the other as fully and as accurately as possible. This is in contrast to conceptualizing the other as a 'selfobject' or as 'the thing in regard to which the instinct achieves its aim'. However, what is lacking in Zachrisson's account, as it is in most psychoanalytic accounts, is an adequate confrontation with the question of the specific processes involved in our understanding of another person as having an 'independent existence', not just in the clinical situation, but in our quotidian interactions.

Intersubjective experience and unconscious mental states

Complicating a psychoanalytic perspective on intersubjective experience and understanding of another's mental states is its primary emphasis on *unconscious* mental states, particularly in the clinical situation. How does one understand another person when what one means by understanding another person focuses primarily on understanding of the person's unconscious mental states? One general answer to this question in the clinical context is that, based on the patient's productions (i.e., free associations, dreams, transference reactions, personal history, and presenting symptoms), as well as the analyst's theoretical knowledge of human nature and psychological functioning, clinical experience, and 'evenly hovering attention' (Freud, 1912a) the analyst makes interpretive inferences regarding the patient's unconscious inner conflicts and mental states.

Countertransference

Another answer that has emerged, based on a reconceptualization of the concept of countertransference, is that the feelings and thoughts that enter the analyst's consciousness constitute a reliable guide to the patient's unconscious mental states. The altered conception of countertransference was initially formulated by Deutsch (1926), Heiman (1950) and more fully elaborated by Racker (1968) who wrote that 'the thoughts and feelings which emerge [in the analyst] will be, precisely, those which did not emerge in the patient, i.e., the repressed and the unconscious' (p. 17). In other words, the analyst's countertransference reactions were now viewed, not as blind spots, but as a reliable guide to understanding the patient's repressed unconscious mental states. Thus, following the new 'totalistic' conception (Kernberg, 1965), countertransference is now viewed by many, if not most, analysts, not as a barrier to successful treatment, but as an indispensable therapeutic tool. Indeed, Gabbard (1995) writes that the view of countertransference as an indispensable therapeutic tool constitutes a 'common ground' among analysts despite different theoretical persuasions.

Mental telepathy

What are the processes that underlie the presumed remarkable phenomenon in which the analyst's feelings and thoughts turn out to be precisely the patient's repressed mental contents? In addressing this question, Freud (1912) writes that 'the analyst must turn his own unconscious like a receptive organ toward the transmitting unconscious of the patient. He must adjust himself to the patient as a telephone receiver is adjusted to the transmitting microphone' (p. 115). In some of his writings, Freud appeals to mental telepathy as the process through which the unconscious of one person communicates with the unconscious of another person. These are not casual and passing references to telepathy. In addition to scattered comments about telepathy in the course of discussing other matters, Freud also devoted three papers to the topic: 'Dreams and Telepathy' (1922); 'The Occult Significance of Dreams' (1925); and 'Psychoanalysis and Telepathy' (1941 [1921]). He also has a lengthy discussion of 'dreams and occultism' in *New Introductory Lectures in Psychoanalysis* (1933[1932]).

On occasion, Freud debunks seemingly mysterious occult phenomena such as prophetic dreams and experiences of *déjà vu*. For example, he attributes the latter to 'unconscious phantasies of which one is unconsciously reminded in a situation of the present time' (Freud, 1901, p. 268). However, in other writings, despite asserting that he is 'strictly impartial' (Freud, 1901, p. 200) and 'unenthusiastic and ambivalent' (p. 181), he views the possibility of its reality sympathetically. A 'strictly impartial' and 'unenthusiastic and ambivalent' attitude toward telepathy is hardly suggested by other comments he makes. For example, in discussing an event described by a patient involving a fortune-teller, Freud (1941 [1921]) writes:

The event becomes completely explicable if we are ready to assume that the knowledge was transferred from [the patient] to the supposed prophetess-by some unknown method which excluded the means of communication familiar to us. That is to say, we must draw the inference that there is such a thing as thought-transference.

(p. 184)

In other passages Freud expresses a positive attitude toward telepathy and thought-transference:

I have often had an impression, in the course of experiments in my private circle, that strongly emotionally colored recollections can be successfully transferred without much difficulty ... I am inclined to draw the conclusion that thought-transference of this kind comes about particularly easy at the moment at which an idea emerges from the unconscious, or, in theoretical terms, as it passes over from the 'primary process' to the 'secondary process'.

(Freud, 1925, p. 138)[13]

The only reason for discussing the relation between dreams and telepathy is that the state of sleep seems particularly suited for receiving telepathic messages. In such cases one has what is called a telepathic dream and, when it is analyzed, one forms the conviction that the telepathic news has played the same part as any other portion of the day' residues and that it has been changed in the same way by the dream-work and made to serve its purpose.

(Freud, 1933[1932], p. 37)

When they [i.e., thought-transference and telepathy] first came into my range of vision more than ten years ago, I too felt a dread of a threat against our scientific *Weltanschauung*, which, I feared, was bound to give place to spiritualism or mysticism if portions of occultism were proved true. Today I think otherwise.

(Freud, 1933[1932], p. 54)

Freud (1933 [1932]) goes on to speculate that what may mediate between 'two mental acts [i.e., between sender and receiver] may easily be a physical process into which the mental one is transformed at one end and which is transferred back once more into the same mental one' (p. 55). He then draws an analogy between the possibility of telepathy and speaking and hearing by telephone. He also observes that 'it is a familiar fact that we do not how the common purpose comes about in the great insect communities' and speculates that 'possibly it is done by means of a direct psychical transference of this kind' and perhaps

that this is the original, archaic method of communication between individuals and that in the course of phylogenetic evolution it has been replaced by the better method of giving information with the help of signals which are picked up by the sense organs. But the older method may have persisted in the background and still be able to put itself into effect under certain conditions …

(p. 55)

Freud is obviously attempting, stated in the language of contemporary discourse, 'naturalize' telepathy and thought-processes, that is, to suggest that such phenomena may be compatible with a scientific world view that limits its accounts to physical processes.

Mental telepathy has continued to be of interest to some psychoanalytic theorists. Perhaps Freud's interest in the topic serves as a stamp of approval. There are a sizable number of papers on this topic in psychoanalytic journals. Let me provide a few examples. I begin with a relatively recent paper entitled 'Becoming a Telepathic Tuning Fork: Anomalous Experience and the Relation Mind' appearing in *Psychoanalytic Dialogues* (Farber, 2017). I think the best way to provide a sense of the paper is to present some representative passages: 'Understanding projective identification as a dissociative process of communication by which the person projected his own unacceptable emotions into the analyst, who could then know experientially what the patient was feeling can be understood scientifically as telepathic communication' (p. 719). Rather than attempting to address the question of how one person's projections of his or her unacceptable emotions can lead the object of the projection to understand one's feelings, – what possible processes are involved? – the author simply proposes that this occurs via 'telepathic communication'.

Although we tend to regard the paranormal as outside the range of scientific explanation and are dismissive of experiences we cannot understand, telepathy and other uncanny experiences fascinate us and are the subject of blockbuster films and best-selling books. Telepathy is the passage of information from one mind to another other than by normal means of communication. An increasing number of scientists globally have studied telepathy and other paranormal phenomena, research that *surpassed* [my emphasis] the ordinary standards of rigorous research … Many scientist found that our mind is not limited by our bodies' boundaries but extends far beyond to alternate realities … Quantum physics does strange things with time space, and causality interconnecting everything in the universe … Prayer was found to have a positive effect on numerous medical conditions, in a process thought to be driven by telepathic empathy.

(p. 719)

Farber (2017) devotes a good deal of space to the writings of Stan Gooch (1978, 2000), 'a British psychic, "little known to the scientific world", 'who became a trained research psychologist, had a Jungian analysis, and published several books on the paranormal' (p. 720). The kind of evidence Farber adduces for the reality of telepathy includes the following: after Elizabeth Mayer's 'hand-carved harp was stolen', Mayer called a dowser

> who specializes in finding lost objects using a twig called a dowsing rod ... Within 2 days and without leaving his home, he found the precise street coordinates where the harp was (Mayer, 2007). Two weeks later, she had the harp back ...
>
> (p. 725)

Farber also informs the reader how she became interested in telepathy.

> While writing this paper, I began thinking about how I became aware of Elizabeth Mayer's (2007) *Extraordinary Knowing: Science, Skepticism, and the Inexplicable Powers of the Human Mind* and Stan Gooch's (2007) *The Origins of Psychic Phenomena: Poltergeists, Incubi, Succubi, and the Unconscious Mind*. My husband, a book collector, likes to go library sales. Often, I'll accompany him but not always. I recall that on two different days I heard an internal voice urging me to go with him, and I did. It was on those days that I came across Mayer's and Gooch's books, which I had never heard of before, and began to wonder whether that internal voice was a telepathic communication.
>
> (pp. 725–726)

In other words, two people who Farber did not know and did not know her, may have sent her a telepathic communication. I leave it to the reader to assess the nature of this and other 'evidence' provided by Farber.

Lazar (2001) writes that

> A skeptical attitude persists despite robust evidence demonstrating the reality of nonlocal phenomena such as telepathy and the impact of mind from a distance ... Newer constructs and research findings in quantum physics ... demonstrate the reality of nonlocal effects and help provide a conceptual framework that encompasses research documenting psi.
>
> (p. 113)

According to Lazar, paranormal phenomena not only influence us and constitute ways of knowing, but also have healing capacities. Among the findings cited by Lazar is a report that prayer led to the survival of a very ill premature infant. She writes that because the infant did not respond despite maximum medical intervention, life support was about to be withdrawn. However, before doing so, however, a prayer circle was held around the dying baby. Forty-five minutes later, there was a sudden dramatic improvement in the infant. Among other things, what is not made clear in this account is the link, if any, between telepathy and the power of prayer.

dePeyer (2016) claims that

> telepathic phenomena transgress the dominantly held Newtonian-based theory of mind that brain and mind must be one and the same and that nonlocal experiences [i.e., telepathy] are nonphysical in nature and thus cannot easily be reduced to theories based on neural function.
>
> (p. 162)

She also points to the phenomenon of blindsight as constituting evidential support for telepathy; and analogizes between the sub-atomic phenomenon of entanglement and 'entangled minds'. Like others who claim the existence of telepathy, de Peyer suggests that quantum physics somehow constitutes the basis for telepathic processes. Just how the sub-atomic entanglement phenomenon – which physicists have a great deal of difficulty understanding – is related to 'entangled minds', that is, to telepathic communication, is, of course, not articulated. It is sufficient that the term 'entanglement' can be used in both contexts. Similarly, with references to quantum physics that are frequently found in papers on telepathy. It is sufficient to refer to it and leave it to the reader to figure out in what way, say, Heisenberg's principle of uncertainty, is somehow related to telepathic processes.

In a paper in which the focus is on the conditions in which thought-transference is likely to occur – which, of course, only makes sense if one assumes that it exists – Silverman (1988) writes:

> As for the question of thought-transference, preliminary findings suggest that the conditions under which it seems to occur involve the simultaneity of (1) the analyst's tendency to repress disturbing thoughts (including activated residuals) because of guilt at being distracted; and (2) qualitatively similar conflictual themes emerging from repression in the patient's unconscious.
>
> (p. 292)

The 'preliminary findings' to which Silverman refers is not made clear. Rather, what he does provide is a clinical vignette that is presumably illustrative of the conditions under which thought-transference occurs.

In a paper on the 'Parallels between Psi Phenomena and the Psychotherapy Process', Rosenbaum (2011) writes that 'psychoanalysis and psi research each provide a different perspective on the same phenomenon – the nature of the unconscious' (p. 58). In support of her thesis, Rosenbaum refers to a paper of which I am a co-author (Gallese et al., 2007). She refers to our comment that some theorists have looked to telepathy as an explanation of certain instances of projective identification in which behavioral cues are not present. The misleading impression is that we are neutral or endorse the appeal to telepathy as an account of projective identification. What Rosenbaum does not refer to are our following comments:

> ... unless the patient's projections generate *some* behavioral cues to which the analyst can respond (consciously or unconsciously), it is difficult to understand how these projections ... can possibly influence the analyst's experience – unless one wants to posit some magical or telepathic processes between patient and analyst
>
> (p. 150)

We then cite Ponsi's (1997) appeal to telepathy and comment that such an appeal suggests 'no apparent recognition that some mechanism must be involved in order to account for this phenomenon' (p. 150).

In a recent paper in the *Journal of the American Psychoanalytic Association*, a flagship journal for American psychoanalysts, Rabeyron et al. (2021) trace the history of the continuing interest in telepathy in the psychoanalytic literature. However, the main purpose of their paper is to demonstrate how 'telepathy has also contributed significantly to the development of fundamental concepts, including transference, projective identification, and primary process forms of symbolization processes', to identify 'the conditions for the emergence of telepathy', to demonstrate 'how this notion relates to the most originary and primary forms of the intersubjective relationship', and finally, to integrate telepathy 'within contemporary psychoanalytic theory' (p. 579). After reviewing the literature, they conclude that: 'Telepathy is thus a key notion in understanding the most primary intersubjective phenomena of psychic life, as well as the profound nature of reality and the links that unite analyst and analysand' (p. 563).

Following this conclusion, Rabeyron et al. (2021) devote much attention to such issues as the conditions that facilitate the emergence of telepathy and the purposes it serves, as if its reality had already been convincingly demonstrated. The conditions for the emergence of telepathy identified by Rabeyron et al. (2021) include 'a desperate attempt by the analysand to maintain a connection with the analyst, in particular during or after a period of separation (Papazian, 2017), one of the main factors at the origin of telepathic dreams'; similarly for Prados (1959), telepathic processes would tend to occur when the patient perceives 'a threat of separation when he feels that the analyst lacks empathy ... the patient might try to capture the analyst's attention through thought-transference if the latter appears psychically absent during the session' (p. 543). Surprisingly, Rabeyron et al. (2021) do not consider the possibility that patients' reports of so-called telepathic experiences during periods of separation and experienced lack of analyst empathy and presence may reflect attempts to feel closer to the analyst and may have little to do with actual telepathy or thought-transference.

Characteristic of many papers on telepathy and thought-transference is the reliance on anecdotal evidence. In Freud's case, the so-called evidence includes letters he received, patients' reports of long past events, and his private experiments with colleagues. With regard to the Rabeyron et al.'s. (2021) paper, consider the following examples of presumed empirical support for telepathy: a report by Petitmengin (2021) that reads as follows:

> One day, at the very moment a patient enters her office, a patient, Sylvie, her psychoanalyst feels a taste of blood in her mouth. 'I had a taste in my mouth. It was strong, it was as if someone had put blood under my nose and my mouth. It wouldn't leave me'. After a while, as this taste persists, she interrupts her patient and asks, 'What happened to you?' The patient began to cry: a few days before, she was rushed to the hospital for a miscarriage. 'And then the taste of blood disappeared immediately'.
>
> (p. 201)

Another example provided by Rabeyron et al. (2021) is that of a presumably telepathic dream reported by a patient of Robert Stoller's. In the dream, an older man carries a large object which smashes through a glass wall. Despite the presence of glass everywhere, the old man was not hurt. Stoller reports that the same night on which his patient had the dream, he, Stoller, was at a party held for a political candidate. At that party, while moving chairs, Stoller crashed through a closed sliding glass door. Stoller reports that 'although glass fell all over, I was scarcely scratched' (as cited in Rabeyron et al., 2021, p. 556). There are many other presumed telepathic phenomena reported by Rabeyron et al. (2021), including incidents in which someone has a sudden alarming sense that someone close to him or her has died, and then learns that that individual died at precisely the time of the alarming experience. Of course, incidents in which an alarming sense that someone has died is *not* associated with an actual death is not of much interest and is not reported. I leave it to the reader to identify the problems inherent in viewing these reported incidents as evidence of telepathy.

There is much more on which one can comment in regard to the above papers. However, my main purpose in discussing these papers is not simply to critique them. Nor is it to debate the issue of whether telepathic processes exist. Nor is it to discourage an open-mindedness that allows one to investigate phenomena that appear to challenge existing conceptions.[14] Rather it is to raise questions regarding the nature and quality of the evidence and arguments on which the claim for the existence of telepathy and thought-transference as significant means of communication and interpersonal understanding are based. Given the poor quality of both the arguments and the evidence adduced to support the arguments in the papers I have discussed (as well as other similar papers not discussed), it is striking that they have been published in virtually every one of the main journals in the field, a state of affairs that generates the following question: what does the publication of papers in respected psychoanalytic journals – and I have presented only a sample – characterized by the kind of arguments made and the kind of evidence presented tell us about the state of psychoanalytic theorizing, not only in regard to the issue of intersubjective experience and understanding, but also more broadly, the state of psychoanalysis as a discipline?

Research and theory on intersubjective experience

Nothing but reductionism and the call to cease all talk of mind and mental states notwithstanding, productive theoretical accounts and a good deal of fruitful research have been devoted to the processes involved in our experience and understanding of others. There is evidence that just as infants are born with a propensity and developing capacity to experience the physical world in terms of what might be thought of as Kantian categories (e.g., causality, unified objects) as well as 'rules' regarding how objects function (e.g., if an object is not supported, it will fall), similarly, they are born with a propensity and developing capacity to experience others as intentional beings. To cite just a few examples, five-month-old infants respond differently to intentional versus non-intentional behavior (Woodward et al., 1999). Further, starting early in life, infants expect behavior to be intentional and rational rather than non-intentional and irrational. For example, as evidenced by differences in the duration of visual focusing, five-month-old infants expect that a person will place a wide object in a wide rather than a narrow box (Ting et al., 2021). Lou and Baillargeon (2005) reported that five-month-old infants attribute goals to self-propelled boxes, that is, to objects that appear to show agency. There is also evidence that the mirror neuron system (MNS) is present by six months of age and that it is activated by the goals and intentions of actions rather than by sheer movements (Nystrom, 2008; Shimada & Hiraki, 2006). Six-month-old infants are capable of other-directed behaviors toward peers in distress (Hay et al., 1981). Infants not only show empathic concern at three months of age, but individual differences in the degree of such concern are associated with social competence at 36 months of age (Davidov et al., 2020; Paz et al., 2021). Although the claim that newborns imitate is controversial, there is reliable evidence that seven-month-old infants imitate happy faces (but not angry faces) (Daytner et al., 2017).

Although the capacity to experience others as intentional beings is a necessary condition, it is not a sufficient condition for our understanding of the specific content of the mental states of others. It is the latter that is referred to as the philosophical problem of other minds. What makes that possible? Of course, one obvious answer to the question is that one can *ask* the other person what s/he is thinking and feeling. However, a good part of the time we understand the other's mental states without needing to ask, a capacity necessary for social interaction. A standard answer to that question is to invoke the concept of *empathy*. However, the term empathy has been understood in many different ways and has been applied to many different phenomena. Cuff et al. (2016) have identified 43 'discrete definitions' of empathy and Batson (2009) writes that the term *empathy* is applied to eight different phenomena. It would, therefore, be more useful to begin with a description of different theoretical accounts of the processes involved in our mindreading capacity. We can then address the question of the degree to which empathy is involved in these accounts as well as the question of which aspects of empathy, if any, are being invoked.

There are at least three theoretical answers to the question of how we understand another's mental states: Theory Theory (TT), Simulation Theory (ST), both of which are really a family of theories, and Interaction Theory (IT).

Theory Theory[15]

One version of Theory Theory, *Child as Scientist Theory*, proposes that, like a scientist, based on observation and inference, the child develops hypotheses, makes predictions, and revises these hypotheses when predictions fail. One of the early formulations of TT is provided by Premack and Woodruff (1978), who write:

> As humans, we assume that others want, think, and the like and thereby infer states that are not directly observable, using these states anticipatorially, to predict the behavior of others as well as our own. These inferences, which amount to a theory of mind are to our knowledge universal in human adults.
> (p. 525)

Importantly, the inferences and hypotheses can be implicit rather than entail reflective reasoning. The specific mental states of particular interest to TT researchers are *beliefs*.

Critical to TT research is the 'false-belief task' (Wimmer & Perner, 1983). In a well-known example, a puppet ('Sally') puts a toy in box A and leaves the room. After Sally leaves the room, another puppet ('Anne') moves the toy to box B. When Sally returns to the room, Anne is asked where Sally will look for the toy. When a 3-year-old child is asked where Sally will look for the ball, s/he will say box B. (Wimmer & Perner, 1983; Baron-Cohen et al., 1985). The 3-year-old is not able to distinguish between what s/he knows and what another child may not know. However, by age 4–5, this ability is present. In the course of development, the child is assumed to become increasingly capable of making inferences regarding someone else's mental state.

Bem's (1972) 'self-perception theory' can be understood as a version of TT, as applied to self-understanding. It holds that one knows another person's inner states in the same way one knows one's own mental states – through observation and inference. The Nisbett and Wilson (1977) study discussed in Chapter 2 can be seen as an example of applying a version of self-observation theory to understanding one's motives for one's decisions. An implication of self-perception theory essentially denies privileged access to large swaths of one's inner states and erases the fundamental distinction between first-person self-knowledge and third-person self-knowledge discussed, among others by Moran (2001). From the view of self-perception theory, virtually all self-knowledge, as well as knowledge of others, is third-person knowledge.

Simulation Theory

Like Theory Theory, Simulation Theory is also a family of theories with a common emphasis on one form or other of simulation processes. Unlike TT, ST does not propose that either explicit or implicit theorizing is the primary basis for understanding another person's mental states. Rather, it proposes that we understand another person's mental states by 'mental simulation' of which there are various forms. One form of commonsense folk psychology, described as understanding another person by imaginatively putting oneself in the other's shoes., and then thinking about what one would do or feel in the other person's situation, can be viewed as a form of ST. In this form of simulation, the process involves imagining what *I would do or feel were I in the same situation*. Although this form of simulation may facilitate understanding of the other when the observer and the observed are very much alike, it may tell us more about ourselves than about the other person when observer and observed are very different in important respects. In that sense, one might think of it as quasi- or pseudo-empathy. What is missing in this account is *taking the perspective of the other and attempting to get a sense of what the other person would do or feel*. It is the inclusion of this latter component that warrants the label of empathy.[16]

In 1996, Rizzolatti, Fadiga, Gallese, and Fogssi serendipitously discovered that when a monkey observes another monkey's motor act (e.g., grasping a cup), the area of the premotor cortex that is activated in the monkey carrying out the action is also activated in the monkey observing the action. Further, the neural response is activated by intentional, goal-related action rather than by mere movements (Rizzolatti & Gallese, 1996). This discovery plus other related findings generated the formulation of Embodied Simulation Theory The brain areas activated in the observer have been referred to as the mirror neuron system. A similar system has been found in humans and is also present when one observes another's emotional expressions. For example, Wicker (2003) found that the left anterior insula was activated not only when subjects experienced disgust in reaction to inhaling odorants, but also when observing a video showing the facial expression of disgust. A similar finding has been reported with regard to the experience of pain. That is, areas of the brain that are activated when experiencing pain are also activated when observing another in pain (e.g., Singer, 2008).

On the basis of this and other evidence, Gallese (2006) concludes that when someone is observing another, the internal representations of the bodily states associated with the actions and emotions observed are activated in the observer, as if the observer 'would be doing a similar action or experiencing a similar emotion or sensation' (p. 15). In short, according to Gallese's version of Simulation Theory, which he refers to as Embodied Simulation Theory, a variation of Simulation Theory, the simulation that occurs does not refer to voluntary and conscious imaginative acts at the personal level, but rather to automatic and sub-personal simulation or implicit imitation at the neural level.

There has been a great deal of controversy and debate around the question of just and what and how much can the MNS explain. As I have stated elsewhere (Eagle, 2022b), there is a plausible case for the role of the MNS in understanding another person's intentional actions, emotional facial expressions, and experiences of sensations of pain and disgust. However, there is probably a very limited role of the MNS in understanding other mental states of another person, for example, beliefs and complex intentions and actions. As Rizzolatti and Sinigaglia (2008) acknowledge, automatic understanding of action intentions 'is based exclusively on the vocabulary of acts and the motor knowledge on which our capacity to act depends {and} is completely devoid of any reflexive [sic], conceptual and/or linguistic mediation' (p. 25).

Following the discovery of mirror neurons, a great deal of research has been carried out on factors that influence shared neural activation between observer and observed and empathic response in the former. There is evidence that in circumstances, shared neural activation and empathy are severely compromised and perhaps even absent. For example, Hein et al. (2010) reported that empathy-related neural responses to observing another in pain vary with such factors as whether one is observing an ingroup rather than an outgroup member in pain. Indeed, they found that observing an outgroup member in pain 'was processed in a reward-related manner' (p. 158). In a related study, Singer et al. (2006) reported that activation of the brain's pain-related areas (the brain's fronto-insular and anterior cingulate cortex) were activated when observing a person who behaved in a fair manner in a game experienced pain, and was significantly reduced when observing a player experiencing pain who behaved in an unfair manner. Indeed, in this condition, there was also increased activation in reward-related brain areas.

These findings bring to mind the fact that history is replete with evidence of failure of empathic response toward other human beings in the form of warfare, ethnic strife, scapegoating, murder and torture generated by group ideology, in which the other is experienced, at one and the same time, as sub-human – an object rather than a subject – as well as a malevolent, even powerful, subject who is representing a danger to one's very existence. In the former case, the other is no longer, just like oneself, a human being; in the latter case, the other is a satanic, sometimes super-human being who is extraordinarily evil. The horrific historical events with which we are all familiar disturbingly indicate the ease with which an empathic response toward certain others can be undone by various factors, including the family and culture in which one is embedded and the ideology generated by authority figures. The remarkable fact is that many individuals who experience the other in this way do not necessarily show a *general* defect in the ability to respond empathically. They can be good and understanding friends, husbands, wives, family members, and so on. This is the sort of reality that undoubtedly led Arendt (1994) to refer to the 'banality of evil'. A critical question that arises is how one gets from an empathic capacity that appears early in infancy to its startling absence in the cruel actions of which we are capable.

In a number of other studies, the greater the overlap between physiological and neural activation in experiencing pain oneself and observing another person in pain, the greater the likelihood of prosocial behavior. In one study, the greater the match between SCR magnitude during the experience of pain oneself and observation of another in pain, the greater the likelihood of 'costly helping' behavior (Hein et al., 2011). In a remarkable finding, Brethel-Haurwitz et al., 2018) reported that the greater the overlap in anterior insula responses to experiencing pain oneself and observing another in pain, the greater the likelihood of the extreme altruistic behavior of a kidney donation. In a study on cultural modulation of neural correlates of observing another in pain. Cheon et al. (2013) reported that compared to Caucasian-American participants, participants from a more collectivist culture that places greater value on focusedness on others (i.e., South Korea) showed heightened neural activation in the affective brain matrix (i.e., interior cingulate cortex and insula) when observing another person in pain.

The above findings, particularly the findings on the influence on the observer of such factors as ingroup versus outgroup membership or fair versus unfair behavior of the observed, suggest that top-down factors may exert an influence on empathic response and the degree of neural circuit sharing between observer and observed. They also suggest that one can understand another's mental state (e.g., experience of pain) independently of robust MNS activation. There is little doubt that despite the absence of shared neural circuits and the low level of activation in the neural empathic network, the observers of an outgroup member and of someone who behaved in an unfair manner clearly perceived and understood that the people they were observing were in pain. Indeed, it is understanding that outgroup members or unfair players were experiencing pain that accounts for the activation of the reward-related neural areas in the observer. Thus, such understanding was possible seemingly without neural sharing or simulation. However, it is not clear that this understanding entailed simulation of any kind. Hence, one needs to entertain the idea that although shared neural activation may be involved in empathic understanding, it cannot be its sole or perhaps primary basis.

Interaction Theory

A number of theorists (e.g., Gallagher, 2008, 2011; Schillbach et al., 2013) have been critical of TT and ST on at least two grounds: one, that the context for the data on which these theories are based is that of a passive spectator observing another individual and two, that the presupposition underlying these theories is that because the mind of the other person is hidden, one must engage in special inferential and simulation processes in order to understand another person's mental states. In contrast to TT and ST, interaction theorists note one, that in everyday life we are not simply passive and detached observers; rather, we engage in interaction with others; and two, that in the course of interaction with others, rather than rely on intervening inferential or simulation processes, not only do we *immediately and automatically* experience the person with whom we are interacting as an intentional being, but we also immediately understand the other's mental states by perceiving the bodily behaviors and expressions of the other person in a particular interactional context. One should add that in the context of interaction, the effect of each participant's behavior on the other person constitutes an additional and important source of information that is not available when one's role is mainly that of a detached observer. An implicit claim of IT is that because the data on which it is based are more directly relevant to real-life situations, its theoretical account of interpersonal understanding is likely to have greater ecological validity than TT and ST.

Gallagher (2008) writes that in ordinary interpersonal interaction, 'knowing the other person's intentions, emotions and dispositions is simply a matter of perceiving their embodied behavior in the situation. In most cases of everyday interaction, no inference is necessary' (p. 164). On this point, IT and ST are in agreement. They are also in agreement regarding the importance of shared neural circuits in enabling intersubjective understanding. Indeed, according to Gallagher (2008), the fact of shared neural circuits may underlie direct perceptual understanding of another person's mental states. As Gallagher (2008) puts it, mirror neuron activation would be viewed 'as part of the neuronal processes that underlie social perception' (Gallagher, 2008, p. 170). He continues: 'The articulated neuronal processes that include activation of mirror neurons or shared representation constitute the neural processes of a non-articulated immediate perception of the other's intentional actions rather than a distinct process of simulating their intentions ...' (p. 170). However, IT differs from ST in arguing that not only inference, but also simulation, is not necessary for understanding the mental states of another person. As Gallagher (2008) writes, '... for the most part, in most of our encounters in everyday life, perception and context deliver sufficient (or close to sufficient) information for understanding others' (p. 168). There is no need for special cognitive processes of either inference or simulation.

The IT position is captured by some comments by Wittgenstein cited by Gallagher:

> Look into someone else's face, and see the consciousness in it, and a particular shade of consciousness. You see on it, in it, joy, indifference, interest, excitement, torpor, and so on ... Do you look into yourself in order to recognize the fury in *his*?
>
> (Wittgenstein, 1967, sect. 229)

> We see emotion – as opposed to what? – We do not see a facial contortion and *make the inference* that he is feeling, joy, grief, boredom. We describe a face immediately as sad, radiant, bored, even when we are unable to give any other description of the features. – Grief, one would like to say, is personified in the face ... In general I do not surmise fear in him – I see it. I do not feel that I am deducing the probable existence of something inside from

something outside; rather, it is as if the human face were in a way translucent and that I am seeing it not in a reflected light but rather in its own.

(Wittgenstein, 1980, sects. 570, 170).

Clearly, Wittgenstein is arguing forcefully for the position that we perceive emotions in others directly and equally forcefully, against the position that we first perceive another's facial expressions (and one can add, gestures and bodily movements) and then infer or deduce emotions in the other, as well as against the position that we understand another's emotions by first perceiving facial expressions, simulate these expressions, and then look inward to infer on the basis of these perceptions. Rather, we directly and immediately perceive the intentions, emotions, and sensations in others.

Wittgenstein's and Gallagher's position regarding the direct perception of intentions, emotions, and sensations is essentially identical to that of the Gestalt psychologists who also argued against the idea of inference based on observation of behavior. For example, Asch (1952) wrote:

When we say that a person is in pain, we see his body as feeling. We do need to 'impute' consciousness to others if we directly perceive the qualities of consciousness in the qualities of action ... it is superfluous to go 'behind' it to its conscious substrate, for consciousness has revealed itself in the act.

(p. 158)

Asch's comments echo Kohler's (1947) statement that 'If I refer to the calmness of a man before me, I refer to a fact which I perceive' (p. 241). They are also very similar to those made by Koffka and Kohler in accounting for one's understanding of another person's mental states, who as Eagle and Wakefield (2007) have shown, also remarkably anticipated the mirror neuron discovery (see also Gallese, 2016). Koffka (1924) writes:

... every form of behavior has a certain articulation or phrasing. This articulation issues from a similar articulation of the central nervous processes of the acting individual. This central articulation in turn corresponds to the individual's 'experience', which is articulated in like manner. Thus, the perception in the mind of an onlooker, if it is so constituted as to embrace what is going on in the agent, must itself possess a similar articulation. And hence the experience of agent A and observant B must resemble each other.

(Koffka, 1924, pp. 130–131)

Although, as Gallagher, as well as the Gestalt psychologists, argue, a good part of the time, direct perception of facial expressions and bodily movements, without any intervening inferential or simulation processes, may suffice to grasp another's affective state, this is not always the case. As Gangopadhyay and Miyahara (2014) in many circumstances, understanding another's mental state may require implicit (and sometimes explicit) inferential and simulating processes. There is also the issue of top-down influences on the perception of another's mental state. As noted earlier, how one reacts to observing another person in pain varies with such factors as whether the other person is viewed as fair or unfair, or whether s/he is a member of an ingroup or outgroup. Although these studies have to do with the effect of these factors on empathic response, they may also exert subtle influences on perception. Further research would be useful.

Neural and behavioral synchrony

Reflecting an increased interest in social interaction, a number of studies during the last 20 or so years have undertaken the simultaneous measurement of brain states during the interaction of two or more people. The evidence suggests the existence of both behavioral and neural synchrony during social interaction. The particular social interactions investigated have included musical interaction (Kahlil, 2022), romantic kissing, mother-child interactions, speaker and listener in conversation, hand kinematics in leaders and followers (as cited in Czuzumanski, 2020), and patient–therapist interaction (Koole & Tschacher, 2016). There is evidence that behavioral and neural synchrony is associated with rapport, interpersonal bonds, marital satisfaction, and co-regulation (Koole & Tschacher, 2016). There is also evidence of physiological synchrony as measured by autonomic nervous system activation of people in interaction.

It is important to note that physiological synchrony is not limited to matching physiological activation, but as is the case, for example, in co-regulation, is seen in *complementary* reactions. It is not clear whether synchrony should be understood as two people having the *same* neural, behavioral, and physiological patterns or whether it can also include *complementary* patterns. For example, mother's appropriate synchronous responses to her infant's distress are not limited to her own distress, but include complementary soothing and comforting behaviors and accompanying neural and physiological processes. In general, a caring and comforting response to another person in distress may entail a two-component process: component one, one's own experience of at least a small dose of the other's distress (perhaps made possible by the activation of the mirror neuron system); and component two, the activation of a caring response.

Although there is obviously a need for much further work and much clarification, one can tentatively address the implications of behavioral, neural, and physiological synchrony for intersubjective experience and understanding. Behavioral and neural synchrony *per se* may not have important implications for intersubjective experience and understanding. After all, ant colonies, for example, show incredible behavioral, and undoubtedly, neural and physiological synchrony. However, at the very least, the findings on behavioral and neural synchrony represent further evidence, not only of our inherent social nature, but also suggest that any adequate understanding of the nature of mind must go beyond the phenomenon of one person passively observing another person and needs to include social interactions.[17]

Different theories of interpersonal understanding focus on different mental states

To an important extent, the different theories regarding understanding of another person's mental states tend to focus on different subjective phenomena. Whereas TT studies deal mainly with the other's *beliefs*, ST and IT focus mainly on understanding the other's actions and emotions. This is important in so far as whereas beliefs may not be easily gleaned from observing another person's behavior, actions and emotional expressions of another person are readily observable. Hence, it is no accident that whereas false beliefs constitute the main paradigm for investigation of TT hypotheses, understanding another's intentional actions, facial expressions, and bodily movements constitute the main phenomena in the investigation of ST and IT hypotheses. The nature of the phenomena being investigated also determine which theories accounting for mindreading can be combined as hybrid theories and which cannot be so readily combined. Thus, as discussed above, whereas ST and IT can be combined, neither theory can be easily combined with TT, particularly in the context of investigating false beliefs phenomena. In short, each of the three theories discussed may have explanatory value in regard to the particular mental states on which they focus.[18]

Somewhat ironic for a theory that emphasizes ongoing social interaction, IT does not seem to take into account the fact that in social interaction with another person, one does not merely perceive the other's intentions, emotions, and actions, but also reacts to them, and that these reactions include both shared and complementary feelings. Indeed, it is shared feelings by observer and observed that is of much importance in ST that appears to be absent in IT. As Gallese (2007) puts it, 'Only the embodied simulation, mediated by the activation of the mirror neuron system enables the capacity of knowing "how it feels" to perform a given action. Only this mechanism enables intentional attunement with the observed agent' (p. 661). It may well be, however, that neither explicit nor implicit simulation is necessary for shared feelings. If that is the case and if the element of shared feelings is added to Gallagher's (2008) formulation of IT, one might justifiably conclude that the 'interpretation of mirror neuron activation offers a tight fit with IT' (p. 170).

Concluding comments

Much of the research and theorizing I have described in this chapter would likely not have been pursued had researchers and theorists taken seriously the fiat to cease all talk of mind and mental states or the claim that all our joys and sorrows are nothing but assemblies of neural cells. This is also the case with a good deal of interesting and important research on intersubjective experience outside the context of the debate among TT, ST, and IT theorists. Obviously, I cannot cover this huge literature. However, let me provide one or two examples of such research. There is evidence that specific brain networks are activated when one engages in mentalization, that is, when one attributes mental states to another person (Frith & Frith, 2003; Gallagher et al., 2000; Grafman et al., 1995; Saxe & Powell, 2006). These networks are activated even when one is presented with animated geometric shapes showing biological movement (Castelli et al., 2000; Frith & Frith, 2010).[19] They are also activated by the perception of eye gaze toward oneself and hearing one's name, both suggesting intention to communicate (Brook & Kempe, 2012). Interestingly, these brain networks are also activated when one engages in self-monitoring (Castelli et al., 2000). As Frith and Frith (2006) note, particularly in the context of social interaction, the capacity for ready-at-hand mentalizing is highly adaptive in so far as it enables one to *predict* what another person is going to do.

There is a great deal of research that does not deal directly with the question of understanding another person's mental states, but would make little sense if one did not make the implicit assumption that we interact with each other as intentional beings. Consider as an example, the following findings on the relation between touch and trust on delay of gratification: in one study, Leonard et al. (2014) reported that a friendly touch on the back had a significant effect on delay of gratification of 5-year-old children. A friendly touch also facilitates social behavior ranging from school children's compliant behavior to tipping at a restaurant (Crusco & Wetezel, 1984). There is evidence that a gentle touch is associated with oxytocin release (Portnova et al., 2020), which in turn, is associated with increased trust (Kosfeld et al., 2005). There is also evidence that trust in a specific individual who is promising a future reward as well as generalized trust in others are lawfully related to delay of gratification (Ma et al., 2018). Michaelson and Munakata (2016) reported that children who observed an adult behaving in a trustworthy manner toward another adult showed greater delay of gratification than children who observed an adult behaving in an untrustworthy manner. The above studies taken together suggest that the ability of a friendly touch to influence delay of gratification may operate through enhancing trust.

It is difficult to imagine that the above studies would be carried out if one did not assume the reality of mental states such as expectations and trust. Thus, ironically, many scientific studies would be proscribed by a philosophical ideology that removes consciousness, subjective experience, mind, and mental states from scientific investigation. This reality exposes the vacuousness of philosophical proposals that have in common the central idea that the discourse of consciousness and subjective experience is illusory and should be replaced by the discourse of neural activity.

Notes

1 There is not much to be said regarding how structuralism and behaviorism deal with intersubjective experience. The issue simply does not arise.
2 Again, recall Renee's experience during her psychosis.

3 Although the early psychoanalytic theorists cited by Bolognini (2004) refer to empathy in the context of the analyst's understanding of the patient's *unconscious* mental states, see Eagle and Wolitzky (1997) and Schlesinger (1981) for a discussion of some problems inherent in the idea of an empathic response to another person's unconscious (and perhaps disavowed) mental states.

4 He also writes that 'psychoanalysis demands nothing more than that we should apply this process to ourselves also – a proceeding to which it is true, we are not constitutionally inclined' (p. 169).

5 It should be noted that in following Kohut's formulation to its logical conclusion, Stolorow does not intend to demonstrate its implausibility through *reductio ad absurdum*. Rather, he views the product of the logical conclusion to be a reasonable description of object relations. One should add that, as we will see, in his later work Stolorow's views diverged from a self-psychology position.

6 Ironically, although different in specific content, the self-psychology and Freudian theory share an instrumental conception of the object. Indeed, one can re-state the Freudian definition of the object as 'the thing in regard to which the instinct achieves its' aim' in self-psychology terms as 'the thing in regard to which the self is enhanced'.

7 This is, in effect, Fairbairn's version of the concept of transference.

8 The target here is a straw man insofar as no one suggests that an individual human mind arises *sui generis* totally independent of others.

9 It is not clear in what way this differs from concepts such as Representations of Interactions Generalized (RIG's) (Stern, 1985); internal working models (IWM's (Bowlby, 1973)); and '"relational configurations"' (Mitchell, 1998).

10 Benjamin's view is congruent with Kant's moral position that human beings are ends in themselves and should never be treated as instrumental means to other ends.

11 There are certain experiences, oceanic feelings, sexual union, for example, in which one does experience little boundary between oneself and the other.

12 It is interesting that the term 'othering' is employed to describe a perspective in which the other is not fully experienced as a being like oneself. In such instances, the other is experienced as so different, so alien that one could not possibly understand his or her mental states.

13 There is an irony here. The Freud of the 'hermeneutics of suspicion' (Ricoeur, 1970), who views manifest content with suspicion, nevertheless shows little of the same skepticism in regard to reports, rife with the possibility of error and contamination, of presumed phenomena that, it appears, he would very much like to believe do exist.

14 Although I am reminded of the adage that it is alright to be open-minded, but not so open that your brains fall out.

15 TT research and theory on intersubjective experience and understanding often go under the misleading heading 'Theory of Mind' – misleading because, as will see, only one of the theoretical accounts proposes that we develop a *theory* of the other's mental states.

16 As early as 1739, Hume wrote that 'When I see the effects of passion in the voice and gesture of any person, my mind immediately passes from these effects to their causes, and forms such a lively idea of the passion as is presently converted into the passion itself' (p. 575). He also wrote that 'Affections readily pass from one person to another, and beget corresponding movements in every human creature' (p. 577). And Adam Smith, approximately 20 years later, wrote 'Whatever is the passion which arises from any object in the person principally concerned, an analogous emotion springs up at the thought of his situation, in the breast of any attentive spectator' (as cited in Sprague, 1967, p. 462).

17 One needs to include an important caution regarding the research on neural synchrony. As Holroyd (2022) has recently noted, the different methods employed to measure neu-

ral synchrony has resulted in a 'lack of a widely accepted definition of synchrony' (p. 346). Also, the different methods 'permit evidence consistent with the idea [i.e., of neural synchrony] to accumulate without providing means to falsify it' (p. 346).

18 This is not unlike the situation that holds with regard to different psychoanalytic 'schools', each school focusing on a particular aspect of psychological functioning.

19 Luo and Baillargeon (2005) reported that five-month-old infants attribute goals to self-propelled boxes, that is, to objects that appear to show agency.

References

Arendt, H. (1994). *Eichmann in Jerusalem: A report on the banality of evil*. Penguin.

Asch, S. (1952). *Social psychology*. Prentice-Hall.

Bacal, H. A., & Newman, K. M. (1990). *Theories of object relations: Bridges to self psychology*. Columbia University Press.

Baron-Cohen, S., Leslie, A. M., & Frith, U. (1985). Does the autistic child have a "theory of mind"? *Cognition, 21*(1), 37–46. https://doi.org/10.1016/0010-0277(85)90022-8

Batson, C. D. (2009). These things called empathy: Eight related but distinct phenomena. In J. Decety & W. Ickes (Eds.), *The social neuroscience of empathy*. Cambridge University Press. https://doi.org/10.7551/mitpress/9780262012973.003.0002

Bem, D. J. (1972). Self-perception theory. In L. Berkowitz (Ed.), *Advances in experimental social psychology* (Vol. 6, pp. 1–62). Academic Press.

Benjamin, J. (1988). *The bonds of love: Psychoanalysis, feminism, & the problem of domination*. Pantheon.

Benjamin, J. (1990). An outline of intersubjectivity: The development of recognition. *Psychoanalytic Psychology, 7*(Suppl.), (33–46). https://doi.org/10.1037/h0085258

Benjamin, J. (1995). *Like subjects, love objects: Essays on recognition and sexual difference*. Yale University Press.

Benjamin, J. (2000). Response to commentaries by Mitchell and by Butler. *Studies in Gender and Sexuality, 1*(3), 308–308.

Benjamin, J. (2013). Thinking together, differently: Thoughts on Bromberg and intersubjectivity. *Contemporary Psychoanalysis, 49*(3), 356–379.

Benjamin, W. (1913). Experience. In M. Bullock & M. W. Jenning (Eds.), *Walter Benjamin's selected writing* (Vol. 1, pp. 3–6). Harvard University Press.

Bohleber, W. (2013). The concept of intersubjectivity in psychoanalysis: Taking critical stock. *The International Journal of Psychoanalysis, 94*(4), 799–823. https://doi.org/10.1111/1745-8315.12021

Bollas, C. (2006). Perceptive identification. *Psychoanalytic Review, 93*(5), 713–717. https://doi.org/10.1521/prev.2006.93.5.713

Bolognini, S. (2004). *Psychoanalytic empathy*. Free Association Books.

Bowlby, J. (1973). *Attachment and loss* (Vol. 2). Basic Books.

Brethel-Haurwitz, K. M., Cardinale, E. M., Vekaria, K. M., Robertson, E. L., Walitt, B., VanMeter, J. W., & Marsh, A. A. (2018). Extraordinary altruists exhibit enhanced self-other overlap in neural responses to distress. *Psychological Science, 29*(10), 1631–1641. https://doi.org/10.1177/0956797618779590

Brooks, P., & Kempe, V. (2012). *Language development*. Wiley-Blackwell.

Carr, D. (1973). The "fifth meditation" and Husserl's Cartesianism. *Philosophy & Phenomenological Research, 34*(1), 14–35. https://doi.org/10.2307/2106777

Castelli, F., Happé, F., Frith, U., & Frith, C. (2000). Movement and mind: A functional imaging study of perception and interpretation of complex intentional movement patterns. *NeuroImage, 12*(3), 314–325. https://doi.org/10.1006/nimg.2000.0612

Chater, N. (2018). *The mind is flat: The remarkable shallowness of the improvising brain.* Yale University Press.

Cheon, B. K., Im, D.-M., Harada, T., Kim, J.-S., Mathur, V. A., Scimeca, J. M., ... Chiao, J. Y. (2013). Cultural modulation of the neural correlates of emotional pain perception: The role of other-focusedness. *Neuropsychologia, 51*(7), 1177–1186. https://doi.org/10.1016/j.neuropsychologia.2013.03.018

Crick, F. H. C. (1994). *The astonishing hypothesis: The scientific search for the soul.* Charles Scribner's Sons.

Crusco, A. H., & Wetzel, C. G. (1984). The Midas touch: The effects of interpersonal touch on restaurant tipping. *Personality and Social Psychology Bulletin, 10*(4), 512–517. https://doi.org/10.1177/0146167284104003

Cuff, B. M. P., Brown, S. J., Taylor, L., & Howat, D. J. (2016). Empathy: A review of the concept. *Emotion Review, 8*(2), 144–153. https://doi.org/10.1177/1754073914558466

Datyner, A., Henry, J. D., & Richmond, J. L. (2017). Rapid facial reactions in response to happy and angry expressions in 7-month-old infants. *Developmental Psychobiology, 59*(8), 1046–1050. https://doi.org/10.1002/dev.21575

Davidov, M., Paz, Y., Roth-Hanania, R., Uzefovsky, F., Orlitsky, T., Mankuta, D., & Zahn-Waxler, Z. (2020). Caring babies: Concern for others in distress during infancy. *Developmental Science, 24.* https://doi.org/10.1111/desc.13016

De Peyer, J. (2016). Uncanny communication and the porous mind. *Psychoanalytic Dialogues, 26*(2), 156–174. https://doi.org/10.1080/10481885.2016.1144978

Dennett, D. C. (1986). The case for rorts. In R. Brandom (Ed.), *Rorty and his critics.* Wiley-Blackwell.

Deutsch, H. (1926). Occult processes occurring during psychoanalysis. In H. Deutsch (Ed.), *The therapeutic process, the self and female psychology: Collected psychoanalytic papers* (pp. 227–228). Transaction Publishers.

Deutsch, H. (1929). The genesis of agoraphobia. *International Journal of Psychoanalysis, 10,* 51–69.

Eagle, M. N. (2022). Two visions of psychoanalysis: An essay in memory of Carlo Strenger. *Psychoanalytic Psychology, 39*(1), 27–36. https://doi.org/10.1037/pap0000394

Eagle, M. N., & Wakefield, J. C. (2007). Gestalt psychology and the mirror neuron discovery. *Gestalt Theory, 29*(1), 59–64.

Eagle, M. N., & Wolitzky, D. L. (1997). Empathy: A psychoanalytic perspective. In A. C. Bohart & L. S. Greenberg (Eds.), *Empathy reconsidered: New directions in psychotherapy* (pp. 217–244). American Psychological Association. https://doi.org/10.1037/10226-009

Eagle, R. (2007). *Help him make you smile: The development of intersubjectivity in the atypical child.* Rowman & Littlefield.

Fairbairn, W. R. (1944). Endopsychic structure considered in terms of object-relationships. *International Journal of Psycho-Analysis, 25,* 70–92.

Fairbairn, W. R. (1952). *Psychoanalytic studies of the personality.* Tavistock, Routledge & Kegan Paul.

Farber, S. K. (2017). Becoming a telepathic tuning fork: Anomalous experience and the relational mind. *Psychoanalytic Dialogues, 27*(6), 719–734. https://doi.org/10.1080/10481885.2017.1379329

Fosshage, J. L. (2017). Emergence of conflict during the development of self: A relational self psychology perspective. In C. Christian, M. N. Eagle, & D. L. Wolitzky (Eds.), *Psychoanalytic perspectives on conflict* (pp. 127–145). Routledge. https://doi.org/10.4324/9781315758589-8

Freud, S. (1901). The psychopathology of everyday life. In *Standard edition* (Vol. 6, pp. 1–290). Hogarth Press.

Freud, S. (1912a). Recommendations to physicians practicing psycho-analysis. In *Standard edition* (Vol. 12, pp. 111–120). Hogarth Press.

Freud, S. (1912b). The dynamics of transference. In *Standard edition* (Vol. 12, pp. 97–108). Hogarth Press.

Freud, S. (1914). On narcissism: An introduction. In *Standard edition* (Vol. 14, pp.73–102). Hogarth Press.

Freud, S. (1915). Instincts and their vicissitudes. In *Standard edition* (Vol. 14, pp. 117–140). Hogarth Press.

Freud, S. (1916 [1915]). On transience. In *Standard edition* (Vol. 14, pp. 305–307). Hogarth Press.

Freud, S. (1916–1917). Introductory lectures on psycho-analysis. In *Standard edition* (Vol. 15–16, pp. 1–482). Hogarth Press.

Freud, S. (1922). Dreams and telepathy. In *Standard edition* (Vol. 18, pp. 195–220). Hogarth Press.

Freud, S. (1925). The occult significance of dreams. In *Standard edition* (Vol. 19, pp. 125–138). Hogarth Press.

Freud, S. (1933). New introductory lectures on psycho-analysis. In *Standard edition* (Vol. 22, pp. 5–182). Hogarth Press.

Freud, S. (1941 [1921]). Psychoanalysis and telepathy. In *Standard edition* (Vol. 18, pp. 174–193). Hogarth Press.

Friedman, M. S. (1955a). *Martin Buber: The life of dialogue.* The University of Chicago Press.

Friedman, M. S. (1955b). *Martin Buber: The life of dialogue.* Routledge.

Frith, U., & Frith, C. D. (2003). Development and neurophysiology of mentalizing. *Philosophical Transactions of the Royal Society of London Series B, Biological sciences, 358*(1431), 459–473. https://doi.org/10.1098/rstb.2002.1218

Frith, U., & Frith, C. D. (2006). The neural basis of mentalizing. *Neuron, 50*(4), 531–534. https://doi.org/10.1016/j.neuron.2006.05.001

Frith, U., & Frith, C. D. (2010). The social brain: Allowing humans to boldly go where no other species has been. *Philosophical Transactions of the Royal Society of London Series B, Biological Sciences, 365*(1537), 165–176. https://doi.org/10.1098/rstb.2009.0160

Gabbard, G. O. (1995). Countertransference: The emerging common ground. *The International Journal of Psychoanalysis, 76*(3), 475–485.

Gallagher, H., Happé, F., Brunswick, N., Fletcher, P., Frith, U., & Frith, C. (2000). Reading the mind in cartoons and stories: An fMRI study of "theory of mind" in verbal and nonverbal tasks. *Neuropsychologia, 38*(1), 11–21. https://doi.org/10.1016/S0028-3932(99)00053-6

Gallagher, S. (2008). Inference or interaction: Social cognition without precursors. *Philosophical Explorations, 11*(3), 163–174. https://doi.org/10.1080/13869790802239227

Gallagher, S. (2011). Narrative competency and the massive hermeneutical background. In P. Fairfield (Ed.), *Hermeneutics in education* (pp. 21–38). Continuum.

Gallese, V. (2006). Mirror neurons and intentional attunement: Commentary on olds. *Journal of the American Psychoanalytic Association, 54*(1), 47–57. https://doi.org/10.1177/00030651060540011101

Gallese, V. (2007). Before and below 'theory of mind': Embodied simulation and the neural correlates of social cognition. *Philosophical Transactions of the Royal Society of London Series B, Biological Sciences, 362*(1480), 659–669. https://doi.org/10.1098/rstb.2006.2002

Gallese, V. (2016). Finding the body in the brain. In B. P. McLaughlin & Kornblith (Eds.), *Goldman and his critics* (pp. 297–317). Wiley.

Gallese, V., Eagle, M., & Migone, P. (2007). Intentional attunement: Mirror neurons and the neural underpinnings of interpersonal relations. *Journal of the American Psychoanalytic Association, 55*(1), 131–176. https://doi.org/10.1177/00030651070550010601.

Gallese, V., Fadiga, L., Fagassi, L., & Rizzolatti, G. (1996). Action recognition in the premotor cortex. *Brain, 119*(2), 593–609.

Gangopadhyay, N., & Miyahara, K. (2014). Perception and the problem of access to other minds. *Philosophical Psychology, 5*, 1–20.

Gooch, S. (1978). *The paranormal*. Harper & Row.

Gooch, S. (2007). *The origins of psychic phenomena: Poltergeists, incubi, succubi, and the unconscious mind*. Inner Traditions.

Grafman, J., Holyoak, K. J., & Boller, F. (Eds.). (1995). *Structure and functions of the human prefrontal cortex*. New York Academy of Sciences.

Grayling, A. C. (2019). *The history of philosophy*. Penguin Press.

Hall, H. (1976). Idealism and solipsism in Husserl's Cartesian meditations. *Journal of the British Society for Phenomenology, 7*(1), 53–55.

Hay, D. F., Nash, A., & Pedersen, J. (1981). Responses of six-month-olds to the distress of their peers. *Child Development, 52*(3), 1071–1075. https://doi.org/10.2307/1129114

Heimann, P. (1950). On counter-transference. *The International Journal of Psychoanalysis, 31*, 81–84.

Hein, G., Lamm, C., Brodbeck, C., & Singer, T. (2011). Skin conductance response to the pain of others predicts later costly helping. *PloS One, 6*(8), e22759. https://doi.org/10.1371/journal.pone.0022759

Hein, G., Silani, G., Preuschoff, K., Batson, C. D., & Singer, T. (2010). Neural responses to ingroup and outgroup members' suffering predict individual differences in costly helping. *Neuron, 68*(1), 149–160. https://doi.org/10.1016/j.neuron.2010.09.00

Hobson, R. P. (1993). *Autism and the development of mind*. Lawrence Erlbaum Associates, Inc.

Holroyd, C. B. (2022). Interbrain synchrony: On wavy ground. *Trends in Neurosciences, 45*(5), 346–357. https://doi.org/10.1016/j.tins.2022.02.002

Hume, D. (1888). *A treatise of human nature*. Clarendon Press. (Original work published 1739).

Husserl, E. (1929–1935). *Zur phänomenologie der Intersubjektivität. Texte aus dem NachlassDritter teil: 1929–1935*. Springer.

Husserl, E. (1973). *Cartesian meditations* (D. Cairns, Trans.). Martinus Nijhoff. (Original work published 1931).

Jones, E. (1946). A valedictory address. *International Journal of Psychoanalysis*, *27*(1–2), 7–12.

Jones, E. (1952). Preface to "psychoanalytic studies of the personality". In W. R. D. Fairbairn (Ed.), *Psychological studies of the personality*. Tavistock, Routledge & Kegan Paul.

Kernberg, O. F. (1965). Notes on countertransference. *Journal of the American Psychoanalytic Association*, *13*(1), 38–56. https://doi.org/10.1177/000306516501300102

Khalil, A., Musacchia, G., & Iversen, J. R. (2022). It takes two: Interpersonal neural synchrony is increased after musical interaction. *Brain Sciences*, *12*(3), 409. https://doi.org/10.3390/brainsci12030409

Klein, M. (1935). A contribution to the psychogenesis of manic-depressive states. In *The writings of Melanie Klein* (Vol. 1). Hogarth Press.

Klein, M. (1975). *Love, guilt, and reparation, and other works, 1921–1945*. Hogarth Press.

Koffka, K. (1924). *Growth of the mind*. Harcourt Brace.

Köhler, W. (1947). *Gestalt psychology; An introduction to new concepts in modern psychology* (Rev. ed.). Liveright.

Kohut, H. (1971). *The analysis of the self: A systematic approach to the psychoanalytic treatment of narcissistic personality disorders*. University of Chicago Press.

Kohut, H. (1977). *The restoration of the self*. International Universities Press.

Kohut, H. (1984). *How does analysis cure?* University of Chicago Press. http://doi.org/10.7208/chicago/9780226006147.001.0001

Koole, S. L., & Tschacher, W. (2016). Synchrony in psychotherapy: A review and an integrative framework for the therapeutic alliance. *Frontiers in Psychology*, *7*, 862.

Kosfeld, M., Heinrichs, M., Zak, P., Fischbacher, U., & Fehr, E. (2005). Oxytocin increases trust in humans. *Nature*, *435*(7042), 673–676. https://doi.org/10.1038/nature03701

Laing, R. D. (1967). *The politics of experience and the bird of paradise*. Penguin.

Lazar, S. G. (2001). Knowing, influencing, and healing: Paranormal phenomena and implications for psychoanalysis and psychotherapy. *Psychoanalytic Inquiry*, *21*(1), 113–131. https://doi.org/10.1080/07351692109348926

Leonard, J. A., Berkowitz, T., & Shusterman, A. (2014). The effect of friendly touch on delay-of-gratification in preschool children. *The Quarterly Journal of Experimental Psychology*, *67*(11), 2123–2133. https://doi.org/10.1080/17470218.2014.907325

Luo, Y., & Baillargeon, R. (2005). Can a self-propelled box have a goal? Psychological reasoning in 5-month-old infants. *Psychological Science*, *16*(8), 601–608.

Ma, F., Chen, B., Xu, F., Lee, K., & Heyman, G. D. (2018). Generalized trust predicts young children's willingness to delay gratification. *Journal of Experimental Child Psychology*, *169*, 118–125.

Mayer, E. (2007). *Extraordinary knowing: Science, skepticism, and the inexplicable powers of the human mind*. Bantam.

Michaelson, L. E., & Munakata, Y. (2016). Trust matters: Seeing how an adult treats another person influences preschoolers' willingness to delay gratification. *Developmental Science*, *19*(6), 1011–1019. https://doi.org/10.1111/desc.12388

Mitchell, S. A. (1988). *Relational concepts in psychoanalysis: An integration*. Harvard University Press.

Mitchell, S. A. (2000). *Relationality: From attachment to intersubjectivity*. Analytic Press.

Moran, R. A. (2001). *Authority and estrangement: An essay on self-knowledge*. Princeton University Press.

Nisbett, R. E., & Wilson, T. D. (1977). The halo effect: Evidence for unconscious alteration of judgments. *Journal of Personality and Social Psychology*, *35*(4), 250–256. https://doi.org/10.1037/0022-3514.35.4.250

Nyström, P. (2008). The infant mirror neuron system studied with high density EEG. *Social Neuroscience*, *3*(3–4), 334–347. https://doi.org/10.1080/17470910701563665

Papazian, B. (2017). 'Telepathic' phenomena and separation anxiety. *International Journal of Psychoanalysis*, *98*(4), 1169–1192.

Paz, Y., Orlitsky, T., Roth-Hanania, R., Zahn-Waxler, C., & Davidov, M. (2021). Predicting externalizing behavior in toddlerhood from early individual differences in empathy. *Journal of Child Psychology and Psychiatry, and Allied Disciplines*, *62*(1), 66–74. https://doi.org/10.1111/jcpp.13247

Petitmengin, C. (2001). *L'expérience intuitive*. l'Harmattan.

Ponsi, M. (1997). Interaction and transference. *International Journal of Psychoanalysis*, *78*(2), 243–263.

Portnova, G. V., Proskurnina, E. V., Sokolova, S. V., Skorokhodov, I. V., & Varlamov, A. A. (2020). Perceived pleasantness of gentle touch in healthy individuals is related to salivary oxytocin response and EEG markers of arousal. *Experimental Brain Research*, *238*(10), 2257–2268. https://doi.org/10.1007/s00221-020-05891-y

Prados, M. (1959). Transference and seemingly parapsychological phenomena. *Psychoanalytic Review*, *46*(3), 29–44.

Premack, D., & Woodruff, G. (1978). Does the chimpanzee have a theory of mind? *Behavioral and Brain Sciences*, *1*(4), 515–526. https://doi.org/10.1017/S0140525X00076512

Rabeyron, T., Edvard, R., & Massicotte, C. (2021). Psychoanalysis and telepathic processes. *Journal of the American Psychoanalytic Association*, *69*(3), 535–571. https://doi.org/10.1177/00030651211022332

Racker, H. (1968). *Transference and countertransference*. International Universities Press.

Ricoeur, P. (1970). *Freud and philosophy: An essay on interpretation*. Yale University Press.

Rizzolatti, G., & Sinigaglia, C. (2008). *Mirrors in the brain: How our minds share actions and emotions* (F. Anderson, Trans.). Oxford University Press.

Rosenbaum, R. (2011). Exploring the other dark continent: Parallels between psi phenomena and the psychotherapeutic process. *Psychoanalytic Review*, *98*(1), 57–90. https://doi.org/10.1521/prev.2011.98.1.57

Sandler, J. (1981). Unconscious wishes and human relationships. *Contemporary Psychoanalysis*, *17*(2), 180–196. https://doi.org/10.1080/00107530.1981.10745658

Saxe, R., & Powell, L. J. (2006). It's the thought that counts: Specific brain regions for one component of theory of mind. *Psychological Science*, *17*(8), 692–699. https://doi.org/10.1111/j.1467-9280.2006.01768.x

Schilbach, L., Timmermans, B., Reddy, V., Costall, A., Bente, G., Schlicht, T., & Vogeley, K. (2013). Toward a second-person neuroscience. *The Behavioral and Brain Sciences*, *36*(4), 393–414. https://doi.org/10.1017/S0140525X12000660

Schlesinger, H. (1981). The process of empathic response. *Psychoanalytic Inquiry*, *1*(3), 393–416. https://doi.org/10.1080/07351698109533411

Schwartz, H. P. (2012). Intersubjectivity and dialecticism. *The International Journal of Psychoanalysis*, *93*(2), 401–425. https://doi.org/10.1111/j.1745-8315.2011.00543.x

Shimada, S., & Hiraki, K. (2006). Infant's brain responses to live and televised action. *NeuroImage*, *32*(2), 930–939. https://doi.org/10.1016/j.neuroimage.2006.03.044

Silverman, S. (1988). Correspondences and thought-transference during psychoanalysis. *Journal of the American Academy of Psychoanalysis*, *16*(3), 269–294. https://doi.org/10.1521/jaap.1.1988.16.3.269

Simpson, E. A., Murray, L., Paukner, A., & Ferrari, P. F. (2014). The mirror neuron system as revealed through neonatal imitation: Presence from birth, predictive power and evidence of plasticity. *Philosophical Transactions of the Royal Society of London Series B, Biological Sciences*, *369*(1644), 20130289. https://doi.org/10.1098/rstb.2013.0289

Singer, T., Seymour, B., O'Doherty, J. P., Stephan, K. E., Dolan, R. J., & Frith, C. D. (2006). Empathic neural responses are modulated by the perceived fairness of others. *Nature*, *439*(7075), 466–469. https://doi.org/10.1038/nature04271

Stern, D. N. (1985). *The interpersonal world of the infant: A view from psychoanalysis and developmental psychology*. Routledge. https://doi.org/10.4324/9780429482137

Stolorow, R. D. (2013). Intersubjective-systems theory: A phenomenological-contextualist psychoanalytic perspective. *Psychoanalytic Dialogues*, *23*(4), 383–389. https://doi.org/10.1080/10481885.2013.810486

Stolorow, R. D., Atwood, G. E., & Orange, D. M. (2002). *Worlds of experience: Interweaving philosophical and clinical dimensions in psychoanalysis*. Basic Books.

Sullivan, H. S. (1953). *The interpersonal theory of psychiatry*. Routledge. https://doi.org/10.4324/9781315014029

Ting, F., He, Z., & Baillargeon, R. (2021). Five-month-old infants attribute inferences based on general knowledge to agents. *Journal of Experimental Child Psychology*, *208*, 105126. https://doi.org/10.1016/j.jecp.2021.105126

Trevarthen, C. B. (1979). Communication and cooperation in early infancy: A description of primary intersubjectivity. In M. Bullowa (Ed.), *Before speech* (pp. 321–347). Cambridge University Press.

Wicker, B., Keysers, C., Plailly, J., Royet, J. P., Gallese, V., &Rizzolatti, G. (2003). Both of us disgusted in my insula: The common neural basis of seeing and feeling disgust. *Neuron*, *40*(3), 655–664. https://doi.org/10.1016/s0896-6273(03)00679-2

Wimmer, H., & Perner, J. (1983). Beliefs about beliefs: Representation and constraining function of wrong beliefs in young children's understanding of deception. *Cognition*, *13*(1), 103–128. https://doi.org/10.1016/0010-0277(83)90004-5

Winnicott, D. W. (1971). *Playing and reality*. Penguin.

Wittgenstein, L. (1967). *Zettel* (G. E. M. Anscombe, Trans.). University of California Press.

Wittgenstein, L. (1980). *Remarks on the philosophy of psychology*. University of Chicago Press.

Wolf, E. S. (1985). The search for confirmation: Technical aspects of mirroring. *Psychoanalytic Inquiry*, *10*(2), 271–282.

Woodward, A. L. (1999). Infants' ability to distinguish between purposeful and non-purposeful behaviors. *Infant Behavior and Development*, *22*(2), 145–160.

Zachrisson, A. (2013). The internal/external issue: What is an outer object? Another person as object and as separate other in object relations models. *The Psychoanalytic Study of the Child*, *67*(1), 249–274. https://doi.org/10.1080/00797308.2014.11785497

Zahavi, D. (2004). Phenomenology and the project of naturalization. *Phenomenology and the Cognitive Sciences*, *3*(4), 331–347.

Chapter 6

Feelings and affects

Although I refer to feelings and affects in different places throughout the previous chapters, given their centrality in consciousness and subjective experience, I think it is important to address them more systematically in a separate chapter. There are 13 different definitions of the word 'feeling' in *Webster's Unabridged Dictionary*. It will be useful to clarify how I use the word 'feeling' in this chapter. The overarching concept is the emotional system which consists of three components: neurophysiological, behavioral, and subjective affective feelings (Damasio, 1999, 2021). I use the term 'affective feeling' or 'feeling' in this chapter to refer to the subjective feeling component of the emotional system or more broadly, to the affective tone of an experience.[1]

I further assume, along with many others, that subjective experience always has an affective tone. This assumption is congruent with Freud's (1915a) insistence that every experience is accompanied by a 'quota of affect' (p. 152), as well as with Wundt and Titchener's inclusion of affect as an element of consciousness. Wundt (1897/1998) not only wrote that affect is a fundamental aspect of the mind, but also that 'we are never in a state entirely free from feeling' (p. 92). And similarly, Titchener (1909) wrote that

> … stimuli do something more than arouse sensation; they give rise to processes of a different kind, to 'feelings' in a special sense; we do not merely take the impressions as they come, but we are affected by them, we feel them.
> (p. 226)

Indeed, Titchener (1909) included *Affectionen*, along with Sensations and Images, as fundamental elements of consciousness.

That affective feeling is a fundamental mode of subjective experience was also recognized by Dewey (see Hohr, 2013) as well as in contemporary characterizations of consciousness. For example, Solms (2013) writes that consciousness as well as conscious states are 'inherently affective' (p. 12), and that consciousness is essentially affective consciousness. And as Langer (1967) writes, 'organic activity is not "psychological" unless it terminates, however remotely or indirectly, as something felt' (p. 4). When philosophers use the term *qualia* in regard to mental

DOI: 10.4324/9781032686967-7

states, they refer to the fact that phenomenal experiences have a qualitative aspect; that is, 'it is something it is like for me to undergo each state, some phenomenology that it has' (Tye, 1997).

Titchener proposed that affects along with the other elements of consciousness, vary along the dimensions of quality, intensity, direction, and clearness; and Wundt identified valence and arousal level as the primary dimensions of affects, a formulation that remains prominent in contemporary discussions of affect (e.g., Barrett & Bliss, 2009). There is wide recognition that affective feelings vary along the qualitative evaluative dimension of pleasurable–painful or positive–negative.[2]

Affective feelings as 'readings' of bodily states

According to Damasio (2018), feelings of pleasure versus unpleasure or of well-being versus distress reflect homeostatic states of the body. As Damasio (2018) puts it, 'feelings are the mental expression of homeostasis' (p. 6). Damasio (2018) writes that whereas primitive organisms maintain homeostasis and life itself through 'sensing' and ensuing automatic approach-avoidance behavior, more advanced organisms, such as human beings, that have a brain and a nervous system, are capable of feelings that provide one with information about one's bodily states. On this view, bodily states underlying emotions constitute automatic and rapid neurophysiological reactions to events; and it is the 'reading' of these neurophysiological reactions that constitute affective feelings which, along with neurophysiological states and behavior, are the third component of the emotional system.

The conception of affective feelings as 'readings' of bodily states implies that the experience of affective feelings *follows* rather than precedes the neurophysiological and behavioral reactions. It will be recognized that this account bears a strong family resemblance to the James-Lange theory of emotions, according to which, one sees the bear, which triggers neurophysiological reactions, and then runs (an automatic flight reaction) (James, 1884). It is only at that point that one experiences the emotion of fear, which is essentially the experience of one's bodily state (e.g., rapid heart rate, surge of energy, muscular changes, etc.). According to James-Lange theory, the commonsensical account in which one assesses danger, experiences the emotion of fear, and then runs, would simply be too slow to serve a survival function. Notably, in this view, the experience of the emotion of fear is essentially epiphenomenal. It plays no causal or motivational role; the neurophysiological and behavioral reactions necessary to escape the danger precede the emotional experience.

Of course, all experiences entail bodily states – we are not disembodied creatures. However, a conception of affective feelings solely in terms of 'readings' of bodily states cannot be an adequate account of their nature and function for a number of reasons. Insofar as bodily states are influenced by external stimulus conditions (e.g., a dangerous situation), feelings not only provide information about bodily states, but also about the external world, in particular, about the external stimuli that triggered the bodily states. With the exception of the word 'either' in the following passage, I think Bowlby (1969) has it just right when he writes that 'affects, feelings, and emotions are phases of an individual's intuitive appraisals either of his own organismic states and urges to act or of the succession of environmental situations in which he finds himself' (p. 104).

Although the conception of affective feelings primarily as 'readings' of bodily states may (or may not) work with regard to the so-called primary emotions such as fear, where rapid emergency reactions are imperative, it does not represent an adequate account of other emotions, particularly social emotions such as love, hate, guilt, embarrassment, shame, feelings of rejection, humiliation, and so on. A conception of these emotions as reflections of bodily states tells us little or nothing about their essential properties, including the interpersonal and interactional contexts in which they are generated, their directedness toward others, the degree to which they entail appraisal processes, and the mediating role of language. Unlike the James-Lange example of running from the bear, the experience of these social emotions is triggered by one's *construals* of events, which take place either simultaneously with or precede the experience of the emotion.[3] The possession of a brain and a nervous system not only allows experiential access to bodily states, but also one to appraise the meanings of events. Thus, compared to understanding, for example, the emotion of shame in terms of violation of some personal and societal standard, little insight into its nature and what triggers it is provided by viewing it as a reflection of bodily states.

Even if one grants that affective feelings are, in some sense, 'readings' of bodily states, as Schachter and Singer (1962) demonstrated in their classic study, how one 'reads' or construes one's bodily states, including the emotional label assigned to them, is influenced by various factors, including cognitive and social contexts in which the bodily states are experienced, as well as one's, so to speak, relation to one's body. For example, with regard to the latter, compared to a non-hypochondriacal individual, a hypochondriacal individual will be far more likely to 'read' a bodily state as a sign of serious illness and will, therefore, experience anxiety. As an example of the importance of social context, there is much clinical evidence that 'good trips' versus 'bad trips' in reaction to bodily states brought about by psychedelic drugs vary with the social context in which the drug is taken: a cold, indifferent social versus a supportive and trustworthy environment.

The relation between affective feelings and how one construes events can be accurately characterized in terms of circular causation. That is, although affective feelings are triggered by one's construals of events, it is also the case that one's construals can be influenced by the affective state one is in – a form of (affective) state-dependent cognition – when reacting to inner and outer stimuli and events. The circular causal relation between construals and affective feelings has implications for how one thinks about the nature of therapeutic interventions, particularly in regard to negative affect. One can attempt to alter the individual's construals that trigger negative affect through psychotherapy. Or one can attempt to alter the negative affect directly through medication. However, given the circular relation between construals and affect – as well as the nature of state-dependent cognition – altering negative affect through medication may also influence construals of past and present events. To complicate matters even further, similar to medication, but through different means, psychotherapeutic interventions such as support and empathic understanding, may also alter negative affect, which in turn, may influence the individual's construals of past and present events.

The motivational primacy of feelings

In the above discussion, I have been critical of Damasio's conception of affective feelings primarily in terms of 'readings' of bodily states on the ground that that conception overlooks central properties of affective feeling such as social and interactional nature, the degree to which they provide information about the external world, their appraisal function, and their link to one's construals of events. Let me now focus on what is right about Damasio's conception of the nature of affective feelings. There is little doubt that in an important sense, affective feelings reflect and provide vital information about one's bodily state. There is also little doubt that, as Damasio (2018) proposes, that in complex organisms, affective states of pleasure and unpleasure motivate appropriate actions that serve to regulate one's homeostatic state.

To take a concrete example of the relation among bodily states, affective feelings, motivation for behavior, and action, consider the experience of feeling thirsty. When intracellular or extracellular fluid volume reach a certain point, one will experience thirst. Thus, feeling thirsty is a signal of a particular bodily state, and also serves as a motive to drink, which will restore fluid volume. In short, the relation between bodily states, affective feelings, and motivation for action describes an adaptive, homeostatic process. Note that there is no direct, unmediated pathway from a drop in fluid volume to drinking behavior. Rather, the subjective feeling of thirst is an integral component of the homeostatic process. Indeed, a situation in which a significant drop in fluid volume was not accompanied by the subjective experience of thirst as well as the desire to quench one's thirst would constitute a failure of the homeostatic process, with the consequence that the survival of the individual would be at risk. In short, rather than a direct pathway between a drop in extracellular fluid volume and drinking behavior, the homeostatic system works by the drop in extracellular fluid volume leading to *wanting* to drink. One could, of course, build an automaton that is programmed so that a deficit in fluid volume would automatically trigger fluid replenishment. One could also program the automaton to emit the words 'I am thirsty' when fluid volume falls below a certain level. However, it would be absurd to believe that because one programmed the automaton to utter 'I am thirsty', it is experiencing thirst.[4]

A similar story can be told in relation to hunger. We know that certain peptides, leptin, for example, are associated with food intake and feelings of hunger and satiety. However, similar to thirst, there is no direct, automatic, and unmediated pathway from peptide level to eating behavior. Subjective feelings of hunger intervene. Without such subjective feelings, whatever the peptide level, one would be less likely to eat, with similar consequences to failing to drink when fluid volume drops below a certain level. Again, one could build an automaton in which level of peptides triggers automatic replenishment, the utterance 'I am hungry', and even some form of 'eating' behavior. However, it would be absurd to attribute subjective feelings of hunger to the automaton.[5]

Proximal motives and distal functions

Feelings of thirst and hunger are but two concrete and straightforward examples of the motivational primacy of affective feelings. As discussed in Chapter 3, such primacy is often obscured by the conflation of proximal motives and distal evolutionary functions. Thus, although the distal function of drinking when thirsty is to restore homeostasis, the proximal motive is the unpleasant feeling of thirst and the desire to replace that feeling with the pleasurable feeling attendant upon quenching one's thirst. Let us say that one is able to directly restore extracellular fluid volume just prior to any feelings of thirst. Feelings of thirst and feelings associated with quenching one's thirst would not be in the repertory of one's subjective experiences. Now let us imagine similar automatic homeostatic mechanisms that bypass feelings with regard to all phenomena that we now view in terms of motivational systems. There would not be any feelings, only bodily states and automatic homeostatic corrective mechanisms. It will be recognized that this is essentially a description of the functioning of primitive organisms discussed by Damasio (2018). In its elimination of subjective feelings, it is also a description of accounts, like Chater's (2018) of human behavior to the effect that the belief that motives influence our behavior is illusory. In effect, any concept of motivation disappears and is replaced by automatic programs that have functional homeostatic properties. Essentially, we become automatons with no inner life of feelings that play a central role in what we do. One can sum things up by saying that we do things because we are programmed to do them; there is no doing things because we *want* to do them or have reasons for doing them. At worst, there is no wanting; at best, although one may experience wanting, the belief that it is motivationally causally linked to doing is illusory.

Although the above description may represent an account of automatons, it is not an accurate account of how biological evolution works. As Damasio (2018) writes, in complex organisms such as human beings, the capacity for feelings that motivate behavior has been selected in the course of evolution as the ordinary adaptive means of serving distal functions. Thus, one drinks when one is thirsty, one eats when one is hungry, one has sex because it is pleasurable, and so on. Of course, evolution may have taken a different course so that, like robots, so that drop in fluid volume automatically triggers replenishment, with no intervening subjective feelings between the two. But that is not the course evolution has taken.[6]

The failure to accord affective feelings motivational primacy or, indeed, any motivational function, has a long history in psychology. As far back as 1948, a highly influential paper by Leeper appeared, which documented and critically evaluated the tendency in the psychological literature to view emotion as a disruptive force that interferes with the integrity of ongoing, organized activity. Emotion reflected the 'loss of cognitive control' over 'lower centers', the consequence of which is the disorganization of behavior (p. 6). According to Leeper (1948), the philosophical origins of this view is the 'age of rationalism', characterized by the belief that 'only in the rational and intellectual functions did mankind reach the proper stature' (p. 8).[7]

Leeper (1948) was very much ahead of his time in recognizing the motivational primacy of emotions. He writes that if his 'argument is sound, it means that emotional processes operate as motives' (p. 17). He also advises the adoption of the 'view that emotional processes are one of the fundamental means of motivation in the higher animals – a kind of motivation that rests on complex neural activities …' (p. 19). Leeper was equally ahead of his time in addressing the role of emotions in psychoanalytic theory. He astutely observes that despite the common belief that psychoanalytic theory challenges the rationalist conception of human nature, the fact is that in important ways it exemplifies the 'rationalistic tradition' (p. 9). As Leeper (1948) notes, according to the id–ego model of the mind, it is the ego that is the 'reality-recognizing and reality-manipulating part of the personality' and the id that represents 'the instinctive tendencies', which 'with their emotional aspects or components, are the trouble-makers … the disruptive factors in the life of the person' (p. 9).

The nature of feelings and their motivational role in Freudian theory

Implicit in Leeper's account is the conclusion that the philosophical origins of the role of emotion in Freudian theory also lie in the 'age of rationalism' and in the Enlightenment vision. There is little doubt that this is the case. For example, according to Freudian theory, at the core of neurosis is the dominance of wishful thinking inherent in the pleasure principle over the reality principle. And the overarching goal of making the unconscious can be understood in terms of enhanced self-knowledge, insight, and diminution of the influence of wish-fulfillment and associated affect over reality-testing.

Freud not only claimed scientific status for psychoanalytic theory, but also viewed the individual's capacity for the dominance of reason over affect – for him, the essence of the scientific spirit – as the most advanced state of human development. In extolling the virtues of 'scientific thinking', Freud (1933) writes that 'it is concerned carefully to avoid individual factors and affective influences' (p. 170). He also writes that 'Our best hope for the future is that intellect – the scientific spirit, reason – may in process of time establish a dictatorship in the mental life of man' (p. 171). However, Freud (1933) also wrote that the dominance of reason and the optimal operation of the reality principle is available to only a few. For the rest of humanity, 'a resistance stirs within us against the relentlessness and monotony of the laws of thought and against the demands of reality-testing' (p. 33). One can add to the above passages the large Freudian literature on religion as wish-fulfillment illusion, and the dependence of civilization on renunciation of instinctual wishes, as well as their associated affect (Freud, 1927, 1930[1929])

Freud clearly recognized that affective feelings are, by definition, conscious and that the concept of unconscious feelings or emotions is an oxymoron. He writes:

> It is surely the essence of an emotion that we should be aware of it, i.e., that it should become known to consciousness. Thus, the possibility of the attribute of unconsciousness would be completely excluded as far as emotions, feelings and affects are concerned.
>
> (Freud, 1915b, p. 177)

He also writes that whereas 'unconscious ideas continue to exist as actual structures in the system *Ucs* ... all that corresponds in that system to unconscious affects is a potential beginning which is prevented from developing' (Freud, 1915b, p. 178). His conclusion: 'Strictly speaking, then ... there are no unconscious affects as there are unconscious ideas' (p. 178).

However, as Freud notes, in clinical work we do speak of unconscious love, hate, anger, guilt, and anxiety. What can such locutions reasonably mean? One answer to that question is provided by Freud in the above passage, namely, that the only reasonable meaning that references to repressed or unconscious affects can have is that of potential affects, that is affects that are 'prevented from developing'.[8] Freud (1915b) writes that 'to suppress the development of affect is the true aim of repression and that its work is incomplete if this aim is not achieved' (p. 178). In other words, in accord with the commonsense understanding of the pleasure principle, the basic motive of repression (as well as other defenses) is to prevent the conscious experience of painful negative affect (frequently, anxiety).Freud (1915b) provides two other answers to the question of what one may reasonably mean when one refers to unconscious affect: one, the affect is transformed into anxiety; and two, there is a 'severance ... between the affect and the idea to which it belongs', with the consequence that the affect is consciously experienced, but is attached to a 'substitutive idea' (p. 179). This latter process seems to be a form of displacement.

Given the centrality of the pleasure principle in Freudian motivational theory, one might expect that feelings of pleasure and unpleasure would play an equally central motivational role. However, as we have seen in Chapter 2, this is not the case in any straightforward way. The pleasure principle in Freudian theory is a theoretical concept that refers to build-up and discharge of excitation rather than to subjective feelings. As Rapaport (1960) notes, when the terms' pleasure' and 'pain' are used in the context of the pleasure principle, they 'must be taken for concepts' (p. xxx), not designations of subjective experience. For example,

> the referent of the concept *pain* is the accumulation of cathexes (which may, but need not be accompanied by a subjective experience of pain), that of *pleasure* the discharge of cathexes (which may, but need not be accompanied by a subjective experience of pleasure).
>
> (Rapaport, 1960, p. xxx)

In short, although there is some systematic relation between them, there is no one-to-one correspondence between the build-up and discharge of excitations and feelings of pleasure and unpleasure.

There are a few places in his writings where Freud seems to link the pleasure principle more directly to conscious feelings of pleasure and unpleasure. For example, he writes that 'what consciousness yields consists essentially of perceptions of excitations coming from the external world and of feelings of pleasure and unpleasure which can only arise from within the mental apparatus' (Freud, 1920, p. 24). He also links conscious feelings of pleasure and unpleasure to 'oscillations in the tension of [the id's] instinctual needs' (Freud, 1940, p. 198).[9] Note that in linking feelings of pleasure and unpleasure closely to oscillations in tension level of instinctual needs, the former is defined entirely in quantitative terms, limiting their motivational efficacy entirely to quantitative levels of tension. The *qualitative* aspect of feelings is entirely overlooked.

Freud was clearly aware of this problem. He writes: '... it cannot be doubted that there are pleasurable tensions and unpleasurable relaxations of tension' (Freud, 1924, p. 160), and refers to sexual excitation as but one example of the former.

> Pleasure and unpleasure, therefore, cannot be referred to as an increase or decrease of a quantity (which we describe as 'tension due to a stimulus'), although they have a great deal to do with that factor. It appears that they depend, not on this quantitative factor, but on some characteristic which we can only describe as a qualitative one.
>
> (p. 160)

Freud goes on to speculate what this 'qualitative characteristic' might be and ends up with 'We do not know' (p. 160).

Freud does not pursue the issue of the 'qualitative characteristic' of affective feelings any further in his writings. Perhaps most important, he does not assimilate recognition of the qualitative nature of affective feelings into his theorizing. To take just one example, Freud (1926) attributes the anxiety linked to the 'danger situations' of loss of the object, loss of the object's love, and castration threats to fact that at the core of all three situations is the common danger that the individual will be left at the mercy of undischarged sexual excitations. In other words, the conception of danger and the explanatory account of anxiety are entirely at the metapsychological level of quantity of excitation. There is no reference to the qualitative feelings associated with such dire situations.

The peripheral role of qualitative feelings in Freud's formulation of the pleasure principle is likely attributable to the underlying assumption that a quantitative account that bypasses conscious qualitative feelings is more scientific. To accord conscious qualitative feelings motivational capacity would be to undermine or dilute the conception of psychoanalytic theory as a discipline that investigates unconscious processes and, in particular, as a theory that accounts for most of psychological life in terms of unconscious motivations derived from instinctual drives. That is, to recognize the inherently qualitative nature of feelings would be to threaten the quantitative conception of the pleasure principle and therefore, its scientific standing. This reading is certainly congruent with the epiphenomenal role given to consciousness in the Freudian theory of the mind (see Chapter 2).

In this regard, it is worth noting Rapaport's (1960) comment that 'Once this [i.e., the dissociation between the pleasure principle and feelings] is grasped, Freud's theory is freed of the misconception by virtue of which it is still so often considered a subjectivist and hedonistic theory' (Rapaport, 1960, p. xxx). This last sentence is especially noteworthy in its implication that the disjunction between the pleasure principle and conscious feelings is necessary in order to allay any concern that Freudian theory may be viewed as a theory that is focused on conscious subjective experience rather than a theory that is primarily concerned with non-subjectivist unconscious processes (such as the accumulation and discharge of cathexes).

According to Rapaport (1960), only the id, that is, only instinctual drives, have motivational force; other factors may play a causal, but not a motivational role in behavior and in the workings of the mind. Rapaport (1960) defines motives as 'appetitive internal forces' and writes that motivational behavior is modeled on the 'defining characteristics of instinctual drives', which include the properties of peremptoriness, cyclical character, selectiveness, and displaceability (p. 866). Based on this conception of motivation, Rapaport (1960) concludes that non-drive factors such as curiosity, novelty seeking, desire for mastery, and competence, which have been referred to as cognitive motives in the psychological literature (e.g., Berlyne, 1950; Harlow et al., 1956), and as 'ego interests' in the psychoanalytic literature (Hartmann, 1939) should be thought of as non-motivational *causes*. However, insofar as Rapaport's conception of motives is modeled on instinctual drives, his conclusion is question-begging. It also leads him to the odd conclusion that because it is an ego function, defense – the essence of which is that it is motivated by the desire to avoid the experience of negative affect – has only a causal, not a motivational role in psychological functioning. (For a further discussion of this issue, see Eagle, 2022.)

Along with the conception of the pleasure principle in terms of quantity of excitations, conceptualizations of motivation, are embedded in metapsychological drive theory, the results of which are the dissociation between motivation and feelings and the failure to recognize the central role of subjective affective feelings in motivating behavior. For Freud and other psychoanalytic theorists to have acknowledged the motivational primacy of affective feelings would have perhaps come too close to diluting the all-embracing motivational influence of unconscious instinctual drives. It would also have entailed recognition of the non-epiphenomenal role of conscious experiences in psychological functioning. Or to put it in another way, to recognize the qualitative nature of conscious feelings and to grant them motivational capacity is to threaten the entire structure of the relation between conscious and unconscious in Freudian theory as well as the conception of psychoanalysis as a study of the unconscious, as a *Tiefenpsychologie*.

I discussed above the failure to adequately distinguish between proximal motives and distal functions. It seems to me that this failure is expressed in the location of motivation in instinctual drives, with the consequence of conflation levels of discourse. There is little doubt that instinctual drives play a causal role in determining the specific nature of our motives as well as their intensity and timing. One can grant that taking some action to reduce the level of tension associated is adaptive and serves a survival function (e.g., reduction of potentially damaging levels of excitation). However, the *proximal motive* for the action is the *conscious feeling* of tension, not the *distal function* of discharging potentially harmful excitations. By acting on proximal motives, one serves distal evolutionary functions. As noted above, that is how evolution generally works. Thus, on this view, instinctual drives – as well as other biological systems – play a *causal* role in influencing the specific conscious feelings we have that motivate our behavior. However, and this is an essential point, it is our conscious feelings that are the proximal motives on which we act. Thus, one needs to stand Rapaport's (1960) account on its head: although instinctual drives causally influence the nature of our desires and feelings, it is our desires and feelings that are the primary motives for our behavior and actions. This has been recognized by a number of psychoanalytic theorists. For example, Sandler (1981) writes: 'A psychoanalytic psychology of motivation related to the control of feeling states should, I believe, replace a psychology based on the idea of an instinctual drive discharge' (p. 188). Note also the following statement by Fenichel (1945), who viewed himself as a Freudian theorist: 'Thus in the last analysis, any defense is a defense against *affects* [emphasis in original] "I do not want to feel any painful sensation" is the first and final motive of defense' (p. 161).

It seems to me that the relation between proximal motives and distal functions can serve as a general framework for the influence of unconscious factors. Generally speaking, the primary way that unconscious factors, including instinctual drives, influence behavior is through their causal influence on the conscious thoughts we think, and the conscious desires and feelings we have, which serve to motivate what we do. The important point is that unconscious factors do not directly trigger behaviors, the way a program triggers a sequence of behaviors in a robot. Rather, they influence us indirectly through the intermediate step of casually influencing our conscious thoughts, desires, intentions, and feelings.[10] Thus, contrary to Freud's (1923) endorsement of Groddeck's (1923) claim that 'we are lived by our id', it is more accurate to say that although they are causally influenced by our id, we live by our aims rather than 'being lived by it' (Pine, 2011, p. 839). Further, it is our aims and their associated conscious thoughts and feelings that constitute the texture and fabric of one's subjective life. One may readily acknowledge that unconscious factors influence one's conscious desires, feelings, and the motives for one's actions. In that sense, one can say that unconscious factors play an *indirect* motivational role through their causal influence on what one thinks, desires, feels, and what one wants to do. However, according to Freudian theory, it is not simply that unconscious factors influence our conscious desires and feelings. Indeed, that claim is not distinctively psychoanalytic; any cognitive psychologist would acknowledge that. What is distinctively psychoanalytic and what makes it a *Tiefenpsychologie* are the claims that the desires that motivate us are themselves unconscious, that the major part of mental life consists of unconscious desires and thoughts. Further, according to Freud (1915a) unconscious desires are no different from conscious desires save for the fact that they lack the property of consciousness.

A host of questions are raised by the concept of unconscious desires. Normally, a desire is inherently accompanied by affective feelings, frequently intense affective feelings. It is difficult to imagine having a desire unaccompanied by any feelings. However, insofar as the idea of unconscious feelings is an oxymoron, an unconscious desire is a strange form of desire, one that is not inherently linked to affective feeling – so much for unconscious desires being identical to conscious desires. Freud was clearly aware of this conceptual difficulty, and attempted to deal with it in two ways. He writes that the true aim of repression is to remove affect from an idea or to prevent affect from developing. This suggests that the ideational or representational aspect of a repressed desire may be conscious, but not necessarily accompanied by affective feelings, normally as noted, a fundamental element of desire. A question that arises is what makes the repressed mental content a desire rather than ideation that is normally accompanied by affective feelings, but not so accompanied in specific cases. The other way that Freud (1915a) tries to deal with the conceptual problems raised by the concept of unconscious desire is to propose that affective feelings are, indeed, consciously experienced, but are no longer connected to the original desire, but rather to new representational content. Before leaving the topic of unconscious desires, I want to briefly note Rubinstein's (1980) lucid discussion of the conceptual issues inherent in the concept of unconscious desires. Rubinstein (1980) weaves a complex argument. But the gist of it is as follows: there exists in the world either conscious motives and desires or neural states – no in-between ontological category that is neither a conscious mental state nor a neurophysiological state. From this perspective, although it may be clinically useful to invoke unconscious motives and desires, it is important to keep in mind that the only defensible (interrelated) meanings unconscious motives and desires can have are one, the individual to whom one attributes an unconscious motive or desire is acting *as if* s/he had that motive or desire; two, unconscious motives and desires can be understood as *pointers* to particular neurophysiological states; and three, unconscious motives and desires can be understood as *dispositions* (which are ultimately neural processes) to experience and act in a particular way.

In important respects, Rubinstein's critical evaluation of the concept of unconscious motives and desires bears a family resemblance to Searle's (1990) critique of certain concepts having to do with unconscious cognitive structures in cognitive psychology. As noted earlier, Searle's (1990) objection to the positing of cognitive structures and processes between subjective experience and brain processes is that it implies a new ontology that is neither accessible to consciousness nor neurophysiological, that is, neither mental (i.e., potentially accessible to consciousness) nor neurophysiological, but something in-between. He suggests that the cognitive structures and processes posited by cognitive psychology constitute 'descriptions of functional aspects of systems, which will have to be explained by underlying neurophysiological mechanisms. In such cases, what looks like mentalistic psychology is sometimes better construed as speculative neurophysiology' (p. 585).[11] Note that Rubinstein's and Seale's positions are versions of James' (1890) arguments against allowing the positing of unconscious mental states as forms of explanation for behavior.

Research on affect and emotions

Before bringing this chapter to a close, I want to note that in contrast to the state of affairs in psychology that prevailed prior to the appearance of Leeper's (1948) paper, the topic of affect and emotion has been accorded enormous attention in the psychological literature. The American Psychological Association journal, *Emotion* was started in 2001. The journal *Emotion Review* first appeared in 2009. The Center for the History of Emotion, supported by the Wellcome Trust, was established in 2008. The Research Center for the History of Emotions of the Max Planck Institute was established in 2008. The *Journal of Affective Disorders* was first published in 1979. One can speculate that the earlier start of this more clinically oriented journal is at least partly due to the fact that researchers interested in clinical issues were more likely to recognize the importance of affects.

As one would expect, given the above developments, journal articles and books on emotions have burgeoned during the last 20–30 years. Obviously, I cannot cover that literature in this chapter. However, I want to provide the reader with some sense of developments in this area during the last number of years. A major topic of research that has appeared in the literature is affect regulation. Handbooks on 'affect regulation' and 'emotion regulation' regularly appear. A common theme is that the capacity to regulate negative affect is a marker of mental health and that impairments in that capacity is a general factor in a wide range of psychopathology. For example, Caspi and Moffitt (2018) have argued that common to different expressions of psychopathology is a general factor that they refer to as a 'p-factor' which, among other features, includes poor control over affective impulses. Tackett et al. (2013) identify chronic negative emotionality as a common factor in psychopathology.[12] This factor of negative emotionality is especially evident in borderline personality disorder (BPD), and is linked to (Cavicchioli & Maffei, 2020) as well as a general tendency to attribute negative intentions to others.

Affect and alexithymia

Another form of impairment in affect regulation, originally termed 'alexithymia' by Sifneos (1973) has been much investigated in the literature. The literal meaning of alexithymia, taken from the Greek, is 'lack of words for emotions', and is employed to describe a group of individuals who show little imagination, have an impoverished fantasy life, tend to somaticize, and have difficulty with verbal expression of emotion (Nemiah & Sifneos, 1970; Ruesch, 1948; Taylor, 1991). The psychoanalyst Joyce McDougall (1989) describes such individuals as emotionally deaf and dumb. Linking alexithymia to Damasio's conception of emotions as 'readings' of bodily states, it is as if alexithymic individuals are aware of bodily states, but are not able to experience and/or label the emotions that are normally linked to these bodily states. Alexithymia is not so much characterized by an impairment in the regulation of negative affect, but rather by a relative inability to experience and differentiate among different emotions. However, insofar as the relative inability to experience affects may be experienced as emptiness and emotional deadness, in a certain sense, alexithymia can be understood as entailing impairment in the capacity to regulate the negative affect of feeling emotionally empty.

There is an extensive body of research on the presence of alexithymia as a feature of various diagnostic categories. I will limit my sampling of such research to a brief sampling of alexithymia and eating disorders (partly because I have worked clinically with anorexic and bulimic individuals and have participated in some research in this area). In my clinical work with anorexic and bulimic individuals, I have been struck by the accuracy of Ruesch's (1948) term 'organic language' (p. 13) as a description of the way in which alexithymic individuals tend to deal with conflictual events that would normally trigger the experience of negative affect in non-alexithymic individuals. Let me describe an illustrative clinical vignette. A female bulimic patient reported the following episode: she had a shopping date with her mother to celebrate a significant job promotion. About an hour before her mother was due to pick her up, mother called to cancel the date, the reason for which was not especially compelling. My patient reported this incident with flat affect and no overt expression of disappointment or any other emotion. She simply said that she went shopping herself, without her mother. When I asked 'anything else?', she casually reported that before leaving her apartment, she stuffed herself with sweets and then vomited. It seemed clear that the bulimic episode represented the 'organic language' that substituted for an array of emotions that a non-alexithymic individual would likely experience in a similar situation.

Coregulation of affect

There is an important area of research and theory on affect regulation, referred to as coregulation and social baseline theory, that has emerged in the last number of years (Hughes et al., 2012; Coan, 2010, 2011). A central focus of work in this area is the role of interpersonal relationships in physiological and affect regulation. For example. Feeney and Kirkpatrick (1996) reported that variations in heart rate were significantly associated with the individual's attachment pattern, partner's availability, and perceived (rather than actual) social support.

Although research and theory on coregulation of physiology and affect is seen as a relatively new development, it has important precursors. One such precursor is the work of Hofer and his colleagues (e.g., 1978, 1984) who have shown that coregulation of physiological and affect responses in rat pups begins immediately after birth. The caregiver's ministrations (i.e., feeding, holding, licking, holding, providing warmth, interacting with) constitute inputs that regulate the rat pup's physiological systems (e.g., heart rate, temperature regulation, secretion of growth hormone, level of activity, and arousal, etc.) and associated feelings of distress versus well-being. Further, the consequences of interference with the caregiver's ministrations are interfered with (e.g., via separation) are physiological dysregulation and accompanied feelings of distress as manifested by distress vocalization and other behavioral indices.

Hofer (1984) has argued that adult relationships also function as physiological and affect regulators, and that one of the consequences of the loss of a long-term relationship is the loss of regulation provided by that relationship. Hofer (1984) cites Darwin's suggestion 'that the emotion of adult human grief has much in common with the separation response of children and with the forms of grief existing in other species of animals' (as cited in Hofer, 1984, p. 183). Hofer (1984) goes on to suggest that the effects of human bereavement may 'result from withdrawal of specific sensori-motor regulators hidden within the many complex interactions of the relationship that has ended' (p. 188). Hofer (1984) cites studies indicating that even long-term members of a group tend to develop some form of physiological synchrony, for example, in menstrual cycles (McKlintock, 1971), and in the level of adrenal cortical output among members of bomber crews while they worked closely together (Mason, 1959). There is also the classic 'broken heart' study of increased mortality among widowers following the death of their spouse (Parkes et al., 1969). Hofer (1984) concludes that 'independent self-regulation may not exist even in adulthood' (p. 194).

Other precursors to the theory of coregulation of physiological responses and affect are also found in the psychoanalytic literature, including in the writings of Freud and Fairbairn. According to Freud (1926), the early 'danger situations', which include loss of the object and of the object's love, are dangerous because they leave the infant or child at the mercy of excessive excitation. If one translates

Freud's metapsychological language of excitation into ordinary discourse, what Freud is essentially saying is that a consequence of the loss of the caregiver's regulating ministrations is that the infant or child is subject to unbearable tension and distress. In short, from the perspective of Freudian theory, the caregiver is essentially a regulator of the infant's or child's physiological and affective states.

Fairbairn (1952) has his own version of what is, in effect, a theoretical formulation of coregulation of affect. According to Fairbairn (1952), the 'ultimate psychopathological disaster' (p. 52) is a psychological state in which the individual experiences no affective connection with another, including with an internalized representation of the other. This state, according to Fairbairn, is a kind of psychological death. There is much clinical evidence that provides general support for Fairbairn's formulation. For example, as Armstrong-Perlman (1994) has observed, despite experiencing much pain and suffering, some individuals cannot relinquish their affective attachment, indeed, spend much of their lives pursuing, a rejecting other. For these individuals, to relinquish their attachment is equivalent to living in an unbearable inner world devoid of affective connections. Some years ago I worked with a woman who could not relinquish her affective attachment to a cruel and sadistic partner. Any serious thought or plan to leave her partner would inevitably be followed by despair, severe depression, and suicidal thoughts and feelings. These clinical phenomena constitute a pathological form of coregulation in which an affective connection to the other, however distressing and painful it may be, serves to ward off what is feared to be even more devastating and overwhelming distress and dysregulation.

According to Kohut (1984), parental failure to provide the infant and child with adequate experience of being empathically understood is a key factor in the development of psychopathology, which is understood in terms of impairments of self-esteem and affect regulation. And correspondingly, at the core of Kohut's approach to treatment is the assumption that the therapist's empathic understanding is the key factor in enabling the patient to develop the capacity to regulate self-esteem and negative affect. Kohut (1984) also writes that an important indication that treatment has been successful is evidence of the patient's increasing capacity to be comforted by a supportive and friendly gesture of another. In short, although not stated explicitly, implicit in Kohut's (1984) above formulation is the central idea that a core factor in adequate regulation of self-esteem and negative affect is one's capacity to avail oneself of the positive benefits of coregulation.

Implicit in attachment theory is the assumption of the coregulation of affect. According to attachment theory, the two main functions of the attachment figure are one, to serve as a safe haven, that is, to provide comfort and soothing when the child is distressed, and two, to serve as a secure base, that is, to be available when the child engages in the exploration of the physical and social world. These two basic functions of the attachment figure, which Marvin et al. (2002) refers to as the 'circle of security', are two sides of the same coin insofar as the child's repeated experiences of being comforted when distressed leads to trust and confidence in the caregiver's availability should she be needed. This brief description makes it clear that from the perspective of attachment theory, that the attachment figure is a regulator of the infant's and child's affect. On this view, insecure attachment can be understood as an impairment of coregulation of affect. That is, because the child does not have a confident expectation in the availability of the attachment figure, s/he must find other ways to regulate negative affect.

Neural basis for affect regulation

Technological advances, such as the availability of fMRI tools, have contributed to a burgeoning of research on the neural basis of psychological phenomena, including the experience and regulation of affect, which has been referred to as 'affective neuroscience', a term coined by Panksepp in 1981. Let me provide a sampling of research in this area. Posner and Rothbart (2000) report that the perception of sad faces activates not only the amygdala, but also the anterior cingulate, which serves to regulate the negative affect triggered by the sad faces. They view this phenomenon as an example of 'effortful control [which] may support empathy by allowing the individual to attend to the thoughts and feelings of another without becoming overwhelmed by their own distress' (p. 435). Similarly, Torre and Lieberman (2018) found that simply verbally labeling a stimulus that evokes negative affect decreases amygdala activation and increases activation of the prefrontal cortex. Interestingly, Young et al. (2017) reported that highly anxious individuals show deficits in cortical dampening of amygdala activation. These findings suggest that neural functional connectivity between limbic and cortical structures is a core factor in regulation of negative affect and more specifically, that deficits in functional connectivity is a key factor in poor regulation of negative affect.[13]

Reappraisal versus suppression as affect regulating strategies

There is a large body of research comparing reappraisal versus suppression as means of affect regulation (e.g., Gross, 2014). However, before proceeding further, it is important to clarify what is meant by reappraisal and suppression in these studies. The overwhelming majority of studies in this area are concerned not with the suppression of emotional *experiences or feelings*, but with suppression of *expressions* of emotions. As for reappraisal, it does not, as the term *re*appraisal suggests, refer to a re-evaluation of an emotion already experienced, but rather as an 'antecedent-focused strategy that acts before the complete activation of emotion response tendencies has taken place' (Catuli, 2014, p. 1). The description of reappraisal as an 'antecedent' strategy, that is, prior to the full experience of the emotion, raises the question of why the strategy is referred to as *re*appraisal rather than simply appraisal. As I understand the way the term is used in the literature, reappraisal refers to the following process: a situation that triggered negative affect in the past and that triggers incipient negative affect in a current situation is re-appraised, which blocks the full development of negative affect.[14]

Although context and cultural factors may play a mediating role, the most frequent research findings in this area is that compared to suppression of emotional expression, reappraisal is a more adaptive strategy in a number of ways, including physiological costs, interpersonal consequences, experience of positive affect and so on (e.g., McRae et al., 2012; Moses, J.S. 2017; Ochsner & Gross, 2008; Silvers, J.A. 2014). There is also evidence that use of reappraisal is associated with greater functional connectivity between limbic and cortical structures (e.g., Davidson, 2008; Ferri, 2016; Minde-Siedlock, 2015; Miu et al., 2012; Zak et al., 2012).

Virtually all the above studies I have cited have focused on minimizing negative affect as the primary means of affect regulation. I am aware of only one study that focuses on the transformation of the 'emotional valence of arousal from negative to positive' through reappraisal (Dore et al., 2017, p. 235). The study demonstrated that although reappraisal that minimizes negative affect decreased activity in the amygdala, successful positive reappraisal increased activity in brain areas 'involved in computing reward value' and 'enhanced positive connectivity between vmPFC and amygdala' (p. 1). Further, individual differences in such connectivity 'predicted greater positive reappraisal success' (p. 1).

Reappraisal and reflective function

What is referred to as reappraisal in the psychological literature on affect regulation bears a strong family resemblance to the concept of reflective function (RF) that has gained much currency in the psychoanalytic and attachment literatures. The most obvious point of convergence between the two concepts is that both strategies are viewed as adaptive, evidenced by the finding that impairment in both the capacity for reappraisal and RF as strategies for affect regulation are associated with psychopathology, including borderline personality disorder. There are, however, differences between the two concepts. One difference is that whereas reappraisal research and theory are primarily focused on external situations, RF theory and research are primarily concerned with inner mental states. Another difference between the two concepts is that whereas research and theory on reappraisal is directly and explicitly concerned with affect regulation, research and theory on RF are generally discussed in broader contexts that are indirectly related to affect regulation. For example, there is a good deal of research on the relation between the caregiver's capacity to reflect on both her own and her infant's mental states and the latter's security of attachment.

One can integrate the two concepts by noting that one's affective states are often inextricably linked to one's automatic appraisal and construal of another's intentions in an interactional situation. Reflecting on one's own and another's mental states provides an opportunity to reappraise one's earlier appraisals and construals and, in particular, the affects they have generated. There is evidence that enhancement of RF in BPD patients who, as noted, tend to show rejection sensitivity, provides an opportunity for such patients to reappraise their typically rapid and automatic attribution to the other of an intention to reject or humiliate them, which has typically led to rage and other negative affect.

Concluding comment

In coming to the close of this chapter, I want to reiterate that, as Solms (2013) writes, consciousness is affective consciousness. That is, to be conscious is not only to be able to make decisions or to process information – these processes can take place without conscious experience. To be conscious is to *feel*. And to feel always possesses an affective component. As Koch (2019) puts it, to be conscious is to have the feeling of being alive.

Notes

1 As research on 'repressive style' indicates, the neurophysiological component of the emotional system can be activated without activation of the affective feeling component.

2 It is interesting to note that, as shown by research employing the Osgood Semantic Differential (1964), that virtually any stimulus can be rated along an evaluative (positive–negative) dimension (along with active-passive and strong-weak), which presumably reflects the feeling tone the stimulus evokes in the rater.

3 In contrast to the James-Lange example of seeing the bear and running, there are many situations in which the experience of fear is the product of appraisal and construal of events. The above discussion regarding emotions as 'readings' of bodily states versus emotions as a function of appraisals and construals of events is, in important respects, a replay of the debate between advocates of the James-Lange versus Cannon-Bard theories of emotions. It seems to me that the empirical data, as well as conceptual analysis, largely support the claim of Cannon-Bard theory, as well as the theories of Arnold (1960) and Lazarus (e.g., 1966, 1991), that emphasize the importance of appraisal, including implicit appraisal, in the experience of affective feelings.

4 Of course, in humans, eating is associated with a wide range of meanings and is embedded in interpersonal and social contexts, and can take place independently of peptides level or feelings of hunger. Consider anorexia nervosa as an example of the complex relationships among eating, hunger, and a variety of other factors, including the subjective meanings associated with eating.

5 The discussion of humanoid robots generally focuses on information processing capacity and tasks that the robot can carry out. I have not seen much discussion, if any, on simulation of such basic human activities as eating and drinking. I suspect that this largely due to the fact that whereas information processing can be independent of subjective experience, the core conceptual meaning of eating as a human activity is linked to feeling hungry; and the core conceptual meaning of drinking is linked to feeling thirsty. Thus, constructing a robot that takes in and even digests food would bear little essential resemblance to eating; and similarly, in the case of a robot that takes in liquids.

6 Unlike traditional black box S–R behaviorism, in the contemporary account of human beings as sophisticated automatons, there is an O between S and R; however, the O is not subjective desires and wants, but rather neural processes and computational programs.

7 It is doubtful that this view was a universal one. For example, Hume (1748) wrote not only that the passions dominated reason, but that that is the way things should be.

8 Note the family resemblance between this idea and Fingarette's (1969) not spelling out one's mental state and Stern's (2003) concept of defense as not formulating the unformulated.

9 Note here some similarity to Damasio's (1991) conceptualization of affective feelings as reflections of bodily states.

10 Advertisers have always known that their job is not to influence, in Svengali-like fashion, the act of purchasing itself, but rather the feeling of wanting or needing something.

11 It is important to distinguish between Rubinstein's and Searle's arguments and the claim that insofar as they possess intentionality (in the Brentano sense) and representationality, brain states can be viewed as mental (see Wakefield, 2018).

12 The positing of impairment in the regulation of negative affect as a general factor in psychopathology is congruent with the Freudian idea that neurosis entails the failure of defense, which is essentially an affect regulating phenomenon, and the consequent 'return of the repressed'. Caspi and Moffitt (2108) make this connection in citing a paper by the psychoanalyst Ernest Jones (1946) (see Eagle, 2022, for further discussion).

13 These findings on the role of neural connectivity between limbic and cortical structures in affect regulation suggests a reformulation of the id-ego or drive-defense model of Freudian theory from an emphasis on the relation between instinctual drives and regulating ego functions to an emphasis on the relation between affects and cognitive or ego functions.

14 Viewing reappraisal in the context of psychoanalytic theory, it is as if 'signal anxiety' is prevented from developing into full-blown anxiety not through repression, but by reappraising the cues that triggered the signal anxiety. One example of reappraisal would entail the recognition that as an adult, one is no longer the helpless infant who is completely dependent on one's caregiver.

References

Armstrong-Perlman, E. M. (1994). The allure of the bad object. In J. S. Grotstein & D. B. Rinsley (Eds.), *Fairbairn and the origin of object relations* (pp. 222–235). Guilford Press.

Arnold, M. B. (1960). *Emotion and personality*. Columbia University Press.

Barrett, L. F., & Bliss-Moreau, E. (2009). She's emotional. He's having a bad day: Attributional explanations for emotion stereotypes. *Emotion, 9*(5), 649–658. https://doi.org/10.1037/a0016821

Bowlby, J. (1969). *Attachment and loss* (Vol. 1). Basic Books.

Caspi, A., & Moffitt, T. E. (2018). All for one and one for all: Mental disorders in one dimension. *American Journal of Psychiatry, 175*(9), 831–844. https://doi.org/10.1176/appi.ajp.2018.17121383

Cavicchioli, M., & Maffei, C. (2020). Rejection sensitivity in borderline personality disorder and the cognitive-affective personality system: A meta-analytic review. *Personality Disorders: Theory, Research, and Treatment, 11*(1), 1–12.

Chater, N. (2018). *The mind is flat: The remarkable shallowness of the improvising brain*. Yale University Press.

Coan, J. A. (2010). Adult attachment and the brain. *Journal of Social and Personal Relationships, 27*(2), 210–217. https://doi.org/10.1177/0265407509360900

Coan, J. A. (2011). The social regulation of emotion. In J. Decety & J. T. Cacioppo (Eds.), *The Oxford handbook of social neuroscience*. Oxford Library of Psychology. https://doi.org/10.1093/oxfordhb/9780195342161.013.0041

Cutuli, D. (2014). Cognitive reappraisal and expressive suppression strategies role in the emotion regulation: An overview on their modulatory effects and neural correlates. *Frontiers in Systems Neuroscience*, 8, 175. https://doi.org/10.3389/fnsys.2014.00175

Damasio, A. R. (1999). *The feeling of what happens: Body and emotion in the making of consciousness*. Harcourt Brace.

Damasio, A. R. (2018). *The strange order of things. The life, feelings and the making of culture*. Pantheon Books.

Damasio, A. (2021). *Feeling and knowing: Making minds conscious*. New York: Pantheon Books.

Davidson, P. S., Anaki, D., Ciaramelli, E., Cohn, M., Kim, A. S., Murphy, K. J., ... Levine, B. (2008). Does lateral parietal cortex support episodic memory? Evidence from focal lesion patients. *Neuropsychologia*, *46*(7), 1743–1755. https://doi.org/10.1016/j.neuropsychologia.2008.01.011

Dore, B. P., Boccagno, C., Burr, D., Hubbard, A., Long, K., Weber, J., ... Ochsner, K. N. (2017). Finding positive meaning in negative experiences engages ventral striatal and ventromedial prefrontal regions associated with reward evaluation. *Journal of Cognitive Neuroscience*, *29*(2), 2350244. https://doi.org/10.1162/joen_a_01041

Eagle, M. N. (2022). *Toward a unified psychoanalytic theory: Foundation in a revised and expanded ego psychology*. Routledge.

Fairbairn, W. R. (1952). *Psychoanalytic studies of the personality*. Tavistock, Routledge & Kegan Paul.

Feeney, B. C., & Kirkpatrick, L. A. (1996). Effects of adult attachment and presence of romantic partners on physiological responses to stress. *Journal of Personality and Social Psychology*, *70*(2), 255–270. https://doi.org/10.1037/0022-3514.70.2.255

Fenichel, O. (1945). *The psychoanalytic theory of neurosis*. W. W. Norton.

Ferri, J., Schmidt, J., Hajcak, G., & Canli, T. (2016). Emotion regulation and amygdala-precuneus connectivity: Focusing on attentional deployment. *Cognitive, Affective and Behavioral Neuroscience*, *16*(6), 991–1002. https://doi.org/10.3758/s13415-016-0447-y

Fingarette, H. (1969). *Self-deception*. University of California Press.

Freud, S. (1915a). Repression. In *Standard edition* (Vol. 14, pp. 141–158). Hogarth Press.

Freud, S. (1915b). The unconscious. In *Standard edition* (Vol. 14, pp. 166–204). Hogarth Press.

Freud, S. (1920). Beyond the pleasure principle. In *Standard edition* (Vol. 18, pp. 7–64). Hogarth Press.

Freud, S. (1923). The ego and the id. In *Standard edition* (Vol. 19, pp. 12–66). Hogarth Press.

Freud, S. (1924). The economic problem of masochism. In *Standard edition* (Vol. 19, pp. 159–170).

Freud, S. (1926). Inhibitions, symptoms, and anxiety. In *Standard edition* (Vol. 20, pp. 77–174). Hogarth Press.

Freud, S. (1933). New introductory lectures on psycho-analysis. In *Standard edition* (Vol. 22, pp. 5–182). Hogarth Press.

Freud, S. (1940). An outline of psychoanalysis. In *Standard edition* (Vol. 23, pp. 139–207). Hogarth Press.

Groddeck, G. (2015). *The book of the it*. Martino Fine Books. (Original work published 1923).

Gross, J. J. (2014). Emotion regulation: Conceptual and empirical foundations. In J. J. Gross (Ed.), *Handbook of emotion regulation* (pp. 3–20). Guilford Press.

Helm, J. L., Sbarra, D. A., & Ferrer, E. (2014). Coregulation of respiratory sinus arrhythmia in adult romantic partners. *Emotion, 14*(3), 522–531.

Hofer, M. A. (1978). Hidden regulatory processes in early social relationships. In P. P. Bateson & P. H. Klopfer (Eds.), *Perspectives in ethology: II. Social behavior* (pp. 135–166). Plenum Press.

Hofer, M. A. (1984). Relationships as regulators: A psychobiologic perspective on bereavement. *Psychosomatic Medicine, 46*(3), 183–197. https://doi.org/10.1097/00006842-198405000-00001

Hohr, H. (2013). The concept of experience by John Dewey revisited: Conceiving, feeling and 'enliving'. *Studies in Philosophy & Education, 32*(1), 25–38.

Hughes, A. E., Crowell, S. E., Uyeji, L., & Coan, J. A. (2012). A developmental neuroscience of borderline pathology: Emotion dysregulation and social baseline theory. *Journal of Abnormal Child Psychology, 40*(1), 21–33.

Hume, D. (1748/1975). An enquiry concerning human understanding. In L. A. Selby-Bigge & P. Niddich (Eds.), *Hume's enquiries*. Clarendon Press.

James, W. (1884). What is an emotion? *Mind, 9*(34), 188–205. http://www.jstor.org/stable/2246769

James, W. (1890). *The principles of psychology* (Vols. 1–2). Holt.

Jones, E. (1946). A valedictory address. *International Journal of Psychoanalysis, 27*(1–2), 7–12.

Koch, C. (2019). *The feeling of life itself: Why consciousness is widespread but can't be computed*. MIT Press.

Kohut, H. (1984). *How does analysis cure?* University of Chicago Press. http://doi.org/10.7208/chicago/9780226006147.001.0001

Langer, S. K. (1967). *Mind: An essay on human feeling*. Johns Hopkins Press.

Lazarus, R. S. (1966). *Psychological stress and the coping process*. McGraw-Hill.

Lazarus, R. S. (1991). *Emotion and adaptation*. Oxford University Press.

Leeper, R. W. (1948). A motivational theory of emotion to replace 'emotion as disorganized response'. *Psychological Review, 55*(1), 5–21. https://doi.org/10.1037/h0061922

Marvin, R., Cooper, G., Hoffman, K., & Powell, B. (2002). The circle of security project: Attachment-based intervention with caregiver-pre-school child dyads. *Attachment and Human Development, 4*(1), 107–124. https://doi.org/10.1080/14616730252982491

Mason, J. (1959). Psychological influences on the pituitary-adrenal cortical system. *Recent Progress in Hormone Research, 15*, 345–389.

McClintock, M. K. (1971). Menstrual synchrony and suppression. *Nature, 229*(5282), 244–245. https://doi.org/10.1038/229244a0

McDougall, J. (1989). *Theatres of the body: Psychoanalytic approach to psychosomatic illness*. Free Association Books.

McRae, K., Gross, J. J., Weber, J., Robertson, E. R., Sokol-Hessner, P., Ray, R. D., ... Ochsner, K. N. (2012). The development of emotion regulation: An fMRI study of cognitive reappraisal in children, adolescents and young adults. *Social Cognitive and Affective Neuroscience, 7*(1), 11–22. https://doi.org/10.1093/scan/nsr093

Miu, A. C., Crisan, L. G., Chis, A., Ungureanu, L., Druga, B., & Vulturar, R. (2012). Somatic markers mediate the effect of serotonin transporter gene polymorphisms on Iowa Gambling Task. *Genes, Brain and Behavior, 11*(4), 398–403. https://doi.org/10.1111/j.1601-183X.2012.00774.x

Moser, J. S., Dougherty, A., Mattson, W. I., Katz, B., Moran, T. P., Guevarra, D., ... Kross, E. (2017). Third-person self-talk facilitates emotion regulation without engaging cognitive control: Converging evidence from ERP and fMRI. *Scientific Reports, 7*(1), 4519. https://doi.org/10.1038/s41598-017-04047-3

Nemiah, J. C., & Sifneos, P. E. (1970). Affects and fantasy in patients with psychosomatic disorders. In O. Hill (Ed.), *Modern trends in psychosomatic medicine*. Butterworth & Co.

Ochsner, K. N., & Gross, J. J. (2008). Cognitive emotion regulation: Insights from social cognitive and affective neuroscience. *Current Directions in Psychological Science, 17*(2), 153–158. https://doi.org/10.1111/j.1467-8721.2008.00566.x

Osgood, C. E. (1964). Semantic differential technique in the comparative study of cultures. *American Anthropologist, 66*(3), 171–200.

Panksepp, J. (1981). The ontogeny of play in rats. *Developmental Psychobiology, 14*(4), 327–332. https://doi.org/10.1002/dev.420140405

Parkes, C. M., Benjamin, B., & Fitzgerald, R. G. (1969). Broken heart: A statistical study of increased mortality among widowers. *British Medical Journal, 1*(5646), 740–743. https://doi.org/10.1136/bmj.1.5646.740

Pine, F. (2011). Beyond pluralism: Psychoanalysis and the workings of mind. *The Psychoanalytic Quarterly, 80*(4), 823–856. https://doi.org/10.1002/j.2167-4086.2011.tb00108.x

Posner, M. I., & Rothbart, M. K. (2000). Developing mechanisms of self-regulation. *Development and Psychopathology, 12*(3), 427–441. https://doi.org/10.1017/S0954579400003096

Rapaport, D. (1960). On the psychoanalytic theory of motivation. In M. Gill (Ed.), *The collected papers of David Rapaport* (pp. 853–915). Basic Books.

Rubinstein, B. B. (1980). On the psychoanalytic theory of unconscious motivation and the problem of its confirmation. *Noûs, 14*(3), 427–442.

Ruesch, J. (1948). The infantile personality: The core problem of psychosomatic medicine. *Psychosomatic Medicine, 10*(3), 134–144.

Sandler, J. (1981). Unconscious wishes and human relationships. *Contemporary Psychoanalysis, 17*(2), 180–196. https://doi.org/10.1080/00107530.1981.10745658

Schachter, S., & Singer, J. (1962). Cognitive, social, and physiological determinants of emotional state. *Psychological Review, 69*(5), 379–399. https://doi.org/10.1037/h0046234

Searle, J. R. (1990). Consciousness, explanatory inversion and cognitive science. *Behavioral and Brain Sciences, 13*(1), 585–642.

Sifneos, P. E. (1973). The prevalence of 'alexithymic' characteristics in psychosomatic patients. *Psychotherapy and Psychosomatics, 22*(2), 255–262. https://doi.org/10.1159/000286529

Silvers, J. A., Buhle, J. T., Wager, T. D., Lopez, R., Onyemekwu, C., Kober, H., ... Ochsner, K. N. (2014). Cognitive reappraisal of emotion: A meta-analysis of human neuroimaging studies. *Cerebral Cortex, 24*(11), 2981–2990. https://doi.org/10.1093/cercor/bht154

Solms, M. (2013). The conscious id. *Neuropsychoanalysis, 15*(1), 5–19. https://doi.org/10.1080/15294145.2013.10773711

Stern, D. B. (2003). *Unformulated experience*. Analytic Press.

Tackett, J. L., Lahey, B. B., van Hulle, C., Waldman, I., Krueger, R. F., & Rathouz, P. J. (2013). Common genetic influences on negative emotionality and a general psychopathology factor in childhood and adolescence. *Journal of Abnormal Psychology*, *122*(4), 1142–1153. https://doi.org/10.1037/a0034151

Taylor, G., Bagby, R., & Barker, J. (1991). The alexithymia construct. A potential paradigm for psychosomaticmedicine. *Psychosomatics*, *12*, 153–164.

Titchener, E. B. (1909). *Lectures on the experimental psychology of the thought-processes*. Macmillan. https://doi.org/10.1037/10877-000

Torre, J. B., & Lieberman, M. D. (2018). Putting feelings into words: Affect labeling as implicit emotion regulation. *Emotion Review*, *10*(2), 116–124. https://doi.org/10.1177/1754073917742706

Tye, M. (1997). Qualia. In E. N. Zalta (Ed.), *The Stanford Encyclopedia of philosophy*. https://plato.stanford.edu/archives/fall2021/entries/qualia/

Wakefield, J. C. (2018). *Freud and philosophy of mind: Reconstructing the argument for unconscious mental states*. Springer International Publishing. https://doi.org/10.1007/978-3-319-96343-3

Wundt, W. (1897). *Outline of psychology* (C. H. Judd, Trans.). Williams and Norgate and Wilhelm Engelmann. https://doi.org/10.1037/12908-000

Young, K. D., Siegle, G. J., Zotev, V., Phillips, R., Misaki, M., Yuan, H., Drevets, W. C., & Bodurka, J. (2017). Randomized clinical trial of real-time fMRI amygdala neurofeedback for major depressive disorder: Effects on symptoms and autobiographical memory recall. *American Journal of Psychiatry*, *174*(8), 748–755. https://doi.org/10.1176/appi.ajp.2017.16060637

Zak, P. J. (2012). *The moral molecule: The source of love and prosperity*. Dutton.

Chapter 7

Consciousness and subjective experience as a continuum

In no other theory of the mind is the distinction between conscious and unconscious mental states as central as in Freudian theory. I return to this theory as a vehicle for a further discussion of the relation between conscious and unconscious mental processes and states. I propose an alternative to the dichotomous division of the mind into conscious and dynamically unconscious mental states, or at least an additional way of thinking about this division. At the center of this proposal is a resuscitation of James' (1890) conception of experience as a continuum from focal to fringe of consciousness.

As we know, psychoanalysis has been defined as a study of the unconscious (Laplanche & Pontalis, 1973). This is somewhat misleading insofar as the primary emphasis of classical psychoanalytic theory is on the *dynamic* unconscious, that is, an unconscious that is the site of a battle between the warring forces of instinctual drives and impulses striving to reach unconsciousness and repressive defenses working to prevent access to consciousness. This is the fundamental conception of the mind, as reflected in the id–ego or drive–defense model of Freudian theory. Unlike the computational unconscious of cognitive psychology, the Freudian dynamic unconscious is an unconscious of wishes and desires striving for expression, 'a cauldron, full of seething excitations' (Freud, 1933, p. 73). Further, whereas the computational unconscious is inherently inaccessible to consciousness, the fully formed wishes and desires of the dynamic unconscious, which Freud claimed are no different from conscious wishes and desires, are accessible to consciousness once repression is lifted. In Mitchell's (2005) analogy, they are like the ants one finds that have been there all along after one has overturned a rock. Thus, in this view the mind can be thought of as a place or site – think of a rectangle with a horizontal bar at its center. Above the bar are conscious mental states, and below the bar are unconscious mental states – the 'depths' of the mind – striving to find expression in consciousness.[1] It should be noted that in this view, repression operates at the level of *retrieval* of contents that have been fully encoded.

Filling out this model of the mind, according to Freudian theory, we are lived by our id. That is, in contrast to conscious wishes and desires, which, as noted earlier, subject to dissimulation, the repressed instinctual wishes and desires represent

DOI: 10.4324/9781032686967-8

the true purpose of one's life. Further, although self-analysis may be possible for the few, for everyone else, an outside objective *Menschenkenner* is necessary to engage the individual in a liberating process that will bring to consciousness the unacceptable truths, against the awareness of which one has been defending. However, this account of the psychoanalytic project has been met with serious skepticism throughout the history of psychoanalysis including the criticism Meehl (1994) referred to as the 'nagging persistence' of the suggestion problem. That is, what the analyst takes to be unacceptable truths that the patient resists confronting are too often based on the analyst's theoretical affiliations, that is, on his or her particular theoretical perspectives on human nature, personality development, and psychopathology. Different theoretical persuasions have different conceptions of the nature of the truths the patient has difficulty confronting. This makes it very difficult to distinguish between uncovering self-truths and theoretical impositions on the patient. It is time to take another hard look at this categorical division of mind into conscious and (dynamic) unconscious, as well as at the general relation between conscious and unconscious mental life. In his famous ten arguments against the appeal to unconscious mental states, James (1890) wrote that the positing of unconscious mental states 'is the sovereign means for believing what one likes in psychology, and of turning of what might become a science into a tumbling-ground for whimsies' (p. 163). He also wrote that those who turn to unconscious mental states for explanation 'will devote themselves to sapping and mining the region roundabout until it is a bag of logical liquefaction, into the midst of which all definite conclusions of any sort may be trusted ere long to sink and disappear' (p. 107).[2]

Although James may have overstated his case – after all, there is much productive research and theory on unconscious processes, as I have stated elsewhere, 'his concerns [regarding the too-ready appeal to unconscious processes] were not entirely unfounded as shown by the misuses of and arbitrary attributions of unconscious mental states found in the psychoanalytic literature' (Eagle, 2018, p. 11). Consider as an example, historical accounts of agoraphobia in terms of unconscious processes and wishes: 'libidinization' of movement (Abraham, 1913); unconscious prostitution fantasies (Freud, 1926); and unconscious murderous wishes toward the patient's trusted companion (Deutsch, 1929). One can add to these historical examples, accounts in the more contemporary psychoanalytic literature in which claims are made that patients somehow unconsciously put their mental states into the analyst, and unconsciously communicate with the analyst through telepathic dreams; and that the analyst can gain reliable and precise access to the patient's unconscious repressed mental contents through examining his or her own countertransference reactions, that is, through attending to the thoughts and feelings that emerge in his or her consciousness (Racker, 1968; Levine, 1997) or through telepathic processes. In short, as James (1890) feared, too often, all one needs to do to is add the term 'unconscious' in order to avoid addressing the thorny questions of evidence regarding one's claims and theoretical formulations.

Continuum from fringe to focal consciousness

Various alternatives to the classical psychoanalytic account of the relation between conscious and (dynamic) unconscious mental states and processes have been proposed. These alternatives speak to two interrelated issues: one, the categorical division of conscious and unconscious; and two, the positing of a special mechanism – repression – that is instrumental in effecting this division. The general context for one alternative perspective is found in the Jamesian (1890) proposal that conscious experience should be thought of as a continuum ranging from focal to fringe. At any given moment we are bombarded by inner and outer stimuli, and given the limited capacity of consciousness, only a selected sample of the array of inputs is relatively fully encoded, experienced in focal consciousness and stored in memory. The remaining information may be only partly encoded, fade after a brief period of 'iconic storage' (Averbach & Sperling, 1961), or remain at the fringe of consciousness, and, under certain circumstances, may be readily available to focal conscious experience.

Although the concept of the fringe of consciousness makes use of a spatial metaphor, most evident in visual perception of an external stimulus, it is also applicable to one's inner thoughts and feelings. As early as the 13th century, [Duns] Scotus (1266–1308) observed that 'in the field of vision there is one point of distinct vision and many indistinct elements'. However, he adds that

> if this is possible in sensation it is much more possible in the sphere of the intellect … Beneath those thoughts which the will makes clear there may be many indistinct or incompletely actualized thoughts; the will turns to these and exerts itself to raise one of them to clearness.
>
> (as cited in Mangan, 1993, p. 89)

Thus, Scotus proposes consciousness as a continuum not only in relation to visual experience, but also in the context of one's inner thoughts and cognitions. In both contexts, whereas focal experience is distinct and articulated, fringe experiences are vague and unarticulated. One experiences 'senses of meanings' rather than sharply articulated and delineated thoughts, what Gendlin (1984) referred to as 'the edge of awareness' (p. 76). It takes an act of 'will' to raise these thoughts to clearness.[3,4]

In proposing the Jamesian view of consciousness as a continuum from fringe to focal, I am not suggesting that one overlook or ignore the phenomena which the concept of the dynamic unconscious is intended to explain. Rather, I am proposing a different explanatory account of these phenomena, one less burdened by theoretical formulations for which there is little evidence and which are incompatible with what we do know about the workings of the mind, but rather a reformulation of it. What remains is the core observation regarding our tendency to avoid the focal conscious experience of unacceptable mental contents. One aspect of the reformulation I am proposing is the replacement of a categorical division between conscious and unconsciousness with the idea of a continuum in which the outer fringe of consciousness shades into what we refer to as unconscious processes and contents. What this alternative does eliminate are the concepts of repression and the dynamic unconscious as they are understood in Freudian theory, namely, in terms of fully formed wishes and desires, pressing for expression in consciousness and action, and prevented from achieving such expression by an unconscious counterforce.

There is little doubt that Freud (1915) was correct in asserting that the major part of mental life goes on outside awareness. This is certainly true of the computational processes emphasized by cognitive psychology and neuroscience that are inherently inaccessible to conscious awareness. That is, we do not experience unconscious processes themselves, but of the *products* of such processing. It is also true, as Freud (1915) argued, – but with a proviso – that only a small sample of what has been unconsciously processed is consciously experienced. The proviso is that although a small sample reaches *focal* consciousness, a larger sample is represented in the more fringe areas of consciousness. Thus far, I have not invoked the dynamic unconscious. That concept enters the picture based on the observation that of the sample of mental contents that are, in principle accessible to focal conscious experience, a selected set of mental contents that are enmeshed in inner conflict are banned from focal awareness.

Freud's (1915) claim is that these banned mental contents (e.g., desires and wishes) are no different from ordinary mental contents experienced in consciousness save for the fact that they are not conscious. On this view, certain fully formed mental contents, which are the products of unconscious processing, are not relayed to consciousness through the operation of certain defenses. Were it not for these defenses, these mental contents would be experienced as ordinary conscious mental contents. In this view, consciousness functions like a camera or a flashlight. It snaps a picture or lights up the products of unconscious processing. However, as Marcel (1983) has argued, consciousness imposes a distinctive structure on the information relayed to it, which means that the representational products of unconscious processing are different from conscious representations. For example, there is evidence that the representational products of unconscious processing of a word include such features as number of syllables, its first letter, its associates, and connotations, and under certain conditions, its sounds. However, in accord with the 'binding' phenomenon, our regular conscious perception of a word is a whole word and its denotative meaning.

The fact that unconscious processing and focal conscious are organized along different principles and dimensions may help us understand the relation between unconscious processing and creativity. The relation between the two may lie in the different organizational principles of unconscious processing and focal conscious experience. I refer here to the differences between primary and secondary process organization. More specifically, one's openness and access to unconscious mental contents may represent an important source of creativity.

As noted earlier, according to Freudian theory, mental contents, such as ordinary desires, wishes, intentions, and fantasies, that are unacceptable to one's self-image and moral values, are barred from access to conscious experience through a special filtering mechanism – repression. Recall Freud's (1915b) earlier quoted comment that repressed unconscious mental contents, such as wishes and desires are no different from conscious mental contents save for the absence of consciousness.

Were it not for repression these mental contents would be accessible to conscious experience as ordinary wishes and desires. Thus, insofar as these mental contents are fully encoded, repression operates at the level of *retrieval*. The focus on retrieval is congruent with Freud's overriding emphasis on the recovery of *memories* in treatment. (See Fonagy's [1999] claim that this is no longer a central feature of psychoanalytic and psychodynamic treatment.)

In an alternative, or at least supplemental, view, the motivated failure of certain mental contents to be consciously experienced is also due to processes at the level of *encoding*. On this alternative view, rather than positing a separate mechanism of repression, general perceptual and cognitive screening processes, such as level of encoding and direction of attention, are co-opted for defensive purposes. Thus, unacceptable intentions and desires are not spelled out (Fingarette, 1963, 1969) or not fully formulated (Stern, 2003) and allowed to remain relatively unformulated, with the result that they are left vague and fuzzy.[5] As he makes clear, Stern's formulation is based on Sullivan's concepts of selective inattention and unformulated experiences. Sullivan (1956) writes that

> experience is either noticed or unnoticed, or, in the first case, formulated. In other words, we note many things which we do not formulate; that is, about which we do not develop clear ideas of what happened to us. And there is also experience we do not notice but which can be demonstrated to have occurred in explaining subsequent events.
>
> (p. 199)

The convergence between these proposals and the formulation of fringe and focal experiences lies in the consideration that non-articulated and not fully formulated mental contents are at the fringe of experience. It is worth noting that Freud (1915b) also refers to not spelling out as a defense in the context of discussing the possibility of unconscious emotions. He writes:

> Surely it is the essence of an emotion that we should be aware of it, i.e., that it should become known to consciousness. Thus, the possibility of the attribute of unconsciousness would be completely excluded as far as emotions, feelings, and affects are concerned.
>
> (p. 177)

Freud goes on to observe that although we are accustomed to speaking of unconscious affects in the clinical context, such discourse can have only two defensible meanings: one, that 'an affective or emotional impulse is perceived but miscon-strued' (p. 177), that is, mislabeled; and the other, that it is a potential affect that has been '*prevented from developing*' [my emphasis] (p. 178). Were one to apply Freud's reasoning here to other mental states, such as intentions, desires, wishes, and fantasies, the categorical distinction between conscious and unconscious would devolve into a continuum from a fringe of unarticulated and unformulated to focal articulated and formulated.

Hierarchy of connotations

G.S. Klein (personal communication) proposed that the meanings and personal significance of experiences are arranged hierarchically from focal to fringe. Thus, what gets activated in experiencing an object are both focal denotative mean-ings as well as a set of connotations that are hierarchically arranged, what Klein referred to as a 'hierarchy of connotations', a concept very similar to those of associative networks and associative strength.[6,7,8] For example, the focal experi-ence of a word is 'surrounded' by fringe meanings, associations, connotations, affective schemas, and features that are hierarchically arranged on the dimension of accessibility to focal conscious experience. Consider the simple example of perceiving a word. In addition to the focal experience of the denotative meaning of the word, at the fringe of experience is a set of connotations and associations hierarchically ordered.

Let me provide some empirical findings that tend to support the above formu-lations. Let us say that one is presented with a list of words. When asked to recall or recognize the words presented, the errors made are not random, but are likely to be related semantically, associatively, or phonetically to the presented words (see Roediger & McDermott, 1995). For example, let us say that one of the words on the list is 'moon'. There is evidence that when an error is made on a recall or recognition test, one is more likely to select a word that is semantically or associa-tively related to 'moon', such as 'sky' rather than a word that is semantically and associatively unrelated to 'moon'. This suggests that hearing or seeing the word 'moon' activates not only its denotative meaning, but also a network of associa-tions and connotations. Further, as word association norms demonstrate, the asso-ciations triggered are organized hierarchically that under certain circumstances, are accessible to conscious experience.[9] That is, some associations are more likely to be elicited than others. Another way of putting this is to say that some associa-tions are more accessible to conscious experience than other associations.

There is also evidence that the level at which one encodes the presented word influences the nature of the activated associative network (Craik & Lockhart, 1972). In one study (Eagle & Ortof, 1967), the degree of attention given to the presented words, and therefore the level at which the words were processed, was manipulated by including a condition in which one set of participants engaged in another task while listening to the presented words. The result was that compared to a focal attention condition, the recognition errors made by the low-attention subjects were more likely to be based on sound rather than semantic meaning. Thus, the recognition error for 'moon' was far more likely to be 'soon' rather than, say, 'sky'. In short, the level at which the word 'moon' was processed (e.g., phonetic or semantic) influenced the hierarchy of connotations or associative network activated.[10]

Using fMRI, Garoff-Eaton et al. (2007) reported different neural substrates for false recognition based on semantic similarity versus physical similarities. Of special relevance in the present context is the finding that only semantic false recognition was associated with activation for frontal cortex regions. Gomez-Ariza et al. (2017) applied transcranial direct current stimulation to the anterior temporal lobe (ATL), an area of the brain that is believed to serve 'as an integration hub specialized in the processing of semantic relatedness …' (p. 133). The control condition was sham stimulation. The words presented were all either categorically or associatively related to a critical non-presented word. For example, when the critical word was *apple*, categorically related words presented were: *pear*, *banana*, *orange*, and so on; the associatively related words were: *rotten, red, peel*, and so on. There were no significant differences in correct recognition between actual and sham stimulation. However, an important interaction was that false recognition was reduced for the associative list only in the stimulation condition, but was not reduced for the category list. This suggests that different brain areas underlie associative and categorical processing.

There is also evidence that although we perceive a unified stimulus, for example, 'moon', we encode and store it in memory in terms of its various features (e.g., number of letters, its first letter, what it rhymes with, its general semantic category, etc.). Consider the tip-of-the-tongue phenomenon when trying to remember a word or name (Brown, 1966). Even when one cannot retrieve the word or name, one often has the (correct) sense of certain of its features, for example, its first letter or the number of syllables it contains, or its general semantic theme. This suggests that in hearing or seeing the word, one has stored in memory features of the word. The tip-of-the-tongue phenomenon is only one example of an experience in which although one cannot bring the item for which one is searching to consciousness, one remembers certain of its features and has the sense that it is accessible to conscious experience.[11] In the present context, one can think of the different features as fringe aspects of experience that are accessible to experience under certain circumstances.

The hypothesis that a hierarchy of connotations and network of associations accompany focal experience likely applies not only to verbal material, but also to perception of nonverbal material. Let us say that one is presented with a baseball bat or golf club. If one were asked what they are, the response would undoubtedly be that they are implements in athletic activities; that is their denotative focal meaning. However, as is the case with presentation of verbal material, perception of these objects is likely to trigger a network of connotations and associations. That is, whereas the focal meaning of baseball bat and golf club as athletic objects is clearly articulated, there is a set of less clearly articulated fringe meanings that 'surround' the focal meaning. Further, there are likely to be significant individual differences in the fringe meanings activated as a function of various factors, including individual history, affective and drive state.

A number of theorists (e.g., Bucci, 2002; Tomkins, 1962–1963) have proposed that experiences are organized not only along symbolic dimensions (e.g., semantic-categorical and associative), but also along subsymbolic and affective dimensions.[12] One can hypothesize that the affective state one is in during an interaction or when perceiving an external object will influence its connotations and associations. For example, in an affective state of rage, the connotative meaning of 'weapon' may rise higher in the hierarchy, as evidenced for example, in the greater likelihood of 'weapon' emerging as a connotation of and association to a baseball bat and golf club. From the perspective of the concept of experience as a continuum, 'weapon' has moved from the fringe of experience closer toward focal experience.

Rapaport (1942) refers to this kind of phenomenon as reflecting the drive organization of cognition and memory, which is perhaps better formulated as affect organization of memory and cognition. The basic idea is that when, say, one's aggressive affect state is low, aggression-related connotations, such as 'weapon' would be at the fringe of consciousness (or low on the connotative hierarchy); and when one's aggressive affect state is high, the connotation of 'weapon' becomes more focal (and higher in the hierarchy of connotations). Another way to put it is to say that the particular *affordance* provided by the external stimulus is influenced by one's drive-affect state. Thus, one can say that not only, as Bucci notes, do we organize experience in terms of emotional schemas, but also that the emotional schemas activated by a particular experience are likely to vary with the affective state one is in at the time of the experience – a form of state-dependent experience.

The fringe of consciousness in clinical work

Up to this point, the discussion of the activation of a hierarchy of connotations and associations has focused on perceptual experience of an external stimulus. I propose that a similar activation occurs in response to the experience of one's inner world of desires, wishes, and intentions. Consider a clinical pattern in which, say, a male patient experiences anxiety, guilt, and other symptoms following success in achieving his goals. According to oedipal theory, these symptomatic experiences are due to the fact that achievement of his ambitions constitutes unconscious and disguised gratification of the (universal) wish to kill father – a fully formed death wish that has been repressed, but remains active from early childhood to adulthood.

Contrast this account with the alternative formulation that the individual's experience of success activates a hierarchy of connotations and associations, which includes the guilt- and anxiety-inducing meaning of outdoing father. Further, the anxiety and guilt-inducing meaning of outdoing father do not arise in a vacuum, but are likely to be based on parental communications to the effect that 'if you outdo me, you will incur my wrath and/or grievously harm me' (Eagle, 1987; Silberschatz, 2005; Weiss & Sampson, 1986, on Control-Mastery Theory).

These different accounts have important implications for process goals in treatment. On the classical Freudian account, the process goal would be to lift repression in order to uncover hostile wishes toward father. On the alternative account I am proposing, the therapeutic work would be directed toward making explicit the patient's implicit symbolic equivalence between achievement of success and angering and harming father or, to put it another way, making fringe meanings more focal (see Eagle, 1987).[13]

Consider as another clinical example, the symptom of what Freud (1912) refers to as 'psychical impotence', that is, sexual impotence in relation to a 'respectable' woman, such as one's wife, due to psychological factors having to do with universal unresolved incestuous wishes toward mother. According to the alternative view proposed, insofar as the representation of 'wife' activates a hierarchy of connotations that includes mother, sexual feelings toward wife become psychologically equivalent to incest wishes, triggering anxiety and conflict related to an incest taboo. It is important to note that although the above account refers to an incest *taboo*, it does not entail the positing of universal unconscious incestuous *wishes*. Rather, a focal subjective experience (representation of 'wife') activates a hierarchy of meanings and associations that include representations of mother, which is made more likely by early maternal behaviors that result in identification of mother with sexual partner. (See Eagle, 2007, for a further discussion of this issue.)

On the logic of the Freudian account, when repression is lifted and the unconscious becomes conscious, the patient would presumably consciously experience oedipal wishes that had persisted from childhood and had not been worked through, repudiated, or sublimated. On the alternative view, were the unconscious to become conscious – or more in tune with this view, were the fringe to become focal or were the implicit to become explicit – the patient would become aware, not of incestuous wishes – there may be no such wishes to be uncovered – but of his or her implicit symbolic equivalences (e.g., between success and harming and angering father; between sexual feelings toward wife and incestuous wishes) (Eagle, 2007). Further, these symbolic equivalences, or what Weiss and Sampson (1986) refer to as unconscious 'pathogenic beliefs', are best understood as implicit, at the fringe of consciousness, rather than deeply buried in the dynamic unconscious.

It seems to me that much day-to-day therapeutic work, including from a psychodynamic perspective, is more directed to implicit desires, wishes, beliefs, fantasies, and symbolic equivalences that are at the fringe of consciousness than to deeply buried repressed infantile instinctual impulses to which, without interpretive intervention, the patient has no conscious access. Further, therapeutic change, including insight and self-knowledge, is more likely to be marked, not by the uncovering of repressed mental contents, but by understanding the relations among experiences and developing new perspectives toward these experiences.

Not infrequently, what are referred to as dynamically unconscious in the psychoanalytic literature are essentially vaguely sensed meanings at the fringe of conscious experience that are kept from focal experience through failure to articulate or formulate. This is especially evident in Freud's early case studies. Consider Freud's (1895) account of repression in the case of Lucy R., Freud (Breuer & Freud, 1893–1895) says to Lucy: 'I believe that you are really in love with your employer, the Director, though perhaps without being aware of it yourself ...' (p. 117). He also says: 'You're afraid of [the servants] having some inkling of your hopes and making fun of you' (p. 117). Lucy R. responds: 'Yes, I think that's true' Freud replies: 'But if you knew you loved your employer why didn't you tell me?' Lucy: 'I didn't know – or rather I didn't want to know. I wanted to drive it out of my head and not think of it again; and I believe latterly I have succeeded' Freud inquires further: 'Why was it that you were unwilling to admit this inclination?' Freud makes it clear here that at this stage of his theorizing, he does not make a sharp distinction between repression and ordinary unwillingness This exchange hardly suggests deeply buried mental contents inaccessible to conscious experience, or perhaps only accessible by virtue of particular (mostly interpretive) interventions.

The above exchange between Freud and Lucy R, which I believe, is likely to represent the normative rather than the exceptional in clinical work, is redolent of the 'close process monitoring' approach of Gray (1994) and his colleagues as well as Freud's own clinical approach, as reflected in some of his comments. With regard to the former, Gray views both defense and the mental contents defended against as preconscious, that is, as just below the surface of consciousness and therefore, accessible to focal conscious experience by directing the patient's attention to his or her defensive processes. As is made clear in clinical vignettes presented by Gray and his colleagues, the mental contents defended against can readily be described in terms of fringe experiences left unarticulated rather than as deeply buried in some mental location referred to as the unconscious. In Gray's approach, directing attention to these meanings furthers the process of articulation and facilitates their access to focal experience.

Consider the following example illustrating Gray's (1994) defense analysis approach:

Patient: "I am so angry with Betty, I could strangle her ... [he elaborated for a while, then he became hesitant] ... On the other hand, she has many fine qualities, etc."

Analyst: "Now you are focused on her fine qualities, a moment before you were experiencing many different feelings, and then your feelings shifted. Can you see what happened here?"

Patient: "I was afraid you would think I'm a brute for feeling angry at her" (Davison et al., 1990, p. 603).

The analyst directs the patient's attention to the latter's passing thought, which would have likely remained unarticulated without the analyst's simple intervention.

(In this sense, the analyst's approach here is quite similar to Gendlin's (1984) emphasis on capturing the 'edge of awareness').

Contrast the above approach to that of Kleinian and Bionian analysts' use of 'deep' interpretations that presumably speak to deeply repressed inaccessible mental contents attributed to the patient. Following are a couple of examples of such interpretive attributions:

> In my experience sadism reaches its zenith in this [early] phase, which is ushered in by the oral-sadistic desire to devour the mother's breast (or the mother herself) ... It is my experience that in the phantasied attack on the mother's body a considerable part is played by the urethral and anal sadism which is very soon added to the oral and muscular sadism. In phantasy the excreta are transformed into dangerous weapons: wetting is regarded as cutting, stabbing, burning, drowning, while the faecal mass is equated with weapons and missiles.
>
> (Klein, 1930, pp. 24–25)

Consider as another example, excerpts of an exchange between Bion (1954) and a schizophrenic patient who had been in analysis for five years:

Patient: I picked a tiny piece of skin from my face and feel quite empty.

Analyst: The tiny piece of skin is your penis, which you have torn out, and all your insides have come with it.

Patient: I do not understand ... penis ... only syllables.

Analyst: You have split my word "penis" into syllables and it now has no meaning.

And on it goes in this fashion for a while. Bion is apparently aware of the seeming arbitrariness of his interpretation. He writes: 'I must warn you that compression has compelled me to leave out many repetitive formulations which in fact would mitigate the baldness of the interpretations as I report them here' (p. 115). This is hardly sufficient. If the reader is not to experience the interpretations as arbitrary and unrelated to the patient's experience, Bion is obligated to provide at least some material that renders the interpretations even somewhat understandable.[14,15]

As is evident in the above passages, 'deep' interpretations and attributions of bizarre unconscious fantasies and mental contents to the patient that are totally inaccessible to conscious experience, may reflect the analyst's projections of mental contents on to the patient that are mainly derived from the former's theoretical perspectives rather than from the patient's experiences. It is as if the patient, not the analyst, is the blank screen onto which the analyst can project his or her theoretical fantasies. (The above examples of 'deep' interpretations, it should be noted, provide additional warrants for James' (1890) concern that references to unconscious mental contents entailed the risk of opening the floodgates to undisciplined attributions of all sorts.)

Reflective function

Making connections and understanding personal significance among experiences

In the above discussion I have focused on motivational influences at the level of encoding that result in certain experiences being kept at the fringe of consciousness. That is, motivational influences operate through co-opting general psychological processes such as deployment of attention and level of encoding. I want to describe another means of co-opting general psychological processes for defensive purposes. I refer to G.S. Klein's (1976) redefinition of repression in terms of a motivated failure to make connections among different experiences, and to recognize and spell out the personal significance of different experiences, which themselves may be fully encoded and consciously experienced. Thus, according to Klein, repression is not directed to fully formed mental contents themselves, but to the connections among these mental contents, including their personal significance. From this perspective, defense may operate not only at the levels of retrieval and encoding of specific stimuli, but also at the level of understanding the relations among experiences as well as the personal significance of these relations. In effect, what Klein is proposing is that personal *meanings* are kept from consciousness.

Implicit in Klein's position is the idea that self-knowledge and discovering truths about oneself may not rely primarily on the uncovering of repressed unconscious impulses, but rather on enhanced awareness of the personal significance and connections among different experiences, which enables a new perspective on these experiences. Note that what is unconscious – or rather, one should say is preconscious – in this formulation are not wishes and desires striving to reach consciousness and kept from doing so by a special mechanism called repression, but rather, what an understanding of connections among, as well as the personal significance, of fully conscious experiences. Further, the means by which such understanding is inhibited are ordinary psychological processes such as not attending and not reflecting. There are neither wishes and desires constantly striving for conscious expression nor a 'constant expenditure of force' (Freud, 1915a, p. 151) in the form of repression that prevents them from finding such expression.

The importance of understanding the relations among experiences alerts us to the fact that subjective experience includes not only direct immediate experience, but also *reflection* on what one has experienced. This capacity is especially prominent in human beings. James (1890) and Mead (1967) captured the distinction between direct and reflective experience by distinguishing between 'I' and 'Me', a distinction reflected in the structure of language. Thus, one says 'I experience such and such', not 'Me experience such and such'. And in reflecting on an experience, one says 'it occurs to me', not 'it occurs to I'. In short, 'I', the subject, experiences as well as acts, including the act of reflection; and what I reflect on is the object of reflection. Or to put it another way, when I reflect on my experience, a representation of my experience is the object of my reflection. Indeed, the therapeutic goal of making the unconscious conscious is essentially accomplished through strengthening what Sterba (1934) referred to as the observing function of the ego, which can be understood as enhancing the capacity for self-reflection.

Sterba's (1934) identification of the strengthening of the observing function of the ego as a central goal of psychoanalytic treatment anticipates the current emphasis on reflective function (RF) in the psychoanalytic literature. This emphasis reminds us that subjective experience includes not only direct, immediate experience, but also *reflection* on what one has experienced. In the context of classical psychoanalytic theory, the context of Sterba's paper, enhancement of the observing function of the ego allows greater reflection on the role of instinctual wishes and desires in one's psychological life. In the contemporary psychoanalytic literature, references to reflective function are more likely to have to do with making the implicit explicit and making the fringe more focal in experience. As we have seen in the above clinical vignette, the analysis of defense approach of Gray and his colleagues, which focuses on mental states and contents just below the surface of consciousness, can be understood in terms of making the implicit explicit and the fringe more focal.

Sterba's (1934) concept of strengthening the observing function of the ego is directed primarily toward the intrapsychic, that is, toward the patient's own mental states. In contrast, the current concept of RF also includes the capacity to reflect on *another's mental state* (e.g., Fonagy & Bateman, 2006). In view of the fact that we spend a good part of our lives in interpersonal and social interaction, this is an important expansion of the concept of reflective function. Indeed, Fonagy and his colleagues employ the term 'reflective function' rather than 'self-reflective function' to make the point that the capacity to reflect is an important function not only in regard to one's own mental states, but also in regard to the mental states of others.

Some clarification is in order here. Although we can reflect on our own mental states, we obviously cannot, in the same way, reflect on the mental states of others. *We can only reflect on our construals of another's mental states.* However, one's construals are, of course, instances of one's own mental states. Another way to put it is to say that we can reflect, not on another's mental states, but on the mental states we *attribute* to the other person. In short, reflecting on the mental states of others is a form of *self-reflection* in an interactional context. It differs from ordinary self-reflection in so far as one reflects on one's thoughts about someone else's mental states rather than on one's thoughts about one's own mental states. To paraphrase Freud, the critical question is the degree to which one's construals and attribution tally with what is real in the other person.

Mentalization and RF

Another needed clarification is the distinction between 'mentalization' and RF, which Fonagy and his colleagues use interchangeably. Indeed, they have labeled their therapeutic approach, the essence of which is enhancement of reflective capacity, Mentalization Based Treatment (MBT). However, to use one of Freud's favorite metaphors, the two concepts are not on all fours. As noted earlier, mentalization refers to the relatively automatic experience of another as, like oneself, a being with mental states. Reflective function refers to reflecting on what one has mentalized. Further, one may be able to mentalize without necessarily being able to reflect on what one has mentalized. For example, patients with a borderline personality disorder (BPD) may have little problem mentalizing, that is, attributing intentions and other mental states to others and connecting others' behavior to their mental states (e.g., their intentions). Indeed, BPD individuals often over-attribute (malevolent) intentions to others. What they have difficulties with is being able to reflect on their attributions. Indeed, they often experience their attributions as absolute reality and their negative emotional reactions accompanying these attributions as entirely justified. In short, the impairment in borderline personality disorder lies not in difficulty in mentalizing, but in *reflecting* on what has been mentalized, that is, on the mental states one has attributed to others.

The distinction between mentalization and RF becomes more evident in light of the findings of a recent study with BPD patients. Compared to healthy controls, female BPD patients show greater mentalizing accuracy in the context of relationship threat. Interpreting these results requires some background information (Miano et al., 2021). The term 'motivational inaccuracy' describes one's tendency to avoid spelling out to oneself thoughts and feelings of their partners that threaten the relationship. In that sense, 'motivational inaccuracy' can be understood as having the adaptive function of protecting the relationship. Rather than showing 'motivational inaccuracy', BPD patients showed heightened accuracy in regard to identifying their partner's negative thoughts and feelings. However, as Miano et al. (2021) note, although BPD patients are able to recognize how their partner feels, they are unable to reflect on the correct reasons for their partner's feelings. In short, although they are able to *mentalize* accurately regarding their partner's negative feelings – indeed, they are especially sensitive in picking up these feelings – they cannot reflect on the reasons for these feelings, which if they were capable of doing, might serve to ameliorate the situation that generated partner's negative feelings and thus protect the relationship.

There is also evidence that level of RF is related to impulsivity in borderline patients (Levy et al., 2006); and that positive therapy outcome changes include enhanced RF, reduced number of hospitalizations, and fewer suicide attempts in borderline patients (Yeomans et al., 2013). Bateman and Fonagy (e.g., 2009, 2010, 2013) have shown that the enhancement of RF serves as an important vehicle for regulation of negative affect. There are also clinical reports indicating that mentalization without a capacity for reflective functioning can be highly maladaptive. For example, Lieberman (1999) describes the case of a single, high-risk mother attributing malevolent motives and intentions to a very young infant without reflection on whether the infant is capable of having such intentions. To sum up, as is seen in the Lieberman case report, reflective function should be thought of as a capacity to be used when mentalization is problematic, that is, when one may need to modulate one's affective state resulting from one's questionable attribution of negative intentions to others.

There are a number of studies that investigate the relation between the level of reflective function and adaptive behavior in a variety of contexts. In all these studies, the capacity for mentalization is taken for granted. Following is a sampling of such studies: Fonagy et al. (1995) reported that a high level of RF in high-risk mothers served as a protective factor in regard to the attachment status of their infants. Similarly, Alvarez-Monjaras et al. (2019) reported that even in a sample of substance-dependent mothers, level of RF was associated with maternal sensitivity, which has been found to be related to infant secure attachment status. A high level of RF in an adolescent sample was found to be a protective factor with regard to the effects of early parental neglect on the security of attachment (Borelli et al., 2015). There is also evidence that therapists high in RF are more therapeutically effective (Cologon et al., 2017).

Notes

1 See Wachtel's (2003) excellent discussion of the metaphors of surface and depth in theoretical formulations of the nature of the mind.
2 Weinberger (2000) maintains that James' ten arguments have been misunderstood in that they were directed against a conception of unconscious in terms of elements of consciousness. Indeed, Weinberger argues, 'James saw unconscious processes as critically important to psychological functioning' (p. 439). However, as Weinberger goes on to note, James' concept of unconscious processes was formulated in terms of the *fringe* of consciousness rather than in terms of a dynamic unconscious of repressed mental contents. It is the latter formulation of unconscious processes that, I believe, is especially susceptible to James' ten arguments.
3 Polanyi's (1962) distinction between *focal* and *subsidiary* awareness, which implies that awareness exists on a continuum, parallels the distinction between focal and fringe experiences. There is also a family resemblance between the concept of fringe and what Freud refers to as preconscious.
4 Note that in certain respects, this formulation is compatible with Freud's (1915b) proposal that conscious experience represents only a sample of unconscious mental life.
5 Both Fingarette's and Stern's formulations are based on Sartre's (1956) critique of the Freudian concept of repression as a reified subpersonal mechanism (as in 'defense mechanism') rather than a disowned mental state carried out by a person who is trying to avoid negative affect and evade responsibility (see Schafer [1976] discussion of 'action language' for a similar perspective).
6 I cannot find a reference for this term in Klein's published writings. However, I recall Klein, who was my mentor, discussing this concept with me during the time that I was a Research Assistant Professor at the New York University Research Center for Mental Health.
7 One should add that what are also activated are the context or framework in which the word is presented (which may influence its connotations), various features of the word (e.g., number of syllables, its first letter' what it sounds like), and its affective valence. Freud (1915b) commented that every experience is accompanied by a 'quota of affect' (p. 178).

8 The concepts of hierarchy of connotations and network of associations bear an affinity to Husserl's (1913) concept of 'horizon' and the concepts of ground and background, respectively, in Gestalt psychology and Merleau-Ponty's (1968) writings.

9 In an unpublished study on age differences in memory that I carried out many years ago, I found that although, as expected, younger participants showed better memory than older participants, when older participants made recognition errors, their errors were not random, but were likely to be in the 'right ballpark' that is, semantically or associatively related to the target words presented to them. In other words, it was as if their 'memory traces' were fuzzier than the younger participants (Eagle, unpublished manuscript).

10 As early as 1919 Jung and Riklin wrote 'Among the psychical facts having supreme influence upon the association process, attention is cardinal' (p. 8).

11 These phenomena make it clear that what is encoded and stored in memory is not a photographic replica of what has been perceived, and that remembering is not calling up that replica, but rather entails a process of construction based on the features and dimensions along which the perceived stimulus has been stored in memory.

12 This proposal is consonant with Freud's (1894) early idea that all experiences are accompanied by 'a quota of affect' (p. 178).

13 Note this implicit symbolic equivalence between achievement of success and angering and harming father as an example of G.S. Klein's (1976) redefinition of repression in terms of failure to make connections among different experiences.

14 It is interesting to note that on the very next page following the above exchange, Bion cites a passage from Freud (1915) in which he links a schizophrenic patient's getting rid of facial blackheads to working out his castration complex. One is tempted to speculate that, at least to some degree, Bion's interpretation is 'borrowed' from Freud rather than emerging from the patient's experiences, concerns, and associations.

15 I recall an early tradition during my education of highly regarded analysts, in their role as consultants, to come up with unexpected and often arcane interpretations that no one else had apparently entertained. The more unexpected, the more arcane, and the more presumably clever, the more these interpretations were greeted with awe. The focus was not on the question of the degree to which they resonated with the patient's experience or how helpful they might be to the patient, but rather on their degree of cleverness and presumed depth.

References

Abraham, K. (1913). A constitutional basis of locomotor activity. In *Selected papers* (pp. 235–243). Basic Books.

Alvarez-Monjarás, M., McMahon, T. J., & Suchman, N. E. (2019). Does maternal reflective functioning mediate associations between representations of caregiving with maternal sensitivity in a high-risk sample? *Psychoanalytic Psychology, 36*(1), 82–92. https://doi .org/10.1037/pap0000166

Averbach, E., & Sperling, G. (1961). Short term storage of information in vision. In C. Cherry (Ed.), *Information theory* (pp. 196–211). Butterworth & Co.

Bateman, A., & Fonagy, P. (2006). *Mentalization based treatment for borderline personality disorder: A practical guide*. Oxford University Press.

Bateman, A., & Fonagy, P. (2009). Randomized controlled trial of outpatient mentalization-based treatment versus structured clinical management for borderline personality disorder. *American Journal of Psychiatry, 166*(12), 1355–1364. https://doi.org/10.1176 /appi.ajp.2009.09040539

Bateman, A., & Fonagy, P. (2010). Mentalization based treatment for borderline personality disorder. *World Psychiatry: Official Journal of the World Psychiatric Association (WPA)*, *9*(1), 11–15. https://doi.org/10.1002/j.2051-5545.2010.tb00255.x

Bateman, A., & Fonagy, P. (2013). Mentalization-based treatment. *Psychoanalytic Inquiry*, *33*(6), 595–613.

Bion, W. R. (1954). Notes on a theory of schizophrenia. *International Journal of Psychoanalysis*, *35*(2), 113–118.

Borelli, J. L., Compare, A., Snavely, J. E., & Decio, V. (2015). Reflective functioning moderates the association between perceptions of parental neglect and attachment in adolescence. *Psychoanalytic Psychology*, *32*(1), 23–35. https://doi.org/10.1037/a0037858

Breuer, J., & Freud, S. (1893–1895). Studies on hysteria. In *Standard edition* (Vol 2, pp. 1–306). Hogarth Press.

Brown, R., & McNeill, D. (1966). The "tip of the tongue" phenomenon. *Journal of Verbal Learning & Verbal Behavior*, *5*(4), 325–337. https://doi.org/10.1016/S0022-5371(66)80040-3

Bucci, W. (2002). From subsymbolic to symbolic—And back: Therapeutic impact of the referential process. In R. Lasky (Ed.), *Symbolization and desymbolization: Essays in honor of Norbert Freedman* (pp. 50–74). Other Press.

Cologon, J., Schweitzer, R. D., King, R., & Nolte, T. (2017). Therapist reflective functioning, therapist attachment style and therapist effectiveness. *Administration and Policy in Mental Health*, *44*(5), 614–625. https://doi.org/10.1007/s10488-017-0790-5

Craik, F. I. M., & Lockhart, R. S. (1972). Levels of processing: A framework for memory research. *Journal of Verbal Learning and Verbal Behavior*, *11*(6), 671–684.

Davison, W. T., Pray, M., & Bristol, C. (1990). Mutative interpretation and close process monitoring in a study of psychoanalytic process. *The Psychoanalytic Quarterly*, *59*(4), 599–628.

Deutsch, H. (1926). Occult processes occurring during psychoanalysis. In H. Deutsch (Ed.), *The therapeutic process, the self and female psychology: Collected psychoanalytic papers* (pp. 227–228). Transaction Publishers.

Deutsch, H. (1929). The genesis of agoraphobia. *International Journal of Psychoanalysis*, *10*, 51–69.

Díez, E., Gómez-Ariza, C. J., Díez-Álamo, A. M., Alonso, M. A., & Fernandez, A. (2017). The processing of semantic relatedness in the brain: Evidence from associative and categorical false recognition effects following transcranial direct current stimulation of the left anterior temporal lobe. *Cortex*, *93*, 133–145.

Eagle, M. N. (1987). The psychoanalytic and the cognitive unconscious. In R. Stern (Ed.), *Theories of the unconscious and theories of the self* (pp. 155–189). Analytic Press.

Eagle, M. N. (2007). Psychoanalysis and its critics. *Psychoanalytic Psychology*, *24*(1), 10–24. https://doi.org/10.1037/0736-9735.24.1.10

Eagle, M. N. (2018). *Core concepts in classical psychoanalysis: Clinical, research evidence and conceptual critiques*. Routledge.

Eagle, M. N., & Ortof, E. (1967). The effect of level of attention upon "phonetic" recognition errors. *Journal of Verbal Learning & Verbal Behavior*, *6*(2), 226–231. https://doi.org/10.1016/S0022-5371(67)80101-4

Fingarette, H. (1963). *The self in transformation: Psychoanalysis, philosophy and the life of the spirit*. Harper & Row.

Fingarette, H. (1969). *Self-deception*. University of California Press.

Fonagy, P. (1999). Points of contact and divergence between psychoanalytic and attachment theories: Is psychoanalytic theory truly different? *Psychoanalytic Inquiry*, *19*(4), 448–480. https://doi.org/10.1080/07351699909534264

Fonagy, P., Steele, M., Steele, H., Leigh, T., Kennedy, R., Mattoon, G., & Target, M. (1995). Attachment, the reflective self, and borderline states: The predictive specificity of the Adult attachment interview and pathological emotional development. In S. Goldberg, R. Muir, & J. Kerr (Eds.), *Attachment theory: Social, developmental, and clinical perspectives* (pp. 233–278). Analytic Press.

Freud, S. (1894). The neuro-psychoses of defense. In *Standard edition* (Vol. 3, pp. 45–61). Hogarth Press.

Freud, S. (1895). Case histories: Miss Lucy R. In J. Breuer & S. Freud (Eds.),*Studies on hysteria. Standard edition* (Vol. 2, pp. 106–125). Hogarth Press.

Freud, S. (1912). The dynamics of transference. In *Standard edition* (Vol. 12, pp. 97–108). Hogarth Press.

Freud, S. (1915). Instincts and their vicissitudes. In *Standard edition* (Vol. 14, pp. 117–140). Hogarth Press.

Freud, S. (1915a). Repression. In *Standard edition* (Vol. 14, pp. 141–158). Hogarth Press.

Freud, S. (1915b). The unconscious. In *Standard edition* (Vol. 14, pp. 166–204). Hogarth Press.

Freud, S. (1926). Inhibitions, symptoms, and anxiety. In *Standard edition* (Vol. 20, pp. 77–174). Hogarth Press.

Freud, S. (1933). New introductory lectures on psycho-analysis. In *Standard edition* (Vol. 22, pp. 5–182). Hogarth Press.

Garoff-Eaton, R. J., Kensinger, E. A., & Schacter, D. L. (2007). The neural correlates of conceptual and perceptual false recognition. *Learning & Memory*, *14*(10), 684–692. https://doi.org/10.1101/lm.695707

Gendlin, E. T. (1984). The client's client: The edge of awareness. In R. L. Levant & J. M. Shlien (Eds.), *Client-centered therapy and the person-centered approach. New directions in theory, research and practice* (pp. 76–107). Praeger.

Gray, P. (1994). *The ego and the analysis of defense.* Jason Aronson.

Husserl, E. (1983). *Ideas pertaining to a pure phenomenology and to a phenomenological philosophy* (F. Kersten, Trans.). Martinus Nijhoff. (Original work published 1913).

James, W. (1890). *The principles of psychology* (Vols. 1–2). Holt.

Jung, C. G., & Riklin, F. (1919). The associations of normal subjects. In C. G. Jung (Ed.) & M. D. Eder (Trans.), *Studies in word association: Experiments in the diagnosis of psychopathological conditions carried out at the psychiatric clinic of the University of Zurich* (pp. 8–172). Yard & Company. https://doi.org/10.1037/13030-002

Klein, G. S. (1976). *Psychoanalytic theory: An exploration of essentials.* International Universities Press.

Klein, M. (1930). The importance of symbol-formation in the development of the ego. *The International Journal of Psychoanalysis*, *11*, 24–39.

Laplanche, J., & Pontalis, J.-B. (1973). *The language of psycho-analysis.* Hogarth Press.

Levine, H. B. (1997). The capacity for countertransference. *Psychoanalytic Inquiry*, *17*(1), 44–68.

Lieberman, A. F. (1999). Negative maternal attributions: Effects on toddlers' sense of self. *Psychoanalytic Inquiry*, *19*(5), 737–756. https://doi.org/10.1080/07351699909534274

Mangan, B. (1993). Taking phenomenology seriously: The "fringe" and its implication for cognitive research. *Consciousness and Cognition*, *2*(2), 89–108.

Marcel, A. J. (1983). Conscious and unconscious perception: An approach to relations between phenomenal experience and perceptual processes. *Cognitive Psychology*, *15*(2), 238–300.

Mead, G. H. (1967). *Mind, self, and society from the standpoint of a social behaviorist*. University of Chicago Press.

Meehl, P. (1994). Subjectivity in psychoanalytic inference: The nagging persistence of Wilhelm Fliess's Achensee question. *Psychoanalysis and Contemporary Thought*, *17*(1), 3–82.

Miano, A., Barnow, S., Wagner, S., Roepke, S., & Dziobek, I. (2021). Dyadic emotion regulation in women with borderline personality disorder. *Cognitive Therapy and Research*, *45*(6), 1077–1092. https://doi.org/10.1007/s10608-021-10206-8

Mitchell, M. (2005). Self-awareness and control in decentralized systems. Working Papers of the Aaai 2005 Spring Symposium on Metacognition in Computation.

Polanyi, M. (1962). Tacit knowing: Its bearing on some problems of philosophy. *Reviews of Modern Physics*, *34*(4), 601–616. https://doi.org/10.1103/revmodphys.34.601

Racker, H. (1968). *Transference and countertransference*. International Universities Press.

Rapaport, D. (1942). *Emotions and memory*. International Universities Press.

Roediger, H. L., & McDermott, K. B. (1995). Creating false memories: Remembering words not presented in lists. *Journal of Experimental Psychology: Learning, Memory, and Cognition*, *21*(4), 803–814. https://doi.org/10.1037/0278-7393.21.4.803

Sartre, J. (1956 [1943]). *Being and nothingness* (H. Barnes, Trans.). Philosophical Library. (Original work published 1943).

Silberschatz, G. (2005). The control-mastery theory. In G. Silberschatz (Ed.), *Transformative relationships: The control-mastery theory of psychotherapy* (pp. 3–23). Routledge.

Sterba, R. (1934). The fate of the ego in analytic therapy. *International Journal of Psychoanalysis*, *15*, 117–126.

Stern, D. B. (2003). *Unformulated experience*. Analytic Press.

Sullivan, H. S. (1956). *Clinical studies in psychiatry*. W. W. Norton.

Tomkins, S. S. (1962–1963). *Affect imagery consciousness* (Vol. 1–2). Springer.

Wachtel, P. L. (2003). The surface and the depths: The metaphor of depth in psychoanalysis and the ways in which it can mislead. *Contemporary Psychoanalysis*, *39*(1), 5–26. https://doi.org/10.1080/00107530.2003.10747197

Weinberger, J. (2000). William James and the unconscious: Redressing a century-old misunderstanding. *Psychological Science*, *11*(6), 439–445.

Weiss, J., Sampson, H., Zion, M., & Psychotherapy Research Group. (1986). *The psychoanalytic process: Theory, clinical observations, and empirical research*. Guilford Press.

Yeomans, F. E., Levy, K. N., & Caligor, E. (2013). Transference-focused psychotherapy. *Psychotherapy*, *50*(3), 449–453. https://doi.org/10.1037/a0033417

Chapter 8

Some summing up and concluding comments

As we have seen in the previous chapters, to a significant extent, the disciplines of psychology, psychoanalysis, and philosophy of mind, each for their own reasons, have had much difficulty dealing with consciousness and subjective experience in a way that recognized and does justice to their centrality in one's existence. In this last chapter, I will review some of the difficulties already discussed, add discussion of some additional ones, and provide examples of ordinary research and other work that are illustrative of fruitful approaches to the investigation of the role of subjective experience in psychological functioning.

Psychology

According to received historical wisdom, the emergence of psychology as a separate discipline is marked by Wundt's establishment of an experimental laboratory in Leipzig in 1879. This was followed by Titchener's experimental laboratory in the United States at Cornell University. Thus, the status of psychology as a separate discipline with scientific credentials is linked to an experimental investigation of human phenomena. Although Titchener defined psychology as the study of consciousness, what was being investigated in the Cornell experimental laboratory was anything but conscious experience in the world outside the experimental laboratory. The use of trained introspection and avoidance of the 'stimulus error', that is, refraining from reporting the actual object perceived, added up to a phenomenological approach that was far removed from ordinary and spontaneous conscious experience in the real world.

Obviously, the purpose of experimentation is to shed light on phenomena that exist outside the experimental laboratory. This is not problematic with regard to most inanimate phenomena found in nature that remain essentially the same inside and outside the experimental laboratory. This cannot be assumed to be the case with regard to human as well as animal behavior and experience. The behavior and experiences that are present in the experimental laboratory are not necessarily representative of the behaviors and experiences in the world outside the experimental laboratory. Thus, experimental findings in investigations of human behavior and experience always face the test of the ecological validity of these

DOI: 10.4324/9781032686967-9

findings, that is, the degree to which one can generalize from them to behavior and experience in the world outside the laboratory. As one historical example, it could be argued that Structuralism did not leave much of a legacy due to the lack of ecological validity of its findings.

Experimental studies of human experience and behavior studies carry the inherent risk that in meeting the methodological demands of experimental design, one may deform the phenomena presumably being studied to the point that what is being investigated in the experimental laboratory is no longer representative of the phenomena in the world outside the experimental laboratory. Recall Neisser's (1982) earlier noted concerns regarding the ecological validity of findings from laboratory studies (see Chapter 1, p. 24, fn. 10). He wrote that '... theories of memory are either so closely bound to particular experiments that they are uninteresting or so vague that they are intellectually dissatisfying' (p. xii). He also writes that

> I believe that a similar state of affairs prevails in many areas of psychology. Perception, too, is studied mostly in laboratory settings that lack ecological validity (that is, settings that are not representative of the environment in which perception usually occurs).
>
> (p. xii)

Although these comments were made in 1982, they continue to be relevant.

The problem of ecological validity is not limited to the experimental laboratory, but also arises in other research contexts and methodologies where we do not know the degree to which the measures employed in the studies reflect real-world referents. Both Blanton and Jaccard (2006) and Kazdin (2006) refer to these measures as 'arbitrary metrics'. In a very important paper, Kazdin (2006) discusses the problem of arbitrary metrics in research on psychotherapy outcomes. Kazdin (2006) notes that the use of the label Evidence-Based Treatments (EBT) notwithstanding, it is entirely possible that all the reported outcomes of EBT approaches (e.g., changes in scores on the Beck Depression Inventory [BDI]) may tell us little or nothing regarding how treated patients are functioning and feeling. As Kazdin (2006) puts it, these scores tell us little about 'how individuals are doing in everyday life' (p. 41). The important point in the present context is that 'how individuals are doing in everyday life' includes not only adaptive functioning, but also their subjective feelings and experiences.

A form of ecological validity that is of special relevance in the context of clinical work with individuals arises in the context of methodologies that report mainly group findings, which makes it difficult, if not impossible, to understand individuals within a group. This is clearly an important factor in accounting for the clinician's not-uncommon lack of interest in research and preference for ideographic rather than nomothetic approaches. However, it is possible to at least partly integrate these two approaches through the use of mixed methods, as well as adapting nomothetic methods so that they yield findings that are applicable to at least sub-groups if not to each individual within a group.[1] One such method is to include, whenever possible, not just main effects, but also interaction effects (see Eagle, 2020). Another related approach is to identify the characteristics of individuals within, say, experimental and control groups, whose responses are *different* from the modal response of the group to which they belong. And still another approach is to ascertain how participants in a study understood and construed the instructions given to them. Such types of information are generally not reported.

As we have seen in the Nisbett and Wilson (1977) and Wegner (2002, 2003) papers, there is a tendency to make questionable and sweeping generalizations from contrived experimental situations to the nature of cognitive functioning in the world outside these contrived situations. As we have also seen, particularly in the studies reported by Nisbett and Wilson (1977), one reason for the relative lack of ecological validity is the failure to investigate adequately the participant's subjective experiences.

There are many exceptions to the above state of affairs, both in the history of psychology as well as in contemporary psychological research and theory. With regard to the latter, in contrast to an earlier preoccupation with, for example, the study of responses to nonsense syllables and rats running mazes, much psychological research has become more concerned with vital human phenomena and is more likely to be characterized by ecological validity. As for the former, there were a number of important developments in the history of psychology that represent exceptions to the state of affairs described above insofar as they entailed the recognition that consciousness and subjective experience are part of the natural world and are subject to systematic empirical investigation. For example, although like Hull, Tolman investigated maze learning in rats, his concept of 'purposive behaviorism' allowed mental states and structures (e.g., 'cognitive maps') back into psychology, a theoretical development that also played a role in the emergence of cognitive psychology. The psychophysics developed by Weber and Fechner demonstrated the possibility of systematic research on the relations between subjective experience and variations in physical dimensions of external stimuli. As still another example, the Gestalt psychologists also demonstrated the possibility of systematic research on subjective experience, and unlike the structuralist approach, did so in an ecologically valid way that preserved the integrity of phenomenal experience.

Research and theory in psychology during the last 50 or so years have yielded a mixed, but somewhat encouraging picture with regard to the related issues of ecological validity and recognition of the centrality of subjective experience. Let me provide a few concrete examples of such research. In one study, the experimenter's gentle touch on a child's shoulder as s/he entered the experimental room enhanced the child's ability to delay gratification (Leonard et al., 2014). In Skinnerian fashion, one can limit one's account to the functional relations between touch and delay of gratification. However, this approach constitutes a barrier to further understanding of the mechanisms and processes involved in these functional relations. A plausible explanation of the relation between touch and delay of gratification is that the touch condition induces feelings of safety and trust in the child. And indeed, there is evidence that the child's trust in the experimenter, as well as generalized trust are significantly related to delay of gratification (Ma et al., 2018).

What gives a study of this kind a high level of ecological validity is the likelihood that the finding on the relation between trust and delay of gratification is not limited to the experimental situation, but also holds in the world outside the experimental situation. There is evidence that touch triggers oxytocin release (Portnova et al., 2020), which is associated with increased trust (Kosfeld et al., 2005). Further, one can empirically test this assumption by carrying out appropriate research on this issue outside the experimental laboratory. One can also examine the relation between individual differences in level of trust and delay of gratification across the touch and no-touch experimental conditions. If level of trust accounts for most of the variance in accounting for differences in delay of gratification, one could more confidently conclude that it is not touch *per se* that accounts for enhanced delay of gratification, but rather the fact that touch tends to induce a state of greater trust. It should be noted that without the assumption that touch activates particular subjective mental contents, the findings would seem rather arbitrary.

Although my next example is very different from the above studies, it illustrates in a powerful way the degree to which the inclusion of data on subjective mental contents contributes to the importance and ecological validity of the study. The study deals with suicidal ideation (SI) among family farmers with small plots of land in two villages in Southern India (Kandlur et al., 2022). The authors note that suicide is very high among small farmers – 285,000 Indian farmers have died by suicide during the last 20 years – and want to contribute to an understanding of what accounts for this distressing reality. Perhaps surprisingly, they found that whereas amount of debt – a serious problem among small farmers – was not significantly associated with suicidal ideation, amount of land owned was significantly associated with SI: the less land owned, the higher SI. However, this relationship was no longer significant after accounting for self-criticism and anxiety. They also found that coping styles played a significant role in SI: the mean score for negative distraction (e.g., use of alcohol, smoking, and eating to feel better) was higher for farmers who reported SI than those who did not; the mean score for positive distraction (e.g., helping others in distress, spending time with children, listening to music) was lower for farmers who did not report SI than those who did; the farmers who employed a denial/blaming coping style (e.g., bad fortune/luck, trying to forget, blaming self) were higher in SI than those who did not. I want to emphasize the same points made with regard to the trust and delay of gratification study: one, the study possesses a high level of ecological validity; and two, if one examined only the relationship between the 'objective' variable – size of a plot of land or amount of debt – and SI, and ignored the experiential variables, one would reach a misleading conclusion low in ecological validity.

Psychoanalysis.

The focus of at least classical psychoanalytic theory of the nature of the mind is on unconscious mental contents and processes. According to that theory, consciousness and subjective experience are viewed as epiphenomenal samplings of the true psychic reality of unconscious mental processes, and have no causal properties of their own (see Wakefield, 2018). Further, consciousness and subjective experience are dissimulating with regard to our 'real' motives and desires.[2] On this view, based largely on the analyst's interpretations, the dissimulating nature of consciousness and subjective experience can be replaced by self-knowledge, particularly of hitherto repressed mental contents.

As we have seen, a major problem here is that what is taken as accurate interpretations that uncover the patient's unconscious mental contents, that is, interpretations that tally with what is real in the patient, too often are based on the analyst's particular theoretical persuasion (Lomas, 1987; Meehl, 1994). Further, in Freud's (1937) later writings, the operational criterion for the accuracy or validity of an interpretation became not independent evidence of its accuracy, such as access to conscious experience of a hitherto repressed wish or the recovery of an early memory that could be shown to correspond to an actual event, but rather the patient's 'assured conviction' of the correctness of the interpretation. In short, the issue of ecological validity is as relevant in the psychoanalytic context as in the other contexts discussed.[3]

There is evidence that in a variety of contexts, in making judgments, including clinical judgments, the greater the degree of inference required, the lower of both reliability and validity. In the psychoanalytic context, one can confidently say that the 'deeper' the interpretation, the more it requires making inferences influenced by one's theoretical perspective, and the lower the degree of both reliability and validity. One can also add that in the context of the clinical situation, the 'deeper' the interpretation, the more support for the interpretation depends on the 'assured conviction' of the patient, and therefore the greater the problem of suggestion. I would hypothesize – and this is an empirical question – the 'deeper' the interpretation, and therefore, the less experience-near it is, the less therapeutically effective it will be.

In view of these considerations, it may not seem shocking to suggest that psychoanalysis should be conceptualized not solely or even primarily, as the study of the dynamic unconscious, as Freud defined it, i.e., repressed unconscious contents and unconscious defenses), but as the study of implicit and fringe mental contents and processes that remain or have been rendered implicit and at the fringe of consciousness due to a variety of factors, including the fact that they have been experienced early in life; and the defensive reason that making them explicit and focal would trigger negative affect and would entail threat to one's self-image.

In contrast to what we now think of as the dynamic unconscious, implicit and fringe contents and processes are more accessible to conscious experience through such ordinary means as deployment of attention and reflective function.

This reconceptualization retains the centrality of the key psychoanalytic ideas of inner conflict, the influence of early experiences, and defensively motivated unawareness. On this view, the mind is no less dynamic; but, the phenomena that were accounted for by reference to the dynamic unconscious in traditional psychoanalytic theory, that is, a struggle between unconscious instinctual wishes striving for discharge and unconscious counterforces, are now understood as the interplay of implicit or preconscious rather than unconscious forces.

Many post-Freudian departures from Freudian theory have already essentially replaced the id-ego model, including the centrality it accords to the dynamic unconscious, with an emphasis on implicit processes and contents. Examples include the internal working models (IWMs) of attachment theory (Bowlby, 1973) the 'implicit relational knowing' of the Boston Change Process Study Group (Lyons-Ruth, 1999), and the unconscious pathogenic beliefs of Control-Mastery Theory (e.g., Silberschatz, 2005). The id–ego model has also been replaced, or at least supplemented, by an emphasis on impairments in ego functioning, including self-defects (Kohut, 1984) and impairments in reflective functioning (RF), both interfering with regulation of negative affect (see Eagle, 2022). The beginnings of this shift could already be seen in the earlier literature on the 'widening scope' of psychoanalysis (Stone, 1954), with its emphasis on developmental defects and arrests (see also Lachmann & Stolorow, 1980). Although perhaps seen as too radical to acknowledge explicitly, the emphasis on implicit processes and contents constituted a markedly decreased emphasis on the dynamic unconscious. Common to these developments is the fact that, although the term 'unconscious' may continue to be used, they all refer to implicit processes and meaning structures that originate in early interactions with parental figures and continue to exert strong influence on one's feelings, thoughts, and behavior patterns.

The emphasis on implicit processes and meanings, which is congruent with the description of consciousness as a *continuum* in Chapter 6, carries a number of implications for clinical work. One such implication is a relatively reduced emphasis on 'deep' interpretations of mental contents and processes that are inaccessible to consciousness and subjective experience, and that tend to be overly influenced by the analyst's theoretical perspective.[4] In the post-Freudian approaches referred to above, when interpretations are made, they are more likely to focus on implicit material just below the surface of consciousness and that can be made accessible to focal conscious experience through a variety of means, including the analyst's test-passing and the resulting facilitation of a sense of safety (Weiss & Sampson, 1986; Silberschatz, 2005) and direction of the patient's attention to the defensive nature of the pattern of his or her thoughts and feelings (Gray, 1994).

As noted in the discussion of working-through in Chapter 2, significant therapeutic change can be thought of in terms of first making implicit patterns explicit (i.e., transforming procedural knowledge into declarative knowledge) and then, partly through the practice of one's new explicit knowledge in action in the world outside the clinical situation, transforming the declarative knowledge into new forms of procedural knowledge (Rosenblatt, 2004). That is, the hitherto declarative knowledge becomes an embodied and integral part of oneself. As Valenstein (1983) puts it, 'Ultimately, the working-through of insight is pivotally related to the function of action and to definitive changes in action patterns as they are consolidated into the action system' (p. 371).

The emphasis on practice and action patterns in the transformation of explicit insights and self-knowledge into new implicit procedures suggests that this process is similar, in certain respects, to the development and honing of a skill. It also suggests that implicit knowledge is not easily changed through explicit knowledge alone. As Polanyi and Prosch (1975) observe, tacit knowledge is relatively unsusceptible to influence by explicit verbalized knowledge. For example, as noted earlier, the explicit knowledge that the two lines in the Muller-Lyons illusion are of equal length does not alter the experience of the illusion. In important respects, the tacit or procedural knowledge represented by schemas, RIGs, and internal working models are like visual illusions in their relative unsusceptibility to change primarily through explicit knowledge. (This is also the case with regard to motor skills.) In short, it is unlikely that explicit insight and self-knowledge is sufficient to change and replace ingrained implicit models, expectations, and representations. Like any skill, it requires practice and integration into a new set of action patterns – and, I would add, affect patterns. However, in the context of the clinical situation, what is also required is repeated experiences with the therapist that serve to disconfirm early expectations, models, and representations and replace them with new ones. As Lyons-Ruth (1999) observes, not only is implicit relational knowledge acquired through nonverbal (early) interactions, but is changed through nonverbal interactions. Of course, what Lyons-Ruth is essentially referring to here are corrective emotional experiences in one form or another, for example, the test-passing of Control-Mastery Theory and the experience of being empathically understood of self-psychology.

There is evidence that the therapist's test-passing alone, without interpretation, may be sufficient to bring about therapeutic change (Silberschatz, 2005). I reported a case some years ago of the dramatic disappearance of an ingrained and troubling symptom in a patient following interactions between us that could be understood as test-passing (Eagle, 1993). One of the discussants of that paper, Gill (1993), was critical of my failure to make those interactions explicit through transference interpretations. I felt then, and continue to feel, that that would have been a mistake in that it could have intellectualized and diluted the therapeutic impact of the interactions.

The evidence suggests that, as Alexander and French (1946) argued, alteration of maladaptive implicit or procedural patterns requires corrective emotional experiences.[5] Recognition of the central role of corrective emotional experiences in changing implicit or procedural knowledge renders the analyst less a *Menschenkenner* who has special knowledge of the patient's deep unconscious mental contents, and more an empathic facilitator in the sense that Winnicott (1956) uses the term in the title of his book, *The Maturational Process and the Facilitating Environment*. Of course, the degree to which the therapeutic approach implicit in this reconceptualization is related to therapeutic effectiveness is an empirical matter. However, whether or not associated with greater therapeutic effectiveness, I believe that the reconceptualizations I describe constitute a more accurate account of the way the mind works than the classical theory of a dynamic unconscious of fully formed unconscious infantile instinctual wishes push for entry into consciousness and are prevented from entry by equally unconscious and subpersonal defense 'mechanisms'.

The great strengths of Freudian theory lie in the fact that it addresses challenging and profound issues regarding the nature of the mind and of human nature, its comprehensiveness, and the way in which different formulations and mini-theories fit together to form an architectural structure. The fact that it is Freudian theory, not post-Freudian theories or 'schools' that has generated an enormous number of papers and books on the nature of the mind and of human nature in various disciplines tells us something regarding its sweep and its fundamental influence in intellectual thought. The criticisms and revisions of Freudian theory, including the cogent and justified ones, have been piecemeal and scattered. What remains to be done is to put these revisions of classical theory together into a coherent and integrated theory (see Eagle, 2022). It seems to me that when that is accomplished, it will raise serious questions, a fundamental one of which is whether psychoanalysis can continue to be defined as a discipline devoted to the investigation of the dynamic unconscious.

Philosophy of mind

There are two basic arguments underlying a dismissive philosophical attitude toward consciousness and subjective experience, both arguments converging on the idea that a scientific-physicalist worldview cannot accommodate these phenomena. One argument is methodological and epistemological and the other is ontological. The methodological-epistemological argument essentially states that because they are not available to public observation, consciousness and subjective experience are not susceptible to empirical scientific study. This was essentially the argument of methodological behaviorism. The second argument, an ontological one, states that insofar as only physical phenomena exist in the natural world, consciousness and subjective experience are reducible to physical processes such as behavioral or neural processes.[6]

In the disciplines I have discussed, the 'expert' – the psychological researcher, the Menschenkenner analyst, and the philosopher of mind inform the rest of humanity that they are mistaken and illusory in thinking that they have access to the reasons and motives for their actions and decisions, and that they act on the basis of their conscious intentions. Rather, we are told by the experimental psychologist that we rely on mini-causal theories to account for our decisions; by the analyst as expert that conscious experience is dissimulating, that is, it hides and disguises what one 'really' wishes and desires; and by the philosopher of mind that we are nothing but assemblies of neural cells.

Living one's personal life in accord with these perspectives and presumed findings would almost certainly culminate in a grand *alienation* from one's sense of oneself as a conscious agent. This is likely one aspect of what Fodor (1987) had in mind when he referred to the catastrophe that would befall us were common sense intentional psychology to collapse. Indeed, if one took these claims personally and utterly seriously and lived and acted in accord with these beliefs, we would likely and justifiably view that person as psychotic. This radical disconnect between what one professes and how one lives one's life suggests that something is amiss.[7]

Coda

In coming to the end of this book, I want to emphasize once more that consciousness and subjective experience are at the center of one's existence. Insofar as they make empirical observation possible, they are also at the center of scientific inquiry. As Kohler (1938) writes, 'There seems to be a single starting point for psychology as for all other sciences: the world as we find it naively and uncritically' (p. 3). One can add that subjective experience is also the starting point for all sentient human life. Given their fundamental role in all inquiry, including scientific inquiry, it is ironic that so many scientifically minded investigators and theorists in the disciplines I have discussed have taken the positions that consciousness and subjective experience cannot be accommodated in a physicalist scientific world view, that they are inherently dissimulating, and that they are reducible to the physical processes of behavior and neural activity.

As we have seen, the above positions notwithstanding, a significant number of representatives from the disciplines discussed have been routinely investigating consciousness and subjective experience. They have been empirically investigating the factors, processes, and mechanisms that underlie, make possible, and shape and influence consciousness and subjective experience. Scientific investigators have also – without worries of dualism – elucidated the mutual interaction among subjective experiences, behavior, and neurophysiological processes. As these investigations suggest, science deals with subjective experience best when 1) it preserves the integrity of lived subjective experience in its investigations; 2) systematically explores the factors (e.g., maternal behavior, social factors, neurophysiological processes, socioeconomic conditions, genetic predispositions, etc.) that underlie, shape and influence experience and behavior, including individual differences in experience; 3) systematically investigates the relations among subjective experiences as well as the influence of experience on other phenomena (e.g., physical and mental health); 4) addresses the ecological validity of findings, particularly from experimental studies; 5) recognizes that how participants in experimental studies construe the experimental situation may play a significant role in the findings obtained; and 6) recognizes that not all aspects of human experience and behavior can be meaningfully studied in the experimental laboratory.

Although scientific method is the most reliable and powerful means of systematically investigating and shedding light on the processes and factors that underlie and influence experience, like any human endeavor, it has its limits. Science cannot and should not be expected to capture the subjective feel of experience. As Edelman (2003) puts it, 'To expect that a theoretical explanation of consciousness can itself provide an observer with the experience of "the redness of red"' (p. 5521) is unrealistic. He goes on to say that 'A scientific theory cannot presume to replicate the experience that it describes or explains' (p. 5521). That project should be left to poetry, literature, the arts and humanities in general, and to the struggle for one's personal development in the living of one's life.

Notes

1 One is reminded of Cronbach's (1957) classic paper on the two scientific methods of psychology: the experimental and the correlational.
2 As noted earlier, there is a seeming inconsistency between this theoretical view of consciousness and subjective experience and the identification of making the unconscious conscious as an overriding goal of treatment.
3 The validity of a measuring instrument is determined by whether it measures what it is supposed to and claims to measure. For example, the validity of a test that purports to predict academic success is determined by the degree of association between scores on the test and academic performance. Similarly, the validity of an interpretation is determined by the degree to which it tallies with what is real in the patient, for example, whether a repressed early memory attributed to the patient can be retrieved, or barring such retrieval, whether one can find evidence of other behaviors or experiences predicted by the interpretation.
4 Although Gray (1994) assumes that defense is activated primarily by drive-related mental contents, the viability of his close process monitoring therapeutic approach does not rest on that assumption.
5 As early as 1924, Ferenczi and Rank decried the over-intellectualized nature of psychoanalysis and called for the greater presence in psychoanalysis of what Alexander and French later referred to as corrective emotional experience. A similar stance is seen in Kohut's (1984) formulation of self psychology.
6 There are, of course, other philosophical takes on the mind–body issue such as type-token theories, monism, double-aspect theory, idealism, and so on; however, these theories need not concern us here.
7 Although it may be an odd idea, perhaps one can assess not only empirical findings, but also philosophical beliefs in terms of their ecological validity.

References

Alexander, F., & French, T. M. (1946). *Psychoanalytic therapy; Principles and application.* Ronald Press.

Blanton, H., & Jaccard, J. (2006). Arbitrary metrics in psychology. *American Psychologist,* *61*(1), 27–41. https://doi.org/10.1037/0003-066X.61.1.27

Bowlby, J. (1973). *Attachment and loss* (Vol. 2). Basic Books.

Cronbach, L. J. (1957). The two disciplines of scientific psychology. *American Psychologist,* *12*(11), 671–684. https://doi.org/10.1037/h0043943

Eagle, M. N. (1993). Enactments, transference, and symptomatic cure: A case history. *Psychoanalytic Dialogues*, *3*(1), 93–110. https://doi.org/10.1080/10481889309538962

Eagle, M. N. (2020). The role of critical thinking and research in psychoanalytic education. M. Leuzinger-Bohleber, M. Solms, & S. E. Arnold (Eds.), *Outcome Research and the Future of Psychoanalysis*, (pp. 249-259). New York & London: Routledge

Eagle, M. N. (2022). Two visions of psychoanalysis: An essay in memory of Carlo Strenger. *Psychoanalytic Psychology*, *39*(1), 27–36. https://doi.org/10.1037/pap0000394

Edelman, G. M. (2003). Naturalizing consciousness: A theoretical framework. *Proceedings of the National Academy of Sciences of the United States of America*, *100*(9), 5520–5524. https://doi.org/10.1073/pnas.0931349100

Ferenczi, S., & Rank, O. (1924). *The development of psychoanalysis* (C. Newton, Trans.). Nervous and Mental Disease Publishing Company.

Fodor, J. A. (1987). *Psychosemantics: The problem of meaning in the philosophy of mind*. MIT Press.

Freud, S. (1937). Constructions in analysis. In *Standard edition* (Vol. 23, pp. 257–269). Hogarth Press.

Gill, M. M. (1993). Interaction and interpretation: Commentary on Morris Eagle's "Enactments, transference, and symptomatic cure". *Psychoanalytic Dialogues*, *3*(1), 111–122. https://doi.org/10.1080/10481889309538963

Gray, P. (1994). *The ego and the analysis of defense*. Jason Aronson.

Kandlur, R., Sardana, S., & Richardson-Vejlgaard, R. (2022). The Agrarian distress: Factors explaining the will to live among rural and distressed family farmers. *Psychiatry Research Communications*, *2*(1). https://doi.org/10.1016/j.psycom.2021.100019.

Kazdin, A. E. (2006). Arbitrary metrics: Implications for identifying evidence-based treatments. *American Psychologist*, *61*(1), 42–49. https://doi.org/10.1037/0003-066X.61.1.42

Köhler, W. (1938). *The place of value in a world of facts*. Kegan, Paul, Trench, Trubner, and Company.

Kohut, H. (1984). *How does analysis cure?* University of Chicago Press. http://doi.org/10.7208/chicago/9780226006147.001.0001

Kosfeld, M., Heinrichs, M., Zak, P. J., Fischbacher, U., & Fehr, E. (2005). Oxytocin increases trust in humans. *Nature*, *435*(7042), 673–676. https://doi.org/10.1038/nature03701

Kunitz, S. (1995). *Passing through: The later poems, new and selected*. W. W. Norton.

Lachmann, F. M., & Stolorow, R. D. (1980). The developmental significance of affective states: Implications for psychoanalytic treatment. *The Annual of Psychoanalysis*, *8*, 215–229.

Leonard, J. A., Berkowitz, T., & Shusterman, A. (2014). The effect of friendly touch on delay-of-gratification in preschool children. *The Quarterly Journal of Experimental Psychology*, *67*(11), 2123–2133. https://doi.org/10.1080/17470218.2014.907325

Lomas, P. (1987). *The limits of interpretation. What's wrong with psychoanalysis?* Penguin.

Lyons-Ruth, K. (1999). The two-person unconscious: Intersubjective dialogue, enactive relational representation, and the emergence of new forms of relational organization. *Psychoanalytic Inquiry*, *19*(4), 576–617. https://doi.org/10.1080/07351699909534267

Ma, F., Chen, B., Xu, F., Lee, K., & Heyman, G. D. (2018). Generalized trust predicts young children's willingness to delay gratification. *Journal of Experimental Child Psychology*, *169*, 118–125.

Meehl, P. (1994). Subjectivity in psychoanalytic inference: The nagging persistence of Wilhelm Fliess's Achensee question. *Psychoanalysis and Contemporary Thought*, *17*(1), 3–82.

Neisser, U., & Hyman, I. (1982). *Memory observed: Remembering in natural contexts*. W. H. Freeman.

Nisbett, R. E., & Wilson, T. D. (1977). The halo effect: Evidence for unconscious alteration of judgments. *Journal of Personality and Social Psychology*, *35*(4), 250–256. https://doi.org/10.1037/0022-3514.35.4.250

Polanyi, M., & Prosch, H. (1975). Meaning. *Philosophy and Rhetoric*, *10*(2), 123–125.

Portnova, G. V., Proskurnina, E. V., Sokolova, S. V., Skorokhodov, I. V., & Varlamov, A. A. (2020). Perceived pleasantness of gentle touch in healthy individuals is related to salivary oxytocin response and EEG markers of arousal. *Experimental Brain Research*, *238*(10), 2257–2268. https://doi.org/10.1007/s00221-020-05891-y

Rosenblatt, A. (2004). Insight, working through, and practice: The role of procedural knowledge. *Journal of the American Psychoanalytic Association*, *52*(1), 189–207. https://doi.org/10.1177/00030651040520011901

Silberschatz, G. (2005). The control-mastery theory. In G. Silberschatz (Ed.), *Transformative relationships: The control-mastery theory of psychotherapy* (pp. 3–23). Routledge.

Stone, L. (1954). The widening scope of indications for psychoanalysis. *Journal of the American Psychoanalytic Association*, *2*(4), 567–594. https://doi.org/10.1177/000306515400200402

Valenstein, A. F. (1983). Working through and resistance to change: Insight and the action system. *Journal of the American Psychoanalytic Association*, *31*(1), 353–373.

Wakefield, J. C. (2018). *Freud and philosophy of mind: Reconstructing the argument for unconscious mental states*. Springer International Publishing. https://doi.org/10.1007/978-3-319-96343-3

Wegner, D. M. (2002). *The illusion of conscious will*. MIT Press.

Wegner, D. M. (2003). The mind's best trick: How we experience conscious will. *Trends in Cognitive Science*, *7*(2), 65–69.

Winnicott, D. W. (1956). Primary maternal preoccupation. In *The maturational process and the facilitating environment* (pp. 300–305). International Universities Press.

Index

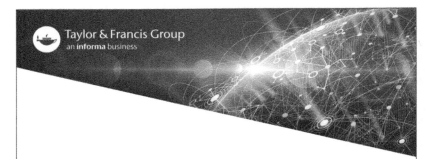